The illustrated
ATLAS OF THE
UNIVERSE

MARK A. GARLICK

Star Maps
WIL TIRION

The illustrated
ATLAS OF THE UNIVERSE

METRO BOOKS
New York

METRO BOOKS
NEW YORK

An imprint of Sterling publishing
387 Park Avenue South
New York, NY 10016

METRO BOOKS and the distinctive Metro Books logo are trademarks
of Sterling Publishing Co., Inc.

Conceived and produced by Weldon Owen Pty Ltd
59–61 Victoria Street, McMahons Point
Sydney, NSW 2060, Australia

WELDON OWEN PTY LTD
Managing Director Kay Scarlett
Publisher Corinne Roberts
Creative Director Sue Burk
Senior Vice President, International Sales Stuart Laurence
Sales Manager North America Ellen Towell
Administration Manager International Sales Kristine Ravn

Managing Editor Averil Moffat
Project Editors Scott Forbes, Dannielle Viera
Designer John Bull
Cartographer Will Pringle/Mapgraphx
Images Manager Trucie Henderson
Picture Research Jo Collard
Design Assistant Emily Spencer
Editorial Assistant Natalie Ryan
Proofreader Bronwyn Sweeney
Indexer Jo Rudd
Production Director Todd Rechner
Production and Prepress Controller Mike Crowton

A WELDON OWEN PRODUCTION

ISBN 978-1-4351-4234-3

For information about custom editions, special sales, and premium
and corporate purchases, please contact Sterling Special Sales at
800-805-5489 or specialsales@sterlingpublishing.com.

Printed by 1010 Printing International Ltd
Manufactured in China

The paper used in the manufacture of this book is sourced from
wood grown in sustainable forests. It complies with the
Environmental Management System Standard ISO 14001:2004

2 4 6 8 10 9 7 5 3 1

www.sterlingpublishing.com

Rope bridge (this page)
Gaspard Mollien, an adventurous French explorer, traveled
widely in Colombia in the 1820s. This engraving shows the
members of his expedition crossing La Plata rope bridge.

Cape Barrow (preceding page)
The two small, open boats shown in this engraving by Edward
Finden are rounding Cape Barrow in heavy, icy seas. The scene
comes from John Franklin's first trip to the Arctic in 1821.

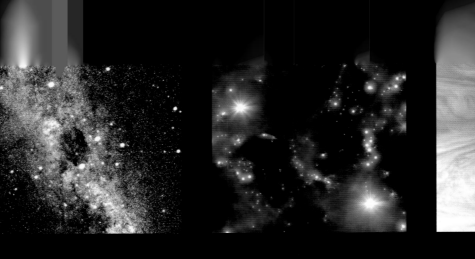

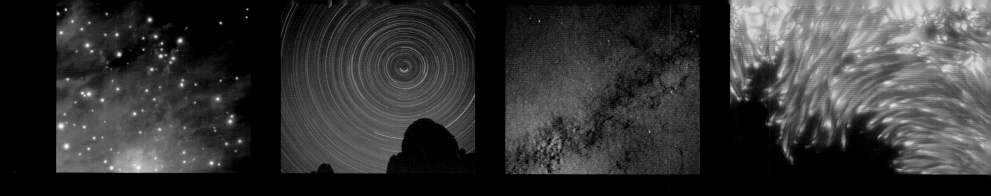

Our dynamic Sun (below left)
This ultraviolet image shows a solar prominence—a huge eruption of relatively cool gas many thousands of miles into space. Prominences are probably related to activity in the Sun's strong magnetic field, though the exact mechanism is not well understood.

Never-ending storm (below)
This color-enhanced view of Jupiter's Great Red Spot was captured by Voyager 1 in 1979. Our understanding of this giant planet was hugely advanced during the 1970s with close encounters by Pioneer 10 and 11, and the later Voyager series spacecraft.

Martian ice lake (above)
In 2005, the Mars Express orbiter captured this image of a large expanse of water ice in an unnamed crater near the Martian north pole. The crater is about 22 miles (35 km) wide. Water ice is found in modest quantities both on the surface of Mars and in the atmosphere.

Rings revealed (left)
This Cassini orbiter image of a section of Saturn's famous rings was taken in ultraviolet light. The colors indicate the types and quantities of minerals detected within the countless particles of water ice that make up the rings. The general pattern is from relatively pure ice at the upper part of the imaged area (blue and turquoise) to particles with high mineral content at the bottom (red).

The Sword of Orion (far left)
The Sword of Orion, in the constellation of the same name, is a group of celestial treasures visible to the naked eye even from a city. At the top of this close-up of the region is a blue reflection nebula with components cataloged under the names NGC 1973, 1975, and 1977. Below this is the famous Orion Nebula (M42), the closest large site of star formation to the Sun.

FOREWORD

Astronomy has captivated humankind for as long as our sense of curiosity has drawn our eyes skyward. Today we are fortunate to live during a great flowering of astronomical knowledge. Never before have so many astronomers had such a range of technology with which to unravel the riddles of our universe. Thanks to powerful telescopes on the ground and in space, images that until very recently would have seemed miraculous are now routinely captured. The once distant planets and satellites of the Solar System have been brought within our reach with technology that has put robotic explorers on Mars, surveyed the surface of Venus through its blanketing clouds, and sent us a picture from the icy surface of a Saturnian moon nearly a billion miles away.

The Illustrated Atlas of the Universe brings all this knowledge and beauty together in the one volume. It reveals what is in the universe and how it all fits together—even how you can best get out there and start seeing it all for yourself. Over a hundred specially commissioned maps and charts make sense of its awesome scale. This is more than an atlas, it is an encyclopedic survey of 21st century astronomy, cosmology, and space exploration.

The Illustrated Atlas of the Universe begins with a study of our planet, Earth, and its natural satellite, the Moon. Then, chapter by chapter, the focus is expanded to survey ever-larger regions of the cosmos until, ultimately, the entire universe and its largest known structures, superclusters of galaxies, are explored in chapter eight. The final two chapters deal with the night sky and are a practical resource for amateur astronomers and everyday stargazers. Chapter nine is a guide through the seasons, mapping out what you can expect to see in the night sky in any given direction—north or south of the equator, any time of year. Chapter ten details all 88 constellations, picking out noteworthy features such as nebulas, stars, and galaxies.

Conceived, written, and illustrated by an international team of astronomers, cartographers, and science educators, and replete with beautiful, full-color photos, maps, charts, and illustrations, *The Illustrated Atlas of the Universe* is your passport to the cosmos, helping to define our place within the universe.

SCALE OF THE UNIVERSE

The universe is much larger than the human mind can truly comprehend. The mind starts to boggle even at the distances to our neighboring stars. But what cannot be comprehended can still be demonstrated. Each of the first eight chapters in this Atlas opens with a map charting the region of principal interest for that chapter. These maps are reproduced over the next four pages, each linked to show how it fits into the next.

Kilometers
Astronomers favor the SI (or metric) system of units, and diagrams and text in this book include SI units alongside US customary units. Some diagrams relating to the Earth–Moon system use kilometers exclusively. One kilometer is equivalent to 0.62 miles.

EARTH AND THE MOON
Pages 14–33

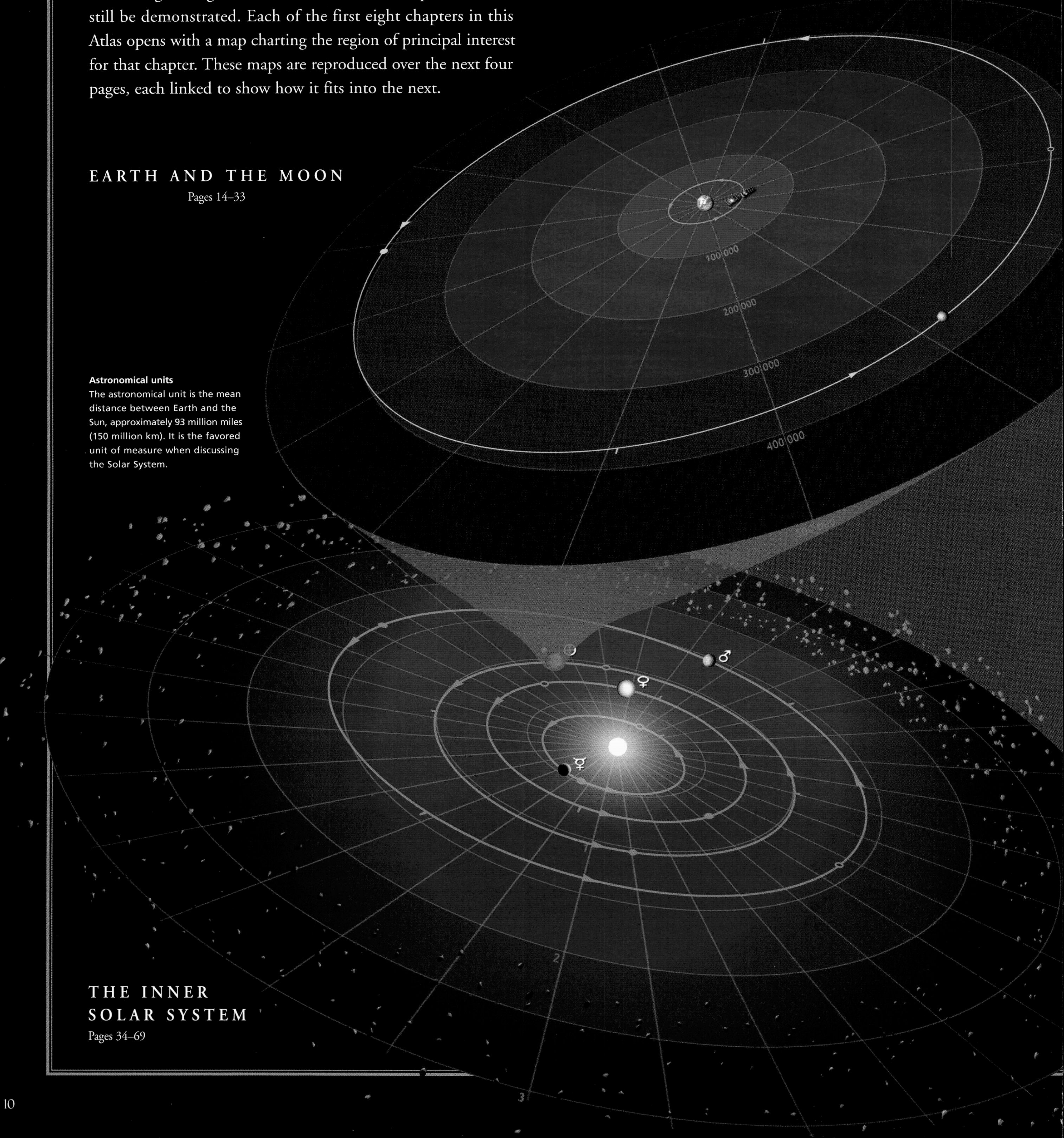

Astronomical units
The astronomical unit is the mean distance between Earth and the Sun, approximately 93 million miles (150 million km). It is the favored unit of measure when discussing the Solar System.

100 000

200 000

300 000

400 000

500 000

THE INNER
SOLAR SYSTEM
Pages 34–69

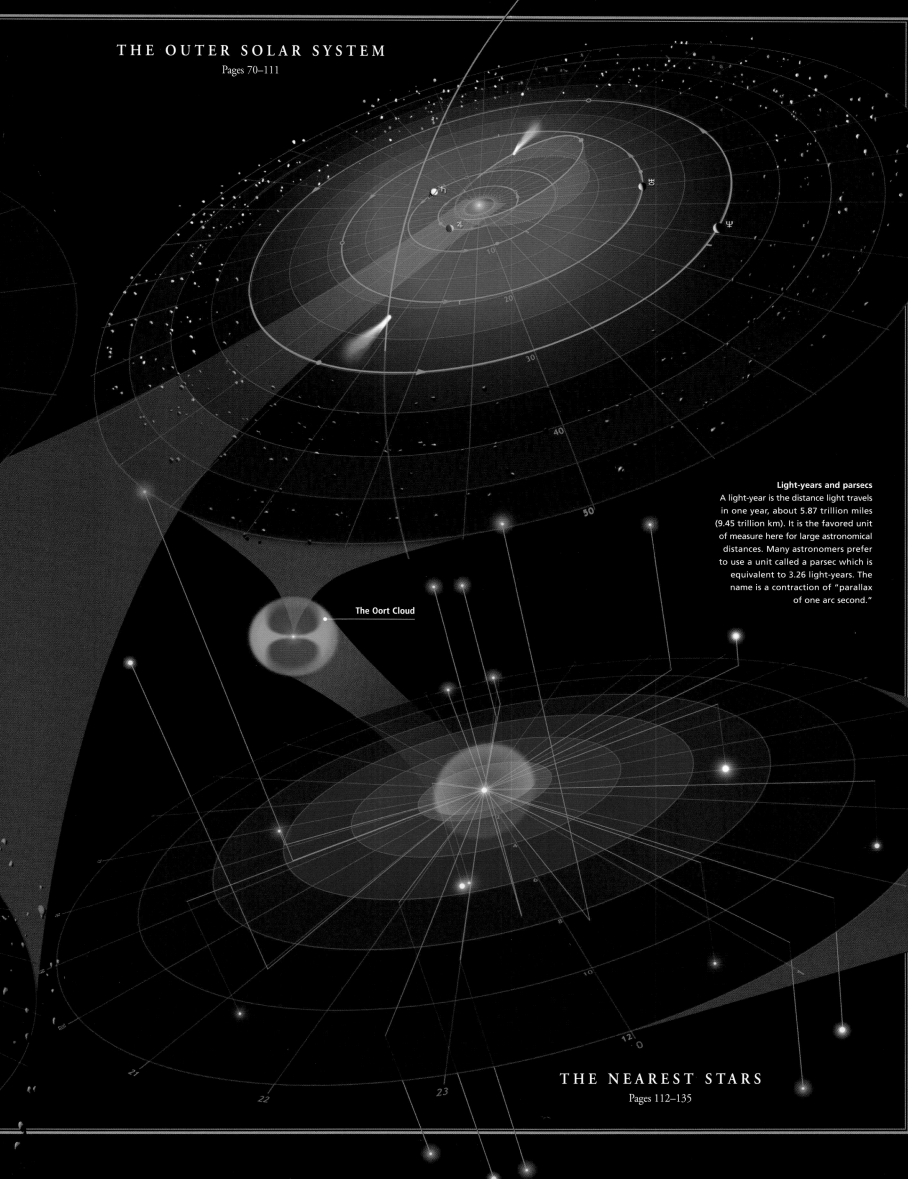

THE OUTER SOLAR SYSTEM
Pages 70–111

Light-years and parsecs
A light-year is the distance light travels
in one year, about 5.87 trillion miles
(9.45 trillion km). It is the favored unit
of measure here for large astronomical
distances. Many astronomers prefer
to use a unit called a parsec which is
equivalent to 3.26 light-years. The
name is a contraction of "parallax
of one arc second."

The Oort Cloud

THE NEAREST STARS
Pages 112–135

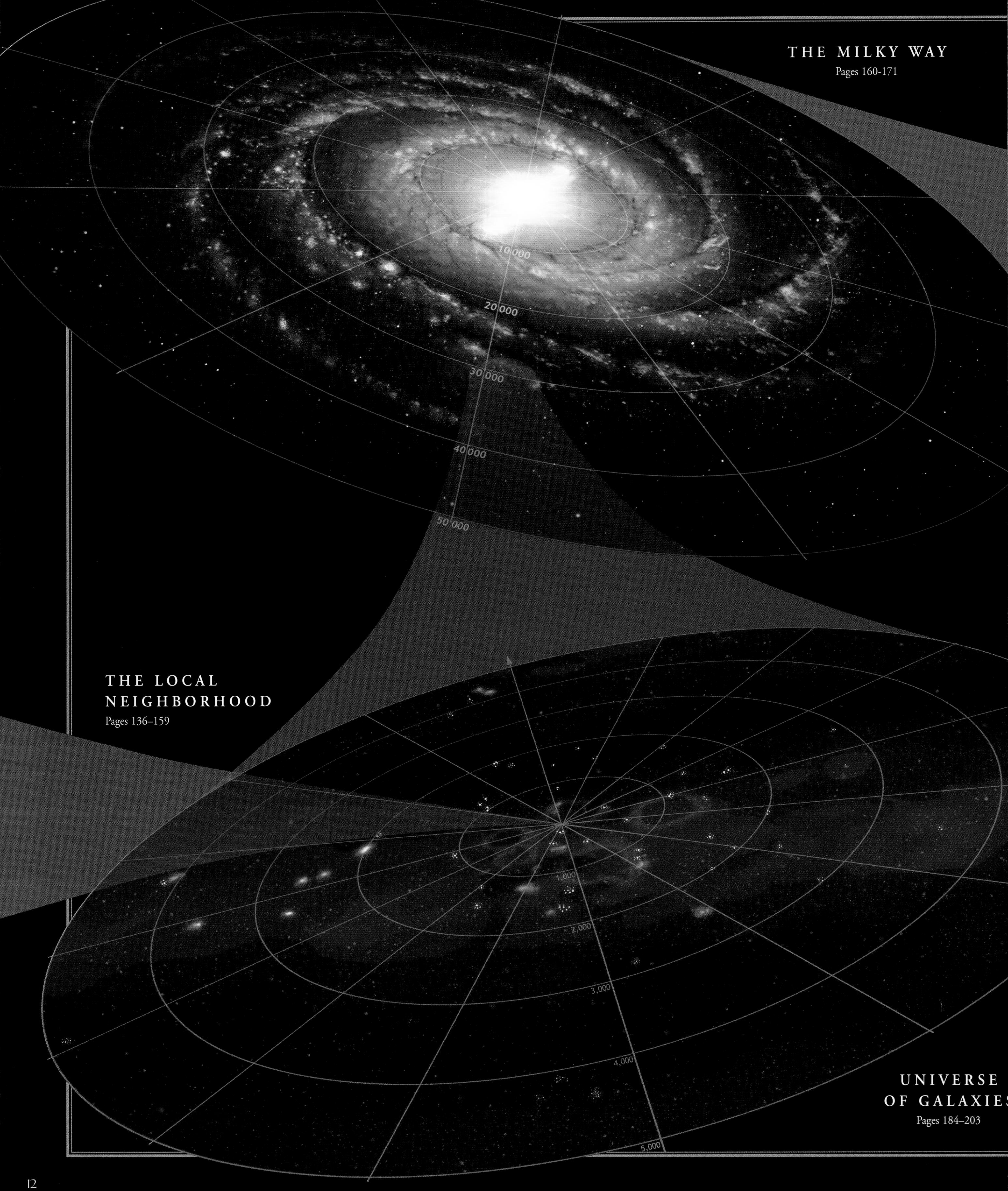
THE MILKY WAY
Pages 160-171
10 000
20 000
30 000
40 000
50 000
THE LOCAL NEIGHBORHOOD
Pages 136–159
1,000
2,000
3,000
4,000
5,000
UNIVERSE OF GALAXIES
Pages 184–203

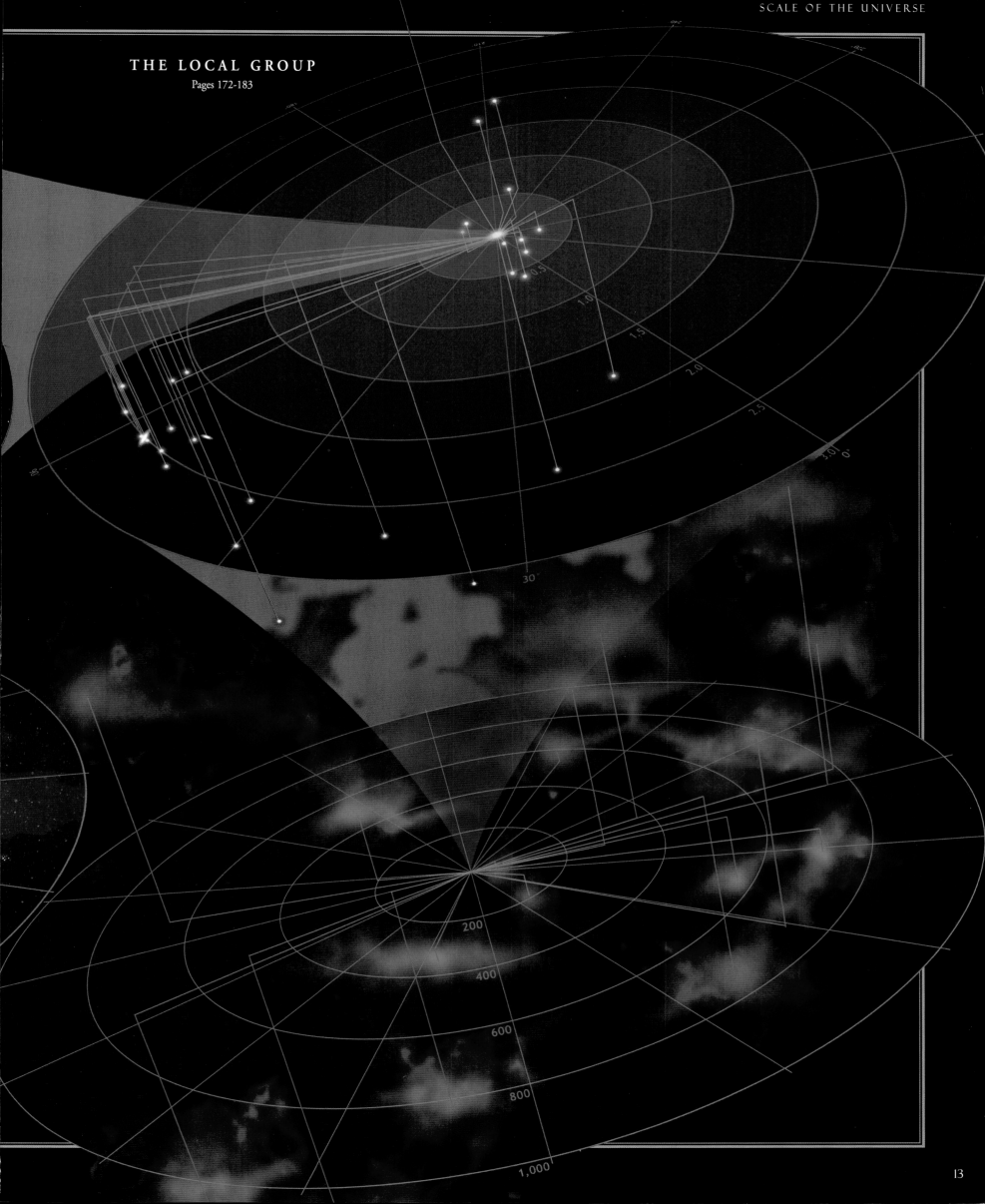

THE LOCAL GROUP
Pages 172-183

In this composite image, the Moon emerges through Earth's blue
atmospheric haze, ascending over a cloudless view of the Sinai Peninsula.
The Moon has been our companion in space for at least 4.5 billion years.

EARTH AND THE MOON

CHARTING EARTH AND THE MOON

Some have argued that Earth and the Moon should be considered a binary planet system, so large is the Moon compared to our world. Our only natural satellite is on average 238,855 miles (384,400 km) distant. It moves in a slightly elongated path, so that in our skies its apparent diameter varies by about ten percent. Strong gravitational forces have locked our satellite into a synchronous rotation with Earth. This means it takes the Moon the same time, 27.32 days, to spin once on its axis as it takes to complete an orbit. The result is that we only ever see the near side or Earth-facing hemisphere—the far side was unknown until the spaceflight era.

Earth and the Moon (below)
The Moon's orbit is somewhat elliptical, its distance from Earth varying by around 24,000 miles (39,000 km). The open and closed circles on the Moon's orbit mark its position closest to (perigee), and farthest from (apogee), Earth, respectively. The farther a satellite is from its parent body, the slower its orbit. The Moon takes almost a month to complete a single revolution whereas some artificial satellites orbit Earth several times a day. Between these extremes is a position—22,300 miles (35,900 km) above the surface—where the orbital period is exactly one day. This is called the geostationary (or geosynchronous) orbit and is shown as the green orbit line on this chart. Astronomers favor the SI (also known as metric) system of units. This is the system used in this diagram, so each increment of the grid represents 62,137 miles (100,000 km).

Tides (left)
The Moon is so large and so comparatively close to Earth that it exerts a considerable gravitational pull on our planet. We witness this force in the daily tides, which are caused by the Moon's gravity pulling at ocean waters. The Sun's gravity also influences the tides, although to a lesser degree. We experience the highest tides, known as spring tides, when Earth, the Moon, and the Sun are aligned.

Earth

The Moon

Earth and the Moon, compared
The Moon is 27 percent the size of the Earth. Only Charon, the largest satellite of the dwarf planet Pluto, is larger compared to its parent world.

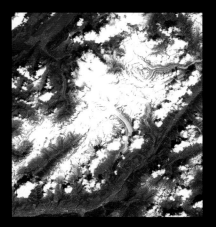

The International Space Station (right)
At least 5,000 artificial satellites have been put into orbit around Earth since the Soviets launched Sputnik in 1957. The vast majority of these have long since burnt up in the atmosphere or constitute orbiting space junk. The International Space Station is the largest and most complex artificial satellite yet constructed.

Water world (left)
Water, in the form of glaciers and rivers, sculpts a rugged mountain landscape in this satellite image of Europe's Central Alps. The vivid green of photosynthesizing plants is a distinctive color over much of Earth's surface.

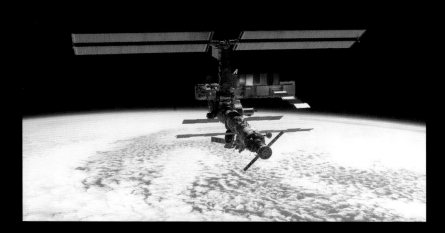

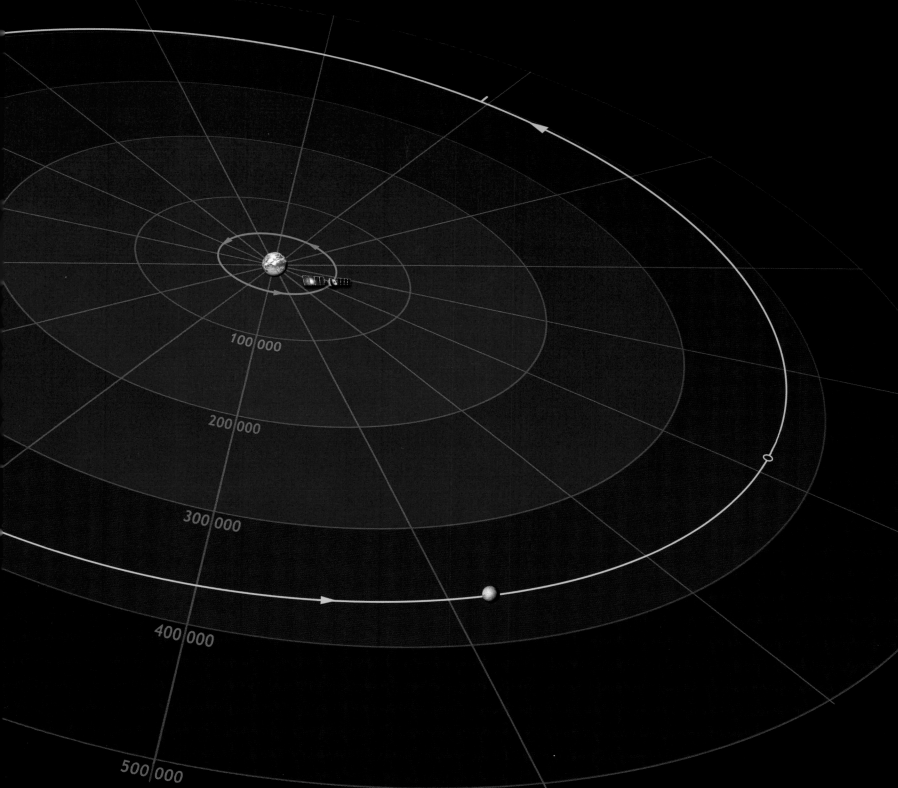

100 000

200 000

300 000

400 000

500 000

EARTH

About 93 million miles (150 million km) from the Sun orbits the third planet, Earth. Like Mercury, Venus, and Mars, Earth is a terrestrial world, a solid sphere made mostly of silicates and metals. Earth is the largest known example of this class of planet, and it is unlike any other in its composition, its climate, and its support of life. Earth's modest atmosphere traps just the right amount of solar energy to raise the ground temperature comfortably above the freezing point of water and its distance from the Sun allows for conditions that are conducive to the presence of liquid surface water. These two factors ensure that well over two-thirds of our planet's surface is covered in this universal solvent—and this is the key to Earth's success as an incubator of life. For if it were slightly cooler here, or hotter, the water would have frozen solid or else evaporated eons ago, and life may never have begun. No other planet in this Solar System or beyond has yet shown conclusive signs of life or habitation.

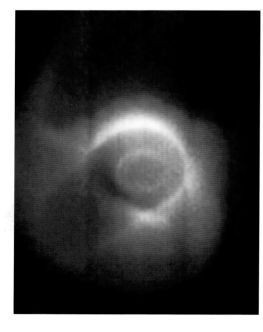

The plasmasphere
Earth is enshrouded in a blanket of plasma or ionized gas called the "plasmasphere" which extends out to a distance of about four Earth radii. The Sun is off to the upper right in this ultraviolet image, a tongue of plasma extending toward it. The faint central ring is the glow caused by north polar aurorae. This image was taken by the Extreme Ultraviolet Imager on NASA's IMAGE spacecraft.

EARTH STATISTICS	
Average distance from the Sun	92.9 million miles (149.6 million km); 1 AU
Equatorial diameter	7,926 miles (12,756 km)
Axial rotation period (sidereal)	23.93 hours
Mass	1.314 x 10^{25} pounds (5.974 x 10^{24} kg)
Volume	0.26 trillion cubic miles (1.08 trillion km^3)
Surface gravity	1 g (9.8 m/s^2)
Average density (water = 1)	5.5
Surface atmospheric pressure	14.7 psi (101.4 kPa)
Escape velocity	6.9 miles/s (11.2 km/s)
Orbital eccentricity	0.017
Highest temperature	136°F (58°C)
Lowest temperature	−126°F (−88°C)
Average albedo (reflectivity)	31%
Number of satellites	1 (the Moon)

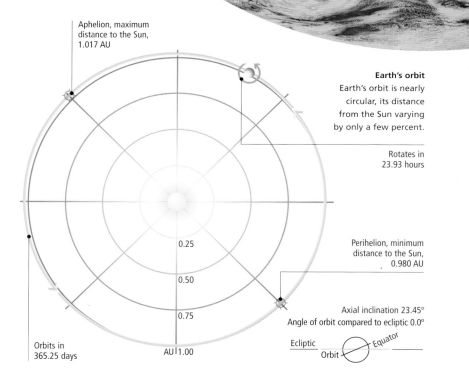

Aphelion, maximum distance to the Sun, 1.017 AU

Earth's orbit
Earth's orbit is nearly circular, its distance from the Sun varying by only a few percent.

Rotates in 23.93 hours

Perihelion, minimum distance to the Sun, 0.980 AU

0.25

0.50

0.75

Axial inclination 23.45°
Angle of orbit compared to ecliptic 0.0°

Orbits in 365.25 days

AU 1.00

Ecliptic

Equator

Orbit

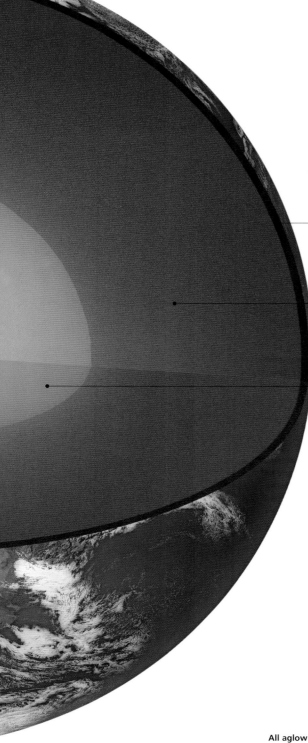

Restless Earth

Earth's landscape is never constant. Volcanoes spew out molten rock that solidifies to form new land, and the vast bodies of water that blanket 71 percent of the surface are sites of creation for sedimentary rocks as well as powerful sources of erosion—as are glaciation, rain, and wind. But perhaps the most important agent of change is the steady march of the continents. The crust is split into gigantic plates that float slowly on a pliable layer called the asthenosphere. Where plates move apart, new material is brought up to the surface to fill in the gaps. And where the plates collide, mountains are created, pushed up many miles high in some places.

Crust
Earth's outermost layer is a thin crust comprised chiefly of volcanic rocks. Its thickness varies, but it is thinnest on the ocean floor where it can be only 5 miles (8 km) deep. Over the continents it is up to eight times thicker.

Mantle
Beneath the crust is a thick mantle, extending down to a depth of about 1,800 miles (2,900 km). Most of the mantle is made up of a compound called olivine, derived from the elements oxygen, magnesium, and silicon.

Core
Earth is the only terrestrial planet with a two-part core. The outer core is liquid, about half the radius of the planet. The inner core is solid and at a very high temperature, similar to that at the surface of the Sun. Both parts are made chiefly of nickel-iron.

The atmosphere and climate of Earth

Our atmosphere is our life-support system and our shield against the dangers of interplanetary space. It harbors about 100 times more gas than the skies of Mars but only 100th the amount of gas that hugs the surface of Venus. The lowest layer, extending from the surface to an average height of 7 miles (11 km), is the troposphere. It is here that we enjoy Earth's mostly temperate climate and experience weather—an everchanging phenomenon driven by the interplay of solar energy, water, land, and Earth's rotation. The layer above this is the stratosphere. It contains the ozone that blocks the Sun's deadly ultraviolet glare. Above this is the mesosphere, the thermosphere, and then the exosphere—a transitional zone between the most rarified atmosphere and interplanetary space.

Atmospheric breakdown
About 78 percent of Earth's atmosphere is nitrogen. Oxygen comprises 21 percent, with argon constituting almost all of the remaining 1 percent. Water vapor is also found in highly variable quantities.

All aglow
Seen from space, Earth at night is aglow with constellations of artificial light. This may look pretty, but for those on the ground trying to peer into space, this light pollution often presents major difficulties.

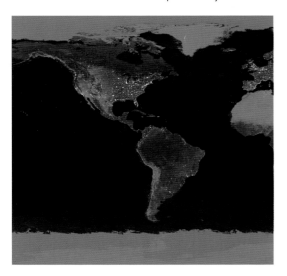

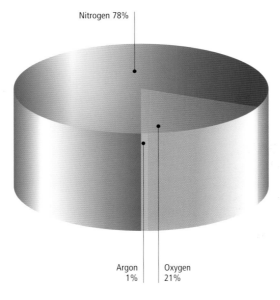

Nitrogen 78%

Argon 1%

Oxygen 21%

Curtain of light
The aurorae (singular, aurora) are caused by charged particles streaming from the Sun. Upon reaching our planet, they get caught up in Earth's magnetic field and collide with molecules in the atmosphere, making them glow.

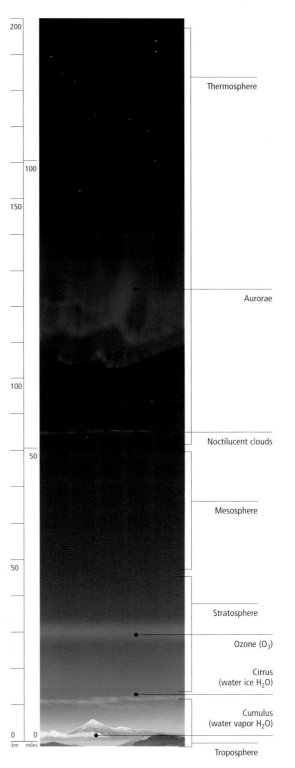

Thermosphere

Aurorae

Noctilucent clouds

Mesosphere

Stratosphere

Ozone (O_3)

Cirrus (water ice H_2O)

Cumulus (water vapor H_2O)

Troposphere

MAPPING EARTH WESTERN HEMISPHERE

Water, water, everywhere: that's a general picture of Earth's western hemisphere. The most prominent feature here is the world's largest ocean, the Pacific, encircled by zones of volcanic and seismic activity called the Ring of Fire. The Pacific Ocean contains twice as much water as the Atlantic, and encompasses an area greater than all of Earth's dry land put together. The North and South American continents are the dominant land features on this hemisphere. The world's largest drainage basin, the Amazon (3°S/60°W), is found here, as is the longest mountain range, the Andes (17°S/68°W).

The western face of Earth (above)
The globe above shows the western hemisphere of Earth as derived from hundreds of satellite photos. The map on the right shows the same area in detail.

Sliding plates (left)
The San Andreas Fault (34°N/118°W) in California marks the boundary where the Pacific and the North American plates meet in a transform boundary, each plate sliding horizontally past the other. This photo shows how strata (layers) in the rock have been deformed by the resultant seismic forces.

Target: Earth (right)
Impact craters are rare on Earth because they are eradicated almost as soon as they form, geologically speaking, by such forces as tectonics, volcanism, and water erosion. However, here is a well-preserved example, Cratère des Pingualuit (or New Québec Crater, 61°N/74°W), now a circular lake in Québec, Canada, with a depth of 876 feet (267 m).

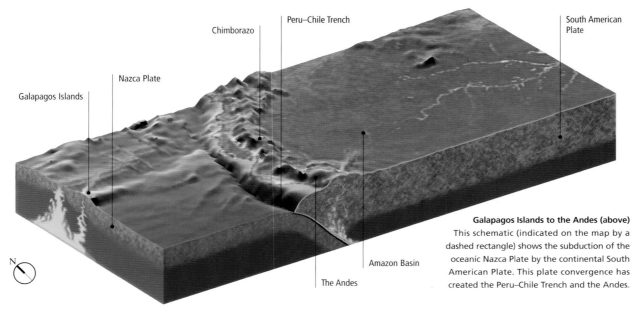

Galapagos Islands

Nazca Plate

Chimborazo

Peru–Chile Trench

South American Plate

Amazon Basin

The Andes

N

Galapagos Islands to the Andes (above)
This schematic (indicated on the map by a dashed rectangle) shows the subduction of the oceanic Nazca Plate by the continental South American Plate. This plate convergence has created the Peru–Chile Trench and the Andes.

Chukchi Sea

Asia

Bering Strait

Bering Sea

Aleutian Basin

Aleutian Islands

Emperor Seamount Chain

Hawaiian Ridge

Midway Islands

Hess Tablemount

Hawaiian

Mid–Pacific Mountains

Christmas

Marshall Islands

Pacific

Howland Island

Central Pacific Basin

Phoenix Islands

Samoa

North Fiji Basin

Fiji

New Hebrides Trench

Norfolk Island Trough

New Caledonia Ridge

Tasman Sea

New Zealand

Kermadec Ridge

Kermadec Trench

Louisville Ridge

Horizon Deep

Tonga Trench

South Fiji Basin

Chatham Rise

Chatham Islands

Campbell Plateau

Pacific–Antarctic

180°E 180°W
90°N
30°N
0°
30°S
60°S
90°S
180°E 180°W

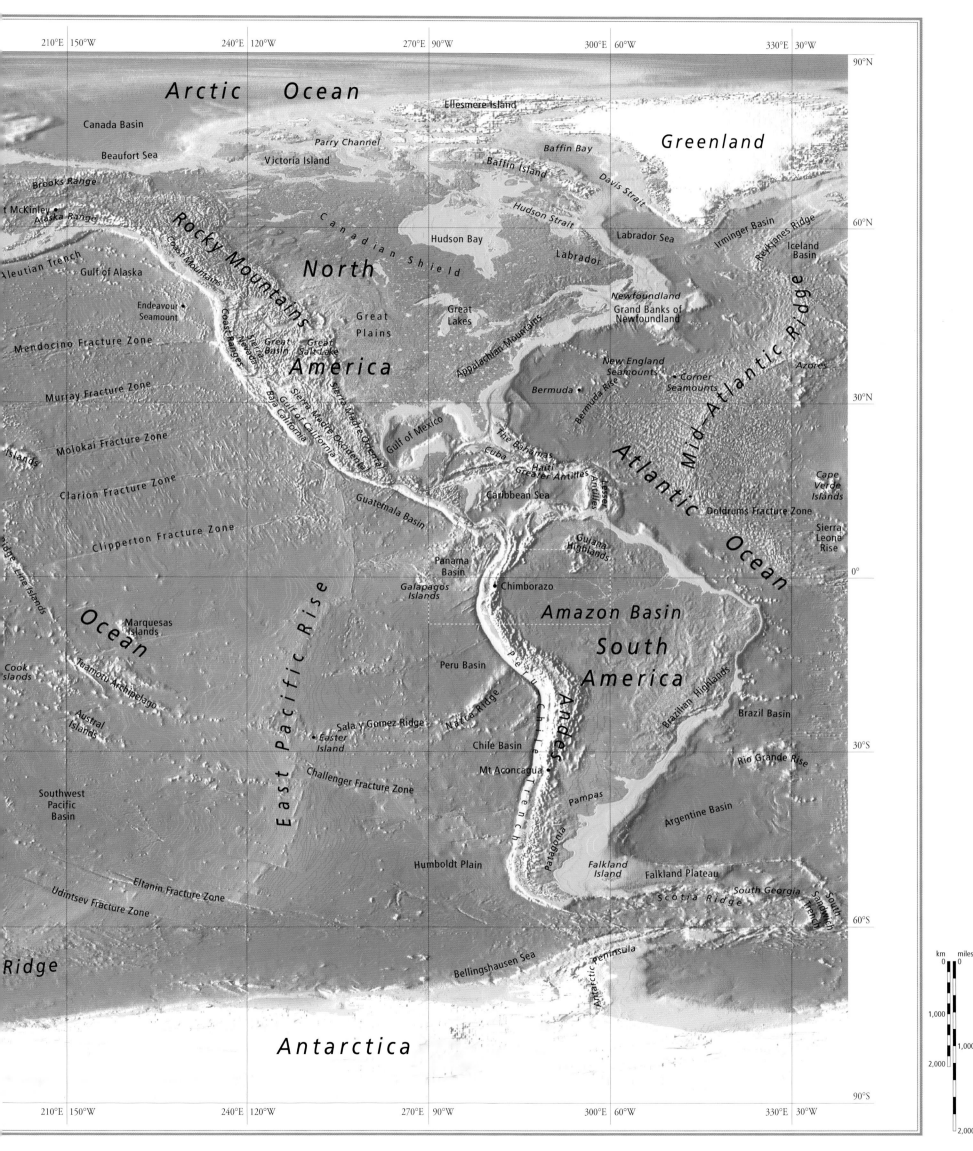

210°E 150°W 240°E 120°W 270°E 90°W 300°E 60°W 330°E 30°W

90°N

Arctic Ocean

Canada Basin

Ellesmere Island

Greenland

Beaufort Sea

Parry Channel

Baffin Bay

Victoria Island

Baffin Island

Davis Strait

Brooks Range

Hudson Strait

Irminger Basin

Reykjanes Ridge

60°N

t McKinley

Alaska Range

Canadian Shield

Hudson Bay

Labrador Sea

Iceland Basin

Aleutian Trench

Gulf of Alaska

North

Great Lakes

Labrador

Endeavour Seamount

Great Plains

Newfoundland

Grand Banks of Newfoundland

Mendocino Fracture Zone

Coast Ranges

Coast Mountains

Appalachian Mountains

New England Seamounts

Corner Seamounts

Azores

America

Great Basin

Great Salt Lake

Bermuda

Bermuda Rise

30°N

Murray Fracture Zone

Sierra Nevada

Baja California

Sierra Madre Occidental

Gulf of California

Sierra Madre Oriental

Gulf of Mexico

The Bahamas

Molokai Fracture Zone

Cuba

Haiti

Greater Antilles

Lesser Antilles

Cape Verde Islands

Clarion Fracture Zone

Caribbean Sea

Doldrums Fracture Zone

Sierra Leone Rise

Islands

Guatemala Basin

Clipperton Fracture Zone

Panama Basin

Guiana Highlands

Atlantic Ocean

0°

idge Line Islands

Galapagos Islands

Chimborazo

Amazon Basin

Mid-Atlantic Ridge

Ocean

Marquesas Islands

South America

Brazilian Highlands

Brazil Basin

Cook Islands

Tuamotu Archipelago

Peru Basin

Peru Chile Trench

East Pacific Rise

Nazca Ridge

30°S

Austral Islands

Sala y Gomez Ridge

Easter Island

Chile Basin

Andes

Rio Grande Rise

Mt Aconcagua

Southwest Pacific Basin

Challenger Fracture Zone

Pampas

Argentine Basin

Humboldt Plain

Patagonia

Falkland Island

Falkland Plateau

South Georgia

60°S

Eltanin Fracture Zone

Scotia Ridge

South Sandwich Trench

Udintsev Fracture Zone

Ridge

Bellingshausen Sea

Antarctic Peninsula

Antarctica

90°S

210°E 150°W 240°E 120°W 270°E 90°W 300°E 60°W 330°E 30°W

km miles
0 0

1,000

1,000

2,000

2,000

MAPPING EARTH EASTERN HEMISPHERE

In contrast to the western hemisphere, the east is dominated by land—Europe and Africa in the west; Asia in the north and center; and Australia in the southeast. There is a lot of movement here. The plates that support Africa and Australia are moving north. India is too, currently colliding into Asia from the south, thrusting up the land and forming the world's highest mountain chain, the Himalaya (28°N/85°E). This hemisphere is also home to the Dead Sea (35.5°E/31.5°N), the lowest point on Earth's continental surface; and the Mariana Trench (16°N/147°E), the deepest ocean trench.

The eastern face of Earth (above)
Earth's eastern hemisphere, as it appears from space, is shown above. The map on the right shows the same area in finer detail.

Volcanic planet (left)
Earth and the distant moons Io and Triton are the only places in the Solar System known to be currently volcanically active. Ol Doinyo Lengai (3°S/36°E) is an example of a cone volcano, still active. Also known as the Mountain of God, it is found in the Great Rift Valley in Tanzania, rising 9,480 feet (2,890 m) above sea level.

Sea stacks (right)
Water is a potent source of erosion, an unceasing agent of change on the surface of our planet. These limestone sea stacks off the coast of Victoria, Australia (41°S/143°E), were once part of the coastline, but constant wave action has eroded the softer rock and left them stranded in the sea.

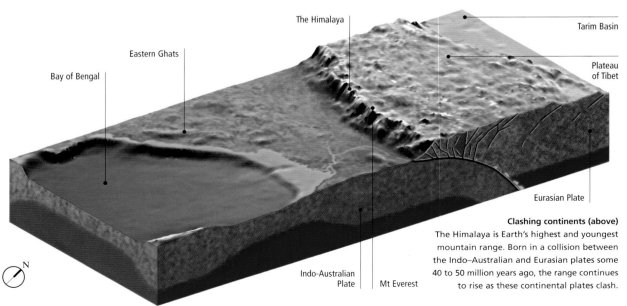

The Himalaya

Eastern Ghats

Bay of Bengal

Tarim Basin

Plateau of Tibet

Eurasian Plate

Indo-Australian Plate

Mt Everest

Clashing continents (above)
The Himalaya is Earth's highest and youngest mountain range. Born in a collision between the Indo–Australian and Eurasian plates some 40 to 50 million years ago, the range continues to rise as these continental plates clash.

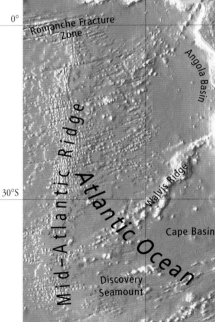

0°E 360°W
90°N

Greenland Basin
East Jan Meyen Ridge
Norwegian Sea
Scandinavia

British Isles
North Sea

English Channel

Bay of Biscay
Mont Blanc

Sardinia
Sicily
Mediterranean

Strait of Gibraltar
Canary Islands

30°N

Hoggar

S a h a
Africa

0°
Romanche Fracture Zone

Angola Basin

Mid–Atlantic Ridge
Atlantic Ocean

Walvis Ridge

30°S

Cape Basin

Discovery Seamount

Atlantic–Indian Ridge

60°S

90°S

0°E 360°W

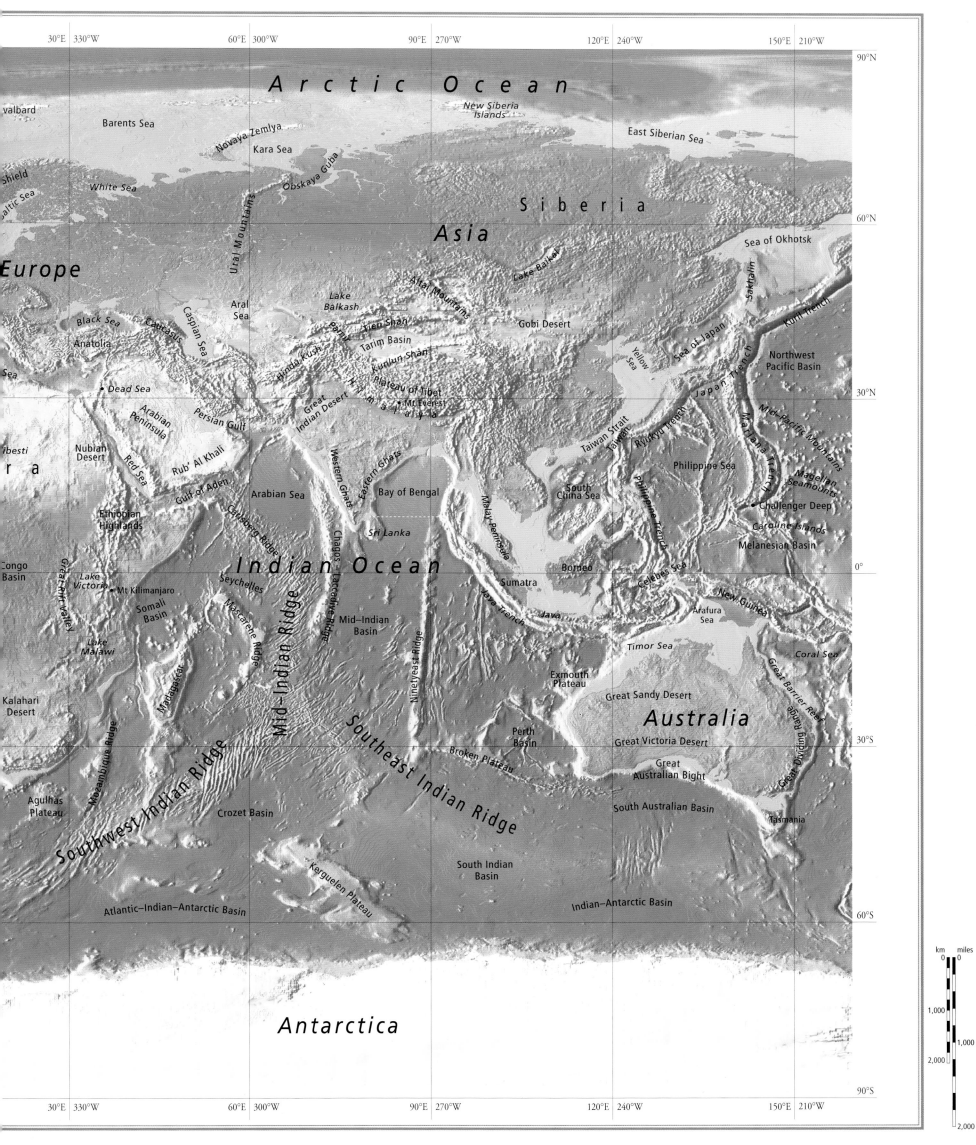

30°E 330°W   60°E 300°W   90°E 270°W   120°E 240°W   150°E 210°W   90°N

Arctic Ocean

Svalbard

Barents Sea

New Siberia
Islands

East Siberian Sea

Novaya Zemlya

Kara Sea

Obskaya Guba

Siberia

60°N

Baltic Sea

White Sea

Shield

Ural Mountains

Asia

Sea of Okhotsk

Europe

Aral
Sea

Lake
Balkash

Altai Mountains

Lake Baikal

Sakhalin

Black Sea

Caucasus

Caspian Sea

Tien Shan

Gobi Desert

Kuril Trench

Anatolia

Pamir

Tarim Basin

Yellow
Sea

Sea of Japan

Northwest
Pacific Basin

Sea

Dead Sea

Hindu Kush

Kunlun Shan

Plateau of Tibet

Mid-Pacific Mountains

30°N

Persian Gulf

Great
Indian Desert

Himalaya

Mt Everest

Taiwan Strait

Taiwan

Ryukyu Trench

Japan Trench

Mariana Trench

Arabian
Peninsula

Tibesti

Nubian
Desert

Red Sea

Rub' Al Khali

Western Ghats

Eastern Ghats

Bay of Bengal

South
China Sea

Philippine Sea

Magellan
Seamounts

ra

Gulf of Aden

Arabian Sea

Sri Lanka

Philippine Trench

Challenger Deep

Ethiopian
Highlands

Carlsberg Ridge

Caroline Islands

Congo
Basin

Great Rift Valley

Lake
Victoria

Seychelles

Mid-Indian
Basin

Malay Peninsula

Sumatra

Borneo

Celebes Sea

Melanesian Basin

0°

Mt Kilimanjaro

Indian Ocean

Chagos-Laccadive Ridge

New Guinea

Somali
Basin

Mascarene Ridge

Java Trench

Java

Arafura
Sea

Lake
Malawi

Timor Sea

Coral Sea

Kalahari
Desert

Madagascar

Mid-Indian Ridge

Ninetyeast Ridge

Exmouth
Plateau

Great Sandy Desert

Great Barrier Reef

Australia

30°S

Mozambique Ridge

Southwest Indian Ridge

Perth
Basin

Great Victoria Desert

Great Dividing Range

Agulhas
Plateau

Broken Plateau

Southeast Indian Ridge

Great
Australian Bight

South Australian Basin

Tasmania

Crozet Basin

South Indian
Basin

Kerguelen Plateau

Atlantic-Indian-Antarctic Basin

Indian-Antarctic Basin

60°S

Antarctica

30°E 330°W   60°E 300°W   90°E 270°W   120°E 240°W   150°E 210°W   90°S

km   miles
0   0

1,000

1,000

2,000

2,000

23

THE MOON

The Moon is our only natural satellite and our nearest neighbor in space. It has been a source of wonder and worship for millennia, and it features in the fables and legends of every culture. Last century, landing a man on the Moon became the greatest prize of the "space race." We are in debt to that contest for much of our knowledge of the Moon, and for technology and techniques of space exploration still in use today. The astronauts who walked on the Moon found an ancient, sterile, and waterless world. But it is fortunate for us that we have it, for its gravity has a stabilizing effect on Earth. Were it not for the Moon, our planet's axis would wobble erratically, adversely affecting the climate and potentially making it difficult for life to have evolved. The currently favored explanation for the Moon's origin is that, shortly after Earth had finished accumulating, it was hit a glancing blow by another partially formed planet, perhaps three times the mass of present-day Mars. The cores of the two protoplanets merged, while debris from the collision went into Earth orbit where it quickly coalesced to form the Moon. Our satellite was a lot closer then, but it has been gradually moving away since. Currently, it is creeping away from us at the rate of about 1.5 inches (4 cm) every year.

Comparing moons
The Moon is a hefty satellite, the fifth largest in the known Solar System, slightly bigger than Jupiter's Europa but smaller than Io, also a Jovian satellite. This image shows the Moon compared to the biggest moon in the Solar System, Jupiter's Ganymede.

MOON STATISTICS	
Discovered	Known from antiquity
Average distance from Earth	238,855 miles (384,400 km)
Equatorial diameter	2,160 miles (3,476 km)
Axial rotation period (sidereal)	656 hours (27.32 days)
Mass (Earth = 1)	0.012
Volume (Earth = 1)	0.020
Surface gravity (Earth = 1)	0.165
Average density (water = 1)	3.35
Escape velocity	1.5 miles/s (2.4 km/s)
Orbital eccentricity	0.055
Highest surface temperature	253°F (123°C)
Lowest surface temperature	−387°F (−233°C)
Sunlight strength	100% Earth's
Albedo (reflectivity)	11%

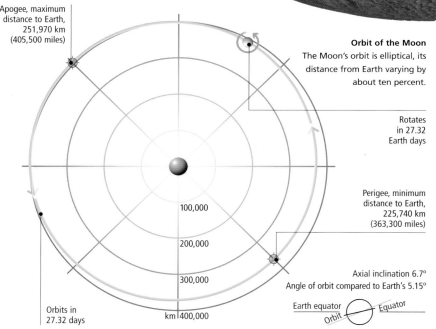

Apogee, maximum distance to Earth, 251,970 km (405,500 miles)

Orbit of the Moon
The Moon's orbit is elliptical, its distance from Earth varying by about ten percent.

Rotates in 27.32 Earth days

Perigee, minimum distance to Earth, 225,740 km (363,300 miles)

100,000

200,000

300,000

km 400,000

Orbits in 27.32 days

Axial inclination 6.7°
Angle of orbit compared to Earth's 5.15°

Earth equator   Equator
Orbit

The geology of the Moon

The Moon's surface is ancient. About 3.9 billion years ago, at the end of a period of heavy bombardment, the lunar highlands looked pretty much as they do now. However, between then and about 3 billion years ago, some parts of the Moon were modified when vast floods of thin lava, with the consistency of motor oil, oozed onto the surface, spread out, and solidified, forming the lunar maria. Aside from this, the lunar surface geology has not changed significantly in billions of years.

The emergent Moon
The Moon is seen forming (right) alongside Earth (left) in this artist's impression. The Moon is coalescing from a disk of debris around the young planet. The debris possibly resulted from a two-planet collision.

Crust
The lunar crust is thought to average about 45 miles (70 km) thick. It is thicker compared with Earth's crust because it cooled and solidified much faster.

Mantle
The Moon's mantle is at least 620 miles (1,000 km) deep. It is made chiefly of rocky materials, and contains few metals. Mild moonquakes originate from deep inside the mantle.

Core
Magnetic data collected by the Lunar Prospector craft in 1999 indicates that the Moon has a small core making up less than four percent of its total mass. It is probably partially molten.

Crater mechanics

Impact craters are formed when an asteroid, meteoroid, or comet smashes into a planetary surface at a speed of several miles per second. This process is illustrated at right. Both the object and the ground immediately where it hits are vaporized upon impact. Shockwaves from the blow travel outward from the impact zone, crushing, melting, or vaporizing the bedrock and excavating a wide cavity (1). This material is thrown radially outward and settles to form an ejecta blanket and, sometimes, secondary craters (2). In the largest craters, the walls can slump to form terraces, and often the ground under the impact site "rebounds" to create a central peak (3).

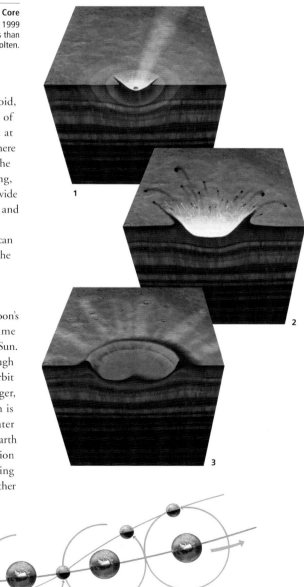

1

2

3

Lunar phases

The phases of the Moon are a consequence of the Moon's orbit around Earth, with the phase at any given time dictated by the position of the Moon, Earth, and the Sun. The diagram below illustrates a single cycle. Although the Moon takes 27.32 days (the sidereal month) to orbit Earth, the time for a complete cycle is slightly longer, at 29.53 days (synodic month). Imagine the Moon is at the start of a phase cycle. One sidereal month later it completes one revolution about Earth. However, Earth itself has moved on in its own orbit, so the illumination on the Moon is not quite what it was at the beginning of the phase cycle. The Moon has to move slightly farther in order for the phase cycle to "catch up."

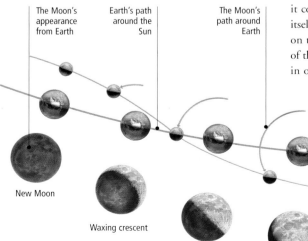

The Moon's appearance from Earth

Earth's path around the Sun

The Moon's path around Earth

New Moon

Waxing crescent

First quarter

Waxing gibbous

Full Moon

Waning gibbous

Last quarter

Waning crescent

New Moon

MAPPING THE MOON NORTHERN NEAR SIDE

The hemisphere of the Moon visible from Earth is distinctive. Most notable are the smooth dark patches that help convey the illusion of a "Man in the Moon"—the so-called maria (singular, mare). Maria is Latin for "seas," for that is what they were at first believed to be. However, the maria are floods, not of water but of solidified lava that oozed onto the lunar crust between 3.9 billion and 3 billion years ago. The northern half of the near side has more maria than the other half. Channels called rimae (or rilles) are also prominent here, as well as several bright ray craters. The Moon is generally shown as it is seen from Earth's northern hemisphere, with the same orientation as the map, right. But southern observers see it "upside down," with north in the lower half.

Moonwalk under Mons Hadley (above)
James B. Irwin, from the Apollo 15 mission, adjusts the Lunar Roving Vehicle at the Hadley-Apennine landing site (26°N/3.5°E). Mons Hadley looms in the background and the extended shadow of the Lunar Module "Falcon" shrouds the foreground.

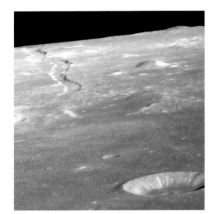

Moon channel (above)
This is Rima Ariadaeus (6°N/14°E, top left) as photographed by the Apollo 10 crew in 1969. A rima (plural, rimae), which means "fissure" or "crack," is a narrow furrow on the lunar surface. Sinuous rimae, such as Ariadaeus, are believed to have once been open channels of lava or underground lava tubes that collapsed when the flow was exhausted.

KEY TO SYMBOLS
- Luna
- Surveyor
- Apollo
- Ranger
- Lunar Orbiter
- Hiten
- Lunar Prospector

North

Pascal
Goldschmid
Carpenter
Pythagoras
J. Herschel
60°N
Oenopides
Mare Frigoris
Harpalus
Xenophanes
Sinus Roris
Plato
Montes Recti
Montes Teneriffe
Montes Jura
Sharp
Sinus Iridum
Promontorium Laplace
Mons Pico
Delisle Gruithulsen
Mairan
von Braun
Helicon
Le Verrier
Mons Rümker
Mare
Malran
Luna 17
Mons Gruithuisen Gamma
Mons Gruithuisen Delta
Montes Spitzbergen
30°N
Montes Agricola
Krieger
Delisle
Archimedes
Vallis Schröteri
Montes Harbinger
Diophantus
Timocharis
Russell
Prinz
Lambert
Montes Archimedes
Schiaparelli
Aristarchus
Euler
Imbrium
Struve
Herodotus
Mons Vinogradov
Seleucus
Brayley
Pytheas
Wallace
Eddington
Montes Apenninus
Luna 13
Montes Carpatus
Krafft
T. Mayer
Oceanus
Eratosthenes
Cardanus
Gay-Lussac
Marius
Sinus Aestuum
Luna 8
Luna 7
Procellarum
Copernicus
Luna 9
Kepler
Olbers
Pallas
Reiner
Cavalerius
Fauth
Hortensius
Schröter
Hedin
Encke
Mare Insularum
Reinhold
Surveyor 2
Hevelius
Gambart
Surveyor 4+6
0°
60°W
30°W

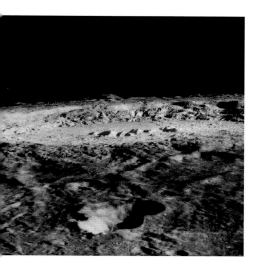

Copernicus crater (left)

Copernicus (9.5°N/20°W) is a prominent crater in Mare Imbrium. Measuring 58 miles (93 km) across, the crater has multiple central peaks and terraced walls. The unmanned Lunar Orbiter 2 craft acquired this oblique image in November 1966.

Lunar landings

The table at right, and those on the following pages, list all known locations of manned, unmanned, crashed, and deliberately impacted lunar craft. The final resting place of two US Explorer satellites and several Soviet Luna craft are undetermined. Other man-made objects on the lunar surface include stages of the Saturn rockets used in the Apollo missions.

LUNAR LANDINGS – NORTHERN NEAR SIDE			
MISSION	**DATE**	**RESULT**	**LANDING SITE**
Luna 2	Sep 14, 1959	Deliberate impact	29°N/0°E
Ranger 6	Jan 30, 1964	Deliberate impact	8.5°N/21°E
Ranger 8	Feb 20, 1965	Deliberate impact	2.5°N/24.5°E
Luna 7	Oct 4, 1965	Crashed	9°N/49°W
Luna 8	Dec 6, 1965	Crashed	9°N/63°W
Luna 9	Feb 3, 1966	Successful landing	7°N/64.5°W
Surveyor 2	Sep 22, 1966	Crashed	4°N/11°W
Luna 13	Dec 24, 1966	Successful landing	18°N/62°W
Surveyor 4	Jul 17, 1967	Crashed	0.5°N/1°W
Surveyor 5	Sep 11, 1967	Successful landing	1.5°N/22°E
Surveyor 6	Nov 10, 1967	Successful landing	0.5°N/1°W
Apollo 11	Jul 20, 1969	Successful landing	0.5°N/23°E
Luna 15	Jul 21, 1969	Crashed	17°N/60°E
Luna 17	Nov 17, 1970	Successful landing	38°N/35°W
Apollo 15	Jul 30, 1971	Successful landing	26°N/3.5°E
Luna 18	Sep 1, 1971	Crashed	3.5°N/56.5°E
Luna 20	Feb 21, 1972	Successful landing	3.5°N/56.5°E
Apollo 17	Dec 11, 1972	Successful landing	20°N/31°E
Luna 21	Jan 15, 1973	Successful landing	26°N/30.5°E
Luna 23	Nov 1, 1974	Successful landing	12.5°N/62°E
Luna 24	Aug 14, 1976	Successful landing	12.5°N/62°E

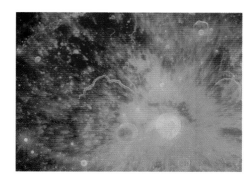

Aristarchus assault (above)

This is a false-color photomosaic of about 500 Clementine lunar orbiter images, showing the vast ejecta blanket surrounding the explosive crater Aristarchus (24°N/47°W, center right). This region is also heavily etched by rimae, including the distinctly arched Vallis Schröteri (26°N/51°W, center left).

Scale is correct for latitude 0° / longitude 0°

MAPPING THE MOON SOUTHERN NEAR SIDE

The southern half of the lunar near side has less maria coverage than the northern half; the landscape is instead dominated by highland regions. Tycho, the Moon's most striking ray crater, is here. Ejecta samples, collected some 1,400 miles (2,200 km) from the crater itself, have dated this relatively young crater as 110 million years old. In general, lunar craters are named after astronomers, astronauts, and philosophers, while mountain ranges are named after those on Earth, such as Montes Pyrenaeus, whose namesake is Earth's famous Pyrenees. Maria have whimsical Latin names, such as Mare Nubium—the "Sea of Clouds."

Lunar excursion (above)
Tracks from a Modular Equipment Transport meander across the Fra Mauro crater floor on the Moon's southern near side. The tracks, only 0.75 inches (19 mm) deep, lead to "Antares," Apollo 14's Lunar Landing Module.

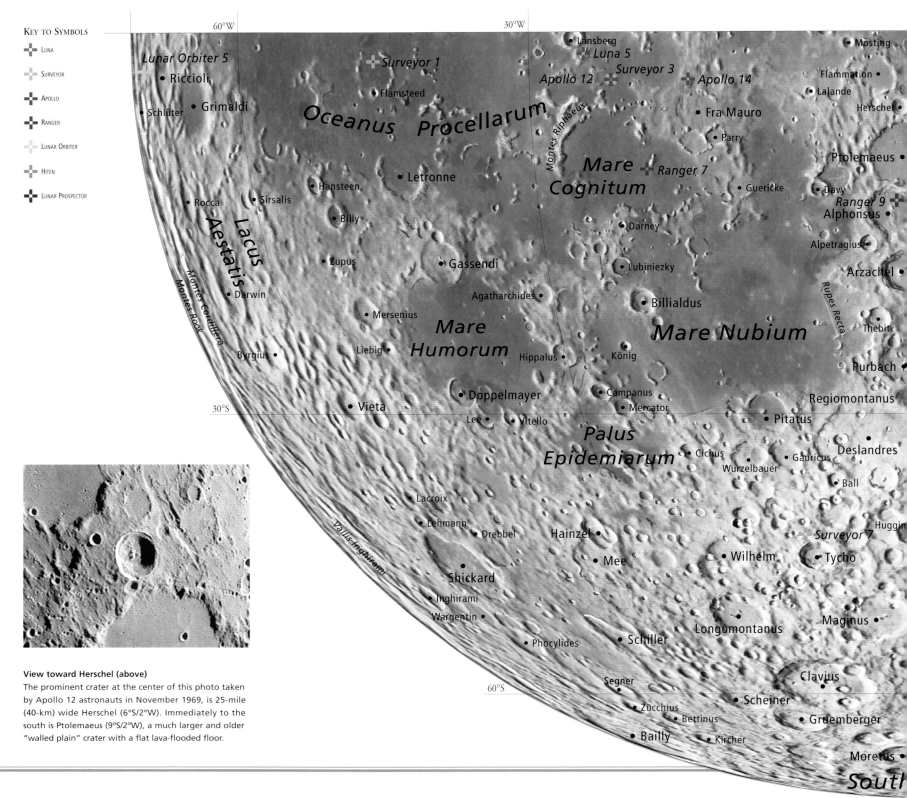

KEY TO SYMBOLS
- Luna
- Surveyor
- Apollo
- Ranger
- Lunar Orbiter
- Hiten
- Lunar Prospector

60°W 30°W

Lunar Orbiter 5
• Riccioli
• Schlüter   • Grimaldi
Surveyor 1
Flamsteed
Oceanus Procellarum

Lansberg
Luna 5
Apollo 12   Surveyor 3   Apollo 14
• Fra Mauro
Mosting
Flammarion
• Lalande
Herschel

Letronne
• Hansteen
Montes Riphaeus
Mare Cognitum   Ranger 7
• Guericke
Ptolemaeus
• Davy
Ranger 9
Alphonsus •

• Rocca   • Sirsalis
• Billy
• Darney
Alpetragius •

Lacus Aestatis
• Zupus
• Gassendi
• Lubiniezky
Arzachel •

Montes Cordillera
Montes Rook
• Darwin
• Mersenius
Agatharchides •
• Billialdus
Mare Nubium
Rupes Recta
Thebit

• Byrgius
Liebig •
Mare Humorum
Hippalus •
König •
• Purbach

Vallis Inghirami
• Vieta
• Doppelmayer
Lee •   • Vitello
• Campanus
• Mercator
Regiomontanus
• Pitatus

30°S

Palus Epidemiarum
• Cichus
Wurzelbauer
• Gauricus
Deslandres
• Ball

• Lacroix
• Lehmann
• Drebbel
Hainzel •
• Mee
• Wilhelm
Surveyor 7
• Tycho
Huggin

Shickard
• Inghirami
Wargentin •
• Phocylides
• Schiller
Longomontanus
Maginus •

60°S

Segner •
• Zucchius
• Bettinus
• Kircher
• Bailly
• Scheiner
Clavius •
• Gruemberger

Moretus •
South

View toward Herschel (above)
The prominent crater at the center of this photo taken by Apollo 12 astronauts in November 1969, is 25-mile (40-km) wide Herschel (6°S/2°W). Immediately to the south is Ptolemaeus (9°S/2°W), a much larger and older "walled plain" crater with a flat lava-flooded floor.

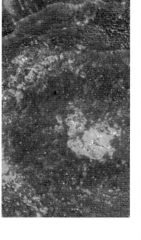
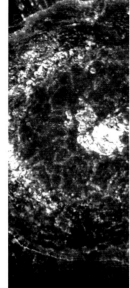

Tycho triptych
Three views of crater Tycho (43°S/11°W) are seen in these
Clementine images. On the left is the true-color version.
The false-color views (center and right) enable the identification of
different minerals in the surface material. Tycho's central peaks are
visible in each view, rising 1 mile (1.6 km) above the crater floor.

LUNAR LANDINGS – SOUTHERN NEAR SIDE			
MISSION	**DATE**	**RESULT**	**LANDING SITE**
Ranger 7	Jul 31, 1964	Deliberate impact	10.5°S/22°W
Ranger 9	Mar 24, 1965	Deliberate impact	13°S/2.5°W
Luna 5	May 1, 1965	Crashed	1.5°S/25°W
Surveyor 1	Jun 2, 1966	Successful landing	2.5°S/43°W
Surveyor 3	Apr 20, 1967	Successful landing	3°S/23°W
Lunar Orbiter 5	Jan 31, 1968	Deliberate impact	3°S/83°W
Surveyor 7	Jan 10, 1968	Successful landing	40.5°S/11.5°W
Apollo 12	Nov 19, 1969	Successful landing	3°S/23°W
Luna 16	Sep 20, 1970	Successful landing	0.5°S/56°E
Apollo 14	Feb 5, 1971	Successful landing	3.5°S/17.5°W
Apollo 16	Apr 20, 1972	Successful landing	8.5°S/5.5°E
Hiten	Apr 10, 1993	Deliberate impact	34°S/55.5°E
Lunar Prospector	Jul 31, 1999	Deliberate impact	87.5°S/42°E

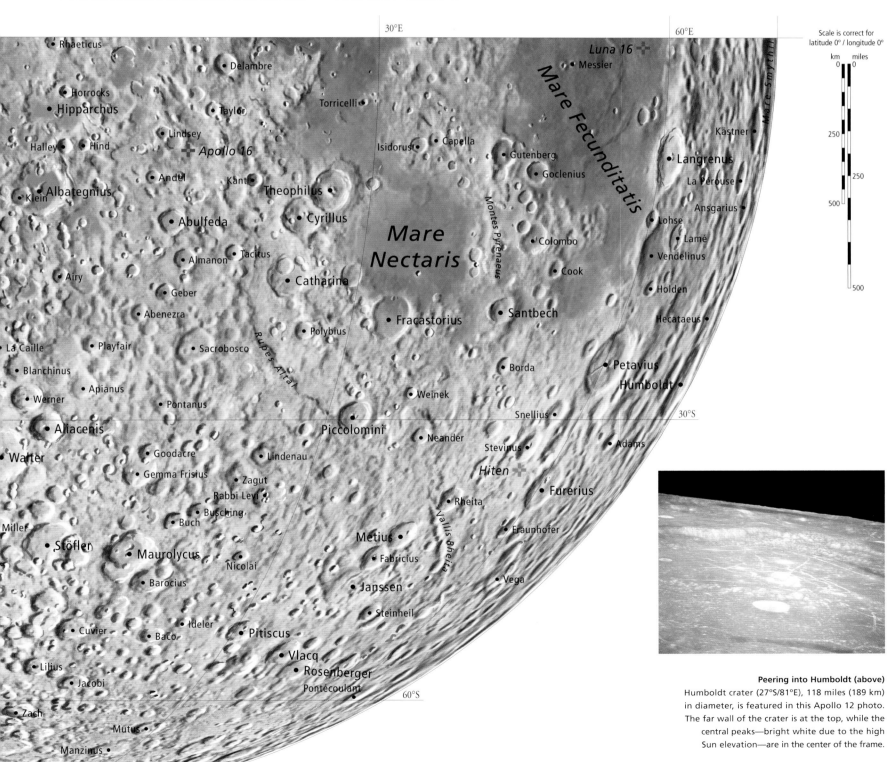

Scale is correct for
latitude 0° / longitude 0°

Peering into Humboldt (above)
Humboldt crater (27°S/81°E), 118 miles (189 km)
in diameter, is featured in this Apollo 12 photo.
The far wall of the crater is at the top, while the
central peaks—bright white due to the high
Sun elevation—are in the center of the frame.

Mapping the Moon Far Side

Because the Moon rotates on its axis in the same time that it takes to orbit Earth (27.32 days), we always see the same lunar face; or, very nearly. In fact, the Moon's orbit is not quite circular, and its rotation axis is not perpendicular to its orbital plane, so it appears to "wobble" slightly—an effect known as libration—enabling us to see just around the near-side Moon edges. In total we can see up to 59 percent of the surface of the Moon from our home planet. The remaining part was a complete mystery until the advent of spaceflight. The first glimpse of the lunar far side was returned by the Luna 3 probe in 1959. Since then, various missions have enabled us to draw up detailed maps of this elusive face of the Moon. These observations have shown that, compared to the near side, the far side has very few maria and an intensely cratered surface. The probable explanation for this difference is that the thicker crust of the far side prevented flow of interior molten material to the surface and, as a result, inhibited the creation of smooth maria.

LUNAR LANDINGS – FAR SIDE			
MISSION	**DATE**	**RESULT**	**LANDING SITE**
Ranger 4	Apr 26, 1962	Deliberate impact	15.5°S/130.5°W
Lunar Orbiter 1	Oct 29, 1966	Deliberate impact	7°N/161°E
Lunar Orbiter 3	Oct 9, 1967	Deliberate impact	14°N/97.5°W
Lunar Orbiter 2	Oct 11, 1967	Deliberate impact	3°N/119°E

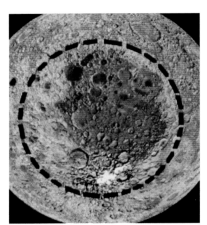

Lunar bull's-eye (above)
Largely hidden over the western edge of the lunar near side is Mare Orientale, the Moon's youngest large impact feature. Unlike similar impact basins on the near side, only the very center of Mare Orientale flooded with lava and its impact structures are otherwise well preserved. From the outermost of its three concentric rings of mountains, the basin is 580 miles (930 km) across, although ejecta from the impact have buried older terrain over a far greater area.

Deep impact (left)
This photograph of the deepest far-side crater, Tsiolkovsky (21°S/128°E), was taken during the December 1968 Apollo 8 mission which rounded the Moon but did not land. Tsiolkovsky measures about 115 miles (185 km) in diameter and is distinguished by an exceptionally dark basaltic lava flow on its floor. As with many far-side features, Tsiolkovsky was discovered and named by Soviet scientists.

Battered surface (left)
Northeast of the crater Tsiolkovsky, on the lunar far side, the landscape is heavily cratered. Impacts of various sizes dot the scene right down to the resolution limit of this Apollo 17 photo. The crater in the center, itself pitted by impacts, is about 47 miles (75 km) in diameter.

Buried scar (left)
Centered on the far side of the Moon near the southern pole is the largest and deepest known impact scar in the entire Solar System: the Aitken Basin. This vast crater is some 1,550 miles (2,500 km) in diameter or seven times the area of France, and an average of 6.2 miles (10 km) lower than the surrounding highlands. Over time, this ancient feature has been disfigured by further impacts so that, despite its size, it is difficult to recognize without color-coded topographical images such as this from Clementine orbiter data.

Swann

H. G. Wells

Giordano
Bruno · Canto
Kidinnu
Szilard

Espin · Seyfert
Maxwell
Artamanov
Vernadskiy
Siedentop
Olcott
Gavrilov
Hoffmeister
Fleming
Hertz
Guyot
Ostwald
Lobachevskiy

Lunar Orbiter 2

Vesalius
Prager
Lane
Chauvenet
Pasteur

Hilbert
Tsiolkovsky

Scaliger
Milne

Bjerknes Clark
Lebede

30°N

0° · 120°E

30°S

North Pole

• Schwarzschild   • Roberts   • Sommerfeld
• Dugan   Gamow   • Avogadro   • Emden   • Stebbins
60°N   • Oliver   Tikhov   Yamamoto   • Rowland   Birkhoff   Dyson   60°N
• Compton   • van Rhijn   • Cooper   • Carnot   Coulomb
D'Alembert   Slipher   • Montgolfier   Esnault-Pelterie   Sarton
• Campbell   • Perkin   • Kulik   • Fowler   Stefan
Millikan   • Duner   • Poczobutt
• Bridgeman   • Ley   • Evershed   • Gadomski
• Wiener   Von Neumann   • Krylov   • Lorentz
• Kurchatov   • Cockcroft   Kovalevskaya
Vijland   • Shayn   • Larmor   • Joule   Parenago
• Trumpler   • Fitzgerald   • Mach   Poynting   Robertson
Mare   • Freundlich   • Dante   • Kekulé   Fersman
Moscoviense   • Komarov   • Morse   • Jackson   Lunar Orbiter 3
• Konstantinov   • Hayford   • McMath   Henyey   Kolhörster
Leonov   • Andersson   Artem'ev
• Tsu Chung-Chi   Kohlschütter   • Spencer   • Valier   • Zhukovskiy   Michelson
• Papaleksi   Tsander   Hertzsprung
Mendeleev Lunar Orbiter 1   • Krasovskiy   • Kibal'chich   Leuschner
• Schuster   150°E   180°   150°W   120°W   0°
• Schliemann   • Vening Meinesz   • Congreve   • Vavilov
Chaplygin   • Daedalus   Icarus   Korolev   • Lucretius
• Marconi   Keeler   • Amici   • Sechenov
• Beijerinck   Heaviside   • Brookes   Paschen
Isaev   • Geiger   • Aitken   Doppler   • Ioffe
Gagarin   • De Vries   • McKellar   Galois   • Houzeau
• Levi-Civita   • Paracelsus   • Bok   Gerasimovich
Pavlov   • Sierpinski   Van de Graaff   • Plummer   Strömgren
ubbotin   • Leeuwenhoek   • Barringer   • Von der Pahlen
30°S   Scobee   Kleymenov
Mare   • Chebyshev
Jules Verne   Ingenii   Oppenheimer   Apollo   • Brouwer
• Obruchev   Leibnitz   • Chaffee   Lovell   Blackett
Roche   • Koch   • Oresme   Maksutov   Borman   • Buffon
Cacyer   • Pauli   Von Karman   • Anders
• Ceraski   • White   • Grissom
Cassegrain   • Hess   • Bose   • Stoney   Mendel
• Fechner   Poincaré   Karrer   Lippmann
60°S   • Planck   • Minkowski   60°S
Vallis Planck   • Lemaître
Vallis Schrödinger   • Lyman   • Antoniadi
Schrödinger   Minnaert   Zeeman

South Pole

Ranger 4

Mare Orientale

Scale is correct for
latitude 0° / longitude 180°

km   miles
0   0
250
250
500
500

MISSIONS TO THE MOON

As our nearest neighbor in space, the Moon has been subject to more study than any other planetary body. The Soviets beat the Americans to much of the glory in the early days of lunar exploration, with their highly successful Luna series of probes starting in 1959. This was just two years after they had launched the first artificial satellite, Sputnik. But the Americans eventually caught up in the "space race" with a whole host of programs of their own, such as Ranger, Surveyor, Lunar Orbiter, and, of course, Apollo—the only manned missions to another world. Fascination with the Moon continues today, and there has even been renewed interest in sending humans there.

First view of the far side (left)
Our first glimpse of the far side of our natural satellite had to wait until October 7, 1959 when the Soviet Luna 3 probe returned this poor-quality but enticing photo of the far side from a distance of 39,500 miles (63,500 km). The dark spot at upper right is Mare Moscoviense (27°N/148°E).

US pre-Apollo programs
NASA managed a battery of lunar missions in the lead-up to Apollo. First came the Rangers—probes which returned photos of the Moon before they crashed into it. Then came five Lunar Orbiters, with the primary mission of finding suitable landing sites for the Surveyor probes, which became the first probes to obtain in-situ compositional data on the Moon.

The Luna program
Between 1959 and 1976, the Soviet Union launched a total of 24 Moon probes named Luna. The program achieved a great many firsts in space exploration: Luna 2 was the first man-made object to hit the Moon; Luna 3 the first probe to return photos of our satellite's far side; Luna 9 the first to make a soft landing on the Moon; and Luna 10 the first to go into lunar orbit.

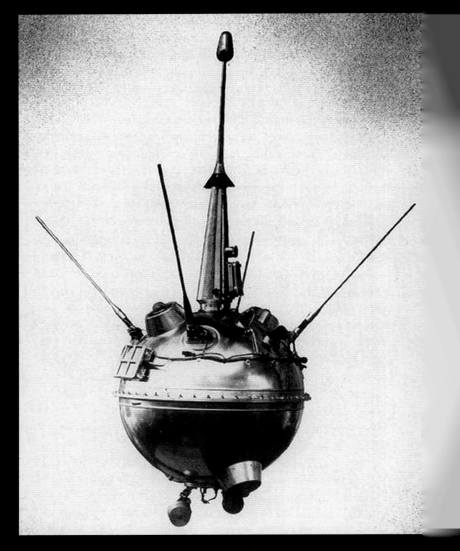

17 minutes to impact (left)
This Ranger 7 image was the first photo of the lunar surface returned by a US spacecraft. The large crater at upper right is Alphonsus (14°S/3°W).

Luna 2 probe (right)
Luna 2 was the first probe to reach another planetary body, when it impacted the lunar surface east of Mare Serenitatis (28°N/17.5°E) on September 14, 1959. Its instrumentation was equipped to measure radiation levels, magnetic fields, and detect any micrometeorite impacts.

Mission Ranger (right)
NASA's Ranger probes were designed to fly directly at the Moon and return images before colliding with the surface. The program was plagued by technical failures until Ranger 6 flew a perfect flight, albeit without transmitting any images. Rangers 7 (illustrated right), 8, and 9 returned many thousands of images showing the lunar surface in unprecedented detail.

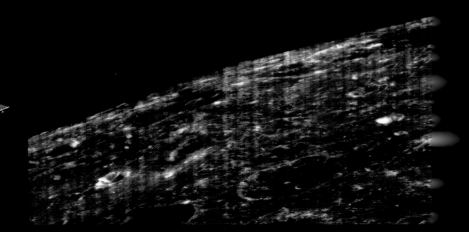

Earthrise (right)
This image, returned by Lunar Orbiter 1 in August 1966, was our first view of Earth from the vicinity of the Moon.

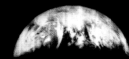

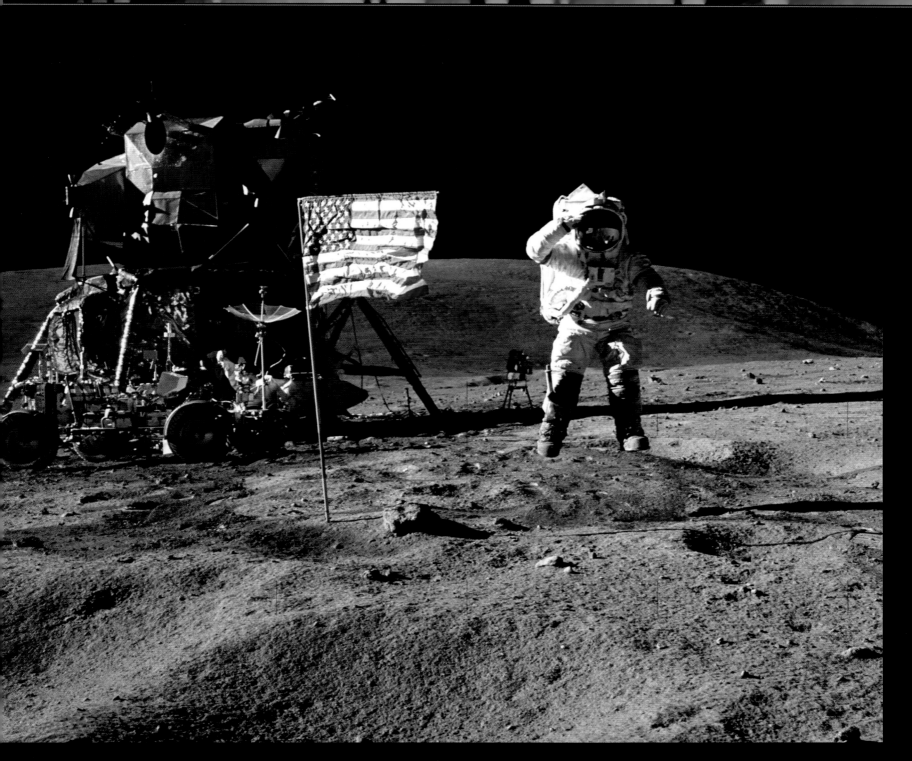

The Apollo program

The Apollo missions were perhaps the most exciting of all missions: a time when human beings walked on the surface of an alien world. However, Apollo got off to a bad start. In 1967, a fire in the Apollo 1 command capsule killed three astronauts who were conducting ground tests. Fortunately, NASA's luck changed. In 1968, Apollo 8 became the first manned craft to leave Earth orbit, ferrying three men around the Moon. Apollo 9 and 10 were practice missions, in preparation for the first actual manned landing, which took place on July 20, 1969. This was Apollo 11, under the command of Neil Armstrong. Sadly, interest in Apollo waned quickly thereafter. The last time man walked on the Moon was during the Apollo 17 mission in December 1972. In total, only twelve people have visited the Moon, all men, all American. The photo above shows John W. Young, commander of Apollo 16, jumping high in the Moon's microgravity beside a lunar rover and the command capsule. The hill in the background is about 3 miles (5 km) distant.

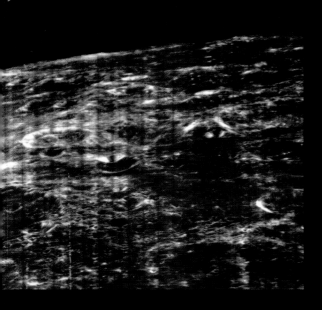

Recent lunar missions

Recent missions to the Moon include Clementine in 1994 and Lunar Prospector in 1998/1999. Clementine mapped the Moon using a set of cameras, though its primary mission was to test missile detection technology. The Clementine photo below shows the Moon partially illuminated by Earthlight, Venus shining brilliantly in the background. Prospector also mapped the lunar surface, and determined the presence of ice buried beneath the ground in deep polar craters.

On June 8, 2004, Venus crossed the face of the Sun in the first transit since
882. Transits of Venus occur in pairs, eight years apart, with the next due
o occur on June 6, 2012. In the past, measurements taken on these occasions
nabled scientists to establish the size of the Solar System.

THE INNER
SOLAR SYSTEM

CHARTING THE INNER SOLAR SYSTEM

The inner Solar System is our immediate neighborhood in space. It is a small and energetic zone, centered on the ordinary yellow star that is our Sun and spanning 2,500 times the Earth–Moon distance, or just over six astronomical units (AU). Defined as the mean Earth–Sun distance, one AU equals 93 million miles (150 million km). Here, snuggled in close to the Sun, basking in the relative heat that such proximity provides, are the four terrestrial or "Earth-like" planets. From the center outward they are Mercury, Venus, Earth, and Mars. All are comparatively small planets composed of rock and metal. A doughnut-shaped ring of rocky debris, the Asteroid Belt, marks the inner Solar System boundary, beyond Mars but before the first gas giant, Jupiter.

Inner Solar System
As illustrated on this map, the inner Solar System to the outer edge of the Asteroid Belt has a radius of about 3.3 AU (the circles on the grid are 0.5 AU apart). Notice that the orbits of Mercury and Mars are clearly elliptical. Earth and Venus have elliptical orbits as well, although they are much closer to a perfect circle. The closed and open circles marked on the orbits indicate each planet's aphelion and perihelion. These are the points when a planet is farthest from and closest to the Sun, respectively. Tick marks denote the orbital nodes, where an orbit crosses Earth's orbital plane, known as the ecliptic. The planets and asteroids shown here are not drawn to scale.

KEY TO SYMBOLS

☿	MERCURY	———	PLANETARY ORBIT
♀	VENUS	◆	APHELION
⊕	EARTH	◯	PERIHELION
♂	MARS	⊤	ORBITAL NODE

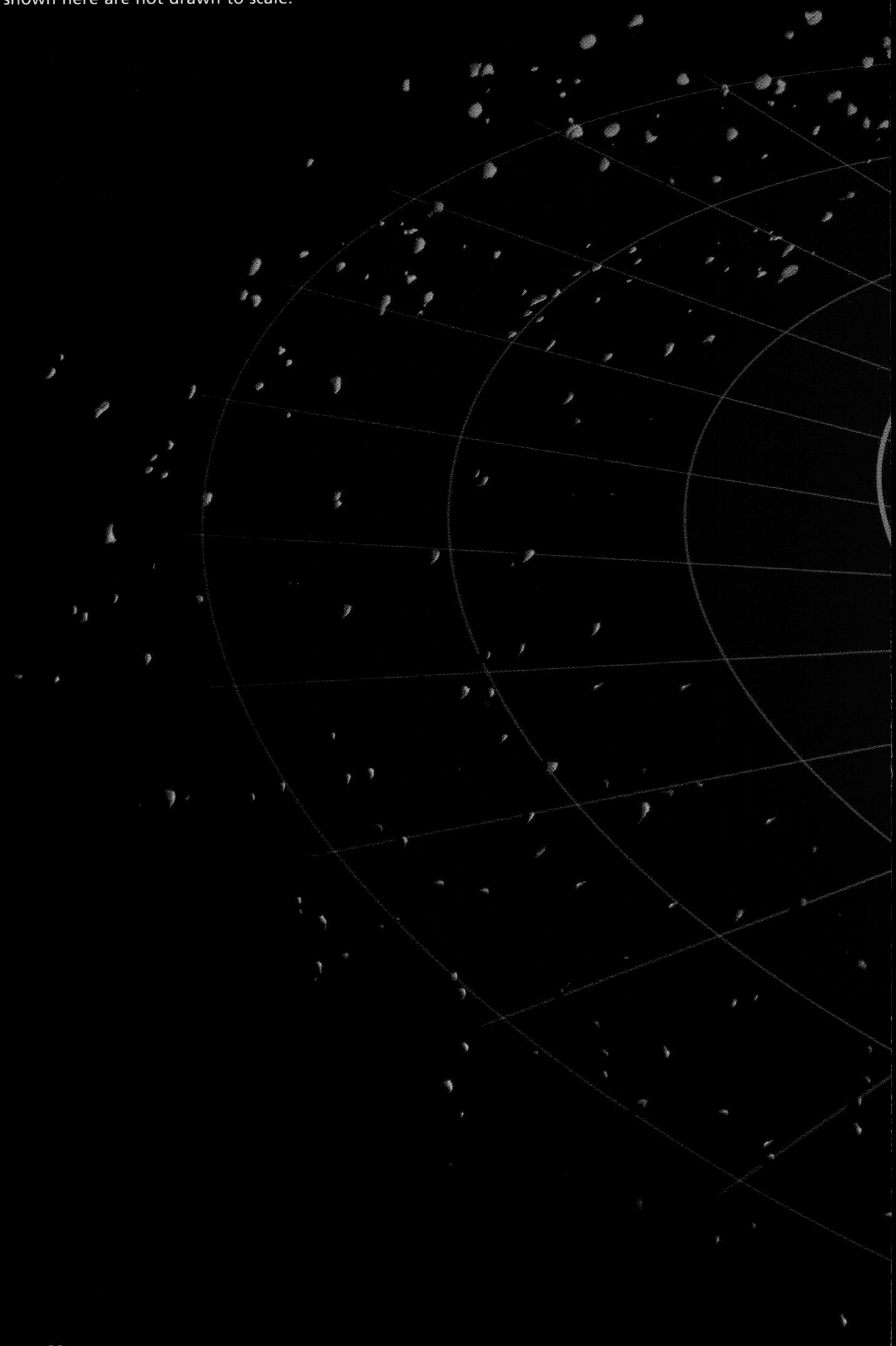

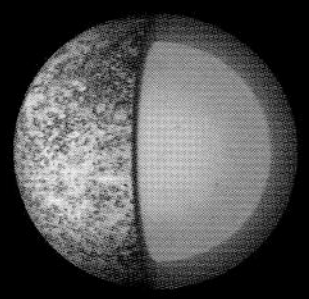

Mercury
Wrapped around Mercury's large iron core is a slender rocky mantle topped with a thin, cracked, and densely cratered crust.

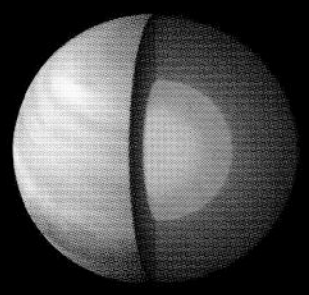

Venus
A blanket of heat-trapping carbon dioxide permanently enshrouds the scorched surface of Venus, making this the hottest planet.

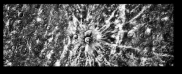

Earth
Earth is the only planet with liquid water on its surface, and, as far as we know, the only one that supports life.

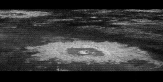

Mars
Mars is a freezing world with an atmosphere much thinner than Earth's. It was probably warmer and wetter in the past.

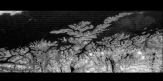

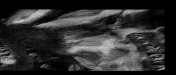

Earth

Venus

Mars

Mercury

The Moon

Ceres

Inner planet size comparison
The largest and smallest terrestrial planets are Earth and Mercury respectively. Venus is almost as large as Earth, and Mars is a mid-sized world about half the size of our own. Ceres, the largest asteroid discovered, is almost as small as a rocky object can go and remain spherical.

Conjunction of the planets
In this scene, all the planets of the inner Solar System are represented. Mercury is just visible between the clouds toward the horizon; Venus is the bright "star" above it and to the left; red Mars is higher up; while distant Saturn shines above the V-shaped Hyades star cluster. The planets, including Earth, are lined up along the plane of the Solar System.

Asteroid Belt
Located between Mars and Jupiter, the Asteroid Belt is home to vast numbers of rocky and metallic fragments. These are remnants from the early Solar System that were never able to agglomerate into a planet, subject as they are to the bullying gravity of Jupiter. The inner and outer edges of the Asteroid Belt lie at distances of 2.1 and 3.3 AU from the Sun, but there are many asteroids that orbit both inside and outside this main belt.

MERCURY

Little Mercury is the closest planet to the Sun. Named by the Romans after their swift-footed messenger to the gods, Mercury is indeed fast, orbiting the Sun in just 88 Earth days. At perihelion, its closest approach to the Sun, Mercury is less than one-third as close in as Earth, but it finds itself at almost half the Earth–Sun distance at the other extreme, aphelion. This combination of a highly elliptical orbit and slow rotation makes for wild temperature swings across this planet's surface. The daytime temperature at perihelion can exceed 800°F (430°C)—enough to melt lead and tin—but at aphelion, in the hemisphere facing away from the Sun, the surface is about 1,100°F (600°C) colder. Mercury spins once on its axis in just under two months. Mercury is an iron sphere, perhaps partially molten, encased in a relatively thin jacket of rock. There is no atmosphere in the usual sense of the word, and no known satellites. Owing to its proximity to the Sun, Mercury is not always easy to see from Earth, as it tends to be buried in the Sun's glare. However, you can sometimes spot the second smallest planet shining near the Sun as a bright evening, or morning, "star."

Iron dwarf
Mercury is the innermost and smallest world of the inner Solar System. As the second smallest of all nine known planets it is only 38 percent the size of Earth, but 1.4 times the diameter of our moon. Mercury, however, has the largest relative core of the planets in the Solar System.

MERCURY STATISTICS	
Discovered	Known from antiquity
Average distance from the Sun	36.0 million miles (57.9 million km); 0.39 AU
Equatorial diameter	3,032 miles (4,879 km)
Axial rotation period (sidereal)	58.65 days (prograde)
Mass (Earth = 1)	0.055
Volume (Earth = 1)	0.056
Surface gravity (Earth = 1)	0.38
Average density (water = 1)	5.43
Surface atmospheric pressure (Earth = 1)	0
Escape velocity	2.8 miles/s (4.3 km/s)
Orbital eccentricity	0.206
Highest surface temperature	800°F (430°C)
Lowest surface temperature	–280°F (–170°C)
Sunlight strength	450–1040% Earth's
Albedo (reflectivity)	11%
Number of satellites	0

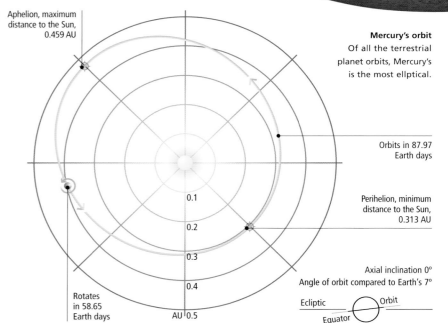

Aphelion, maximum distance to the Sun, 0.459 AU

Mercury's orbit
Of all the terrestrial planet orbits, Mercury's is the most elliptical.

Orbits in 87.97 Earth days

Perihelion, minimum distance to the Sun, 0.313 AU

0.1
0.2
0.3
0.4

Rotates in 58.65 Earth days

AU 0.5

Axial inclination 0°
Angle of orbit compared to Earth's 7°

Ecliptic — Orbit
Equator

The geology of Mercury

At first glance Mercury's battered facade resembles that of the Moon. However, Mercury has none of the maria—smooth plains flooded with ancient lava—that dominate the Earth-facing hemisphere of our satellite. Instead, most of the surface is composed of heavily cratered regions known as highlands, similar to the lunar highlands. There are somewhat smoother regions also, lowlands, that appear to have been flooded with lava, but they are not as extensive as the lunar maria. As far as we can tell (since only half of Mercury has been mapped), there is only one significant impact basin, a vast circular scar called Caloris, perhaps 800 miles (1,300 km) across. The other significant surface features are the scarps, also known as rupes (Latin for rock or cliff)—gigantic cracks that probably formed when the planet cooled and shrank.

Crust
Little is known about Mercury's crust, but it is thought to extend down less than 60 miles (100 km).

Mantle
The mantle is a relatively thin blanket of silicate material that occupies the outermost 25 percent or so of Mercury's radius.

Core
The interior of Mercury is dominated by a gigantic core of iron, part of which may be molten. The core is about as large as the Moon, taking up 70 percent of the planet's interior.

The atmosphere and climate of Mercury

Mercury does not have any significant atmosphere. However, it does harbor a tenuous shell of gases, barely more substantial than a vacuum. These gases derive from various sources. Some hydrogen and helium molecules are captured from the Sun; other elements are blasted from the surface during micrometeorite impacts; and others slowly leak from surface rocks or ice buried deep in craters. The resulting climate features the most extreme temperature variations in the inner Solar System.

Atmospheric breakdown
The gases that have been identified in Mercury's rarefied "atmosphere" include hydrogen, helium, sodium, potassium, and oxygen. The relative quantities are poorly determined, and vary depending on the position of Mercury in its orbit. The Mercury Messenger probe, launched in August 2004, should greatly increase our knowledge on this subject.

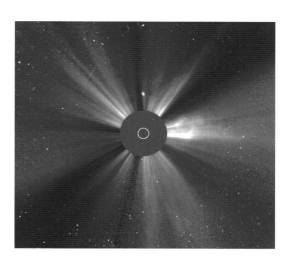

Mercury and the Sun
This photo emphasizes just how close Mercury is to the Sun. The Sun (center) has been blocked by a disk to expose the planet, just above it. Mercury's thin "atmosphere" is continually lost to space, but proximity to the Sun allows Mercury to replenish its lost gases with those from captured solar wind.

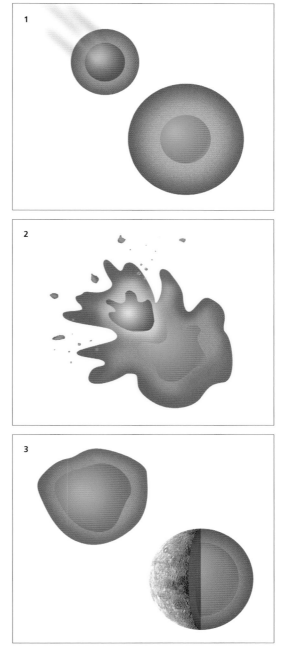

Large core, little planet
Billions of years ago, Mercury may have had a much more substantial silicate mantle (1). However, the cataclysmic impact of a large protoplanet (2) could have removed much of this outer shell without much affecting the iron core, leaving the unusually heavy planet we see today (3).

Mercury's south pole
Recent radar analysis has found that a number of south and north polar craters have high radar reflectivity, a discovery that may indicate the presence of ice, possibly even water ice. The interiors of these polar craters are permanently shaded from the Sun's searing heat, making the preservation of ice possible.

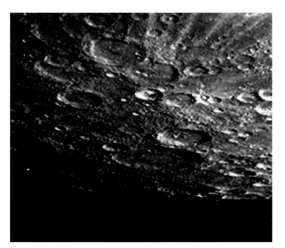

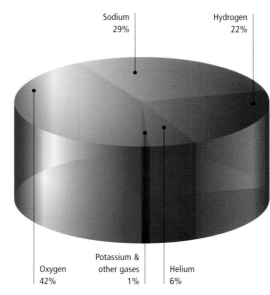

Sodium 29%

Hydrogen 22%

Oxygen 42%

Potassium & other gases 1%

Helium 6%

MAPPING MERCURY

All of our detailed knowledge of Mercury's surface comes courtesy of the NASA spacecraft Mariner 10, which photographed about half of the planet's surface in three flybys in 1974 and 1975. Its visits revealed a battered and ancient crust, somewhat like that of the Moon, with several scarps, or "rupes," testifying to a period of cooling in the planet's ancient history. A single large impact basin, Caloris, 800 miles (1,300 km) across, dominates one hemisphere. On Mercury, planitiae are named after the word for Mercury (either the planet or an equivalent deity) in various languages; craters are named after great figures in the arts; while rupes or scarps take the names of famous ships of discovery.

The unmasked hemisphere of Mercury
Above is an artist's representation of Mercury's known hemisphere, the smooth region being where no data has been obtained. The same hemisphere is shown in more detail in the map on the right.

Mariner 10 Mercury mosaic (left)
This is a false-color photomosaic composed of many smaller photos taken by Mariner 10 during its visits in 1974 and 1975. The large circular feature on the left, only half of which is illuminated, is the Caloris impact basin. This feature, officially named "Caloris Planitia," can be found at the northeastern edge of the map opposite. At the top of the image, bright rays from the impact crater Degas (37°N/126°W) can be seen extending across much of the shown hemisphere. Both Degas and Caloris are representative of the dominant agent of topographical change on Mercury: bombardment by interplanetary debris.

Caloris Planitia and Caloris Montes (above)
This surface schematic reveals the topography of the surface of Mercury between the Caloris impact basin and the region east of Caloris Montes, and is indicated on the map (right) by a dashed rectangle.

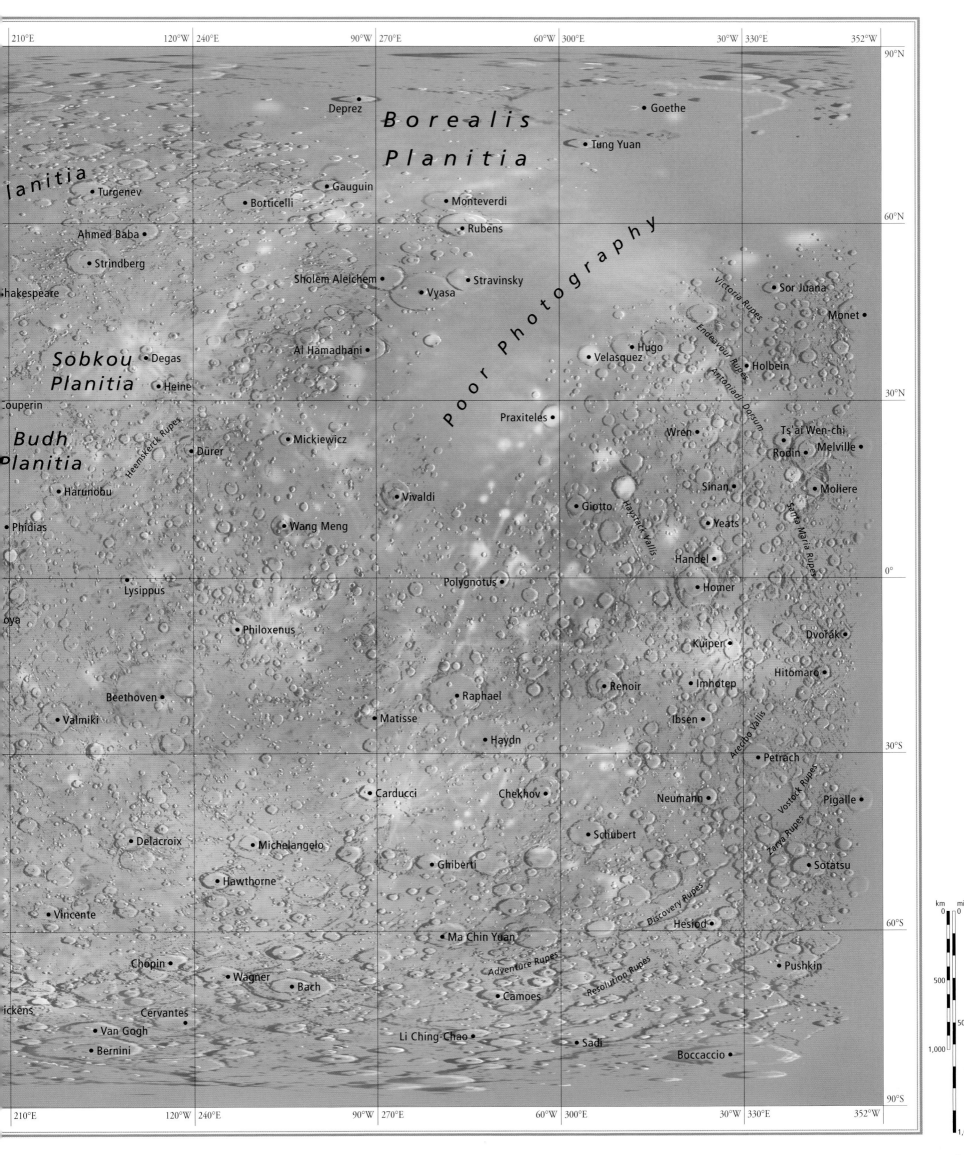

210°E   120°W   240°E   90°W   270°E   60°W   300°E   30°W   330°E   352°W

90°N

• Deprez

Borealis

Planitia

• Goethe

• Tung Yuan

60°N

lanitia

• Turgenev

• Gauguin

• Botticelli

• Monteverdi

• Rubens

Poor Photography

Ahmed Baba •

• Strindberg

Sholem Aleichem •

• Stravinsky

• Sor Juana

Victoria Rupes

hakespeare

• Vyasa

• Monet

Sobkou
Planitia

• Degas

• Heine

• Al Hamadhani

• Velasquez

• Hugo

Endeavour Rupes

Holbein

Antoniadi Dorsum

30°N

Couperin

• Praxiteles

Wren •

Ts'ai Wen-chi

Budh

• Mickiewicz

Rodin •

• Melville

Planitia

• Dürer

Heemskerck Rupes

Sinan •

• Moliere

• Harunobu

• Vivaldi

Giotto •

• Yeats

Santa Maria Rupes

• Phidias

• Wang Meng

Haystack Vallis

Handel •

0°

• Lysippus

Polygnotus •

• Homer

oya

Dvořák •

• Philoxenus

Kuiper •

Arecibo Vallis

• Hitomaro

Beethoven •

• Renoir

• Imhotep

• Valmiki

• Raphael

Ibsen •

• Matisse

30°S

• Haydn

• Petrach

• Carducci

Chekhov •

Neumann •

Vostok Rupes

Pigalle •

Zarya Rupes

• Delacroix

• Michelangelo

• Schubert

• Sotatsu

• Hawthorne

• Ghiberti

Discovery Rupes

• Vincente

Hesiod •

60°S

• Ma Chin Yuan

• Pushkin

Chopin •

Adventure Rupes

• Wagner

• Bach

Resolution Rupes

• Camoes

ickens

Cervantes •

• Van Gogh

Li Ching-Chao •

• Sadi

• Bernini

Boccaccio •

90°S

210°E   120°W   240°E   90°W   270°E   60°W   300°E   30°W   330°E   352°W

km miles
0   0

500

500

1,000

1,000

41

MERCURY SURFACE FEATURES

Mercury's battered surface is truly ancient. With no significant atmosphere, tectonic movement, or water, the planet's rugged landscape has remained essentially as we see it now for almost 4 billion years—something like 80 to 85 percent of its entire history. Mercury is little but an orbiting fossil, its craggy, cratered face a testimony to the heavy bombardment that characterized the last stages of the formation of the planets. The cratered highlands are the oldest features, while the lowland plains are somewhat younger. The most recent structures, however, are the rupes, vast cracks, hundreds of miles long, formed as the planet cooled and shriveled, billions of years ago.

Caloris impact
Mercury's largest known feature, Caloris, probably formed 3.85 billion years ago. The impact sructure is likely the result of an object about 90 miles (150 km) across slamming into Mercury, sending shockwaves through the entire planet (below). Antipodal to Caloris is what is known as "weird terrain"—depressions, hills, and valleys that are the result of wrinkling of the crust.

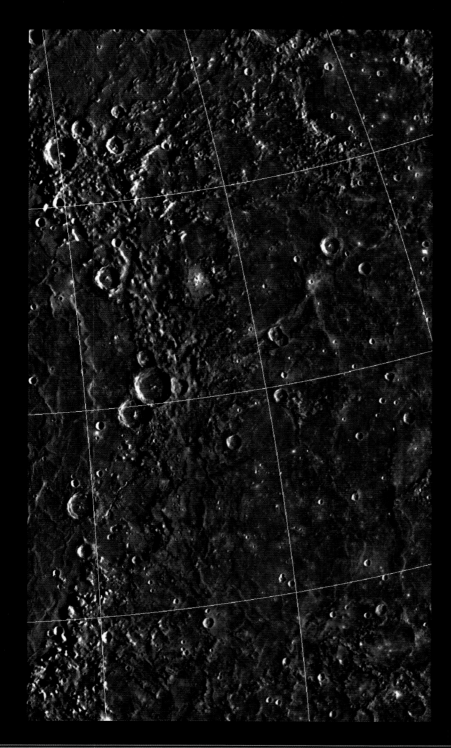

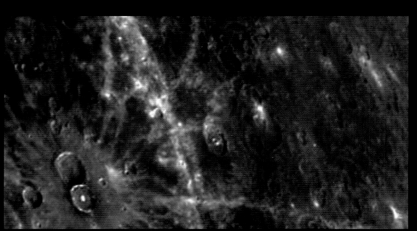

Prominent rayed crater: Degas (above)
Often when craters form, the blanket of material thrown out (the ejecta) during the impact makes a series of bright rays as it settles on the surrounding terrain. These rays are a hallmark of comparatively young craters, like Degas at 37°N/126°W, whose bright central peak is visible here.

Topographical variations (right)
This Mariner 10 image captures two types of distinctive terrain in juxtaposition on Mercury: a smooth plain occupying the expansive floor of Petrarch Crater (30°S/26°W), and the hilly and fractured landscape that encircles it. The area imaged measures 125 miles (200 km) across.

Edge of the Caloris basin (left)
The partial circle of rugged hills in this Mariner 10 image forms the outer edge of the Caloris basin. Unfortunately much of Caloris lies outside the area that was imaged by Mariner 10. Three decades later, we still do not know what the rest of Caloris looks like.

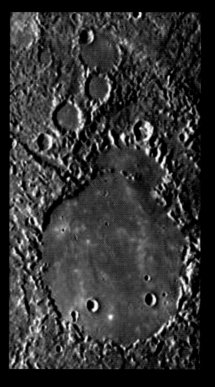

Plains

While Mercury is heavily cratered, there are also extensive, smooth plains or lowlands known as planitia. These are found in and around impact structures such as Caloris, and as such they were probably formed when lava flooded the surface following large impacts, and buried older terrain, somewhat like the maria on the Moon. Alternatively, it is possible that the plains could be blankets, not of lava from the interior, but of surface rock that melted during the impacts that formed Mercury's basins.

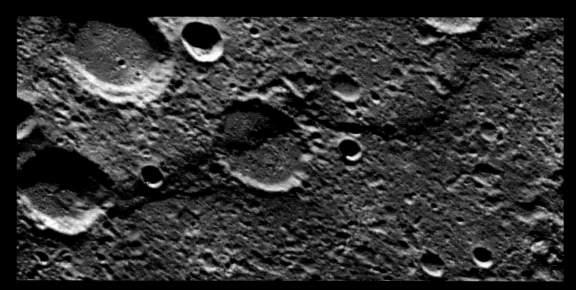

Santa Maria Rupes (below)
This Mariner 10 photo shows typical rupes on Mercury. Known as the Santa Maria Rupes, this feature, 620 miles (1,000 km) long, runs through many large craters, indicating that it formed more recently than the craters themselves, a result of compressional stress in the Mercurian crust.

Rupes

Mercury's surface is home to many rupes, or scarps. These tectonic features, unique to Mercury, can cut across entire craters. Where this occurs, the craters often have shorter diameters perpendicular rather than parallel to the rupes. The explanation is most likely that the rupes are thrust faults, regions where lateral compression fractured the crust of Mercury, pushing parts of the crust above others. What caused the compression? The favored hypothesis is that Mercury shrank as its mantle cooled, splitting and buckling the surface like the skin of a rotting fruit (see illustration left). Some rupes extend for hundreds of miles and jut up to 2.5 miles (4 km) above the adjacent surface. Judging from the fact that none of the rupes has been flooded by plains material, they must be younger than the plains themselves, and probably date to around the time of the Caloris impact, or possibly slightly later.

Mercury's polar plains (above)
The Borealis Planitia on Mercury is located in the planet's northern hemisphere. This image, in which the north pole is at the top, right of center, shows the dominant topographical features of Mercury. Note the distinct difference between the heavily cratered highlands on the left, and the smooth lowland plains of Borealis Planitia and crater Goethe on the right. Borealis Planitia or "Northern Plain" and Caloris Planitia or "Hot Plain" are the only planitiae with names that are not derived from forms of the word "Mercury."

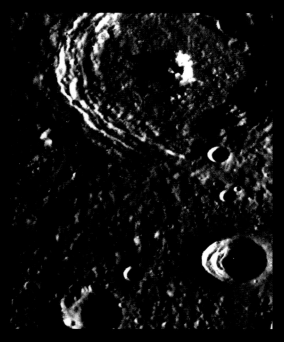

Brahms at 59°N/176°W (above)
When an object a few miles across strikes the crust of a rocky planet like Mercury, the stresses are so great that the rocks of the crust behave as if they were liquid. In fact, the physics at work is essentially the same as when a body of water is disturbed by a drop falling from above. Brahms (top right), 60 miles (96 km) in diameter, is typical of Mercurian craters of this size, exhibiting an extensive field of secondary craters, a rim of concentric terraces, and a pronounced central peak. The terracing and peak are a result of the collapse of the narrow and deep transient crater formed on impact.

DISCOVERING MERCURY

Planetary scientists still know comparatively little about the closest planet to the Sun. Indeed, they know more about the distant Galilean moons of Jupiter, for example, than they do about the scorched ball of iron that is Mercury. Only one probe has ever seen Mercury up close, NASA's Mariner 10. During three flybys in 1974 and 1975, this robotic envoy mapped about half of the planet's surface and discovered its cracked and cratered terrain. To see what the other hemisphere looks like, however, we will have to wait until the Messenger probe arrives in 2011.

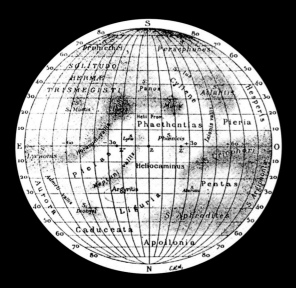

Antoniadi's map of Mercury (above)
Although it bears scant resemblance to the surface revealed by Mariner 10, this map of Mercury published by Franco–Greek astronomer Eugène Michel Antoniadi in 1934 was the most detailed pre-space age map of the planet.

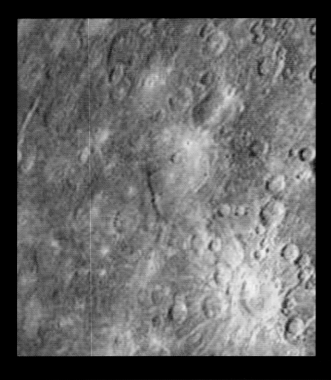

Metallic treasures (left)
To our eyes little Mercury is an overwhelmingly gray planet but the sensitive cameras on board Mariner 10 were designed to record information invisible to the naked eye. This computer-enhanced false-color image of Mercury, a mosaic of several individual Mariner 10 images, illustrates surface material differences. The bright blue areas, for example, are titanium rich. The prominent rayed crater at lower right is Kuiper at 11°S/31°W.

Mariner 10—the first close-up view of the innermost planet

Mariner 10, launched in November 1974 (1), was the last of NASA's Mariner-series of space missions, which spanned more than a decade, and the only spacecraft to photograph Mercury up close. After a flyby of Venus in February 1974 (2), the gravity of that planet boosted the craft's speed and put it into an orbit about the Sun, taking it past Mercury on March 29, 1974 (3). Mariner 10's orbital period was 176 days—exactly twice that of the planet Mercury. This ensured that when the probe completed its first solar orbit, it would again encounter Mercury (itself having orbited twice) at the same point in space, on September 21, 1974 (4). A final flyby took place on March 16, 1975 (5). Almost everything we know about Mercury comes from these three encounters, which accumulated some 7,000 photos.

Mariner 10's flight path (below)
In common with every other interplanetary craft, Mariner 10 had to travel a considerable distance with next to no fuel. To achieve this the craft swung by Venus in a procedure known as "gravity assist," in effect stealing a tiny bit of the planet's orbital energy for a huge boost in speed.

3, 4, 5

2

1

Messenger to Mercury

The MESSENGER (MErcury Surface, Space ENvironment, GEochemistry, and Ranging) mission is expected to significantly improve astronomers' understanding of Mercury. This NASA probe will study Mercury's surface composition and magnetic field, mapping almost the entire surface, revealing at last those regions unseen by Mariner 10. The craft was launched from Cape Canaveral, Florida, on August 3, 2004, on a circuitous journey that will take seven years to complete. In August 2005, Messenger flew past Earth, gaining a velocity boost that will sling it past Venus in October 2006, and again in June 2007. The craft encounters Mercury in January 2008, but only briefly. Two other flybys will follow, in October 2008 and September 2009, before it settles into an orbit around Mercury in March 2011. There the probe will begin a year-long study of the planet, armed with a battery of nine different scientific instruments—each of them shielded behind a heat-resistant ceramic fabric, protecting them from the intense heat this close to the Sun.

Messenger in orbit (left)
This is an artist's impression of the Messenger spacecraft, showing the probe in orbit around the diminutive Mercury in 2011. The two large solar panels, as well as a nickel-hydrogen battery, provide the spacecraft with its power.

Future missions
Another mission to Mercury, due for launch between 2009 and 2012, is the European–Japanese BepiColombo, named for the engineer and mathematician Giuseppe "Bepi" Colombo (1920–84). The mission comprises two orbiters (above) and a possible lander.

VENUS

Moving away from the Sun, the planet we come to after Mercury is Venus, 0.72 AU, or 67.2 million miles (108.2 million km), from the center of the Solar System. This is a world, only slightly smaller than Earth, entirely cloaked in clouds. There is not even a hint of the surface visible from space. Indeed, for many decades, before radar penetrated the Venusian clouds for the first time, people assumed that Venus was much like Earth. Some even likened it to a sister world, a warm lush forested planet, inhabited by exotic creatures. Now we know the truth. Venus is in fact not unlike most visions of Hell, with searing temperatures that are hot enough to melt tin, zinc, and lead. This is because the planet's dense atmosphere of carbon dioxide, a greenhouse gas, traps whatever heat reaches the surface. Still, the thick, cloudy atmosphere does at least make Venus a very bright planet. You can frequently see it from Earth as an evening or morning "star," where it is more brilliant than any other astronomical object except the Sun and Moon. Venus spins in the opposite direction compared with the other terrestrial planets. This unusual retrograde rotation is thought to be the result of a massive impact early in the planet's life. Venus has no natural satellites.

Sister planet
Venus is similar in size and mass to Earth. As a result the Venusian surface gravity is high, being 91 percent as strong as our own.

VENUS STATISTICS	
Discovered	Known from antiquity
Average distance from the Sun	67.2 million miles (108.2 million km); 0.72 AU
Equatorial diameter	7,521 miles (12,104 km)
Axial rotation period (sidereal)	243 days (retrograde)
Mass (Earth = 1)	0.82
Volume (Earth = 1)	0.86
Surface gravity (Earth = 1)	0.91
Average density (water = 1)	5.24
Surface atmospheric pressure (Earth = 1)	92
Escape velocity	6.4 miles/s (10.4 km/s)
Orbital eccentricity	0.007
Surface temperature (negligible variation)	867°F (464°C)
Sunlight strength	190% of Earth's (cloud tops), 5% (surface)
Albedo (reflectivity)	65%
Number of satellites	0

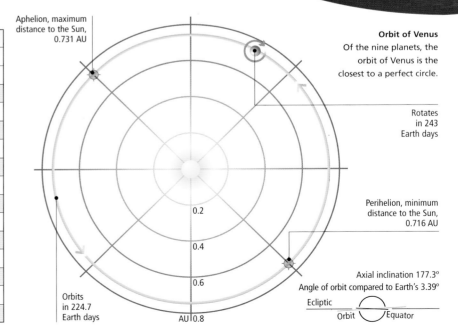

Aphelion, maximum distance to the Sun, 0.731 AU

Orbit of Venus
Of the nine planets, the orbit of Venus is the closest to a perfect circle.

Rotates in 243 Earth days

0.2

Perihelion, minimum distance to the Sun, 0.716 AU

0.4

Orbits in 224.7 Earth days

0.6

AU 0.8

Axial inclination 177.3°
Angle of orbit compared to Earth's 3.39°

Ecliptic

Orbit   Equator

The geology of Venus

Venus is a world dominated by volcanic features. There is no evidence that the planet is active now, but it could be, and certainly was in the recent geological past. Some of the planet's many volcanoes are like those on Earth; others have no terrestrial analog. These have classifications such as pancake domes, coronae, and arachnoids. Venus also has craters, but they are rare. This is because most of the older ones have been eradicated by more recent volcanic activity, and also because the thick atmosphere destroys smaller meteors before they can impact.

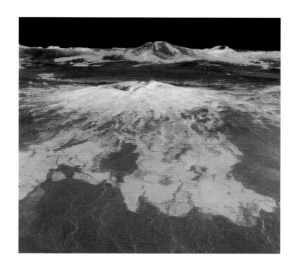

Sapas Mons (8.5°N/172°W)
This false-color, vertically exaggerated image of Sapas Mons was produced from Magellan radar data. Sapas Mons is some 250 miles (400 km) across with sides composed of numerous overlapping lava flows. Maat Mons towers in the background.

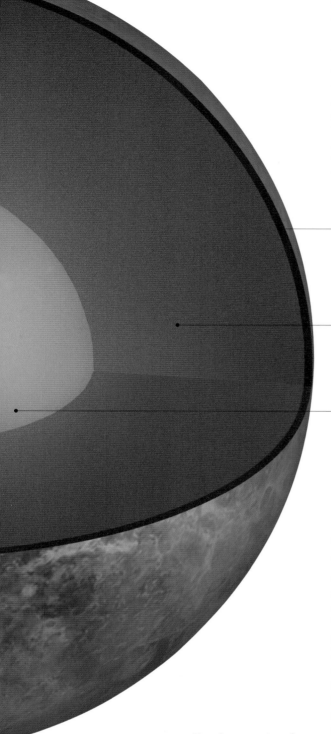

Crust
The rocky crust of Venus is presumed to be quite thin in order to account for the planet's recent volcanic activity. It may be about 30 miles (50 km) thick.

Mantle
Beneath the crust, Venus has a thick silicate mantle that extends perhaps halfway down to the planet's center.

Core
Venus probably has a large nickel-iron core occupying some 50 percent of its radius. The core is likely solid, since there is no appreciable magnetic field.

The atmosphere and climate of Venus

Venus is no place to go for a picnic. The noxious atmosphere is almost entirely comprised of carbon dioxide, and it pushes down on the surface with a pressure 92 times that experienced on Earth. That's equivalent to the pressure some 3,000 feet (900 m) beneath the surface of Earth's oceans. High above the scorching surface are dense clouds of concentrated sulfuric acid. And as if all that were not enough, the greenhouse atmosphere has turned this world into a global heat-trap. Although not the closest planet to the Sun, Venus is the hottest, with temperatures averaging 900°F (480°C). There is little temperature variation across the planet due to the effect of the thick atmospheric blanket.

Venusian upper atmosphere
The bright uppermost clouds of Venus lie at an altitude of about 40 miles (65 km) and circulate around the planet in four Earth days at speeds of up to 225 miles per hour (360 km/h) relative to the surface.

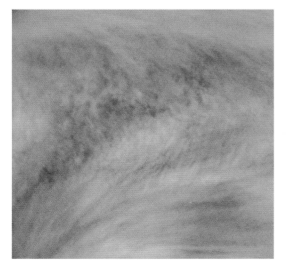

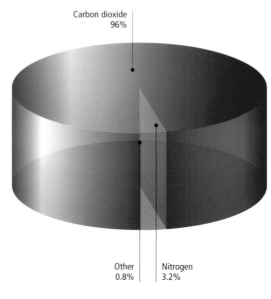

Carbon dioxide
96%

Other
0.8%

Nitrogen
3.2%

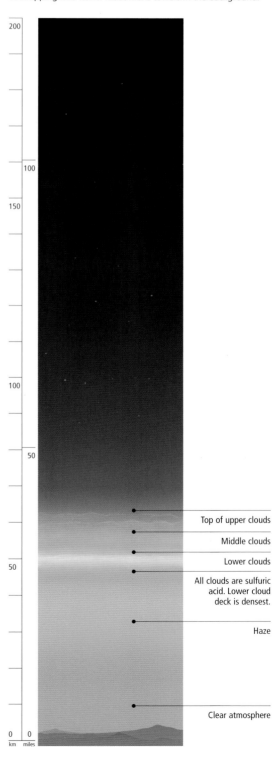

Top of upper clouds

Middle clouds

Lower clouds

All clouds are sulfuric acid. Lower cloud deck is densest.

Haze

Clear atmosphere

MAPPING VENUS WESTERN HEMISPHERE

Venus has surprisingly little surface relief; some 80 percent of the planet has a height variation no greater than 0.6 miles (1 km). That said, the western hemisphere includes the 5-mile (8-km) high Maat Mons (0.5°N/165°W); much of the far northern Ishtar Terra region, including the high plateau, Lakshmi Planum (68.5°N/20.5°W); and the volcanic highlands of Beta Regio (25.5°N/77°W) and Phoebe Regio (6°S/77°W), both accompanied by huge trenches. With very few exceptions, major features on Venus are named after female figures from mythology and large craters are named in honor of notable women in history.

The western face of Venus (above)
This composite image shows the western hemisphere of Venus. In Magellan's radar imaging, the rougher topography of the highland regions shows up as a lighter shade than the smoother plains and lowlands.

LANDING SITES: WESTERN VENUS	
PROBE (LANDING DATE)	**LANDING SITE**
Venera 7 (Dec 15, 1970)	5°S/9°W
Venera 8 (Jul 22, 1972)	10°S/25°W
Venera 9 (Oct 22, 1975)	32°N/69°W
Venera 10 (Oct 25, 1975)	16°N/69°W
Pioneer Venus 2 (Dec 9, 1978)	
Day probe	31°S/43°W
Large probe	4°N/56°W
Venera 11 (Dec 25, 1978)	14°S/61°W
Venera 12 (Dec 21, 1978)	7°S/66°W
Venera 13 (Mar 1, 1982)	7.5°S/57°W
Venera 14 (Mar 5, 1982)	13°S/50°W

Probes to the western hemisphere of Venus (above)
A host of probes has visited western Venus, most belonging to the Soviet Venera series. Venera 7 was the first craft to return data after landing on another planet, while Venera 9 took the first photos from the Venusian surface. Owing to the intensely hostile environment, no probes survived long on the surface.

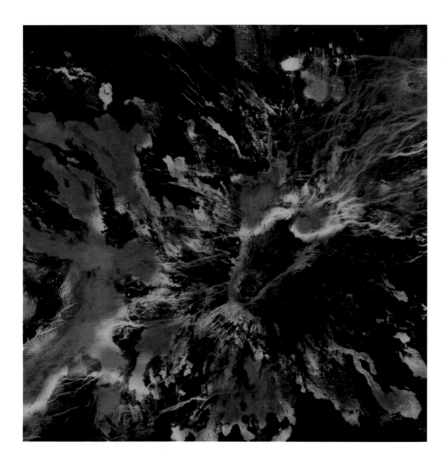

Crowned with pyrite (above)
The colors in this Magellan image of an unnamed volcano in the Phoebe Regio region correspond to a measure of electromagnetic properties of the surface materials. Red corresponds to high radio-thermal emission values, blue to low values. Low values at high elevations are found across Venus and suggest the presence of minerals such as pyrite which would be more stable at the pressures and temperatures found at higher elevations. The image shows an area 310 miles (500 km) across.

Phoebe Regio   Devana Chasma   Hyndla Regio   Beta Regio

Beta Regio and Phoebe Regio (above)
This surface schematic corresponds to the dashed region on the map. Beta Regio and Phoebe Regio are volcanic highlands connected by Devana Chasma, a rift valley some 1,000 miles (1,600 km) long and averaging 125 miles (200 km) wide.

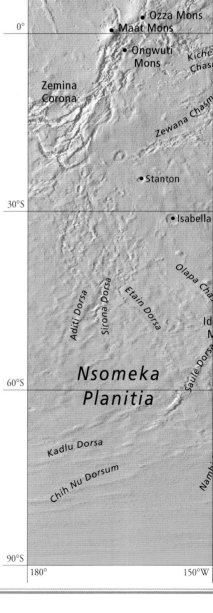

Vinmara Planitia
Cassatt Corona
Lauma Dorsa
Pandrosos D
Cerridwin Corona
Neyterk Coron
• Nijole Mons
Ganiki Planitia
Nokomis Montes
Fornax Rupes
Atla
Ganis Chasma
Tkashi-mapa Chas
Regio
Zewan Chas
• Sapas Mons
• Ozza Mons
• Maat Mons
• Ongwuti Mons
Kiche Chas
Zemina Corona
Zewana Chasm
• Stanton
• Isabella
Aditi Dorsa
Sirona Dorsa
Etain Dorsa
Olapa Cha
Saule Dorsa
Id M
Nsomeka Planitia
Kadlu Dorsa
Chih Nu Dorsum
Nanb

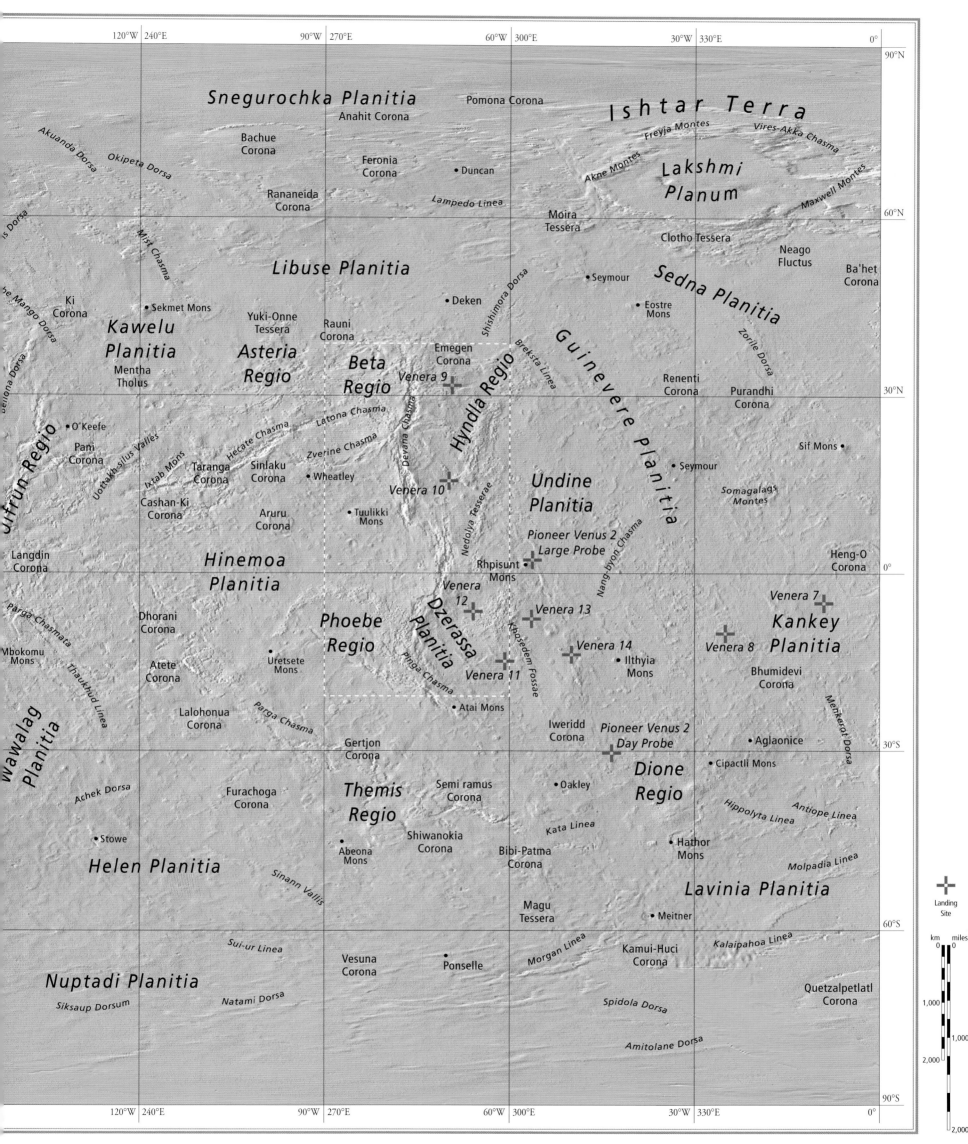

Snegurochka Planitia

Pomona Corona

Ishtar Terra

Anahit Corona

Freyja Montes

Vires-Akka Chasma

Bachue
Corona

Akuanda Dorsa

Okipeta Dorsa

Feronia
Corona

• Duncan

Akne Montes

*Lakshmi
Planum*

Maxwell Montes

Rananeida
Corona

Lampedo Linea

Mist Chasma

Moira
Tessera

60°N

Clotho Tessera

Neago
Fluctus

Ba'het
Corona

Ki
Corona

Libuse Planitia

• Sekmet Mons

Yuki-Onne
Tessera

• Deken

• Seymour

Sedna Planitia

the Mango Dorsa

*Kawelu
Planitia*

*Asteria
Regio*

Rauni
Corona

*Beta
Regio*

Emegen
Corona

• Eostre
Mons

Zorile Dorsa

Mentha
Tholus

Venera 9
✛

Guinevere Planitia

Renenti
Corona

Purandhi
Corona

30°N

• O'Keefe

Hyndla Regio

Breksta Linea

Sif Mons •

Ulfrun Regio

Pani
Corona

Uottakh- silus Valles

Latona Chasma

Ixtab Mons

Hecate Chasma

Taranga
Corona

Sinlaku
Corona

Zverine Chasma

• Wheatley

Venera 10
✛

*Undine
Planitia*

• Seymour

*Somagalags
Montes*

Cashan-Ki
Corona

Aruru
Corona

Nedolya Tesserae

Devana Chasma

• Tuulikki
Mons

Pioneer Venus 2
Large Probe

Nang-byon Chasma

Heng-O
Corona

Langdin
Corona

*Hinemoa
Planitia*

Rhpisunt
Mons ✛

0°

Venera
12 ✛

Venera 13
✛

Venera 7
✛

Parga Chasmata

Dhorani
Corona

*Dzerassa
Planitia*

*Phoebe
Regio*

Khosedem Fossae

*Kankey
Planitia*

Venera 8 ✛

Mbokomu
Mons

Atete
Corona

Uretsete
Mons •

Pinga Chasma

Venera 14
✛

• Ilthyia
Mons

Bhumidevi
Corona

*Wawalag
Planitia*

Thaukhud Linea

Venera 11 ✛

• Atai Mons

Menkerot Dorsa

Lalohonua
Corona

Parga Chasma

Gertjon
Corona

Iweridd
Corona

Pioneer Venus 2
Day Probe

• Aglaonice

30°S

Achek Dorsa

Furachoga
Corona

*Themis
Regio*

Semi ramus
Corona

• Oakley

*Dione
Regio*

• Cipactli Mons

Hippolyta Linea

Antiope Linea

• Stowe

Shiwanokia
Corona

Kata Linea

• Hathor
Mons

Helen Planitia

• Abeona
Mons

Bibi-Patma
Corona

Molpadia Linea

Sinann Vallis

Magu
Tessera

Lavinia Planitia

• Meitner

60°S

Sui-ur Linea

Vesuna
Corona

• Ponselle

Morgan Linea

Kamui-Huci
Corona

Kalaipahoa Linea

Nuptadi Planitia

Natami Dorsa

*Quetzalpetlatl
Corona*

Siksaup Dorsum

Spidola Dorsa

Amitolane Dorsa

90°S

120°W 240°E

90°W 270°E

60°W 300°E

30°W 330°E

0°

✛

Landing
Site

km   miles
0   0

1,000

1,000

2,000

2,000

MAPPING VENUS EASTERN HEMISPHERE

The eastern hemisphere of Venus is where many of the planet's most interesting features are to be found. It is dominated by Aphrodite Terra, a vast highland region stretching for 11,000 miles (17,500 km) or almost halfway around the planet. Maxwell Montes (65°N/3°E)—a long mountain range that includes the planet's highest peak—is here, as is Diana Chasma (18°S/155°E), the deepest Venusian trench. Maxwell Montes peaks at 7 miles (11 km) above the average surface level— nearly 1.3 times higher than Mount Everest—while Diana Chasma reaches to depths of about 2 miles (3 km).

The eastern face of Venus (above)
The Magellan radar image above shows the eastern hemisphere of Venus. The map on the right presents the same area in more detail.

LANDING SITES: EASTERN VENUS	
PROBE (LANDING DATE)	**LANDING SITE**
Venera 4 (Oct 18, 1967)	19°N/38°E
Venera 5 (May 16, 1969)	3°S/18°E
Venera 6 (May 17, 1969)	5°S/23°E
Pioneer Venus 2 (Dec 9, 1978)	
North probe	59°N/5°E
Night probe	29°S/57°E
Vega 1 (Jun 11, 1985)	7.5°N/177°E
Vega 2 (Jun 15, 1985)	7.5°S/180°E

Probes to the eastern hemisphere of Venus (above)
The eastern hemisphere was visited by both the earliest probes (in 1967) and also by the most recent (in 1985). Veneras 4 to 6 were primarily atmospheric explorers, but it was hoped they would make a soft landing. All were crushed before doing so, however. After deploying their descent modules at Venus, both the Vega 1 and 2 spacecraft continued on to a close encounter with Comet Halley. The Pioneer Venus 2 probes transmitted data during descent but perished soon after landing on the Venusian surface.

Eastern Venusian pancakes (above)
This image, created from Magellan radar data, shows three distinctive "pancake domes" on the eastern edge of the Alpha Regio highland plateau. These volcanic features are about 16 miles (25 km) in diameter and 2,400 feet (750 m) high. The vertical scale here has been exaggerated about 23 times.

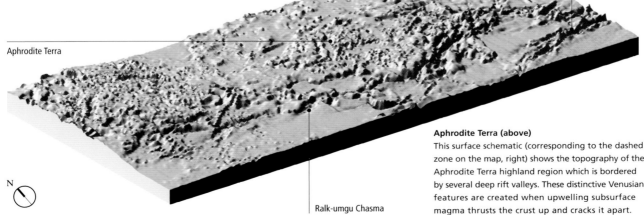

Diana Chasma

Aphrodite Terra

N

Ralk-umgu Chasma

Aphrodite Terra (above)
This surface schematic (corresponding to the dashed zone on the map, right) shows the topography of the Aphrodite Terra highland region which is bordered by several deep rift valleys. These distinctive Venusian features are created when upwelling subsurface magma thrusts the crust up and cracks it apart.

0°   330°W
90°N

Ishtar

• Cleopatra

Maxwell Montes

Pioneer Venus 2
North Probe

Onatah
Corona

Haumea
Corona

Nuna-Buluku
Corona

*Bereghinya
Planitia*   30°N

Mona Lisa

Sappho
Patera

Gour Linea   Metalisa

*Eistla
Regio*

0°   Ca

Venera 5

Kuan-Yin   Venera
Corona

Cybele
Corona

Fatua
Corona

*Tinitan
Planitia*

*Alpha
Regio*   30°S

• Stuart

Carpo
Corona

Vaidilute Rupes

Sehi
Corona   *Astkhik
Planum*

Eithinoha   60°S
Corona   Otg
Cor

*Lad
Ter*

Ngyandu Vallis

*Aibarchin
Planitia*
90°S
0°   330°W

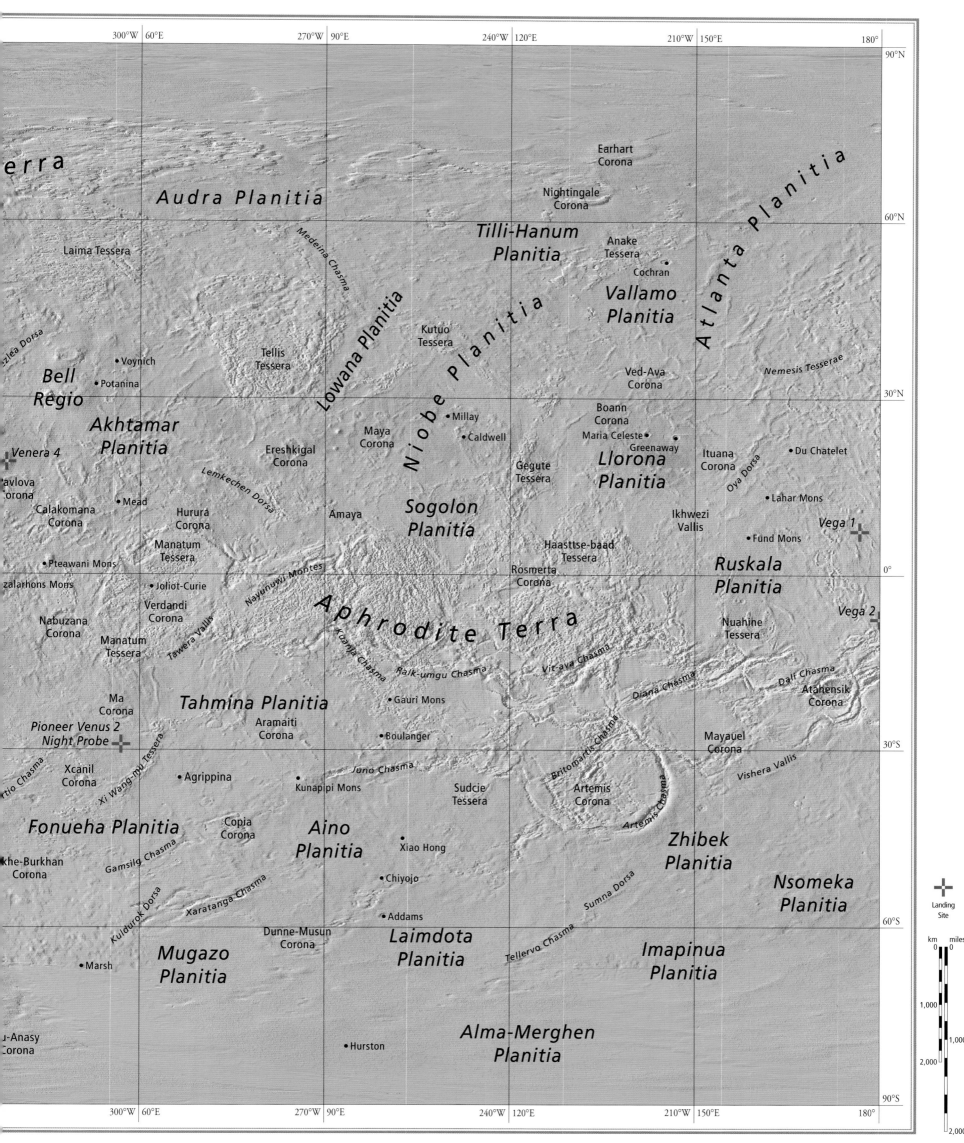

erra

Audra Planitia

Earhart
Corona

Nightingale
Corona

Atlanta Planitia

Laima Tessera

*Tilli-Hanum
Planitia*

Anake
Tessera

Medeina Chasma

Cochran

*Vallamo
Planitia*

zzlea Dorsa

• Voynich

Tellis
Tessera

Kutuo
Tessera

Lowana Planitia

Niobe Planitia

Ved-Ava
Corona

Nemesis Tesserae

• Potanina

*Bell
Regio*

Boann
Corona

Maria Celeste •

• Millay

Greenaway

Ituana
Corona

• Du Chatelet

*Akhtamar
Planitia*

Maya
Corona

• Caldwell

*Llorona
Planitia*

Ereshkigal
Corona

Oya Dorsa

Venera 4

Gegute
Tessera

• Lahar Mons

avlova
orona

Lemkechen Dorsa

Amaya

*Sogolon
Planitia*

Ikhwezi
Vallis

Vega 1

Calakomana
Corona

• Mead

Hururá
Corona

Haasttse-baad
Tessera

• Fund Mons

Manatum
Tessera

Rosmerta
Corona

*Ruskala
Planitia*

• Pteawani Mons

Nayunuwi Montes

Aphrodite Terra

zalarhons Mons

• Joliot-Curie

Verdandi
Corona

Vit-ava Chasma

Nuahine
Tessera

Vega 2

Nabuzana
Corona

Kuanja Chasma

Ralk-umgu Chasma

Diana Chasma

Dali Chasma

Manatum
Tessera

Tawera Vallis

Atahensik
Corona

*Ma
Corona*

Tahmina Planitia

• Gauri Mons

Britomartis Chasma

Mayauel
Corona

Pioneer Venus 2
Night Probe

Aramaiti
Corona

• Boulanger

Artemis
Corona

Juno Chasma

Artemis Chasma

Vishera Vallis

rtio Chasma

Xcanil
Corona

• Agrippina

Sudcie
Tessera

*Zhibek
Planitia*

Xi Wang-mu Tessera

Kunapipi Mons

*Nsomeka
Planitia*

Fonueha Planitia

Copia
Corona

*Aino
Planitia*

• Xiao Hong

khe-Burkhan
Corona

Gamsilg Chasma

• Chiyojo

Sumna Dorsa

Kuldurok Dorsa

Xaratanga Chasma

• Addams

*Imapinua
Planitia*

• Marsh

Dunne-Musun
Corona

*Laimdota
Planitia*

Tellervo Chasma

*Mugazo
Planitia*

-Anasy
orona

*Alma-Merghen
Planitia*

• Hurston

Landing
Site

km   miles
0   0

1,000

1,000

2,000

2,000

VENUS SURFACE FEATURES

Thanks to the Magellan space probe of the 1990s, planetary scientists have finally penetrated the Venusian clouds with high-definition radar and studied its landforms. It is unlikely that the plains of Venus ever saw liquid water, or at least not in very large quantities, therefore the landscape is entirely free of fluvial erosion. Wind erosion has nothing like the influence it has on Earth, since there are relatively slow wind speeds at the surface. Instead, volcanism is the main agent of topographical change. Volcanoes are ubiquitous on the planet; every known type has been found there as well as others seen nowhere else. Between 500 and 300 million years ago their action completely resurfaced the Venusian landscape. Because of this recent activity, craters—especially small ones—are comparatively rare, for many have been erased.

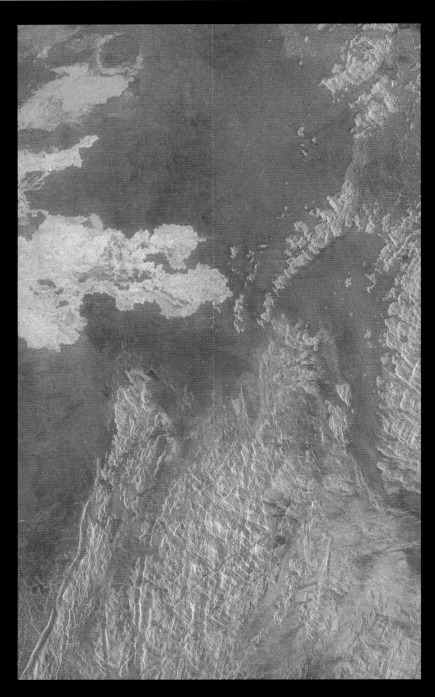

Highlands and tesserae

While most of the scorching surface of Venus consists of lowland plains, some 15 percent is classified as highland: mountainous and comparatively old regions out of the reach of volcanic flooding. In some places, these rugged highland plateaus are highly jumbled and deformed, forming a terrain planetary astronomers refer to as a tessera (plural, tesserae). The name, which derives from Latin and Greek, means a tile or a small block used in the construction of a mosaic. The tesserae, covering 8 percent of Venus, are not extensive, and often exist as small "islands" surrounded by smoother plains.

Contrasts in Eistla Regio (10.5°N/21.5°E) (right)
The bright regions at the bottom and right of this Magellan image are rugged highland tesserae while the dark areas are plains, possibly formed when lava flows swamped low-lying ground. The flow at top left is the result of more recent volcanic activity; its rugged surface appearing bright in radar imagery. The image shows an area about 130 miles (210 km) across.

Longest channel in the Solar System (below)
The thin line winding its way to the top right corner of this Magellan spacecraft image, centered at 49°N/165°E, is one section of the longest channel ever found on Venus—and indeed anywhere in the Solar System to date. It measures 1.1 miles (1.8 km) across, and snakes across Venus for over 4,200 miles (7,000 km). It was probably formed by ancient lava flows.

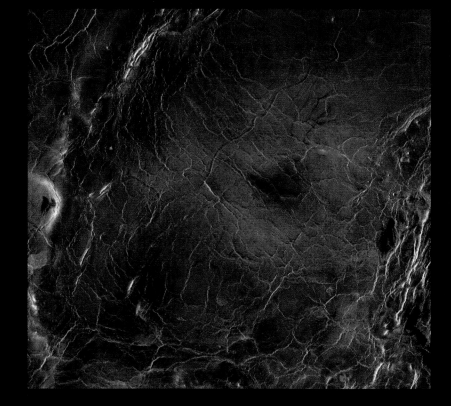

Impact craters

Curiously, of the 1,000 or so known Venus impact sites, few are smaller than 16 miles (25 km) in diameter, and none at all is smaller than about 2 miles (3 km). This is the result of the planet's dense atmosphere, which destroys any smaller, would-be projectiles before they can make an impression on the landscape.

Volcanic plains

The landscape of Venus is dominated by vast, rolling plains, stretching for thousands of miles and covering some 85 percent of the hostile surface. These lowland plains are composed of solidified basalt, which suggests that they are volcanic in origin. They probably formed as recently as a few hundred million years ago when lava, leaking out of the crust from sources not readily apparent, flooded almost the entire surface. Because the rolling plains are essentially fossilized oceans of lava, they are remarkably flat, and are mostly found at low altitudes. In general they have a relief of less than 0.6 miles (1 km).

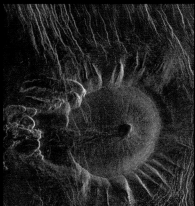

Gigantic bloodsuckers (left)
This feature in Eistla Regio, known as a tick-type or arachnoid volcano, is one of several of this type on Venus. Measuring a few tens of miles across, it has a slightly concave summit, while ridges and valleys radiate down its flanks.

Volcanic pancakes (far right)
These fractured, circular, volcanic objects are known as pancake domes and are unique to Venus. Here at 30°S/12°E, near Alpha Regio, they average about 15 miles (25 km) across and about 2,500 feet (750 m) in height. Scientists think they were created when viscous lava oozed onto the surface, where it spread out and solidified.

Coronae (right)
This Magellan mosaic shows a corona—an unusual volcanic feature on Venus which has no Earth analog. This example, known as Ba'het (50°N/0.1°W), is about 138 miles (230 km) long and 90 miles (150 km) across.

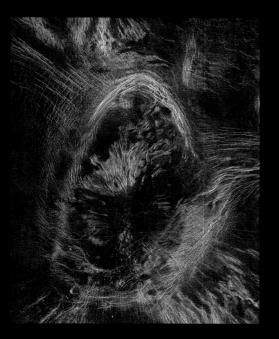
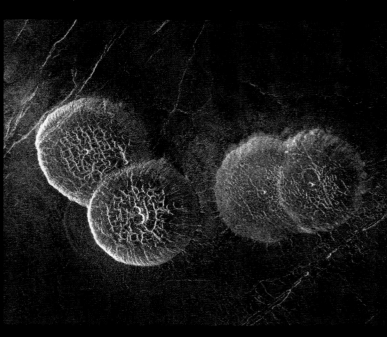

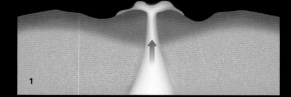
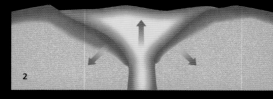
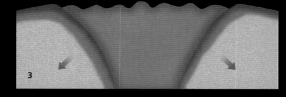

Venusian mountains

Volcanoes are by far the most prominent feature on the surface of Venus—more than 1,100 volcanic features are known. Astronomers do not know for sure if they are now active, but they may be, and certainly they have significantly changed the entire Venusian landscape in the last 500 to 300 million years. Some of the volcanoes are shield volcanoes, similar to the Hawaiian Islands on Earth or the giant Tharsis volcanoes on Mars. But others are types that are unique to Venus.

Formation of coronae (above)
The creation of a corona begins when lava flows out of a volcanic vent, creating the corona's central bulge (1). Eventually the weight of the volcanic material breaks the crust below (2). The dome then sinks into the crust, buckling surrounding terrain. Sometimes the dome itself may also crumple and fracture as it slowly cools (3).

Maat Mons (0.5°N/165°W) (below)
By combining Magellan radar imagery and altimetry data, scientists have reconstructed this three-dimensional model of a Venusian volcano. Called Maat Mons, this volcano reaches a height of around 5 miles (8 km). We see it from a vantage point about 1 mile (1.6 km) above the terrain and 348 miles (560 km) from the summit. The foreground features fractured plains partially covered in solidified lava flows. Although the volcano is high, it is very wide and its slopes are therefore gentle. However, the vertical scale in this image has been increased more than twenty times to emphasize the topography.

DISCOVERING VENUS

For much of human history, Venus has been an enigma. Its surface, permanently shielded by clouds, remained unknown until Earth-based radar first penetrated them in 1961. Even the planet's rotation period could only be guessed at until then, because the surface does not spin at the same rate as the atmosphere. Other Earth-based radar studies followed in the 1970s but it is from space probes that we have obtained most of our knowledge of the Venusian surface. The most celebrated missions were the Soviet Venera probes, which took the first images from the Venusian surface, and the NASA mission Magellan, which showed us almost the entire planet at high resolution for the first time.

The sky was brighter than expected, similar to an overcast day on Earth, and appeared a rusty burnished yellow.

These flat rocky slabs were determined to be a type of basalt and are probably volcanic in origin.

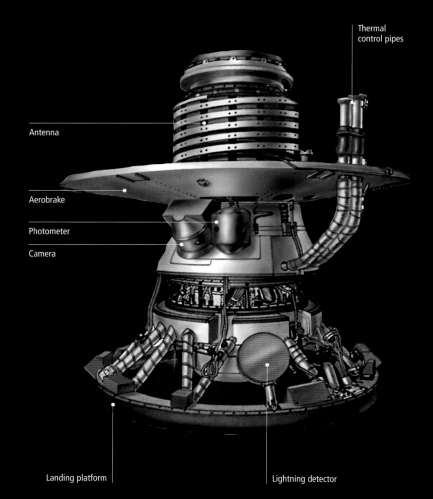

Thermal control pipes

Antenna

Aerobrake

Photometer

Camera

Landing platform

Lightning detector

The Soviet programs: Venera and Vega

The Soviet Venera program comprised sixteen separate probes designed to study the planet Venus—from orbit, from within its atmosphere, and from the surface. On October 18, 1967, the first successful Venera, number 4, arrived at Venus and ejected a capsule into the atmosphere. This capsule briefly transmitted atmospheric data such as temperatures and chemical composition on its way through the clouds, verifying that the atmosphere was dominated by carbon dioxide. Veneras 5 and 6 were of similar design. On December 15, 1970, the Venera 7 capsule became the first man-made object to land on another planet. And on October 22, 1975, Venera 9 became the first probe to orbit Venus, its landing capsule sending back the first photos from the surface. The last Venera probe, 16, arrived at Venus in October 1983. The later Vega probes, both launched in December 1984, each comprised a separate lander and an atmospheric balloon probe. They arrived at Venus in June 1985, the landers being the last man-made objects to touch down on the planet. The balloon probes were released at an altitude of about 30 miles (50 km) and returned data on conditions in the upper atmosphere as they were swept around the planet in hurricane-speed winds. Above is a panoramic photograph returned from the surface of Venus by Venera 13 on March 1, 1982.

Venera lander (left)
This illustration shows the odd design of the Venera landers 9 to 14. The probes were slowed by parachute, but fell freely for the last few miles through the soupy atmosphere and hit the surface at about 25 feet per second (8 m/s). The probes had to be designed to absorb this shock as well as withstand the crushing atmospheric pressure and high temperatures at the surface. During descent electrical discharges were measured using a lightning detector.

Pioneer's portrait of Venus (below)
Radar mapping by the Pioneer Venus orbiter gave scientists the first complete picture of the Venusian surface, although at a resolution of some 30 miles (50 km) the finer details were missing. This color-coded map of the northern hemisphere reveals a planet dominated by relatively smooth lowlands, which are here shaded blue and green. The yellow regions are highlands, topped in the north by the Maxwell Montes chain depicted in red and white.

Pioneer Venus

The Pioneer Venus program consisted of two NASA probes, both launched in 1978. Their objectives were to photograph the planet and to map its surface using cloud-penetrating radar. Pioneer 1 (right) simply went into orbit around the planet, where it remained, sending back data until August 1992. Pioneer 2 released four sub-probes, each of which returned data on the composition and clouds of the Venusian atmosphere on their way to the surface. One of the sub-probes (Day Probe) landed intact and sent back data for over an hour.

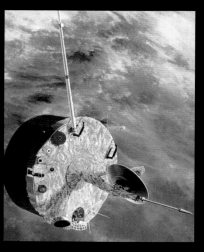

Discarded camera lens
protective cover

Tests on the soil
indicated that it was
a fine volcanic ash.

Part of the circular landing
foot, used to absorb the
shock of the landing

Color calibration strip

Magellan: Venus unmasked

Our knowledge of Venus took a huge leap forward with
the NASA probe Magellan. Magellan was deployed from
the space shuttle Atlantis in May 1989. Arriving at Venus
fifteen months later, it went into a near-polar orbit,
from where it mapped almost the entire surface using
radar at a resolution of about 330 feet (100 m). In 1993,
the probe mapped the gravity of Venus. It was then put
into gradually lower orbits until it finally disintegrated
in the planet's atmosphere in October 1994, its mission
a resounding success. The image, left, is a view of Venus
looking straight down on the planet's north pole. It was
obtained by compiling several years of Magellan radar
imagery with additional data from Pioneer Venus, and the
Arecibo radio telescope in Puerto Rico. The topographic
coloring is similar to that used in the Pioneer Venus map
below left and shows Maxwell Montes as a white patch
near the center.

Venus Express—rediscovering Venus

The 2005 launch of the European Space Agency's Venus
Express from the Baikonur Cosmodrome in Kazakhstan
signified a renewal of interest in our closest planetary
neighbor after years in the shadow of missions to Mars
and the outer planets. Reaching the planet in 2006,
Europe's first Venus mission is making the most detailed
study yet of the atmosphere of the planet. Analyses of the
planet's extreme greenhouse effect, hurricane force winds,
and weak magnetic field, will enhance our understanding
of Venus and its unique features. Above is an artist's
impression of Venus Express in orbit. Venus Express is
closely modeled on the Mars Express spacecraft and
shares many of the same instruments.

MARS

Named after the Roman god of war, the so-called Red Planet has
captured our imagination more than any other. Mars is not even
remotely as hospitable as Antarctica. Yet, compared with the
other inner planets, Mercury and Venus, it seems almost friendly.
Indeed, there may even have been life there once—and some
argue that this may be true even today. Mars is a modestly-sized
sphere of rock and iron, and the next world out from the Sun
after Earth. Its eccentric orbit carries it from 1.41 to 1.64 times
farther from the Sun than Earth, making it bitterly cold.
Curiously, the length of the Martian day—24 hours and
37 minutes—is remarkably similar to Earth's; but physically,
these worlds differ enormously from each other. Mars is just
half the diameter of Earth and has only 11 percent of its mass.
Its boulder-strewn surface, red with oxidization, is constantly
ravaged by planet-wide dust storms and riddled with immense
craters, volcanoes, and canyons, all of which dwarf their earthly
counterparts. And the Red Planet's scant atmosphere—which
is almost pure carbon dioxide and lacks a protective ozone
layer—would be lethal to any unprotected interplanetary visitor.
The two Martian moons, Phobos and Deimos, are most likely
captured asteroids, just a few miles in diameter each.

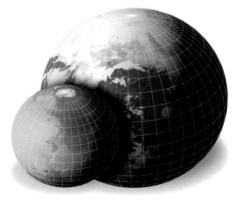

Red dwarf
Mars is the second smallest terrestrial
planet after Mercury, just over half the
size (53 percent) of Earth. However, water
covers two-thirds of our planet, so Earth
and Mars have similar land areas.

MARS STATISTICS	
Discovered	Known from antiquity
Average distance from the Sun	142 million miles (228 million km); 1.52 AU
Equatorial diameter	4,222 miles (6,794 km)
Axial rotation period (sidereal)	24.62 hours (prograde)
Mass (Earth = 1)	0.11
Volume (Earth = 1)	0.15
Surface gravity (Earth = 1)	0.38
Average density (water = 1)	3.93
Surface atmospheric pressure (Earth = 1)	0.007
Escape velocity	3 miles/s (5 km/s)
Orbital eccentricity	0.09
Highest temperature	80°F (27°C)
Lowest temperature	–207°F (–133°C)
Sunlight strength	36–52% of Earth's
Albedo (reflectivity)	15%
Number of satellites	2

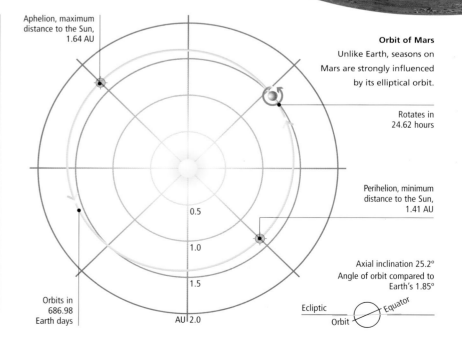

Aphelion, maximum
distance to the Sun,
1.64 AU

Orbit of Mars
Unlike Earth, seasons on
Mars are strongly influenced
by its elliptical orbit.

Rotates in
24.62 hours

Perihelion, minimum
distance to the Sun,
1.41 AU

0.5

1.0

1.5

Axial inclination 25.2°
Angle of orbit compared to
Earth's 1.85°

Orbits in
686.98
Earth days

AU 2.0

Ecliptic
Orbit
Equator

The geology of Mars

Mars has two distinct terrains: the heavily cratered southern highlands and the lowland plains of volcanic origin in the north. The comparatively few craters in the north suggest that this is the younger region. Mars does not have continental plates. The crust is probably thick, solid, and immobile, which explains how Martian volcanoes have grown to the extent that they are the largest in the known Solar System—the lava merely leaked out of the surface and kept on piling up. As well as volcanoes and craters, Mars is home to some vast canyons, again larger than any seen on Earth, and other features that seem to have resulted from flowing surface water. Perhaps the Red Planet was once a Blue Planet.

Crust

The Martian crust is probably much thicker than Earth's, extending down 75 miles (120 km). This solid crust has no plate tectonics and is able to support the mass of huge volcanoes.

Mantle

Beneath the crust is the mantle, a thick shell of rocks such as olivine. This compound, made from silicate, iron, and magnesium, is common to all terrestrial planets. The mantle may also contain some iron oxide.

Core

The Martian core is comparatively small, occupying perhaps 30 to 40 percent of the planet's diameter (shown here with a core at the upper end of that scale). The low density of Mars indicates that the core may be of iron and iron sulfide, lighter than the nickel-iron core of Earth. The weak magnetic field of Mars (Earth's is 800 times stronger) suggests a relatively solid core.

The atmosphere and climate of Mars

Mars is far colder than Earth, a result of its relative distance from the Sun. Temperatures do sometimes rise above freezing in rare instances during the Martian summer, but otherwise they average −58°F (−50°C) and dip down to −190°F (−123°C) in the winter. The eccentric orbit makes for huge seasonal variations, with the polar caps alternately evaporating in the summer and then reforming in the winter from carbon dioxide snowfalls. Dust storms are also typical, smothering the planet in shrouds of fine red powder for weeks or even months.

Atmospheric breakdown

Evidence suggests that Mars was once wet, its surface perhaps covered in rivers, lakes, and seas. Therefore, the Red Planet may also have had a substantial atmosphere in the past. Now, though, much of it has been lost to space, and it is less than one percent as dense as Earth's. The surface pressure is equivalent to 22 miles (35 km) above Earth, or about three times the cruising altitude of a typical passenger jet.

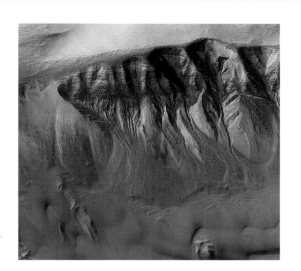

Wet world evidence
This photo, returned by the Mars Global Surveyor spacecraft, shows what appear to be recently formed gullies on the rim of a Martian crater. The gullies were possibly carved by flowing water or liquid carbon dioxide.

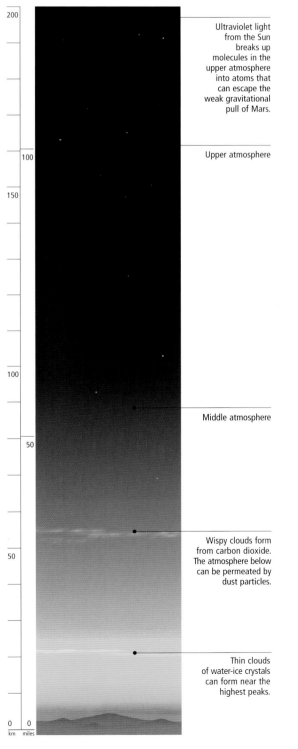

Ultraviolet light from the Sun breaks up molecules in the upper atmosphere into atoms that can escape the weak gravitational pull of Mars.

Upper atmosphere

Middle atmosphere

Wispy clouds form from carbon dioxide. The atmosphere below can be permeated by dust particles.

Thin clouds of water-ice crystals can form near the highest peaks.

A cloudy day on Mars
Like Earth, Mars has clouds, but they are not extensive. This photo shows the Tharsis region, with the volcano chain Tharsis Montes on the left. The clouds tend to cling to the summits, up to 17 miles (27 km) above the surface. The clouds are made of water-ice crystals that freeze out of the high, cold air.

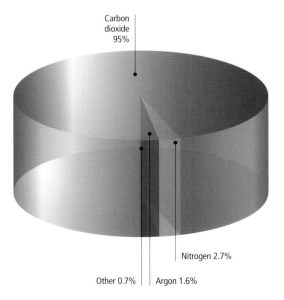

Carbon dioxide 95%

Nitrogen 2.7%

Other 0.7% | Argon 1.6%

MAPPING MARS WESTERN HEMISPHERE

The western hemisphere of Mars contains the planet's most well-known and recognizable features. Both the highest peak, Olympus Mons (18.5°N/133°W), and the deepest valley, Valles Marineris (12°S/65°W), are on this face of Mars. The earliest landing site, that of the failed Soviet lander Mars 3, was in Terra Sirenum (45°S/158°W), and Viking 1, the first successful mission, landed in Chryse Planitia (22.5°N/48°W). Prominent features on Mars generally carry the names given them in the 19th or early 20th centuries while large craters are named after scientists and writers who have contributed to Martian knowledge or lore.

The western face of Mars (above)
From space, the western hemisphere's most striking features, Olympus Mons, the Tharsis Montes volcanoes, and Valles Marineris, are all clearly seen.

LANDING SITES: WESTERN MARS

PROBE (LANDING DATE)	LANDING SITE
Mars 3 (Dec 2, 1971)	45°S/158°W
Mars 6 (Mar 12, 1974)	24°S/19°W
Viking 1 (Jul 20, 1976)	22.5°N/48°W
Pathfinder (Jul 4, 1997)	19°N/33.5°W
Opportunity (Jan 25, 2004)	2°S/6°W
Phoenix (May 25, 2008)	68°N/ 126°W

Probes to the western hemisphere of Mars (above)
Soviet probes were the first to land on Mars, starting with the arrival of Mars 3. Only 20 seconds after a soft landing Mars 3 lost contact, possibly due to a planet-wide dust storm that was raging at the time. Mars 6 crash-landed in Margaritifer Terra. Viking 1 was the first mission to successfully send back images of Mars from the ground. The Pathfinder Sojourner rover was the first mobile explorer of the planet's western hemisphere, joined later by the Mars Exploration Rover (MER), Opportunity.

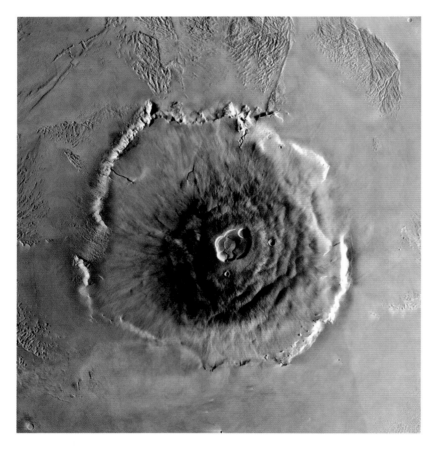

Olympus Mons (above)
Olympus Mons is the largest mountain in the Solar System. Its summit soars 17 miles (27 km) above the local surface and its base is approximately 340 miles (550 km) across. Observations by the Mars Global Surveyor suggest that this shield volcano may have last erupted 10 to 20 million years ago.

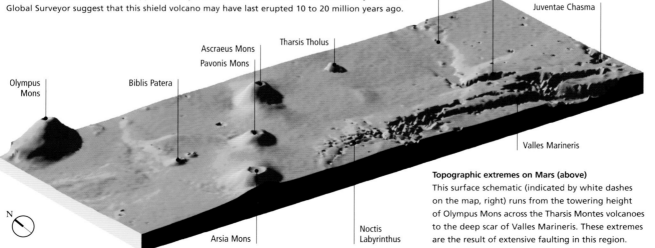

Topographic extremes on Mars (above)
This surface schematic (indicated by white dashes on the map, right) runs from the towering height of Olympus Mons across the Tharsis Montes volcanoes to the deep scar of Valles Marineris. These extremes are the result of extensive faulting in this region.

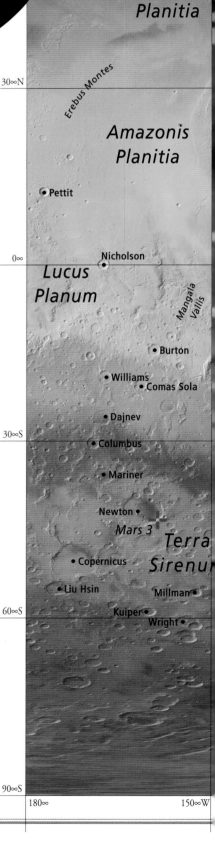

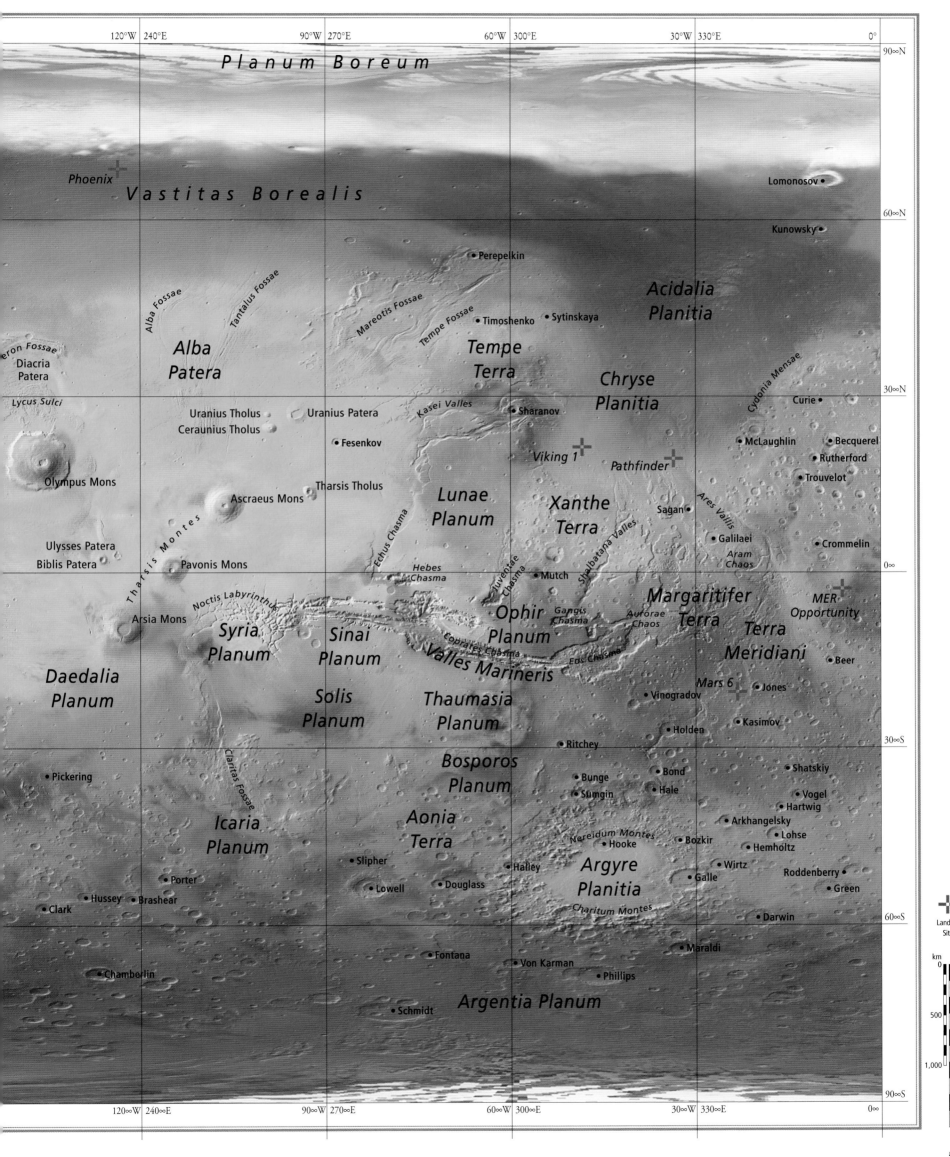

Planum Boreum

Vastitas Borealis

Phoenix

Lomonosov

Kunowsky

Perepelkin

Acidalia
Planitia

Alba Fossae

Tantalus Fossae

Mareotis Fossae

Tempe Fossae

Timoshenko   Sytinskaya

Alba
Patera

Tempe
Terra

Chryse
Planitia

eron Fossae
Diacria
Patera

Cydonia Mensae

Curie

Lycus Sulci

Kasei Valles

Sharanov

Uranius Tholus   Uranius Patera

Ceraunius Tholus

McLaughlin   Becquerel

Fesenkov

Viking 1   Pathfinder

Rutherford

Olympus Mons

Ascraeus Mons   Tharsis Tholus

Lunae
Planum

Xanthe
Terra

Trouvelot

Sagan

Ares Vallis

Ulysses Patera

Biblis Patera   Pavonis Mons

Galilaei

Crommelin

Tharsis Montes

Echus Chasma

Hebes
Chasma

Juventae Chasma

Mutch

Aram
Chaos

Shalbatana Valles

Noctis Labyrinthus

Margaritifer
Terra

MER
Opportunity

Arsia Mons

Syria
Planum

Sinai
Planum

Ophir
Planum

Gangis
Chasma

Aurorae
Chaos

Terra
Meridiani

Daedalia
Planum

Coprates Chasma

Valles Marineris

Eos Chasma

Beer

Solis
Planum

Thaumasia
Planum

Mars 6   Jones

Vinogradov

Ritchey

Holden

Kasimov

Bosporos
Planum

Bunge   Bond

Sumgin   Hale

Shatskiy

Pickering

Claritas Fossae

Vogel

Hartwig

Icaria
Planum

Aonia
Terra

Arkhangelsky

Nereidum Montes

Hooke   Bozkir

Lohse

Hemholtz

Slipher

Halley

Argyre
Planitia

Wirtz

Galle

Roddenberry

Porter

Lowell   Douglass

Green

Hussey   Brashear

Clark

Charitum Montes

Darwin

Landing
Site

Maraldi

Fontana

Von Karman

Phillips

Chamberlin

Schmidt

Argentia Planum

km   miles
0   0

500

500

1,000

1,000

MAPPING MARS EASTERN HEMISPHERE

This half of the planet lacks the majestic Tharsis volcanoes and the vast Valles Marineris of the western hemisphere but it is not without interest. Hellas Planitia is a huge, lowland impact basin centered around 43 degrees south, 66 degrees east, measuring some 1,370 miles (2,200 km) in width and about 5 miles (8 km) in depth—the lowest point on Mars in fact. It is often seen from Earth as a bright spot because it tends to fill with iridescent clouds of ice crystals. The planet's darkest region is also in this hemisphere, called Syrtis Major Planum (9.5°N/70.5°E).

The eastern face of Mars (above)
This hemisphere, much like the west, is markedly smoother in the north. Scientists speculate that this may be due to a bygone seabed or that lava flows erased the older terrain in the north.

LANDING SITES: EASTERN MARS	
PROBE (LANDING DATE)	**LANDING SITE**
Mars 2 (Nov 27, 1971)	45°S/47°E
Viking 2 (Sep 3, 1976)	48°N/134°E
Polar Lander (Dec 3, 1999)	76°S/165°E
Beagle 2 (Dec 25, 2003)	11°N/90°E
Spirit (Jan 4, 2004)	15°S/175°E

Probes to the eastern hemisphere of Mars (above)
Several probes have touched the surface of the eastern Martian hemisphere, but not all of them successfully. NASA's Mars Polar Lander, the British Beagle 2 rover, and the early Soviet craft Mars 2 all came to grief on this side of the Red Planet. Only Viking 2 and, more recently, the Mars Exploration Rover (MER), Spirit, have made successful landings on this hemisphere.

Evidence of water on Mars (above)
This photo, returned by NASA's Mars Global Surveyor spacecraft, is one of many that are convincing planetary scientists that Mars once had plentiful water. The image, which spans about 1.9 miles (3 km), shows layers of sediment within the crater Schiaparelli (3°S/16°E), possibly deposited by running water. The dark areas—which look like water, complete with ripples—are actually composed of sand.

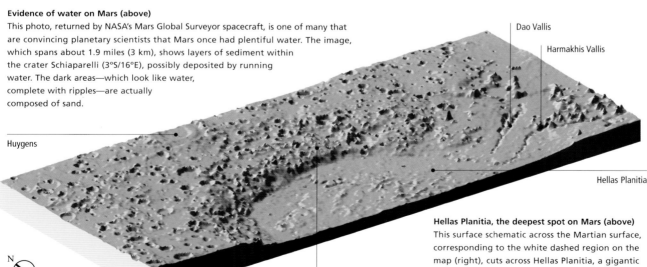

Huygens

Dao Vallis

Harmakhis Vallis

Hellas Planitia

N

Hellespontus Montes

Hellas Planitia, the deepest spot on Mars (above)
This surface schematic across the Martian surface, corresponding to the white dashed region on the map (right), cuts across Hellas Planitia, a gigantic impact structure which, at a depth of 5 miles (8 km), contains the planet's lowest point.

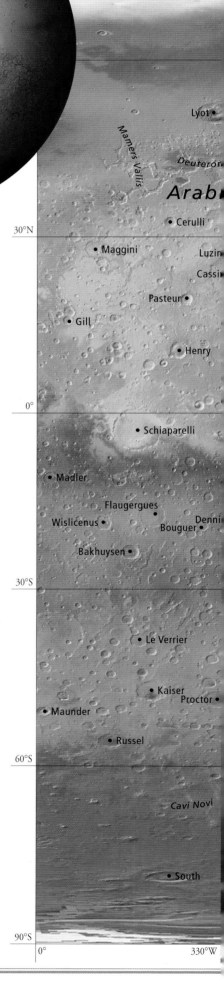

0°   330°W
90°N

Lyot

Mamers Vallis   Deuteror

Arabi

Cerulli

30°N   Maggini   Luzin

Cassi

Pasteur

Gill

Henry

0°   Schiaparelli

Madler

Flaugergues   Denni

Wislicenus   Bouguer

Bakhuysen

30°S

Le Verrier

Kaiser

Proctor

Maunder

Russel

60°S

Cavi Novi

South

90°S
0°   330°W

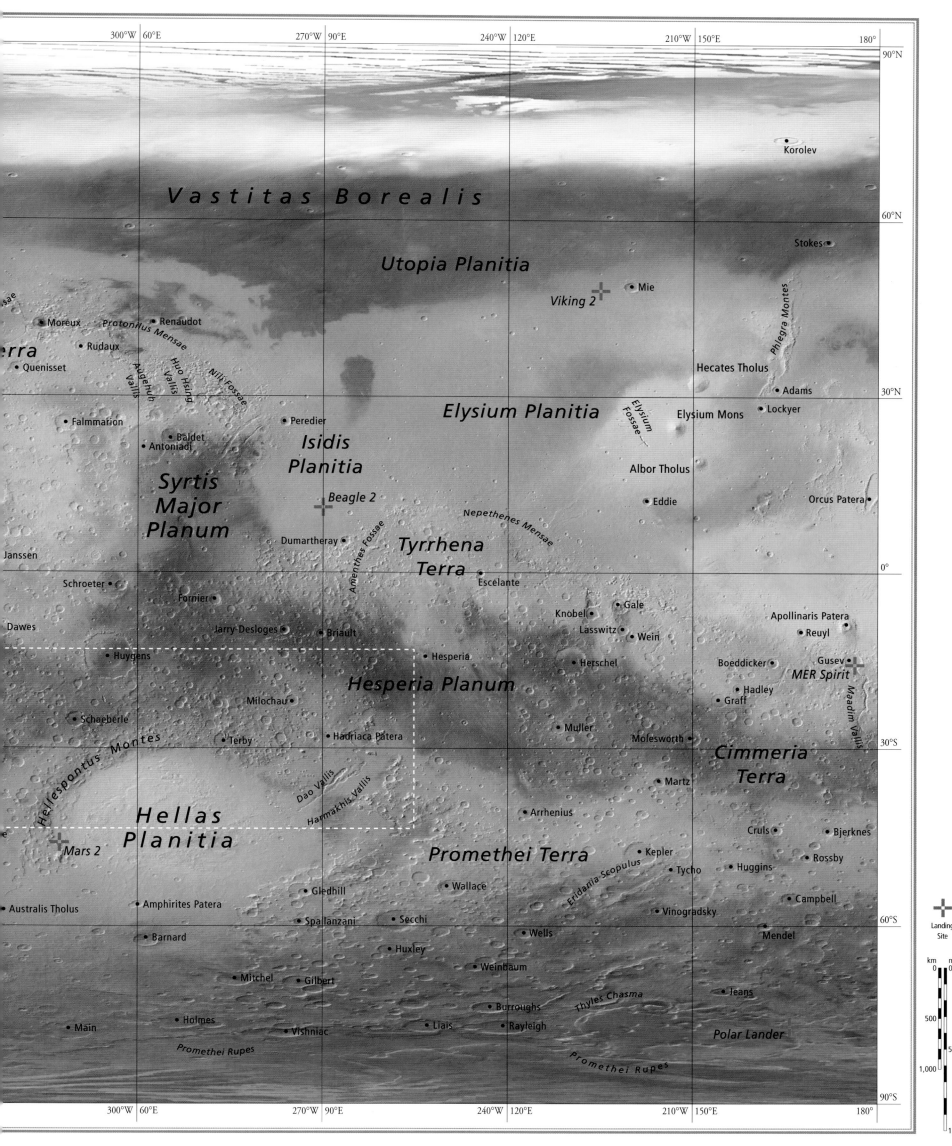

Vastitas Borealis

Korolev

Stokes

Utopia Planitia

Mie

Viking 2

Moreux

Renaudot

Protonilus Mensae

Phlegra Montes

erra

Rudaux

Hecates Tholus

Quenisset

Augehuh Vallis

Huo Hsing Vallis

Nili Fossae

Adams

Elysium Planitia

Elysium Fossae

Elysium Mons

Lockyer

Falmmarion

Peredier

Baldet

Antoniadi

Isidis Planitia

Albor Tholus

Syrtis Major Planum

Beagle 2

Eddie

Orcus Patera

Janssen

Dumartheray

Amenthes Fossae

Tyrrhena Terra

Nepethenes Mensae

Schroeter

Fornier

Escelante

Knobel

Gale

Apollinaris Patera

Dawes

Jarry-Desloges

Briault

Lasswitz

Wein

Reuyl

Huygens

Hesperia

Herschel

Boeddicker

Gusev

MER Spirit

Hesperia Planum

Hadley

Graff

Milochau

Schaeberle

Muller

Molesworth

Maadim Vallis

Terby

Hadriaca Patera

Cimmeria Terra

Hellespontus Montes

Dao Vallis

Harmakhis Vallis

Martz

Hellas Planitia

Arrhenius

Cruls

Bjerknes

Mars 2

Promethei Terra

Kepler

Tycho

Huggins

Rossby

Australis Tholus

Amphirites Patera

Gledhill

Wallace

Eridania Scopulus

Vinogradsky

Campbell

Spallanzani

Secchi

Wells

Mendel

Barnard

Huxley

Weinbaum

Mitchel

Gilbert

Thyles Chasma

Jeans

Main

Holmes

Burroughs

Liais

Rayleigh

Polar Lander

Vishniac

Promethei Rupes

Promethei Rupes

Landing
Site

km   miles

500

500

1,000

1,000

MARS
SURFACE FEATURES

The surface of Mars is a treasure trove for planetary scientists. Its volcanoes, the largest in the entire Solar System, are truly enormous—equivalents on Earth are mere blisters by comparison. Martian canyons and craters are no less impressive and evidence is everywhere that Mars once had lakes, seas, even oceans, in the distant past. But most exciting of all are certain features, like gullies, that may have been carved by running water in geologically recent times. The big question is: where is the water now? Possibly much of it dissipated into the atmosphere and was lost to space, or maybe it was absorbed into the ground where it remains frozen beneath the surface. Some geologists speculate that liquid water might remain in certain, low-altitude regions where the conditions are just right.

Valles Marineris: largest canyon in the Solar System

Valles Marineris is the Red Planet's most famous landmark, visible telescopically from Earth as a dark scar spanning virtually an entire hemisphere. This tectonic feature—actually a network of separate, gigantic canyons—is a rip in the Martian crust up to 4.5 miles (7 km) deep and stretching some 2,400 miles (3,800 km) in length. It is the largest canyon system in the known Solar System. Scientists believe that Marineris was created when sub-surface magma welled up and effectively ripped the crust apart laterally. Toward the top and just left of center of this Viking 1 orbiter image (right), a large subsidiary canyon, Candor Chasma (6.5°S/71°W), can be seen, possibly formed by water flowing out of the main channel long ago.

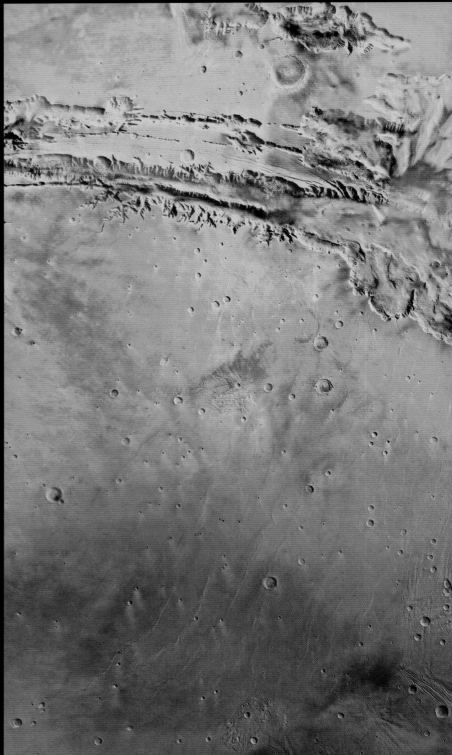

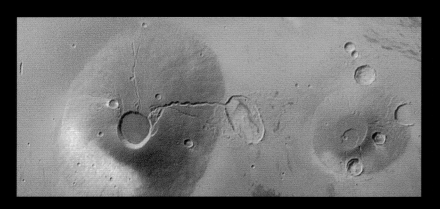

Volcanoes on Mars

Volcanoes are common on Mars, and they grow to enormous dimensions because the planet lacks plate tectonics—the lava just piles up in one place. The image above, captured by the Mars Global Surveyor, shows two examples of shield volcanoes at the northern end of the Tharsis Montes chain. They are, on the left, Ceraunius Tholus (24°N/97°W), and on the right, Uranius Tholus (26.5°N/98°W). The caldera at the summit of Ceraunius Tholus is about 15 miles (25 km) across. Although these volcanoes are almost certainly extinct, there is evidence that other volcanoes have been active within the last 10 million years and Mars cannot be declared volcanically inactive just yet.

Evidence of water erosion

Mars is replete with canyon and channel systems, whose tree-like branching suggests that, like their counterparts on Earth, they were formed by rivers and streams. Very few of these channels are found on the young lowland plains, suggesting they date from early in the planet's history. There is also evidence of catastrophic flooding—as may have occurred when water locked up in a canyon, or buried underground at high pressure, was suddenly released. The photo at right shows what appear to be gullies running down the sides of a small crater within the larger Newton Crater (41°S/158°W). These gullies were likely formed by flowing water and debris.

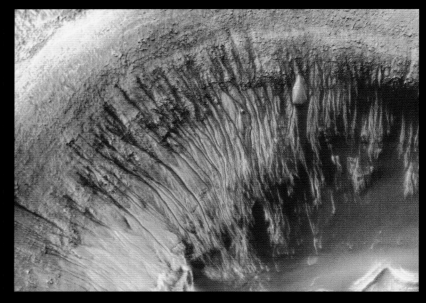

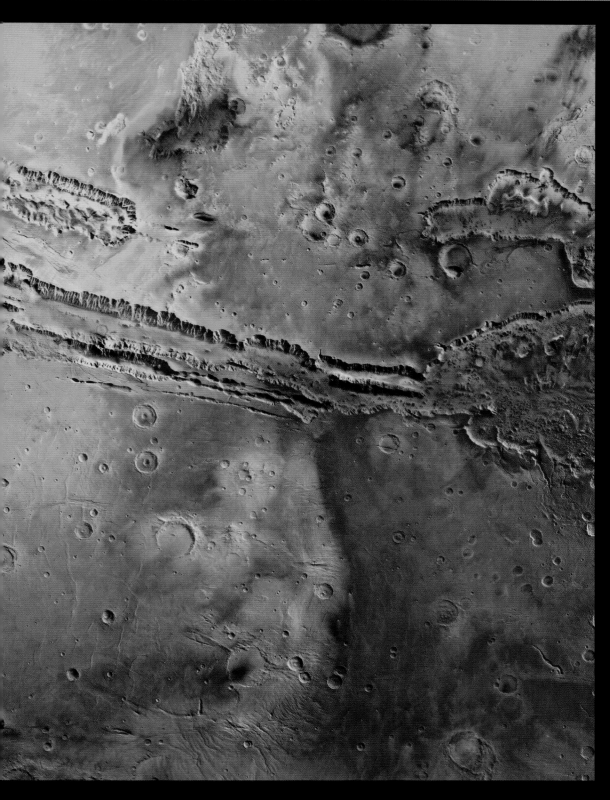

Wind erosion

As well as volcanism and erosion by water, wind has played a role in sculpting the barren Martian surface. Sandstorms are common on Mars, and can smother much of the planet for months. The long sculpted features visible in the Mars Global Surveyor image below were probably sandblasted into the bedrock by loose particles carried by the prevailing winds. The relatively smooth regions presumably contain more durable material, which the wind has not yet eroded. Such features on Earth are called "yardangs." The foreground of the image shows an area about 12 miles (20 km) across just south of Olympus Mons (18.5°N/133°W).

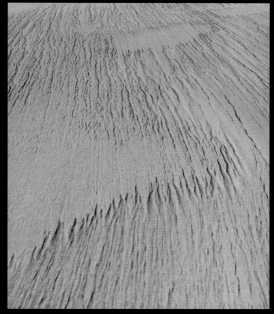

Craters

Like all planetary bodies, the surface of Mars began to accumulate impact craters as soon as it solidified. Oddly, most of the craters on the Red Planet occupy the southern hemisphere—the so-called highlands. The northern hemisphere, by contrast, is younger and therefore much smoother; its craters have been eroded by wind and more recent volcanic activity.

Frosty winter crater (below)
This image shows a western hemisphere crater called Lomonosov (65°N/9°W), 93 miles (150 km) across, as seen during the Martian winter. The crater rim is white, coated in frost, while fog and higher patches of cloud are also visible.

Polar caps

Like Earth, Mars has a pair of polar caps. However, whereas ours are made entirely of water ice, those on Mars contain, in addition, vast quantities of carbon dioxide, or dry ice. When Mars is closest to the Sun, the southern hemisphere warms up and the polar cap shrinks as the carbon dioxide evaporates. In winter, the carbon dioxide falls to the ground as snow and the polar cap grows back to full size.

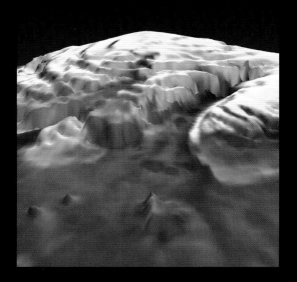

The Martian north pole (left)
The terraced, northern polar cap of Mars pops out in three dimensions in this image derived from Mars Global Surveyor altimetry data. Approximately 2.6 million altitude measurements were made, by laser altimeter, to construct this image, whose vertical scale has been greatly exaggerated for clarity.

Discovering Mars

More than any other planet, Mars has inspired the human imagination. A century ago, astronomers thought of it as a habitable world populated by "Martians"—an idea that was fueled in part by the discovery of what were believed to be irrigation canals there. H.G. Wells's novel, *The War of the Worlds*, with its fictional account of a Martian invasion, added to the Mars mania. And when this novel was serialized for American radio in 1938, many people really did think that aliens were invading. But now we have discovered the true Mars. This is an arid, bitterly cold world, rocky and barren, strewn with craters and mammoth volcanoes—and it is, as far as we can tell, lifeless.

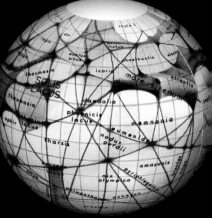

Channeled Mars (left and below)
These Mars globes are modeled on the maps drawn by Franco–Greek astronomer Eugène Michel Antoniadi early last century. While the representation of dark and light regions is quite accurate, the long, straight "channels" turned out to be tricks of the eye. Antoniadi became a leading critic of the canal theory later in his career.

Early speculations
Before Mars had been seen up close, many people believed the planet to be populated, in particular the wealthy American amateur astronomer Percival Lowell (1855–1916). Following the report by the Italian Giovanni Schiaparelli (1835–1910) of "channels" on Mars, Lowell—misinterpreting the Italian word for channels as "canals"—convinced himself that Martians were ferrying water from the planet's poles to its arid but fertile equatorial regions.

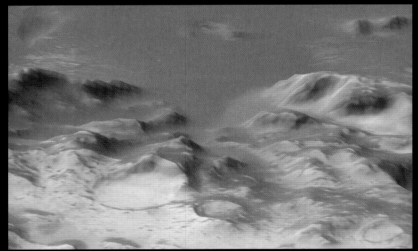

Early missions to Mars
When Mariner 4 became the first craft to fly past Mars in 1965, it found no canals, no signs of civilization—just a cratered desert world. Eleven years later two US landers, Viking 1 and 2, touched down on the surface. Tests on the soil found no signs of life. The photo above, the first ever taken from the surface of Mars, was returned by Viking 1 just minutes after it touched down near Chryse Planitia (22.5°N/48°W).

Mars Global Surveyor
Perhaps the most successful Mars mission to date is Mars Global Surveyor. The craft arrived at the Red Planet in September 1997 and began an extensive orbital survey. The photos returned reveal the planet in hitherto unimagined detail. The image at right is an example, showing Martian mountains and craters in the southern hemisphere dusted with a frost of carbon dioxide, or dry ice, during the spring.

A cocoon of airbags ensured that Pathfinder made a soft (if extremely bouncy) landing.

The size and distribution of rocks confirmed that the Ares Vallis region, where Pathfinder landed (19°N/33.5°W), was once the site of a catastrophic ancient flood.

Pathfinder's meteorology mast recorded the temperature, pressure, and wind speed at the landing site.

Far Knob, 19 miles (30.6 km) distant

PHOBOS STATISTICS	
Discovered	1877
Dimensions	12 x 14 x 17 miles
	(20 x 23 x 28 km)
Mean orbit	5,827 miles (9,378 km)
Orbital period	7.65 hours

DEIMOS STATISTICS	
Discovered	1877
Dimensions	6 x 7 x 10 miles
	(10 x 12 x 16 km)
Mean orbit	14,577 miles (23,459 km)
Orbital period	1.26 days

Phobos and Deimos

Of the inner planets, only Earth and Mars have natural satellites and only Mars has two. However, the Martian moons are tiny, most likely strays snatched from the nearby Asteroid Belt. American astronomer Asaph Hall (1829–1907) discovered them in 1877, when Mars came relatively close to Earth. Naming them Phobos (right) and Deimos (far right), Hall calculated their orbits and from this obtained the mass of Mars. Phobos is closer to its parent planet than any other moon in the Solar System.

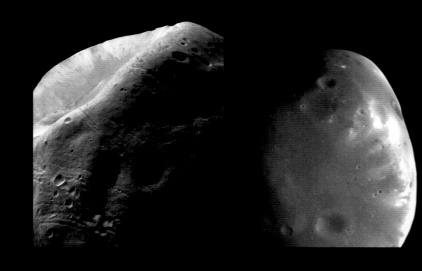

A postcard from Mars (right)
The Spirit rover had covered more than 2.2 miles (3.5 km) of the Martian surface, inside the 90-mile (145-km) wide Gusev Crater (15ºS/175ºE), when it took this panorama. The crater wall can be seen on the horizon with smooth plains leading up to it. The foreground shows a rock outcrop in the crater, which the rover partially climbed.

Pathfinder

On American Independence Day, 1997, Mars Pathfinder became the first craft to touch down on the Red Planet since the Viking landers 21 years earlier. The lander (shown deployed below) also released a milk-crate-sized exploration rover called Sojourner, which was operated from Earth via remote control. Mars Pathfinder continued to send data for two months before communications were lost.

Mars Express

In 2003, the European Space Agency launched its first ever mission to Mars, dubbed Mars Express. The probe arrived in Mars's orbit in December 2003 where it dispatched a rover named Beagle 2. Unfortunately, Beagle 2 was lost, but the orbiter is performing well, and in February 2005 discovered strong evidence for the existence of a frozen sub-surface ocean in the Elysium Planitia (20ºN/120ºE) region.

Mars Exploration Rover mission

NASA's success on Mars continues with its twin Mars Exploration Rovers, individually known as Spirit and Opportunity, which arrived on opposite hemispheres of Mars in January 2004. Each identical golf-cart-sized rover (illustrated right) is equipped with a panoramic camera, a microscopic imager, a self-guiding navigation system, and tools for analyzing the atmosphere and the composition of rocks.

Twin Peaks:
South Peak, 0.6 miles
(1 km) distant

Twin Peaks:
North Peak, 0.5 miles
(0.85 km) distant

The rover's wheel tracks were closely studied in order to determine the physical properties of Martian soil.

Here the Sojourner rover is examining the rock "Yogi" which was found to be a type of fine-grained basalt.

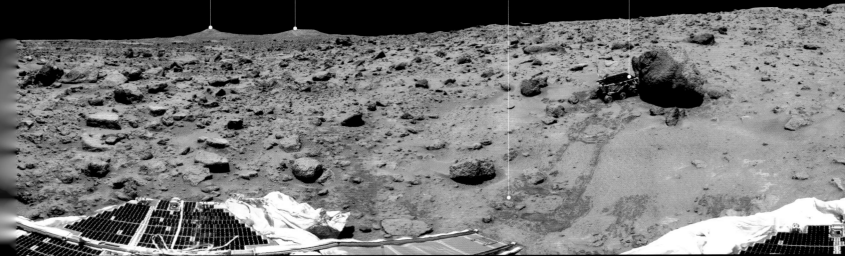

Asteroids

Orbiting between Mars and Jupiter is a cosmic junk-pile of leftovers, stranded after the Solar System formed from a cloud of gas and dust. These are the asteroids, or minor planets. These bodies are numbered in their millions, but their combined mass is only one-twentieth that of the Moon. There would have been many more originally, enough to make a small terrestrial planet the size of Mars. However, under the gravitational influence of the Sun and Jupiter, many were flung from the Solar System or swallowed by the Sun. The presence of Jupiter even now prevents the rest from coalescing into a planet. Today, these objects survive as fossils of the planet-forming process. Most are just a few tens or hundreds of feet across, but a rare few are small worlds in their own right.

Trojan asteroids

Some asteroids, known as the Trojans, actually share the orbit of Jupiter. These asteroids occupy two positions in the orbit of Jupiter, as illustrated below. More than half of them are bunched up around 60 degrees ahead of Jupiter and the rest are 60 degrees behind. Both lots are herded into these locations by the gravitational interplay between the giant planet and the Sun. Some 1,500 Trojans have been identified since the first, Achilles, was discovered in 1904.

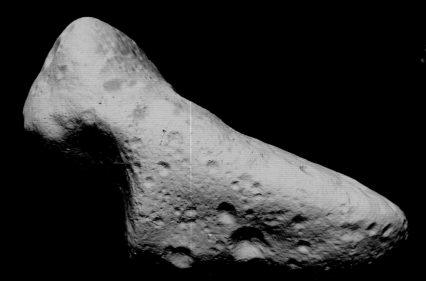

433 Eros

The asteroid 433 Eros made history in February 2000 when it became the first such world to be orbited by a spacecraft. The probe in question was NEAR-Shoemaker, which orbited Eros for a year before landing on the asteroid in a bid to study its surface composition. Saddle-shaped Eros (left) is one of only three so-called Near-Earth Asteroids larger than 6 miles (10 km) in diameter, measuring 25 x 9 x 9 miles (40 x 14 x 14 km). The map below was made from a mosaic of several images returned by NEAR-Shoemaker. It reveals a surface strewn with numerous craters and boulders.

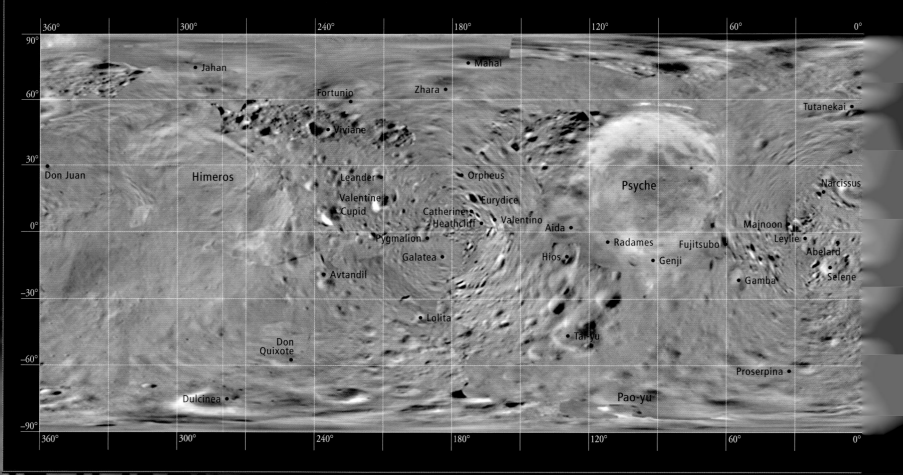

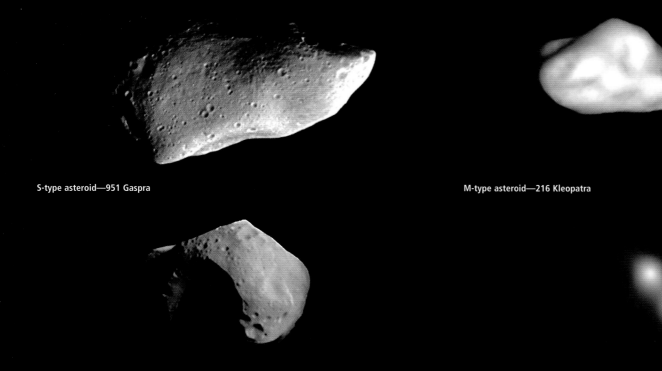

Near-Earth Asteroids

Not all asteroids occupy the Asteroid Belt. Near-Earth Asteroids (NEAs) are those that orbit within 1.3 AU of the Sun and include asteroids that come close to the orbit of our planet. As many as 100,000 NEAs larger than 330 feet (100 m) are estimated to exist, but only a few thousand have so far been found. Eros, photographed up close in 2000, is a Near-Earth Asteroid.

Dimensions of the Asteroid Belt

Most asteroids—although by no means all—are found in a zone around the Sun, between the orbits of Mars and Jupiter, called the Asteroid Belt. It extends from about 2.1 to 3.3 astronomical units (AU) from the Sun. Those asteroids on the innermost edge take about three years to complete an orbit, while for the outermost ones, the trip takes about twice that. The Asteroid Belt is not uniformly thick, but is instead tapered. On its outskirts the thickness is about 1 AU, but on its inside edge the belt is only about one-third as deep. Often the Asteroid Belt is imagined as a dense and dangerous field of crazily spinning boulders, an impediment to interplanetary travel. In reality, asteroids take hours or even weeks to complete a single rotation. Moreover, the belt is so extensive, and yet the asteroids so few, that you could easily spend your entire life on an asteroid and never see a neighboring one up close.

Asteroid types

Asteroids come in several classes, depending on their composition, spectrum, and albedo (reflectivity). S-type asteroids are common in the inner part of the main belt. The "S" stands for "silicaceous," for these worlds tend to be largely of silicate (stony) materials. Making up 75 percent of all known asteroids are the very dark C-types. These are "carbonaceous," containing large amounts of carbon. They are the most common asteroids in the outer regions of the main belt. M-type asteroids are common in the middle of the main belt. They are metallic, made of nickel and iron. In addition, while some asteroids have tiny moons, others comprise two worlds of comparable size orbiting a common center of mass. An example is 90 Antiope, seen below. It comprises two separate 50-mile (80-km) wide bodies separated by about 100 miles (160 km), orbiting each other once every 16.5 hours.

S-type asteroid—951 Gaspra

M-type asteroid—216 Kleopatra

C-type asteroid—253 Mathilde

Mutually orbiting double asteroid—90 Antiope

DISCOVERING ASTEROIDS

Asteroids are important to astronomers because, hailing as they do from the earliest stages of the Solar System, they offer clues to the formation of the planets. Yet, until 1991, no asteroid had been seen close-up. That changed when the Galileo probe, bound for Jupiter, flew past 951 Gaspra in 1991, and then by 243 Ida in 1993, returning detailed photos of each. In February 2000, the NEAR-Shoemaker probe went into orbit around the asteroid 433 Eros. The minor planets are finally getting their share of the limelight, and a number of asteroid missions are planned for the near future.

 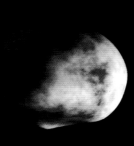

The discovery of asteroids

On January 1, 1801, Italian monk and astronomer Giuseppe Piazzi (1746–1826) discovered an unknown world between Mars and Jupiter. Piazzi named it Ceres and heralded it as a new planet. But subsequent discoveries of similar worlds—several hundred of them by the 20th century—forced a rethink. Instead of a single large world, there seemed to be a whole wealth of small "planetoids"—Piazzi's name for them—that came to be known as asteroids. Today, many thousands are cataloged, each with a name and a number representing the order in which they were discovered, but millions more remain undetected. 1 Ceres, 580 miles (933 km) in diameter, remains the largest, containing one-third the estimated combined mass of all the asteroids. However, fewer than twenty asteroids measure more than 155 miles (250 km) across, and most are just a few tens of feet across. Meteorites, rocks or metal fragments from space that fall to Earth, are usually splinters chipped off asteroids during collisions. The 4-inch (10-cm) meteorite shown above left is widely believed to come from 4 Vesta (above right), a uniquely basaltic-crusted olivine asteroid with evidence of volcanic activity in its past.

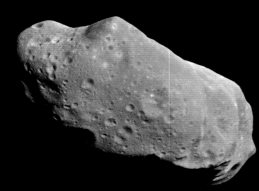

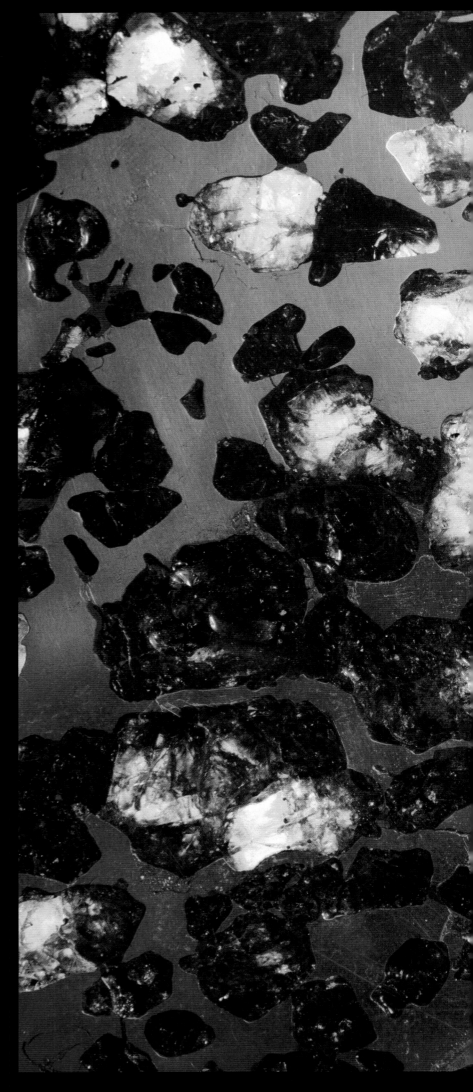

Ida and its moon (above and right)
The image above, captured by the Galileo probe en route to Jupiter in 1993, shows the first confirmed example of an asteroid (243 Ida, above left) with its own tiny moon (Dactyl, above right). Ida is 34 miles (54 km) across at its widest, while Dactyl (seen in close-up at right) is no wider than 1 mile (1.6 km) and is shaped like an egg.

Finding asteroids from Earth

Asteroids reveal themselves telescopically as faint points of light moving against the background of distant stars. In a typical year hundreds of new asteroids are discovered in this way, most by means of semi-automated systems dedicated to asteroid discovery. Others are found accidentally when they drift into the field of view while other astronomical observations are being made. The discovery and tracking of asteroids is of more than purely scientific interest. Asteroid strikes are believed to have caused environmental catastrophe and mass extinctions several times in the past and there is no reason to think that Earth will be spared in the future. However, if we get sufficient warning of an asteroid on a collision course with Earth, perhaps human ingenuity will find a way to avert disaster.

Approaching Itokawa (right)
Hayabusa heads toward its encounter with the asteroid 25143 Itokawa in this artist's impression. The probe utilizes a new technology called ion propulsion. The engine first ionizes its stock of propellant, xenon. Then, as it expels these ionized (electrically charged) particles out the back, the reaction—based on Newton's laws of motion—provides thrust to drive the craft toward its goal.

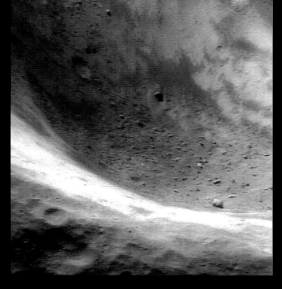

Psyche, close-up (above)
The NEAR-Shoemaker probe took this image of Psyche Crater on 433 Eros from an altitude of 31 miles (50 km). From this height it is possible to see that the crater floor is covered in a loose layer of dust and boulders called regolith. The colors are representative but have been enhanced for clarity. Psyche is 3.3 miles (5.3 km) across.

Asteroids at home (left)
It is not necessary to go into space to study asteroids up close: they often come to us in the form of meteorites. This slice from the Imilac meteorite, discovered in Chile in 1822, reveals golden-colored silicate materials embedded within a translucent nickel-iron matrix. This material probably formed billions of years ago at the boundary between an asteroid's molten core and solid crust.

Discovery of an asteroid (right)
In 2003 scientists using the Hubble Space Telescope to study a Sagittarian galaxy were surprised to find a previously unknown asteroid showing up in an image as a series of thirteen arcs. The trail is broken up because Hubble was making successive exposures of the same patch of sky. The asteroid's apparent wavy trajectory is due to the orbital motion of Hubble. Based on the observed brightness of the asteroid, its diameter is estimated to be about 1.5 miles (2.4 km).

Hayabusa mission

Not content with simply orbiting an asteroid and landing on it, as with the NEAR-Shoemaker probe, Japanese engineers have devised a mission that will actually bring back samples from one. The mission, called Hayabusa (originally MUSES-C), was launched on May 9, 2003, toward the asteroid 25143 Itokawa. Hayabusa, which is Japanese for "falcon," reached the tiny asteroid (just 0.4 miles or 0.7 km across) in 2005, and is expected to return to Earth with its precious sample in June 2007.

NEAR-Shoemaker mission

NEAR, short for Near-Earth Asteroid Rendezvous, was the first and so-far only man-made object to go into orbit around an asteroid. Later named NEAR-Shoemaker in honor of a famous planetary geologist, the craft was launched in 1996, its objective the 20-mile (33-km) long asteroid named 433 Eros. In June 1997, NEAR passed 253 Mathilde at a distance of only 745 miles (1,200 km), then reached Eros in late 1998. In February 2000, NEAR went into orbit around Eros, where it spent a year photographing the surface in great detail. Finally, NEAR made a low-speed descent to the surface of Eros, where it will rest, intact, for countless millennia.

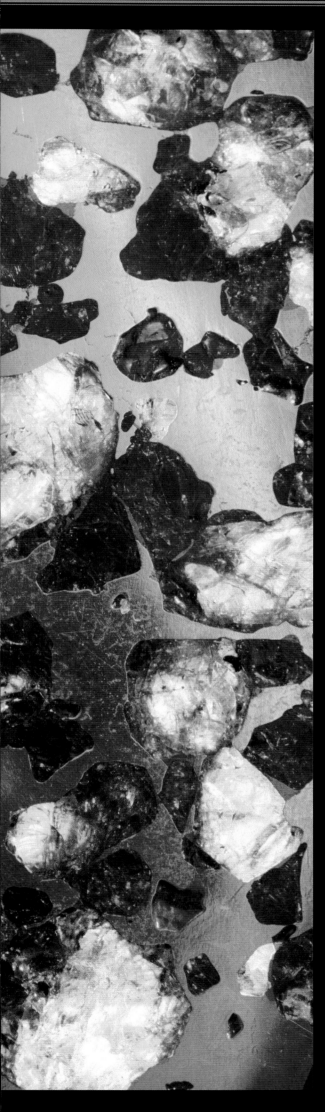

Majestic gas giants, encircled by ring systems, dominate the outer regions
of our Solar System. Above is a false-color view of the gas giant Saturn
and its abundant rings, taken by the Cassini probe on May 3, 2005.

The Outer
Solar System

Charting the Outer Solar System

Beyond Mars and the asteroids is the realm of the Outer Solar System. The innermost planet here, Jupiter, is five astronomical units from the Sun, while Neptune is six times more distant still. The two largest—Jupiter and Saturn—are gas giants, fluid worlds made of super-compressed hydrogen and helium. Uranus and Neptune are ice giants—with thick atmospheres surrounding dense, slushy mantles of ice-rich compounds. Beyond the planets is the Kuiper belt, a donut-shaped region containing tens of millions of rocky and icy worldlets. Some of them are substantial, such as the dwarf planets Pluto and Eris. Finally, stretching perhaps as far as one-third of the way to the nearest star, resides the Oort Cloud—and the beginnings of interstellar space.

The outer Solar System
This map of the outer Solar System extends to the outer edge of the Kuiper Belt or 50 AU (each concentric ring is 5 AU apart). The closed and open circles marked on the orbits indicate each planet's aphelion and perihelion. Tick marks denote the orbital nodes, where an orbit crosses Earth's orbital plane. Typical long-period and short-period comet orbits are also indicated. The planets and comets shown here are not drawn to scale.

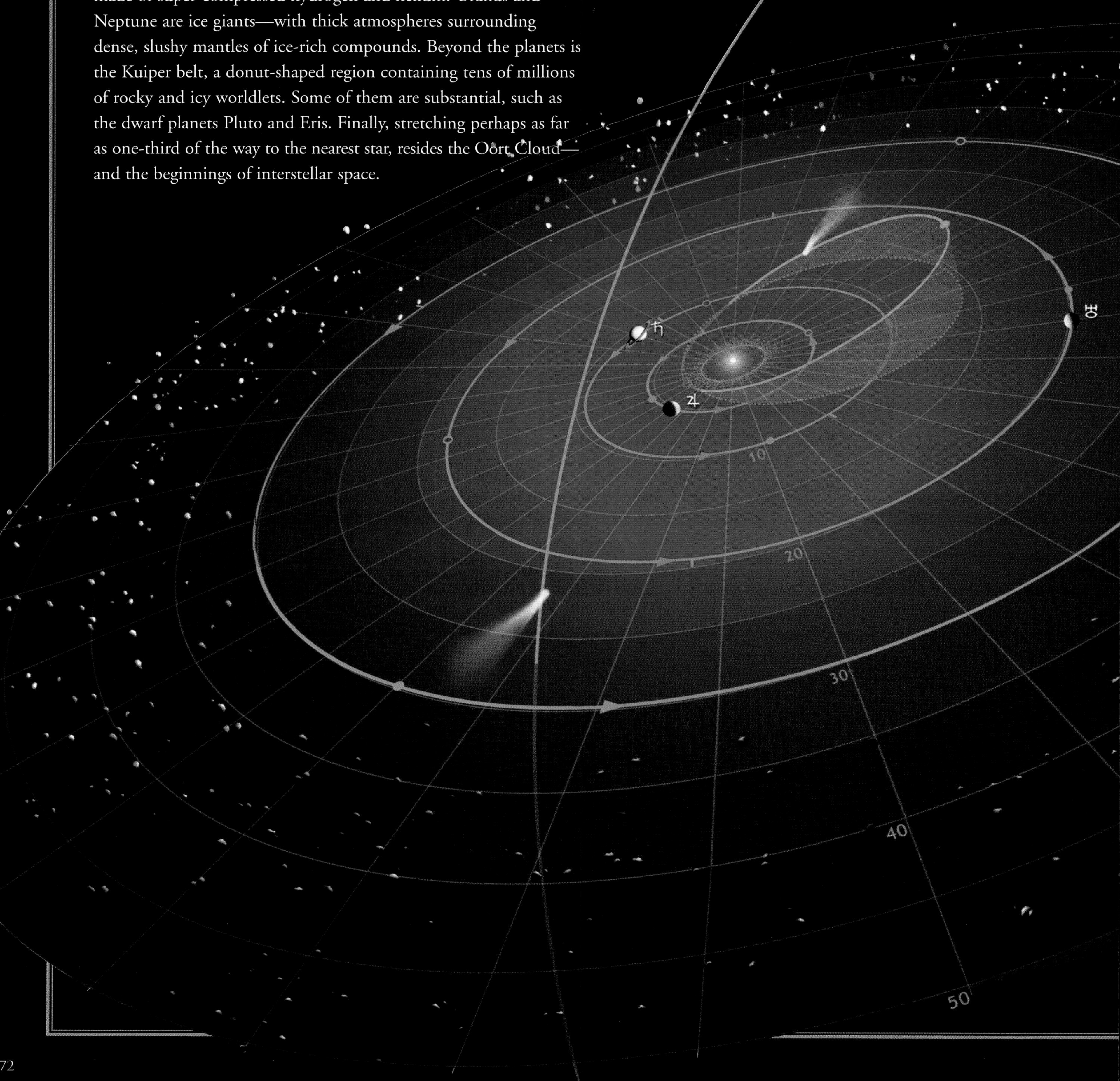

Key to Symbols

Symbol	Name	Symbol	Name
		—	Planetary Orbit
♃	Jupiter	●	Aphelion
♄	Saturn	○	Perihelion
♅	Uranus	⊤	Orbital Node
♆	Neptune	—	Short-Period Comet
		—	Long-Period Comet

Voyagers to the outer Solar System

In 1977, NASA launched the Voyagers, a pair of space probes that were to profoundly advance our understanding of the outer Solar System. Each flew past Jupiter and Saturn, from where Voyager 1 was directed out of the plane of the Solar System. But Voyager 2 stayed the course, becoming the first (and so far only) probe to reach Uranus (1986) and Neptune (1989)—visiting more planets than any other probe in history. The Voyagers continue to return data from their remote vantage points, well beyond the Kuiper belt.

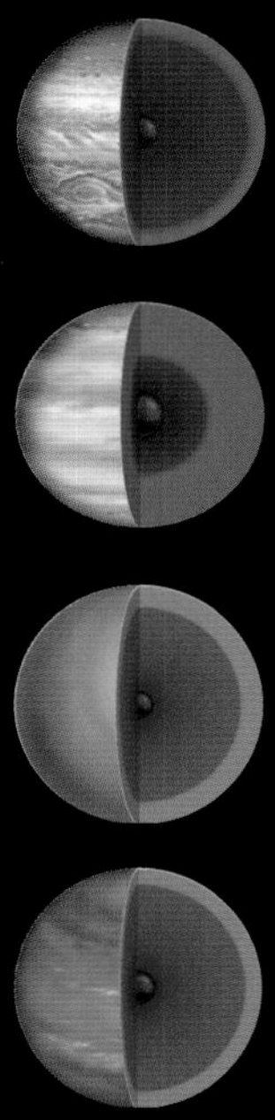

Jupiter

Jupiter's most distinctive features are its size and colorful, banded atmosphere, where storms can last for centuries.

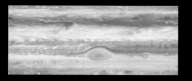

Saturn

Saturn is famous for its rings, and rightly so. These beautiful structures are composed of fragments of ice and rock.

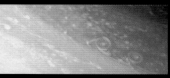

Uranus

Unlike the other planets, Uranus is tipped on its side. Uranus has a dark ring system and a plain green atmosphere.

Neptune

Neptune is similar to Uranus in composition and color, but its atmosphere is more dynamic and stormy.

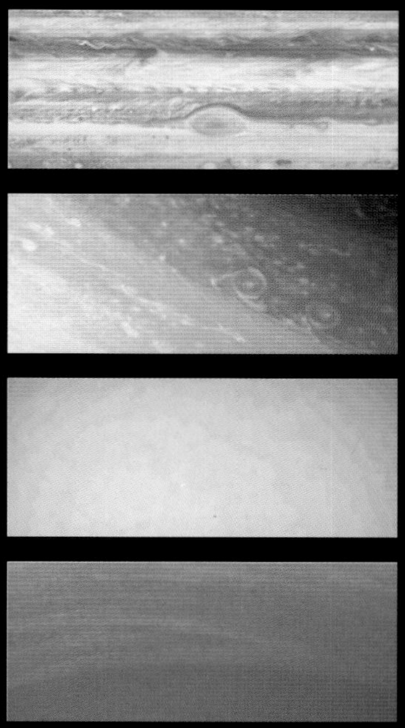

Ψ

Giants of the Solar System

The four outer planets of the Solar System, seen here on the same scale, are also the largest. Jupiter is the biggest of all, while Neptune and Uranus are the smallest, but still four times bigger than Earth.

Jupiter

Saturn

Uranus

Neptune

Earth

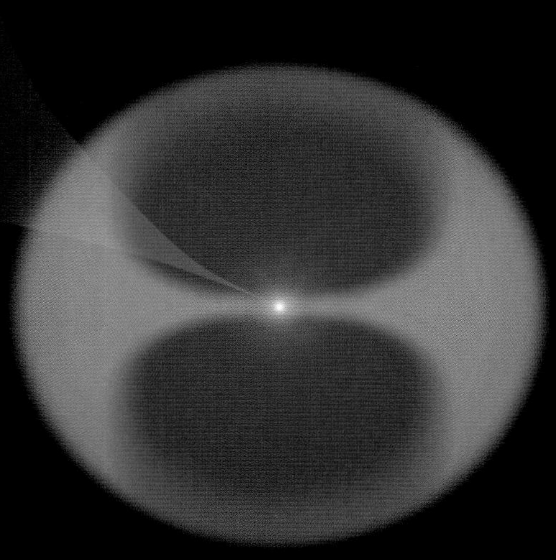

The Oort Cloud

The Kuiper belt does not mark the outer boundary of the Solar System. Extending perhaps as far as 100,000 AU (1.6 light-years) from the Sun is the Oort Cloud, a spherical swarm of icy comet nuclei and the source of the Solar System's long-period comets.

JUPITER

Beyond the inner planets and the asteroids we encounter the realm of the giant planets—and its innermost as well as largest member, Jupiter. Jupiter is composed primarily of hydrogen and helium in super-compressed liquid form. There is no surface as such, although there may be a solid core of rock and ice at the center. Jupiter is a colorful place, dotted with vibrant, swirling storms and encircled by distinctive bands. The latter are cloud formations that have been stretched longitudinally by the planet's rapid rotation period of just 9.92 hours. Above the cloud tops, at the equator, there is a ring system, but it is thin and dark, invisible even to the most powerful optical telescopes. You can frequently see Jupiter in the night sky, where it is more brilliant than any planet save Venus, and sometimes brighter even than the brightest star, Sirius. The planet has at least 63 moons, and there are undoubtedly more yet to be discovered. Most are little more than small fragments of rock, but the four Galilean moons are fascinating worlds in their own right.

Goliath planet
Jupiter is the largest planet of all, 11.2 times the diameter of Earth. Its volume is such that it could easily contain all of the other planets in the Solar System.

JUPITER STATISTICS	
Discovered	Known from antiquity
Average distance from the Sun	483.8 million miles (778.6 million km); 5.2 AU
Equatorial diameter	88,846 miles (142,984 km)
Axial rotation period (sidereal)	9.92 hours
Mass (Earth = 1)	317.8
Volume (Earth = 1)	1,321
Gravity at cloud tops (Earth = 1)	2.64
Average density (water = 1)	1.3
Escape velocity	37 miles/s (59.5 km/s)
Axial tilt from orbit	3.13°
Sunlight strength	3–4% of Earth's
Albedo (reflectivity)	52%
Number of satellites	≥63

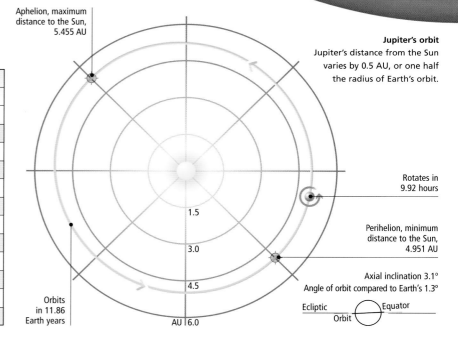

Aphelion, maximum distance to the Sun, 5.455 AU

Jupiter's orbit
Jupiter's distance from the Sun varies by 0.5 AU, or one half the radius of Earth's orbit.

Rotates in 9.92 hours

Perihelion, minimum distance to the Sun, 4.951 AU

Axial inclination 3.1°
Angle of orbit compared to Earth's 1.3°

Ecliptic — Equator
Orbit

Orbits in 11.86 Earth years

1.5
3.0
4.5
AU 6.0

The structure of Jupiter

Jupiter's huge size does not keep it from rotating faster than any other planet in the Solar System: a Jovian day is only 9.92 hours. As a result Jupiter is visibly oblate, its equatorial diameter being about seven percent greater than the polar value. The deep inner mantle—about 30,000 miles (50,000 km) thick—conducts huge electric currents which drive the planet's magnetic field, the most powerful in the Solar System. The temperature at Jupiter's center has been estimated at 36,000°F (20,000°C), and the core pressure is about 100 million atmospheres.

Jupiter's true colors
This photo shows Jupiter as seen by the Hubble Space Telescope in 1991. The atmospheric colors are close to those that would be seen by a human observer.

Outer mantle
Around 600 miles (1,000 km) below the top of Jupiter's thin atmosphere is a liquid molecular hydrogen and helium mantle reaching more than 6,000 miles (10,000 km) deeper into the planet.

Core
If Jupiter has a solid core it may well be several times the mass of Earth, and is most likely made of ice and rock under enormous pressure.

Inner mantle
At more than two-thirds of the total radius, the inner mantle is the most extensive layer. It is composed almost entirely of very dense liquid metallic hydrogen, from which Jupiter's strong magnetic field most likely derives.

The Jovian atmosphere

Unlike the terrestrial planets, whose atmospheres interface with planetary surfaces, the atmosphere of Jupiter (and all other giants) gradually grows denser with depth before merging seamlessly with the fluid interior hundreds of miles down. The stormy outermost atmosphere that we can see is composed of three separate cloud layers of ammonia ice, ammonium hydrosulfide ice, and water ice spanning a vertical range of just 50 miles (80 km).

Atmospheric breakdown
Jupiter's atmosphere is 90 percent hydrogen and 10 percent helium, with traces of compounds such as methane and ammonia.

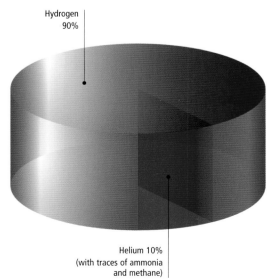

Hydrogen
90%

Helium 10%
(with traces of ammonia
and methane)

Mighty magnetosphere
Jupiter has a very powerful magnetic field that extends all the way to the orbit of Saturn. This illustration shows how flows of electrons within the field (the pink loops) connect three of Jupiter's large moons with areas of auroral activity at the poles.

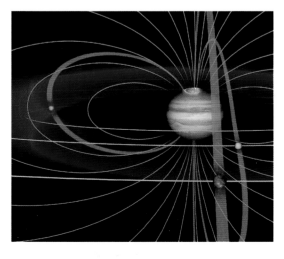

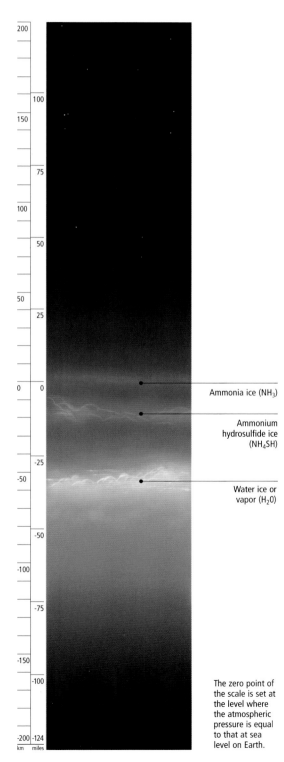

Ammonia ice (NH_3)

Ammonium
hydrosulfide ice
(NH_4SH)

Water ice or
vapor (H_2O)

The zero point of the scale is set at the level where the atmospheric pressure is equal to that at sea level on Earth.

km   miles

MAPPING JUPITER

Jupiter may have no solid surface, but the main features that comprise its upper atmosphere are so long-lived that they can still be mapped. In general the planet has a stripy appearance. This is a direct consequence of the planet's rapid rotation, which stretches its clouds parallel to the equator. The stripes themselves are driven by heat in Jupiter's interior. Gases under high pressure rise up through the atmosphere where they form the brighter stripes, which are called zones. Zones are bright and cool because of their higher position in the atmosphere. At their peak altitude, the gases in the zones spread apart in a latitudinal direction and then sink. This forms the darker, low-pressure stripes, which are known as belts. Between the belts and zones, strong winds resulting from the pressure differences whip up atmospheric disturbances which develop into gigantic storm systems somewhat like hurricanes on Earth—but on truly vast scales.

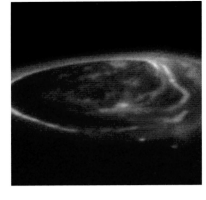

Eerie polar glow (above)
The polar regions of Jupiter show up electric blue in this ultraviolet Hubble image of auroral activity on the giant planet. Auroras, also common on Earth, are caused when solar particles are caught up in planetary magnetic fields and then interact with the atmosphere.

Perpetual tempest (right)
This close-up Voyager 2 view of the Jovian atmosphere shows the long-lived storm system known as the Great Red Spot. The smaller white-colored storm (bottom) has been in existence since about 1940.

Great Red Spot cross-section (below)
The Great Red Spot is Jupiter's most celebrated storm system. It is a region of high pressure that rises above the surrounding atmosphere and rotates once in seven days. Its red color probably comes from chemical reactions within the storm's heart. Known since the 17th century, the Great Red Spot is big enough to contain about three Earths.

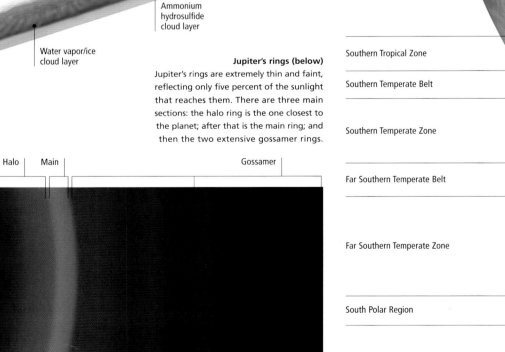

Ammonia cloud layer

Ammonium hydrosulfide cloud layer

Water vapor/ice cloud layer

N

Jupiter's rings (below)
Jupiter's rings are extremely thin and faint, reflecting only five percent of the sunlight that reaches them. There are three main sections: the halo ring is the one closest to the planet; after that is the main ring; and then the two extensive gossamer rings.

Jupiter   Halo   Main   Gossamer

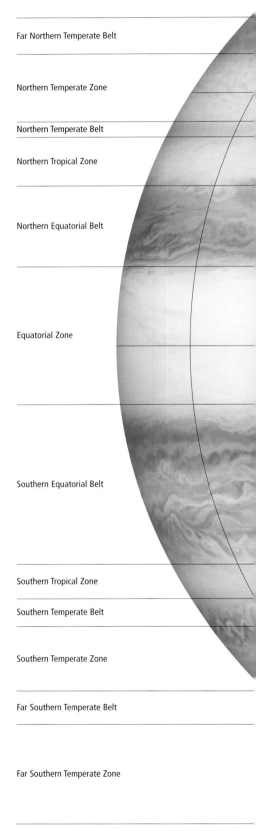

North Polar Region

Far Northern Temperate Zone

Far Northern Temperate Belt

Northern Temperate Zone

Northern Temperate Belt

Northern Tropical Zone

Northern Equatorial Belt

Equatorial Zone

Southern Equatorial Belt

Southern Tropical Zone

Southern Temperate Belt

Southern Temperate Zone

Far Southern Temperate Belt

Far Southern Temperate Zone

South Polar Region

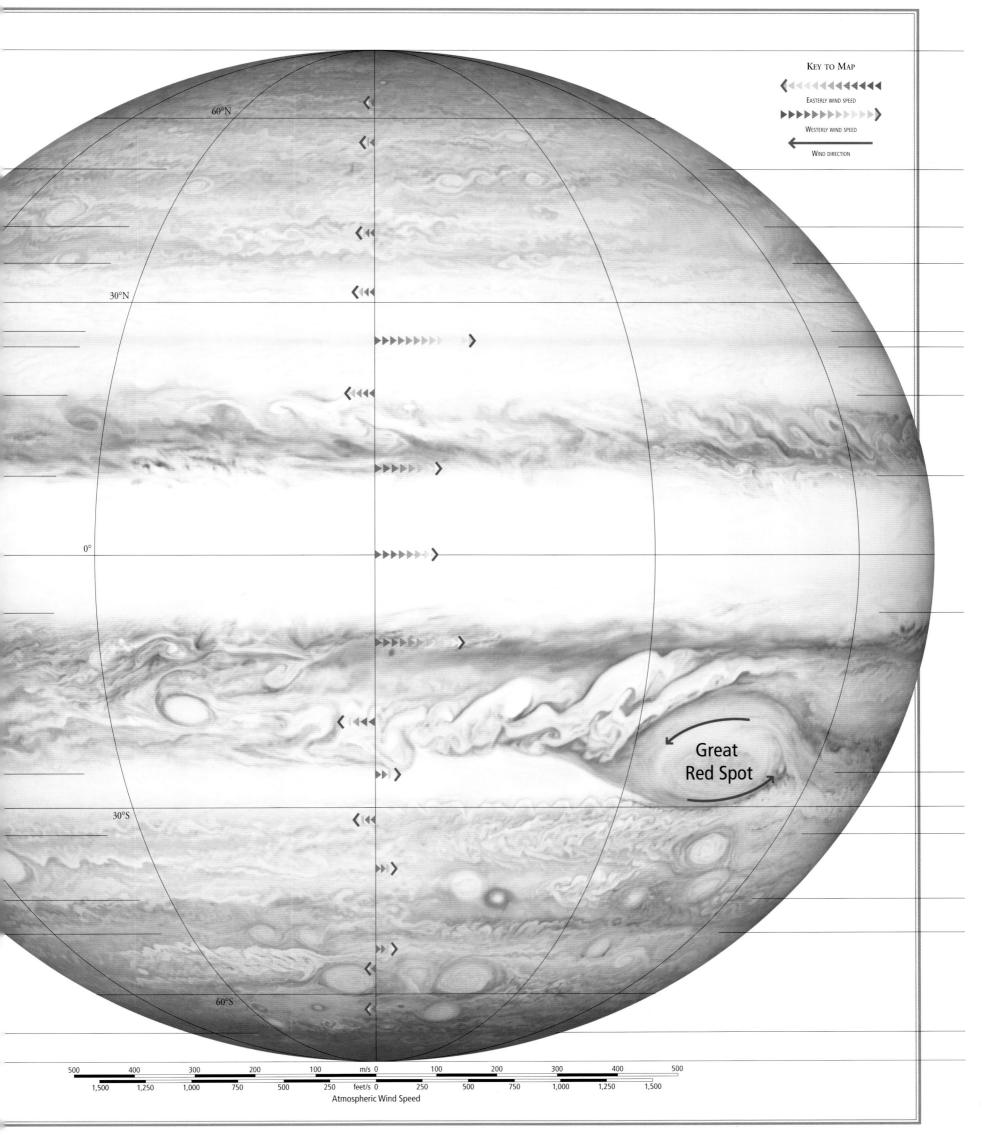

EASTERLY WIND SPEED

WESTERLY WIND SPEED

WIND DIRECTION

60°N

30°N

0°

30°S

60°S

Great
Red Spot

500   400   300   200   100   m/s 0   100   200   300   400   500

1,500   1,250   1,000   750   500   250   feet/s 0   250   500   750   1,000   1,250   1,500

Atmospheric Wind Speed

DISCOVERING JUPITER

As the nearest and largest gas planet to Earth, Jupiter has been relatively easy to study from home. However, that study had to wait at least until the invention of the telescope. In 1610, Galileo Galilei (1564–1642) found the first (and by far the largest) four Jovian satellites. They are called the Galilean moons in his honor. Jupiter's rotation period was first measured by the Italian astronomer Giovanni Cassini (1625–1712) in about 1665. English scientist Robert Hooke (1635–1703) is often credited with discovering the Great Red Spot in 1664, but he may have found an earlier but different spot. The Great Red Spot itself was first unequivocally drawn by German scientist Heinrich Schwabe (1789–1875) in 1831. These were all important discoveries, but detailed understanding of our giant neighbor did not come until the advent of very large telescopes and, more importantly, the first unmanned missions to Jupiter in the 1970s.

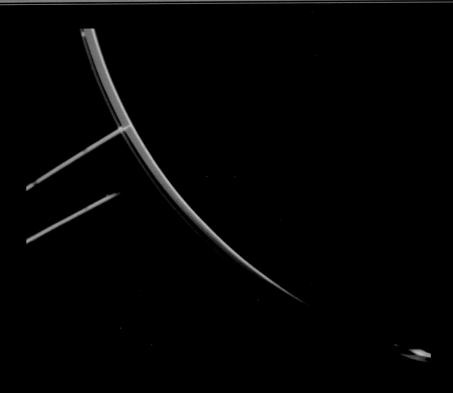

Pioneer and Voyager—viewing the Jovian giant

Without a doubt, the two programs Pioneer and Voyager provided almost all of our detailed knowledge of Jupiter up to the mid-1990s. Pioneers 10 and 11, launched in 1972 and 1973 respectively, took the first close-up pictures of Jupiter and its moons, as well as measuring the planet's magnetic field, radiation belts, atmosphere, and interior. Voyagers 1 and 2, both launched in 1977, discovered the ring system and mapped some of the moons in detail. The orange lines in the Voyager 2 image above are the rings of Jupiter seen from the planet's shadow.

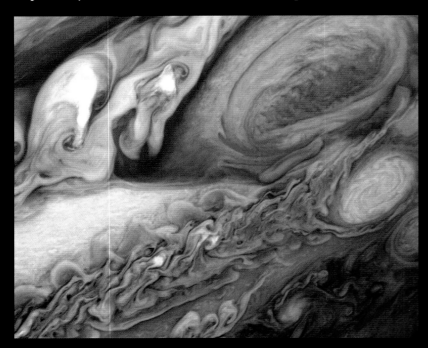

Revealing the Great Red Spot (left)
This color-enhanced view of Jupiter's Great Red Spot was created from data returned by Voyager 1 during its visit to the planet in March 1979. Until Voyager, this famous feature had never been seen in such detail.

Voyager 2 snapshot (right)
Voyager 2 made its closest approach to Jupiter four months after its twin. The dark oval in the upper middle of this color-enhanced image is a long-lasting storm feature in the Northern Equatorial Belt. At lower right, the turbulent clouds west of the Great Red Spot continue to churn.

Diving into Jupiter

When the comet Shoemaker-Levy 9 impacted the Jovian atmosphere in 1994, it afforded astronomers a chance to study such an event at fairly close range. While the fragments from the comet—more than twenty in all—hit Jupiter on the hemisphere that was facing away from Earth, the impact scars were immediately apparent when the affected hemisphere rotated into view (pictured right). Every available telescope was pulled into service to examine the effects. The fragments punched holes in the planet's atmosphere during the course of a week, producing black scorch marks that were readily visible even in amateur telescopes. These observations enabled scientists to refine their models of Jupiter's atmosphere.

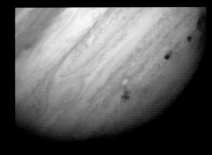

Collision course (below)
This Hubble Space Telescope image of Shoemaker-Levy 9 was taken two months before the first impact with the Jovian atmosphere and about two years after a previous close encounter with Jupiter had torn the comet's nucleus into fragments. The train of twenty icy fragments seen below extended about three times the Earth–Moon distance and was about 140 million miles (660 million km) from Earth when this picture was taken.

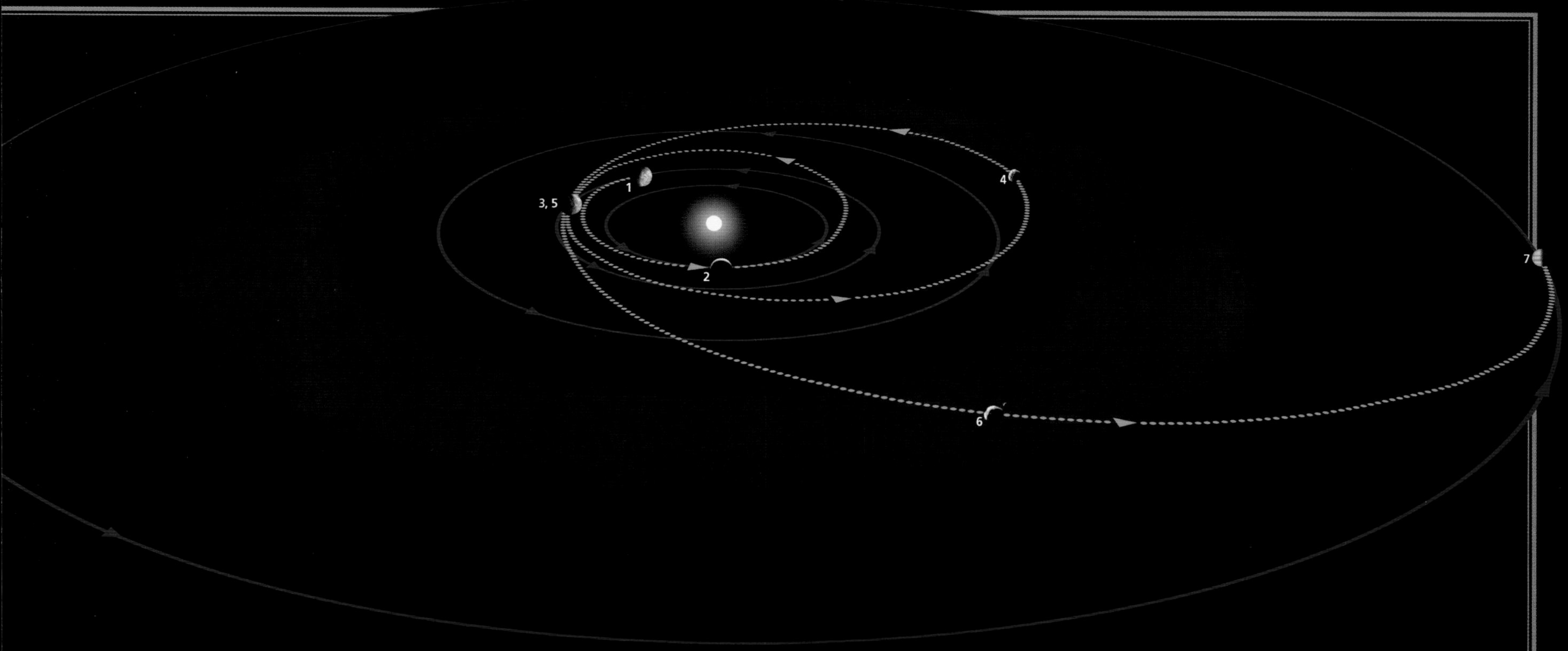

Galileo trajectory (above)

The Galileo spacecraft was launched on October 18, 1989 (1), and flew past Venus in February 1990 (2). It passed Earth in December 1990 (3), then went on to encounter the asteroid 951 Gaspra in October 1991 (4) and Earth again in December 1992 (5). Galileo flew past a second asteroid, 243 Ida, in August 1993 (6), and finally reached Jupiter in December 1995 (7).

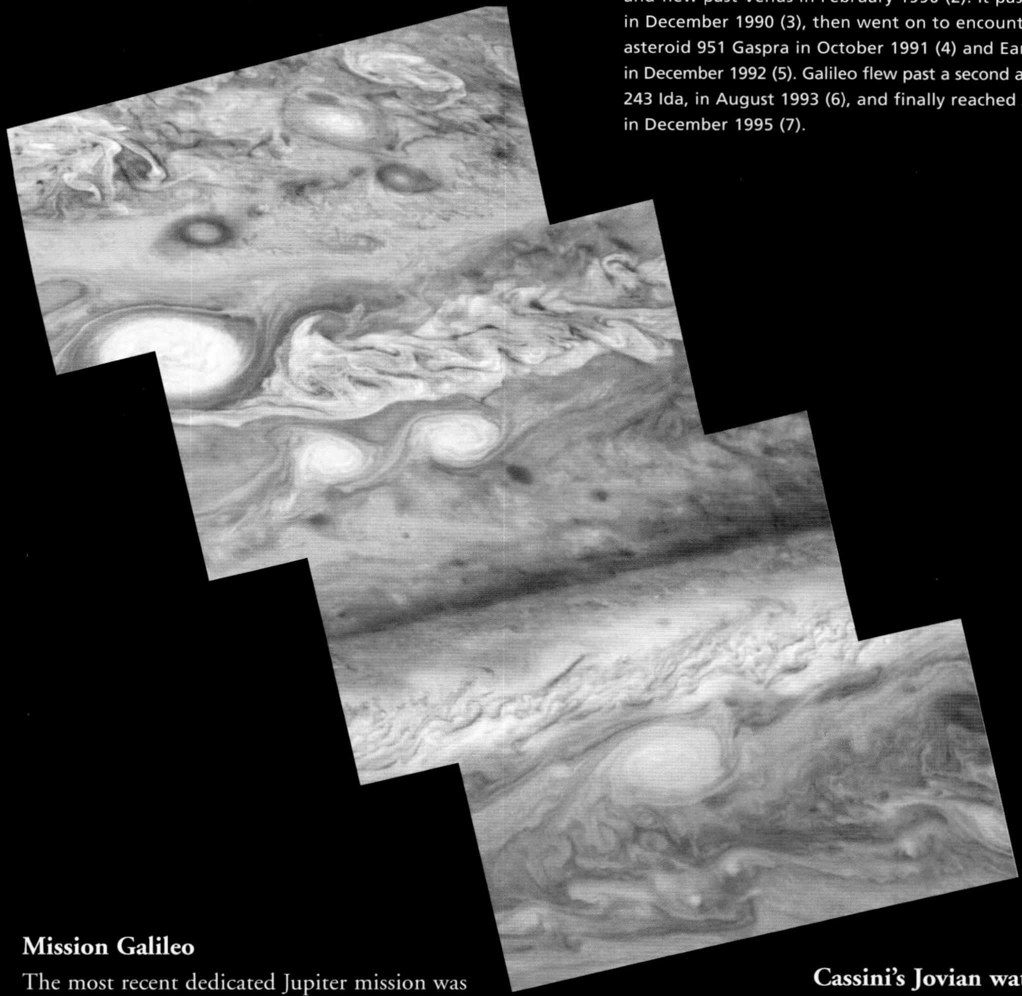

Mission Galileo

The most recent dedicated Jupiter mission was Galileo, which was launched in 1989 and reached the planet in 1995. Once there, the spacecraft released an atmospheric probe which took readings of the various gases it encountered as it descended into the atmosphere. The main craft remained in orbit for eight years, studying the planet's weather and satellites. Galileo was the first spacecraft able to distinguish cloud layers on Jupiter. The colors in the near-infrared mosaic image of Jupiter's northern hemisphere, above, indicate cloud height and thickness.

Cassini's Jovian watercolors

Although the primary objective of the Cassini mission is Saturn and its satellites, the spacecraft also took a close look at Jupiter on its way, hurtling by the planet in December 2000 at a minimum distance of 6 million miles (9.7 million km). Cassini returned data complementing that of the successful Galileo mission, which had arrived at Jupiter five years before. The probe also took some of the most detailed and beautiful images of Jupiter yet seen, such as this true-color mosaic, right.

SATELLITES OF JUPITER

Jupiter has more documented satellites than any other planet, with 63 known to date and no doubt many others awaiting discovery. Only four of the moons—the Galilean satellites Io, Europa, Ganymede, and Callisto—are very large. Indeed they are among the largest in the Solar System. The others are far smaller, some only a few miles across, and are probably captured asteroids or comets. Many of these are yet to be named. The large satellite count is to be expected. Firstly, Jupiter has the strongest gravity of all the planets, governing the motion of many asteroids and ensnaring some of them. Secondly, Jupiter is closer to Earth than the other giants and so its moons are easier to discover.

Galilean moon orbits

The Galilean satellites occupy a band around Jupiter between 262,000 miles and 1,170,000 miles (422,000–1,880,000 km). These moons are primordial—that is, they probably formed around Jupiter when the planet itself was being born.

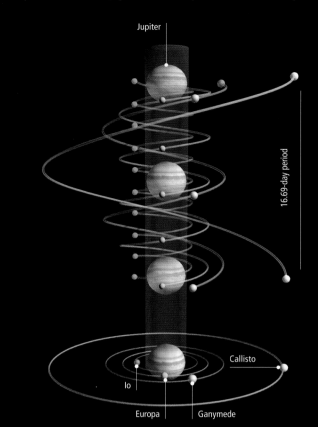

Jupiter

16.69-day period

Callisto

Io

Europa

Ganymede

Ganymede

Callisto

Io

Europa

Galilean moons compared (left)
The Galilean moons make up four of the six largest satellites in the Solar System. Our Moon is slightly larger than Europa, while Saturn's Titan is the second largest satellite after Ganymede.

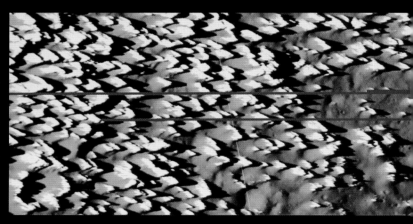

Callisto's jagged peaks (above)
This Galileo close-up view of one small patch of Callisto's surface reveals a unique terrain of bright spires of eroded icy material. The spires are up to 330 feet (100 m) high. The imaged area is about 6 miles (10 km) across.

Cliffs of Callisto (below)
The prominent scarp in this Galileo image is part of a huge impact structure on Callisto called Valhalla. Callisto is the most heavily cratered object in the Solar System. The imaged area is about 15 miles (25 km) across.

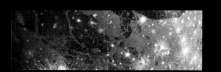

Ganymede
Discovered: 1610
Diameter: 3,270 miles (5,262 km)
Mean orbital radius: 665,116 miles (1,070,400 km)
Orbital period: 7.15 days

Callisto
Discovered: 1610
Diameter: 2,996 miles (4,821 km)
Mean orbital radius: 1,169,855 miles (1,882,700 km)
Orbital period: 16.69 days

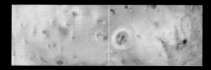

Io
Discovered: 1610
Diameter: 2,264 miles (3,643 km)
Mean orbital radius: 261,970 miles (421,600 km)
Orbital period: 1.77 days

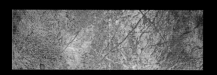

Europa
Discovered: 1610
Diameter: 1,940 miles (3,122 km)
Mean orbital radius: 416,878 miles (670,900 km)
Orbital period: 3.55 days

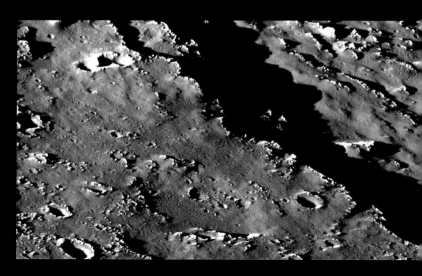

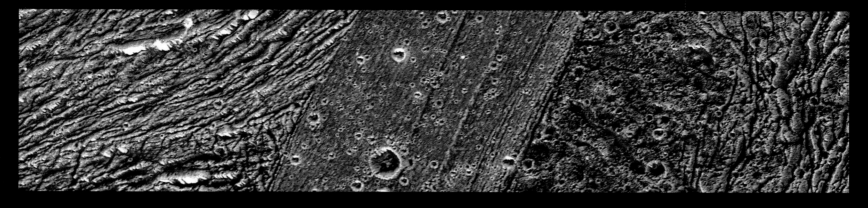

Grooves and wrinkles on Ganymede (above)
The relatively smooth central strip in this Galileo image of the surface of Ganymede is the 15-mile (24-km) wide Arbela Sulcus. Such features, which separate regions of much older terrain, show that Ganymede's icy crust was tectonically active in the past.

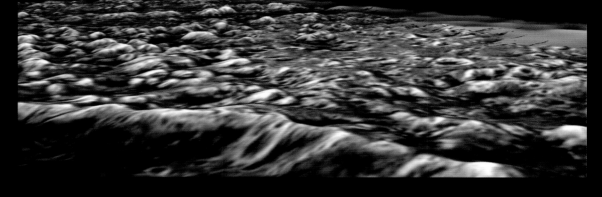

Ganymede (right)
This computer-generated low-altitude perspective of Ganymede's surface was constructed from Galileo data. It reveals a cratered and furrowed terrain that is typical of this huge moon.

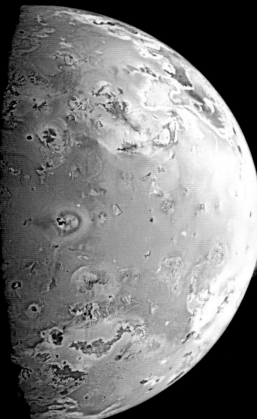

The Jovian moons (right)
This diagram plots the orbits of every known Jovian moon outside the orbit of Callisto (whose orbit is shown in white). The outermost moons orbit at a distance greater than sixty times the Earth–Moon separation. A further four minor moons can be found inside the orbit of Io, the innermost of the Galilean satellites.

Surface in motion (right)
Europa has almost no craters, which suggests a relatively young and probably still active surface. The smooth gray area in this photo is where the older crust has broken apart and been renewed. The thin double ridge line is a type of feature called a flexus, thought to result from faulting in the crust.

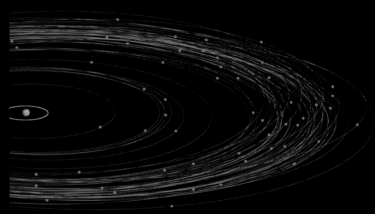

Fiery moon (above)
Although Io's volcanoes are among the hottest spots in the Solar System, conditions are otherwise so cold that the eruptions of superheated gas quickly freeze into plumes of frozen sulfur dioxide. This Galileo image shows a volcanic plume rising 87 miles (140 km) above the surface.

Ice world (right)
This color-enhanced Galileo image shows a typical region of Europa some 500 miles (800 km) across. Numerous brown linear ridges—believed to have resulted from when water erupted onto the freezing surface—overlie an older bluish surface of almost pure water ice.

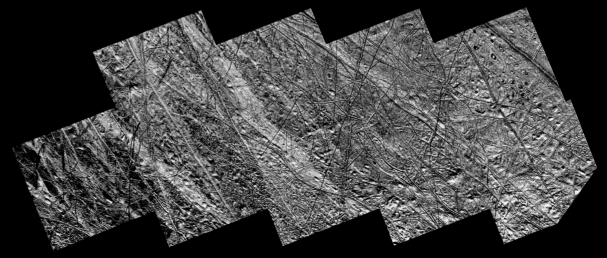

Mapping Io and Europa

Io and Europa are the innermost of the four Galilean satellites of Jupiter and are among the most curious objects in the Solar System. Multicolored Io, constantly wrenched by the gravitational pull of its parent planet and neighboring moons, is the most volcanically active body in the Solar System—spewing across its surface a noxious mixture of molten and gaseous sulfur dioxide. Europa, too, is subject to these forces, the tidal pull heating a vast ocean of water beneath its smooth, icy exterior. Following late 1970s encounters with these moons by the Voyager probes, and the more recent Galileo probe, most of their surfaces have been mapped, though not all at high resolution.

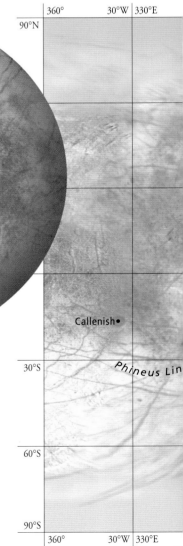

Io (above and right)
Jupiter's colorful Io, with the distinctive volcano, Prometheus, at center left, is shown above. Its surface, mapped on the right, is dotted with volcanoes, lava flows, and lakes of molten sulfur. There are few, if any, craters.

Europa (below and right)
Below, the prominent Asterius Linea marks a cross, center right, on Europa's face. At right, the moon's icy surface is mapped. Some areas are tinged brown with rocky material derived from the interior or delivered via impacts.

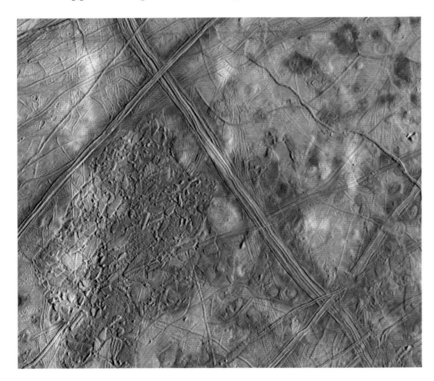

The push and pull of an ocean (above)
This Galileo orbiter image of Europa's surface is one of many that suggest that this satellite harbors an ocean of liquid water beneath its crust. The surface, made of water ice, is in places broken into blocks which have shifted and rotated, presumably driven by activity beneath the surface. Some of the crustal fractures seen here are more than 1,850 miles (3,000 km) long.

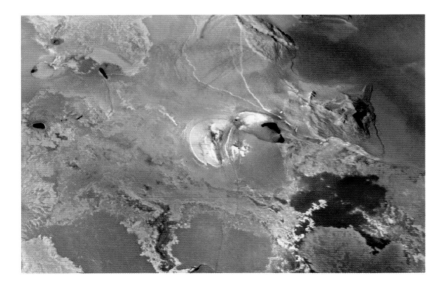

Fire and brimstone (left)
This image of Io's active surface, taken by the Voyager 1 probe during its Jupiter encounter in 1979, shows features such as lava flows and calderas—volcanic craters. The exact surface composition of Io is unknown, but sulfur is definitely a primary constituent. This image spans about 620 miles (1,000 km).

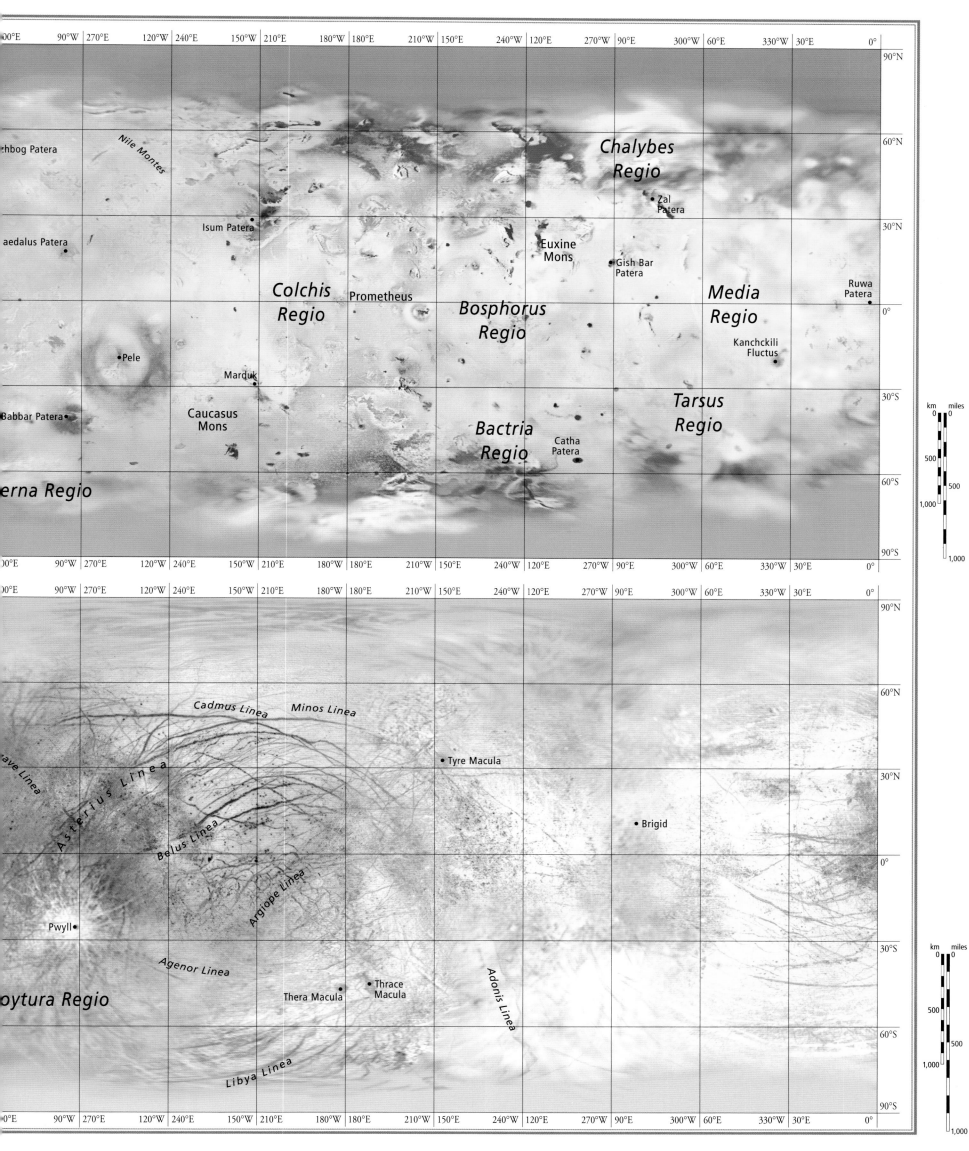

00°E 90°W 270°E 120°W 240°E 150°W 210°E 180°W 180°E 210°W 150°E 240°W 120°E 270°W 90°E 300°W 60°E 330°W 30°E 0°

90°N

hbog Patera

Nile Montes

Chalybes
Regio

60°N

Zal
Patera

30°N

aedalus Patera

Isum Patera

Euxine
Mons

Gish Bar
Patera

Ruwa
Patera

Colchis
Regio

Prometheus

Bosphorus
Regio

Media
Regio

0°

Pele

Kanchckili
Fluctus

Marduk

30°S

Babbar Patera

Caucasus
Mons

Bactria
Regio

Catha
Patera

Tarsus
Regio

erna Regio

60°S

90°S

00°E 90°W 270°E 120°W 240°E 150°W 210°E 180°W 180°E 210°W 150°E 240°W 120°E 270°W 90°E 300°W 60°E 330°W 30°E 0°

km   miles
0   0

500

500

1,000

1,000

00°E 90°W 270°E 120°W 240°E 150°W 210°E 180°W 180°E 210°W 150°E 240°W 120°E 270°W 90°E 300°W 60°E 330°W 30°E 0°

90°N

60°N

Cadmus Linea   Minos Linea

Tyre Macula

30°N

ave Linea

Asterius Linea

Belus Linea

Brigid

0°

Argiope Linea

Pwyll

30°S

Agenor Linea

Adonis Linea

oytura Regio

Thera Macula

Thrace
Macula

60°S

Libya Linea

90°S

00°E 90°W 270°E 120°W 240°E 150°W 210°E 180°W 180°E 210°W 150°E 240°W 120°E 270°W 90°E 300°W 60°E 330°W 30°E 0°

km   miles
0   0

500

500

1,000

1,000

SATURN

Moving outward from Jupiter, the next planet we come to is the Solar System's second largest. This is Saturn, roughly twice as far from the Sun as Jupiter, or nearly ten times farther out than Earth. Like Jupiter, Saturn is a gas giant—a spinning sphere of hydrogen and helium, flattened at the poles. As soon as this world was seen through a telescope, it was obvious that there was something different about it. This difference is, of course, Saturn's beautiful rings. This ring system is not unique—all four of the giant planets have them—but Saturn's are by far the brightest and most extensive. Composed of countless individual particles, the rings are predominantly made of highly reflective water ice, making them bright and also highly visible through a telescope. Saturn itself is visible to the naked eye, appearing as a yellowish, relatively bright "star." At least 54 natural satellites orbit Saturn, including Titan, the Solar System's only known satellite with a substantial atmosphere.

Ringed giant
Saturn is more than nine times the size of Earth and could contain our planet 764 times.

SATURN STATISTICS	
Discovered	Known from antiquity
Average distance from the Sun	890.7 million miles (1,433.5 million km); 9.6 AU
Equatorial diameter	74,898 miles (120,536 km)
Axial rotation period (sidereal)	10.66 hours
Mass (Earth = 1)	95.2
Volume (Earth = 1)	763.6
Gravity at cloud tops (Earth = 1)	0.92
Average density (water = 1)	0.7
Escape velocity	22 miles/s (35.5 km/s)
Axial tilt from orbit	26.7°
Sunlight strength	1% of Earth's
Albedo (reflectivity)	47%
Number of satellites	≥54

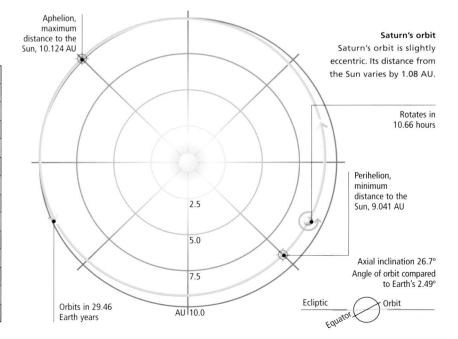

Aphelion, maximum distance to the Sun, 10.124 AU

Saturn's orbit
Saturn's orbit is slightly eccentric. Its distance from the Sun varies by 1.08 AU.

Rotates in 10.66 hours

Perihelion, minimum distance to the Sun, 9.041 AU

2.5

5.0

7.5

Axial inclination 26.7°
Angle of orbit compared to Earth's 2.49°

Orbits in 29.46 Earth years

AU 10.0

Ecliptic   Orbit

Equator

The structure of Saturn

Because of its rapid rotation and low density, Saturn is easily the most oblate planet, with a bulging equator readily discernible to the eye. Because this is a fluid world, it rotates slightly slower at the equator than it does at the poles. In appearance, Saturn is a bit like a pale Jupiter. Both worlds have bands of clouds, but on Saturn they are more subdued and subtle due to their greater depth in the atmosphere. The liquid metallic hydrogen in the lower mantle provides Saturn with a magnetic field with an intrinsic strength 600 times greater than that of Earth's.

Outer mantle
Hundreds of miles beneath the outer edge of Saturn's atmosphere, the pressure increase causes gaseous hydrogen to become liquid hydrogen. This liquid hydrogen forms the outer mantle and occupies the outermost 50 percent of the planet.

Core
The core of Saturn, about 15,000 miles (25,000 km) across, is possibly differentiated into a rocky inner core and an outer shell of ice.

Inner mantle
Beneath the outer mantle is the inner mantle. As on Jupiter, this is liquid metallic hydrogen, but it is much less extensive on Saturn because, as a smaller planet, Saturn has a lower internal pressure.

Atmosphere of Saturn

As on Jupiter, the atmosphere of Saturn consists of three main cloud layers, and blends gradually into the liquid hydrogen mantle beneath it. Again, as with its larger cousin, these cloud layers are composed of the hydrogen-rich compounds ammonia ice, ammonium hydrosulfide ice, and water ice. However, because of the relatively low gravity afforded by Saturn's mass, the Saturnian clouds span a height range of about 100 miles (160 km)—twice as deep as Jupiter's.

Atmospheric breakdown
Most of Saturn, about 96 percent of it, is composed of hydrogen. Helium makes up about 4 percent, with traces of methane, ammonia, and other compounds completing the inventory.

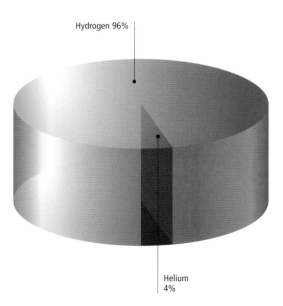

Hydrogen 96%

Helium 4%

Family portrait
Saturn looms alongside three of its satellites in this Voyager 2 photo from 1981. From the top they are Tethys (casting a shadow on Saturn's southern hemisphere), Dione, and Rhea.

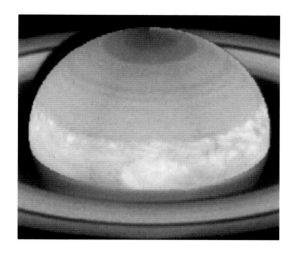

Stormy Saturn
The white band across the Saturnian equator in this Hubble image is a planet-wide storm that raged for several months in 1990. Large storms occur on Saturn every 30 years or so, but storms of this size are rare. The previous such event was observed in 1933.

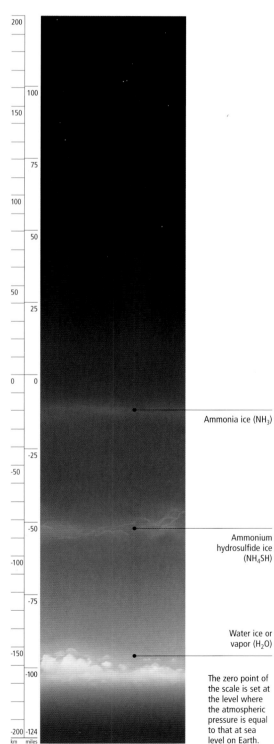

Ammonia ice (NH_3)

Ammonium hydrosulfide ice (NH_4SH)

Water ice or vapor (H_2O)

The zero point of the scale is set at the level where the atmospheric pressure is equal to that at sea level on Earth.

km   miles

MAPPING SATURN

Saturn is somewhat like Jupiter in appearance. This is not surprising, given that both worlds have very similar compositions. However, because Saturn is twice as far from the Sun as Jupiter and therefore colder, its clouds develop deeper in the atmosphere, buried under haze. This makes Saturn somewhat paler than its larger cousin. Still, there are similarities, most notably the overall structure of the Saturnian atmosphere, which is banded like Jupiter's, again the product of rapid rotation. The darker stripes are low-pressure regions called belts, and the brighter ones under higher pressure are called zones. Generally, Saturn's atmosphere is fairly calm, but there are nonetheless storm systems, especially at 30-year intervals in the northern hemisphere, when this half is experiencing summer. Some of these storms can last several years. Winds on Saturn also tend to be fast, up to a bracing 1,600 feet per second (500 m/s) at the equator.

Lord of the rings (above)
In this true-color Cassini image the rings of Saturn cast a shadow on the subtle shades of the giant planet. The gap in the rings at top right is the 2,980-mile (4,800-km) wide Cassini division.

Groovy (right)
The rings of Saturn are made up of countless individual ringlejts, a structure that is due to the gravitational influence of Saturn's many satellites. This stunning ultraviolet image was captured by the Cassini orbiter.

Anatomy of an atmosphere (below)
A cross-section through the upper atmosphere of Saturn reveals how its clouds are arranged in three distinctive layers, with ammonia at the top, ammonium hydrosulfide beneath that, and a water ice/vapor layer at the base. The bright areas, called zones, are high-pressure regions high up in the atmosphere. The darker areas, called belts, are deeper.

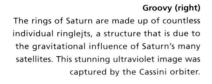

Ammonia
cloud layer

Ammonium
hydrosulfide
cloud layer

Water vapor/ice
cloud layer

Rings of Saturn (below)
In total Saturn has seven main rings, which are identified by the first seven letters of the alphabet. These main rings are divided into many thousands of ringlets. The bulk of the ring system spans 170,000 miles (274,000 km).

North Polar Region

Far Northern Temperate Zone

Far Northern Temperate Belt

Northern Temperate Zone

Northern Temperate Belt

Northern Tropical Zone

Northern Equatorial Belt

Equatorial Zone

Southern Equatorial Belt

Southern Tropical Zone

Southern Temperate Belt

Southern Temperate Zone

Far Southern Temperate Belt

Far Southern Temperate Zone

South Polar Region

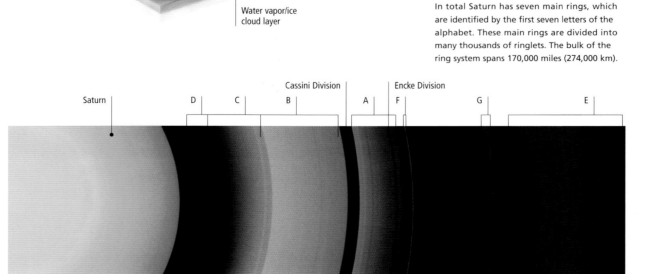

Saturn   D   C   B   Cassini Division   A   F   Encke Division   G   E

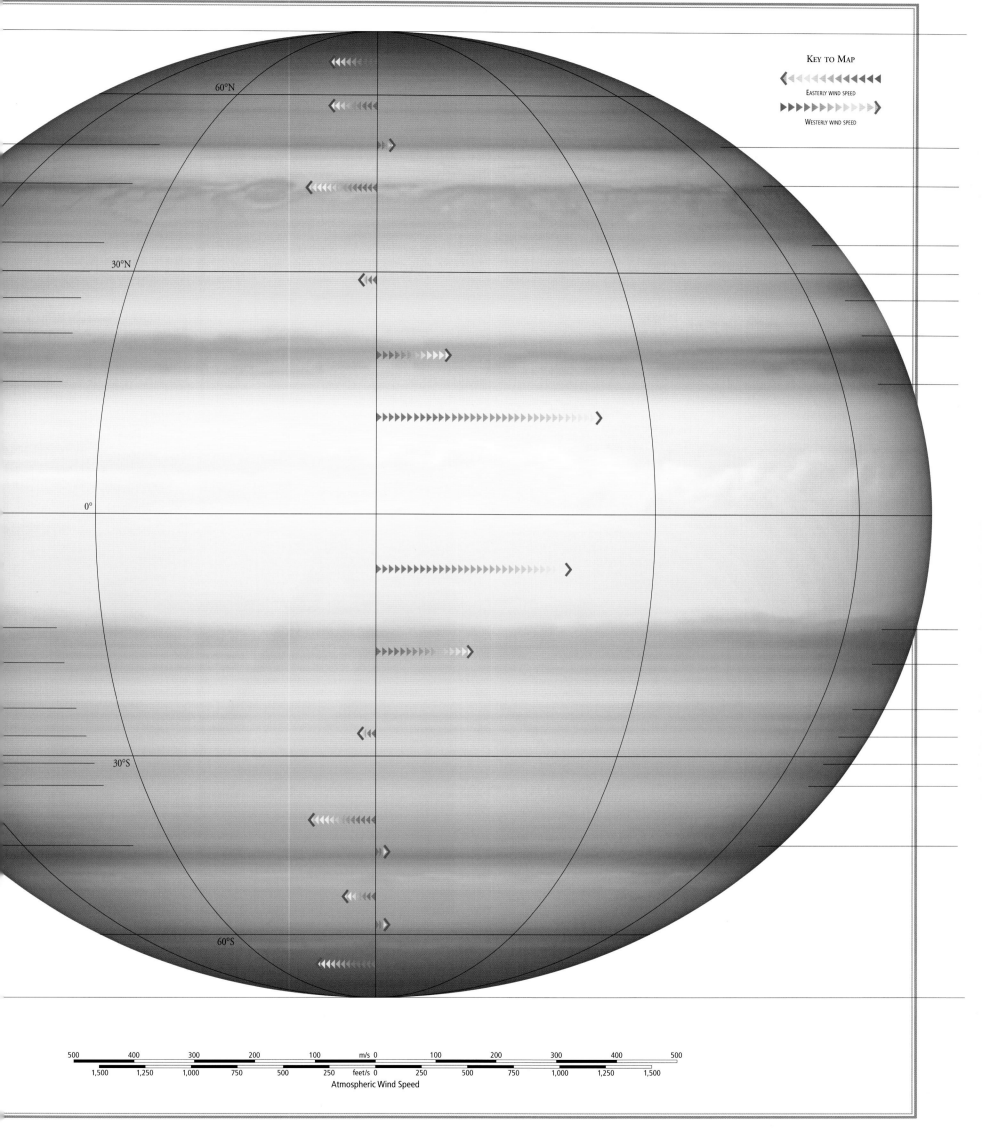

EASTERLY WIND SPEED

WESTERLY WIND SPEED

60°N

30°N

0°

30°S

60°S

500	400	300	200	100	m/s 0	100	200	300	400	500
1,500	1,250	1,000	750	500	250	feet/s 0	250	500	750	1,000	1,250	1,500

Atmospheric Wind Speed

Discovering Saturn

Saturn is readily visible to the naked eye and has been known for millennia as the slowest-moving "wandering star." However, as soon as the telescope was invented and used for astronomy, it became obvious that Saturn was a world unlike any other. It was the Italian astronomer Galileo Galilei (1564–1642) who first saw Saturn telescopically. He made drawings of it which showed a round object with "handles" protruding from the sides. He had unwittingly discovered the famous rings. Slowly, our initial perceptions of Saturn improved and changed. But it was not until the advent of spaceflight that we really began to gain a greater understanding of this enigmatic world. First this was via Pioneer 11, then Voyagers 1 and 2, and more recently the Cassini-Huygens mission, named for two scientists who were influential in early Saturn research.

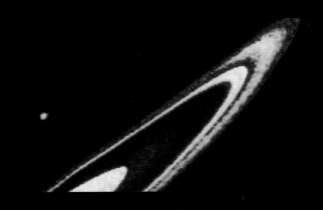

Pioneer and Voyager—seeing Saturn up close

Close-up exploration of Saturn, its rings, and moons was first conducted by the NASA missions Pioneer and Voyager. In September 1979, Pioneer 11 became the first probe to reach Saturn, flying within 13,000 miles (21,000 km) of the ringed planet. Pioneer 11 discovered two previously unknown moons as well as the F ring and took the image above, which was one of the first close-up photos of Saturn's rings. The Voyager probes 1 and 2 reached Saturn in 1980 and 1981 respectively, adding greatly to our knowledge of the rings and moons in particular. In the image below, taken by Voyager 1 in October 1980, the moons Tethys, Enceladus, and Mimas can be seen as tiny specks in orbit around a velvety Saturn.

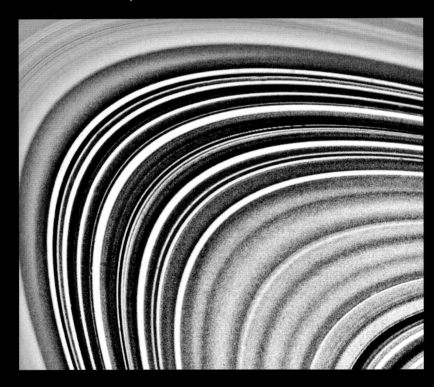

False-color rings (above)
This false-color Voyager 2 image, taken 1.7 million miles (2.7 million km) from the planet, shows Saturn's C ring (blue) and B ring (yellow). The colors indicate differing surface materials of the fragments that make up the rings and accentuate almost 60 bright and dark ringlets within each visible ring section.

Huygens's Saturn sketch (below)
As well as being a brilliant scientist, Christiaan Huygens was an expert lens grinder and telescope maker. In this sketch Huygens considers how the rings might be seen from the surface of Saturn, noting, for example, that at positions C, A, and D, Saturn's most famous feature would be out of view.

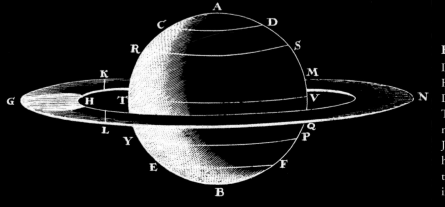

Early observations

In 1610, Galileo Galilei noted the strange shape of Saturn through his telescope. However, an accurate description of this odd object had to wait until 1656, when Dutchman Christiaan Huygens (1629–95), having already discovered Saturn's moon Titan, correctly deduced that "Saturn is surrounded by a thin, flat ring, which nowhere touches the body." It would be another 200 years before Scottish scientist James Clark Maxwell (1831–79) would prove mathematically that the rings of Saturn had to be particulate in nature. Another scientist, prominent in early Saturn studies, was the Italian-born French astronomer Giovanni Cassini (1625–1712). He noted the gap in the rings that now bears his name, and also discovered four more Saturnian moons.

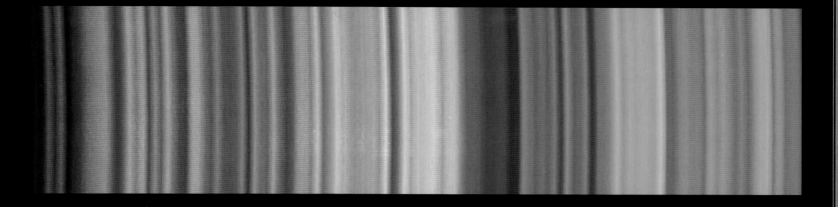

Rings in ultraviolet (above)
The Cassini probe has been able to resolve features in Saturn's rings about 100 times finer than Voyagers 1 and 2. This ultraviolet image shows the outer portion of the B ring (left) and the inner part of the C ring (right). Blue and turquoise indicate particles of ice, whereas red colors show that the ice is mixed with a high concentration of minerals.

Cassini-Huygens—mission to the ringed giant

The most recent voyage to Saturn has been made by the joint NASA/European Space Agency Cassini-Huygens mission. Launched in 1997, Cassini spent eight years coasting through space before reaching the ringed planet in July 2004. Once in Saturn's orbit it began a four-year survey of the planet and its moons at close range. On Christmas Day 2004, Cassini released a smaller car-sized probe called Huygens. Huygens sped toward Saturn's largest moon, Titan, and on January 14, 2005 descended through the thick atmosphere and landed on the surface.

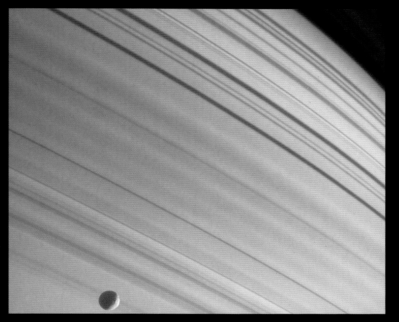

Portrait in blue (left)
This true-color Cassini image shows the moon Mimas (lower left) against the northern hemisphere of Saturn. The blue coloring is due to the scattering of shorter (blue) wavelengths of sunlight at this latitude. The dark lines are shadows cast by the rings.

The flight of Cassini (below)
Following its launch in 1997 (1), Cassini flew past Venus in April 1998 (2) and again in July 1999 (3), each time receiving a velocity kick. It picked up more speed passing Earth in August 1999 (4), then crossed the Asteroid Belt to reach Jupiter in December 2000 (5). It finally reached its destination, Saturn, in July 2004 (6).

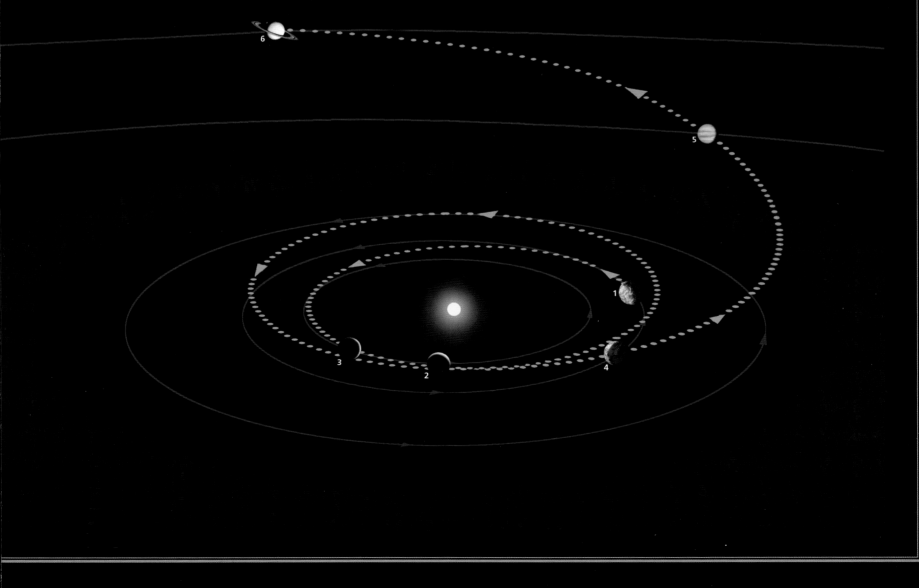

SATELLITES OF SATURN

The planet Saturn plays host to a large entourage of satellites. At least 48 are known, falling into three size categories. The largest by far, in a class of its own, is Titan; at 3,200 miles (5,150 km) across, it is second only to Jupiter's Ganymede and significantly larger than our own Moon. Titan is the only satellite with a substantial atmosphere, and was the target of the Huygens probe in January 2005. There are six Saturnian moons that occupy a mid-sized category, between 250 and 950 miles (400–1,500 km) in diameter. These are (in decreasing order of size) Rhea, Iapetus, Dione, Tethys, Enceladus, and Mimas. Like Titan, they are large enough for their gravity to make them essentially spherical. The remaining satellites are small and irregularly shaped—some of them, no doubt captured asteroids, only a few miles across.

Moon orbits

This diagram compares the orbits of four large satellites of Saturn. From the center outward they are Tethys (yellow), Dione (orange), Rhea (green), and Titan (blue). Many other satellites exist that are outside the range of orbits shown here.

Saturn

15.95-day period

Titan completes one revolution about Saturn in the same time that Tethys, much closer in, makes more than eight circuits.

These four satellites are among the earliest known. Along with Iapetus (not shown), they were all found in the 17th century.

Titan

Tethys

Dione

Rhea

Rhea

Iapetus

Dione

Tethys

Enceladus

Mimas

Titan

Size comparison (below)

Titan, below, easily dwarfs the other six large satellites of Saturn. The second largest is Rhea, while Mimas is the smallest of this group.

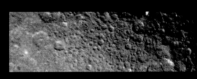

Titan
Discovered: 1655
Diameter: 3,200 miles (5,150 km)
Mean orbital radius: 759,210 miles (1,221,830 km)
Orbital period: 15.95 days

Rhea
Discovered: 1672
Diameter: 949 miles (1,528 km)
Mean orbital radius: 327,490 miles (527,040 km)
Orbital period: 4.52 days

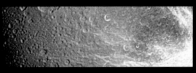

Iapetus
Discovered: 1671
Diameter: 892 miles (1,436 km)
Mean orbital radius: 2,212,890 miles (3,561,300 km)
Orbital period: 79.33 days

Dione
Discovered: 1684
Diameter: 696 miles (1,120 km)
Mean orbital radius: 234,510 miles (377,400 km)
Orbital period: 2.74 days

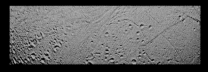

Tethys
Discovered: 1684
Diameter: 659 miles (1,060 km)
Mean orbital radius: 183,090 miles (294,660 km)
Orbital period: 1.89 days

Enceladus
Discovered: 1789
Diameter: 310 miles (499 km)
Mean orbital radius: 147,900 miles (238,020 km)
Orbital period: 1.37 days

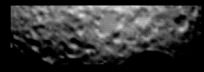

Mimas
Discovered: 1789
Diameter: 247 miles (397 km)
Mean orbital radius: 115,280 miles (185,520 km)
Orbital period: 22.62 hours

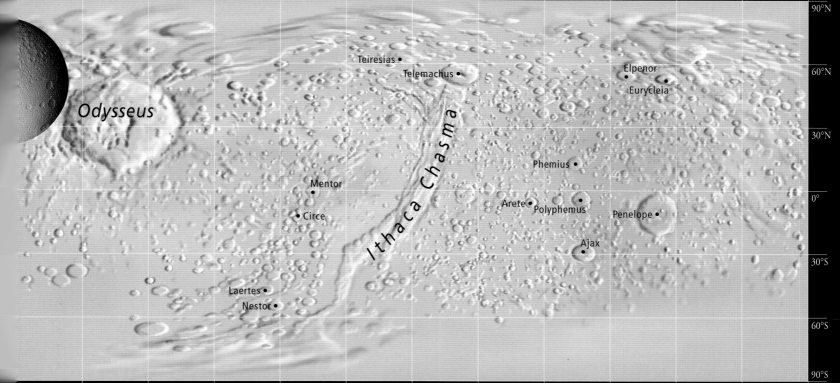

Odysseus

Ithaca Chasma

Teiresias •
Telemachus •

Elpenor •
• Eurycleia

Mentor •
• Circe

Phemius •

Arete •
• Polyphemus

Penelope •

Ajax •

Laertes •
Nestor •

180° | 150°W | 210°E | 120°W | 240°E | 90°W | 270°E | 60°W | 300°E | 30°W | 330°E | 360°W | 0°E | 330°W | 30°E | 300°W | 60°E | 270°W | 90°E | 240°W | 120°E | 210°W | 150°E | 180°

90°N
60°N
30°N
0°
30°S
60°S
90°S

180° | 150°W | 210°E | 120°W | 240°E | 90°W | 270°E | 60°W | 300°E | 30°W | 330°E | 360°W | 0°E | 330°W | 30°E | 300°W | 60°E | 270°W | 90°E | 240°W | 120°E | 210°W | 150°E | 180°

...pping Tethys (above)

...ys, whose surface is mapped here, is the fifth largest
...lite of Saturn at about 660 miles (1,060 km) across.
... the satellites Mimas, Dione, and Rhea, Tethys is
...ably composed mostly of water ice. Tethys is notable
...Odysseus, a huge impact basin, and Ithaca Chasma,
...mile (65-km) wide valley that may have formed
...n an original watery mantle froze, splitting as it
...mmodated the ice's extra bulk.

The surface of Enceladus (below)

Enceladus is a fairly small moon with a diverse
range of surface types. This Cassini mosaic shows
mostly cratered, older terrain criss-crossed by
numerous fault lines that attest to a history of
tectonic activity. At top right is a younger region
of sharply delineated ridges and troughs.

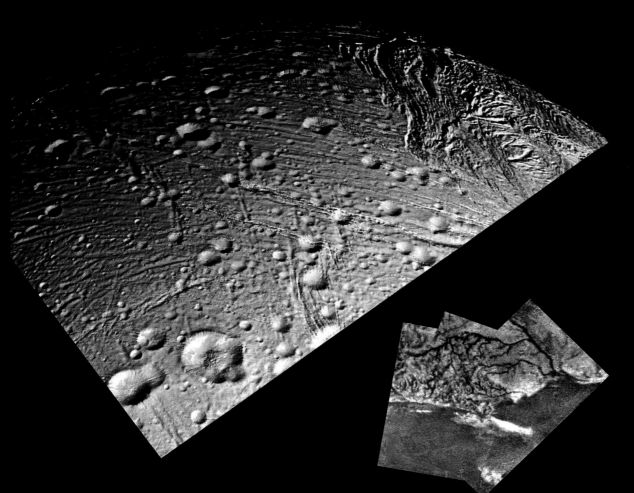

A billion miles from home (above)

On touching down on Titan's surface, the
Huygens probe became the first such craft
to land on a world outside the inner Solar
System. Before its batteries ran out it returned
this tantalising glimpse of Titan's landscape.
The rounded, bubble-like rocks (possibly
chunks of ice) seem to have been shaped
by the action of flowing liquid.

Titan's rivers (left)

The Huygens probe took these detailed
images of Titan's surface in 2005 as it made
its 2.5-hour descent through the moon's
hazy atmosphere. The dark area may be a
region flooded by liquid hydrocarbons such
as ethane or methane. Evidently the liquid
has cut numerous rivers into the terrain,
creating the veined, delta-like region visible
near the top of the image.

URANUS

Leaving the Saturnian system and heading deeper into space, the next world encountered is the pallid, blue-green Uranus. It orbits almost twice as far from the Sun as Saturn, at an average distance of nineteen astronomical units. Like the two planets before it, Uranus is a fluid world whose atmosphere blends smoothly into its interior. Unlike these gas giants though, Uranus has a relatively high density, suggesting that its interior consists of a hot slush of various ice molecules such as water and methane, not just hydrogen alone. Curiously, Uranus's axial tilt is so great that the planet orbits on its side—the result, astronomers think, of a collision between Uranus and another world in the distant past, perhaps during the formation of the Solar System. Uranus also has a ring system, but, unlike the brilliant rings of Saturn, those of Uranus—eleven in all—are made of individual fragments of rock and ice coated in a sooty grime and are consequently very dark. There are at least 27 natural satellites, although only five are larger than 290 miles (470 km) in diameter. Although Uranus can be observed with the naked eye under clear dark sky conditions, it was not recognized as a planet until 1781.

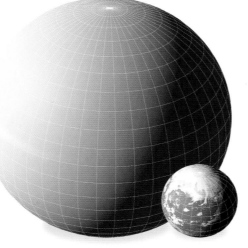

Blue giant
Uranus, almost exactly four times the size of Earth, is often called an ice giant, mid-way in size between the terrestrial planets and the gas giants.

URANUS STATISTICS	
Discovered	March 13, 1781, by William Herschel
Average distance from the Sun	1,784.7 million miles (2,872.5 million km); 19.2 AU
Equatorial diameter	31,763 miles (51,118 km)
Axial rotation period (sidereal)	17.24 hours
Mass (Earth = 1)	14.5
Volume (Earth = 1)	63.1
Gravity at cloud tops (Earth = 1)	0.86
Average density (water = 1)	1.3
Escape velocity	13.2 miles/s (21.3 km/s)
Axial tilt from orbit	97.8°
Sunlight strength	0.2–0.3% of Earth's
Albedo (reflectivity)	51%
Number of satellites	≥27

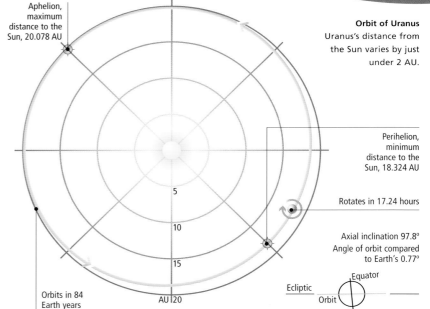

Aphelion, maximum distance to the Sun, 20.078 AU

Orbit of Uranus
Uranus's distance from the Sun varies by just under 2 AU.

Perihelion, minimum distance to the Sun, 18.324 AU

Rotates in 17.24 hours

Axial inclination 97.8°
Angle of orbit compared to Earth's 0.77°

Ecliptic
Equator
Orbit

Orbits in 84 Earth years

AU 20

Structure of Uranus

Uranus is a relatively dense world compared to Jupiter and Saturn. Hydrogen is certainly present, but only 15 percent of the planet's mass is attributed to this element in its pure form, compared to 80 percent in Jupiter. The rest of the hydrogen in Uranus must be locked up in heavier compounds such as water, methane, and ammonia, within the planet's inner mantle. A magnetic field with an intrinsic strength about 50 times stronger than Earth's is generated in the mantle, offset from the planet's axis.

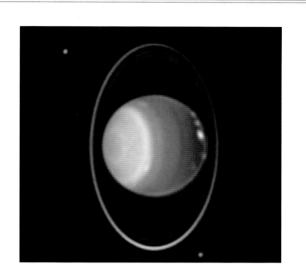

The Uranian system
Uranus, its ring system, and some of its 27 known satellites, are seen in this infrared Hubble Space Telescope image. Red patches indicate high-altitude clouds.

Outer mantle
Beneath Uranus's gaseous atmosphere lies a mantle composed of liquid hydrogen and other elements. It extends to a depth of about 6,000 miles (9,600 km).

Core
There is probably a core of rock and ice within Uranus, with a mass slightly greater than our own planet.

Inner mantle
Below the outer mantle is a slushy layer composed of icy compounds of water, methane, and ammonia. This layer is probably the source of the planet's magnetic field.

Atmosphere of Uranus

The atmosphere of Uranus has none of the vibrant cloud belts that typify Saturn and Jupiter. However, there are signs that as the northern hemisphere's decades-long summer draws to a close the atmosphere is becoming more active and strongly banded. Voyager 2 detected only one cloud deck on Uranus, composed of methane. This was situated low in the atmosphere where the temperature is about 185°F (85°C). It drops off to a chilly –364°F (–220°C) at the top of the atmosphere, which is too cold for cloud formation. Below the methane layer, clouds of ammonia ice, ammonium hydrosulfide crystals, and water ice, are expected theoretically.

Atmospheric breakdown
The Uranian atmosphere has much higher levels of methane compared to those of Jupiter and Saturn. Red light is absorbed by methane which accounts for the planet's blue-green color.

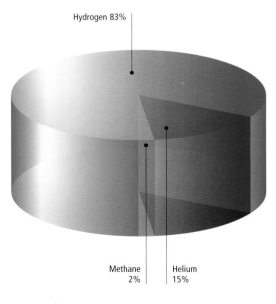

Hydrogen 83%

Methane 2%

Helium 15%

Subtle banding
Uranus's atmosphere is largely lacking in detail in the visible spectrum. However, this false-color, contrast-enhanced photo—obtained during the Voyager 2 flyby in January 1986—reveals subtle banding within the atmosphere.

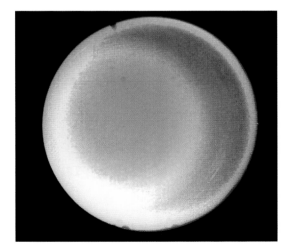

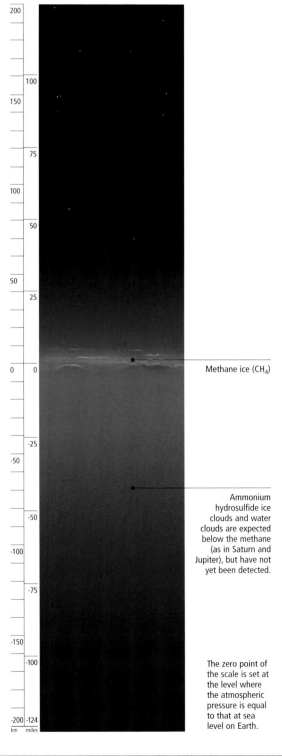

Methane ice (CH_4)

Ammonium hydrosulfide ice clouds and water clouds are expected below the methane (as in Saturn and Jupiter), but have not yet been detected.

The zero point of the scale is set at the level where the atmospheric pressure is equal to that at sea level on Earth.

MAPPING URANUS

To the human eye, Uranus appears more or less featureless. Nevertheless, Uranus has an active atmosphere; it just requires the right instrumentation to see and map it. In the infrared, dark belts, bright zones, a ring system, and storm systems like those found on Saturn and Jupiter are revealed. Specialized telescopes unveil similarly ferocious winds—blowing up to 530 feet per second (160 m/s) at mid-latitudes. The atmospheric features remain hidden because, with no apparent internal heat source, Uranus is extremely cold, which causes the clouds to condense too low down in the atmosphere, behind haze, to be readily observed. However, Uranus's mysteries are not all atmospheric. The ice giant features one of the most unusual magnetic fields in the Solar System, about 50 times stronger than Earth's and centered 60° to its rotational axis.

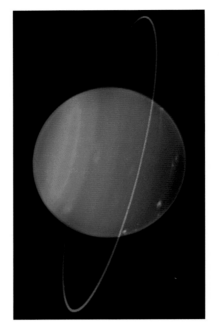 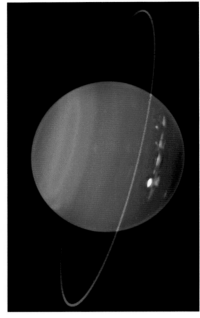

Viewing both sides (above left and above right)
These two near-infrared photos of Uranus were obtained not from space but from Earth, using an image-sharpening adaptive optics system on one of the two Keck telescopes in Hawaii. They were taken half a Uranian day apart and thus show opposite sides of the planet. Infrared images such as these are useful in bringing out the rings (seen here in red), as well as highlighting cloud features. The white clouds of a northern hemisphere storm system, for example, are clearly visible in the photo on the right.

Rings in detail (below)
When Voyager 2 was 147,000 miles (236,000 km) from Uranus and in the planet's shadow, it took this 96-second exposure of the planet's ring system. The angle of the shot allowed scientists to observe that, while the rings are bunched into discrete ringlets, there is an underlying continuous distribution of ring material throughout the system. Most likely this ring material consists of fine dust-coated icy particles up to 3.2 feet (1 m) across. The short white streaks across the image are the result of trailed background stars.

Magnetic mystery (above)
Uranus has a fairly powerful magnetic field, whose intrinsic strength is about 50 times Earth's. Unlike our planet's magnetic field, which is more or less centered on the core and only slightly tilted relative to the spin axis, the field of Uranus is offset from the center and is not aligned with the spin axis at all. The reason for this anomaly is unknown, but it could be that the source of Uranus's magnetic field is in the slushy mantle and not in the core. The illustration above shows Uranus's magnetic field (1) deflecting the solar wind (2), creating a bow shock (3). Note that Uranus's magnetic pole (4) is nowhere near the planet's geographic pole, or spin axis (5).

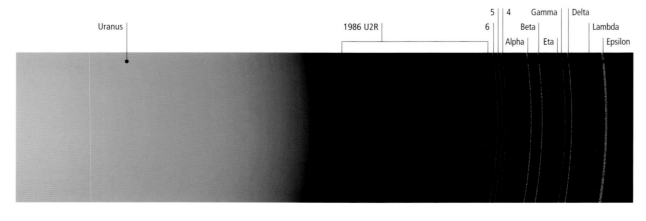

The Uranian ring system (left)
The eleven rings of Uranus are generally narrow, apart from the innermost ring that is continuous and very wide. The seven outermost rings are labeled with letters of the Greek alphabet. All rings are dark, composed of icy particulates most likely covered in organic compounds.

The southern hemisphere of Uranus
Given Uranus's unique tilt, there is some debate over which is the north pole and which the south. The map here has taken the planet's rotation as prograde and therefore the south pole is at the left. The southern hemisphere is often populated by storm systems. These storms result in streaks of methane ice clouds forming parallel to the equator. Such clouds are rarely visible, however, as they condense deep within the thick, hazy methane atmosphere.

The northern hemisphere of Uranus
With its spin axis tilted almost parallel to its orbital plane and an orbit of 84 Earth years, Uranus's polar regions experience 42-year days and 42-year nights. The hemisphere adopted as north on this map was found to be facing the Sun during the Voyager 2 flyby in 1986. At this time it was only beginning its long day, which is due to end in 2027.

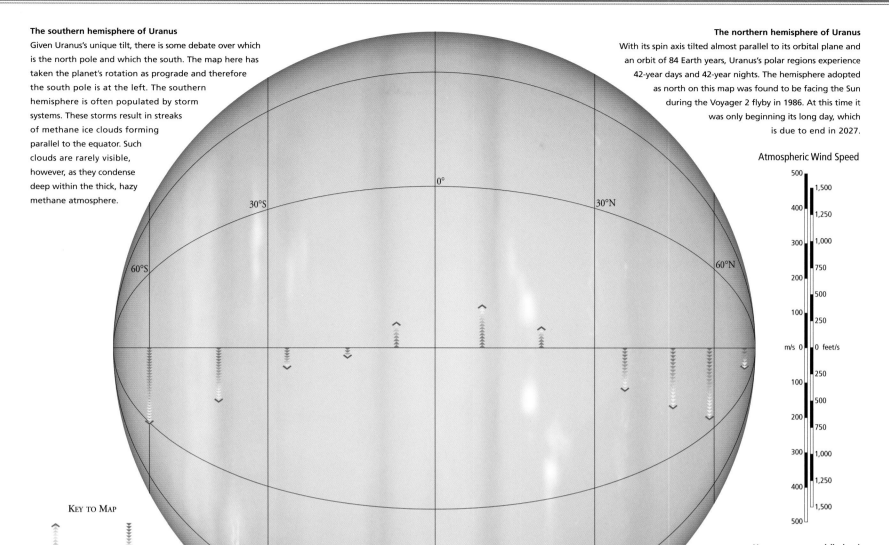

Atmospheric Wind Speed

m/s	feet/s
500	1,500
400	1,250
300	1,000
	750
200	500
100	250
0	0
100	250
200	500
	750
300	1,000
400	1,250
	1,500
500	

KEY TO MAP

EASTERLY WIND SPEED   WESTERLY WIND SPEED

Colored rings (below)
In this Voyager 2 image, the very slight color differences between the dark rings of Uranus have been greatly enhanced in the search for clues to their nature and origin. Almost the full width of the rings is shown, from the diffuse 1986 U2R ring at the top to the bright Epsilon ring at the bottom.

Uranus uncovered (below)
In January 1986, the Voyager 2 probe recorded these two photos of the planet Uranus from a distance of 11 million miles (18 million km). The image at the top shows how Uranus would appear to the human eye at that range, while on the bottom is a false-color enhancement. In the false-color image the atmospheric structure of Uranus is uncovered, revealing a possible polar cap of smog-like haze, southern and northern storm systems, and equatorial bands.

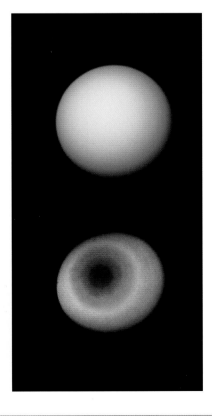

Satellites of Uranus

Uranus boasts at least 27 satellites. The five largest, the so-called classical moons, were discovered between 1787 and 1948. They are Titania, Oberon, Umbriel, Ariel, and Miranda. Because Uranus is so far away, no other satellites were found until the Voyager 2 flyby of 1986, which brought the total up to fifteen. However, these, and all others found since then, are little more than shards of rock and ice, barely a few dozen miles across or smaller. Even the classical moons are on the small side, with the largest, Titania, less than half the diameter of Earth's moon. All have fairly dark surfaces, and are thought to be made of rock and ices. All the satellites of Uranus are named after characters in the works of William Shakespeare and Alexander Pope.

Moon orbits
This diagram shows the relative sizes of the orbits of the five largest Uranian moons. Of the remaining 22 satellites (not shown), some are found much closer in than Miranda, while others are a great deal farther away than Oberon. Sycorax, for example, is 21 times farther from Uranus.

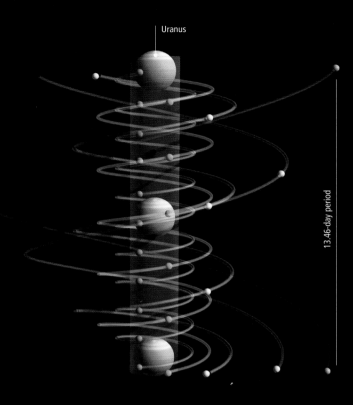

Uranus

13.46-day period

Oberon

Miranda | Ariel | Umbriel | Titania

Titania

Oberon

Uranian moons compared
The five largest moons of Uranus, seen here to scale, are comparable in dimensions to the mid-sized satellites of Saturn, such as Enceladus and Rhea.

Umbriel

Miranda

Ariel

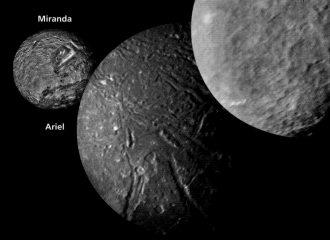

Titania
Discovered: 1787
Diameter: 981 miles (1,578 km)
Mean orbital radius: 270,860 miles (435,910 km)
Orbital period: 8.71 days

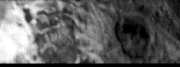

Oberon
Discovered: 1787
Diameter: 946 miles (1,523 km)
Mean orbital radius: 362,580 miles (583,520 km)
Orbital period: 13.46 days

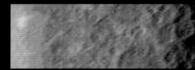

Umbriel
Discovered: 1851
Diameter: 726 miles (1,169 km)
Mean orbital radius: 165,470 miles (266,300 km)
Orbital period: 4.14 days

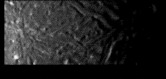

Ariel
Discovered: 1851
Diameter: 720 miles (1,158 km)
Mean orbital radius: 118,690 miles (191,020 km)
Orbital period: 2.52 days

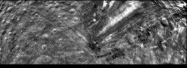

Miranda
Discovered: 1948
Diameter: 293 miles (472 km)
Mean orbital radius: 80,400 miles (129,390 km)
Orbital period: 1.41 days

Mapping Miranda

Miranda, whose surface is mapped here, has one
of the most bizarre landscapes in the Solar System.
In places, two or more utterly different types
of terrain juxtapose, with sharp boundaries
between them. This may be because the
moon's internal heat was exhausted at
a time when heavy rocky materials
were sinking and lighter icy
material was rising to the
surface. An alternative
explanation is that
Miranda reassembled
in orbit after it was
somehow shattered.

Verona Rupes

30°S

Dunsinane Regio

Sicilia Regio

Prospero

Alanso

Argier Rupes

60°S

Inverness Corona

Arden Corona

Ephesus Regio

Elsinore Corona

90°W

90°E

SP

Stephano

Mantua Regio

Scale is correct for
latitude 80°S / longitude 0°

km   miles
0 — 0

25

50   25

50

Tectonics and flooding (below)

The surface of Ariel is covered in vast cracks and faults. Planetary
scientists think the faults are the result of tectonic activity that
caused the crust to crack apart and split open. More recently,
these fissures have been partially filled with frozen deposits—
although exactly what kind of material this could be is uncertain.

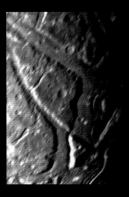

Patchwork world (below)

Miranda, the smallest of the principal moons of Uranus, is the
subject of this Voyager 2 photo from January 1986, taken from
a range of just 19,000 miles (31,000 km). The terrain at the left
is heavily cratered, and so must be older than the grooved
region immediately to the right. Miranda is just one-seventh
the size of Earth's moon and it is not quite spherical.

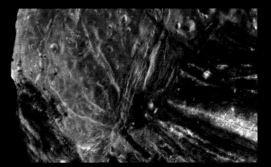

Solar System's highest cliff (below)

Despite being a fairly diminutive Moon, Miranda can boast
the highest known cliff in the Solar System. Seen right of
center in this Voyager 2 image, Verona Rupes (18.5°S/12°W)
is about 12 miles (20 km) high—ten times higher than the
walls of the Grand Canyon.

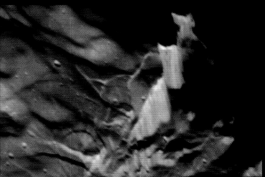

NEPTUNE

Neptune is the last giant outpost, the most distant of the Solar System's eight major planets, just over 30 times farther from the Sun than the Earth. From this far out, the Sun is some 900 times fainter than we are used to on Earth. And yet, despite this gloomy and wintry location, Neptune is a remarkably active planet. Considering how similar Neptune and Uranus are in terms of size and structure, it is surprising how visually dissimilar they are. For while our brief views of Uranus show a pale and relatively featureless world, Neptune is a beautiful icy blue jewel, streaked with cloud bands—not as prominent as Jupiter's but still unmistakable—and dotted with giant storm systems. Not surprisingly, there is also a system of rings, but they are very dark, their particles probably coated in dark organic compounds. As with the other giant worlds, there is the usual array of satellites, at least thirteen in total. Neptune, which is visible through binoculars as a blue-green dot, was discovered in 1846 though its existence had been predicted some years before due to peculiarities in the orbit of Uranus.

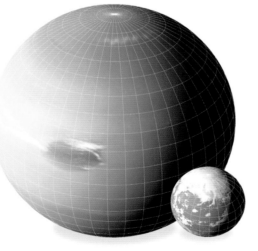

Blue colossus
Neptune, left, is another ice giant, just fractionally smaller than Uranus, but still 3.9 times the size of Earth, right.

NEPTUNE STATISTICS	
Discovered	September 23, 1846, by Johann Galle
Average distance from the Sun	2,793.1 million miles (4,495.1 million km); 30 AU
Equatorial diameter	30,775 miles (49,528 km)
Axial rotation period	16.11 hours
Mass (Earth = 1)	17.1
Volume (Earth = 1)	57.7
Gravity at cloud tops (Earth = 1)	1.2
Average density (water = 1)	1.6
Escape velocity	14.6 miles/s (23.5 km/s)
Axial tilt from orbit	28.3°
Sunlight strength	0.1% of Earth's
Albedo (reflectivity)	41%
Number of satellites	≥13

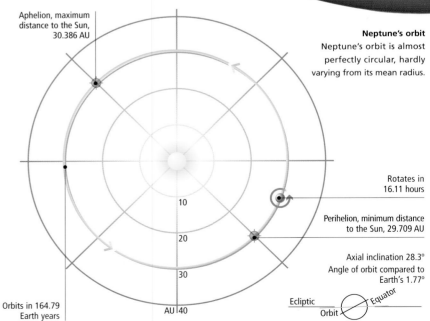

Aphelion, maximum distance to the Sun, 30.386 AU

Neptune's orbit
Neptune's orbit is almost perfectly circular, hardly varying from its mean radius.

Rotates in 16.11 hours

Perihelion, minimum distance to the Sun, 29.709 AU

Axial inclination 28.3°
Angle of orbit compared to Earth's 1.77°

Ecliptic
Equator
Orbit

Orbits in 164.79 Earth years

AU 40

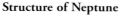

Structure of Neptune

Neptune's interior is probably much like that of Uranus, but there is a striking difference: Neptune has an internal heat source that keeps it warmer than it would otherwise be, so far from the Sun. The heat is probably generated through a process called differentiation: as denser materials fall toward the planet's core, pushing up lighter materials, some of the energy of motion is converted into thermal energy. Neptune also has a magnetic field with an intrinsic strength about 25 times greater than Earth's and offset relative to the axis of the planet.

Outer mantle
Below the atmosphere of Neptune is a mantle of hydrogen and other compounds mixed into an icy liquid form, similar to the equivalent layer in Uranus.

Core
Neptune may have an inner core of rock, possibly encased by a shell of ice, or the rock and ice may be mixed together.

Inner mantle
Below the outer mantle, as on Uranus, the majority of the planet consists of a slushy region made of a mixture rich in water, methane, and ammonia.

Atmosphere of Neptune

Considering that it is so much farther from the Sun than Uranus, Neptune has a markedly dynamic atmosphere. Its clouds ought to condense at lower altitudes and be lost in the haze as they are on Uranus. But an internal heat source keeps its atmosphere stormy, active, and dynamic. The main clouds are methane ice crystals, and there may be additional layers of ammonia ice, ammonium hydrosulfide, and water ice lower down.

Atmospheric breakdown
Most of Neptune's atmosphere is hydrogen. Helium makes up 18 percent and methane accounts for the remainder. This is essentially the same make-up as the atmosphere of Uranus, but Neptune has slightly more methane.

One last shot
This false-color view of Neptune was one of the last photos taken of this world at close range by Voyager 2 before the craft began its endless journey into interstellar space.

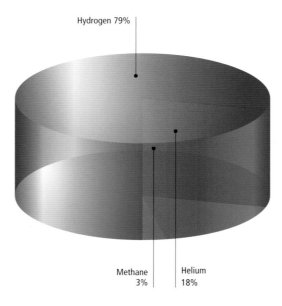

Hydrogen 79%

Methane 3%

Helium 18%

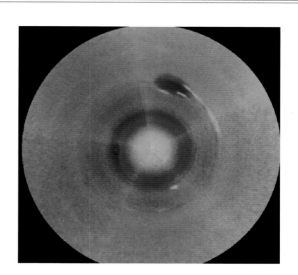

Transient storms
Voyager 2's photos of Neptune revealed cloud bands and multiple storm systems, including the Great Dark Spot seen in the top half of this polar perspective image. However, this huge storm has vanished since the image was obtained in 1989.

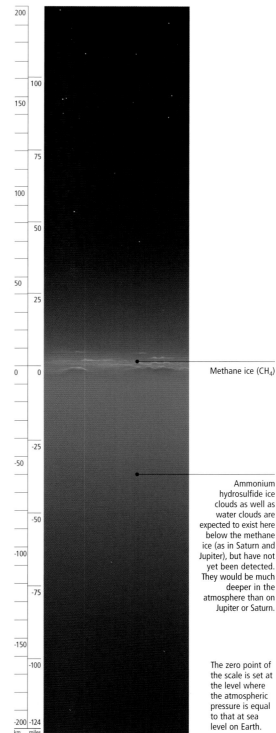

Methane ice (CH_4)

Ammonium hydrosulfide ice clouds as well as water clouds are expected to exist here below the methane ice (as in Saturn and Jupiter), but have not yet been detected. They would be much deeper in the atmosphere than on Jupiter or Saturn.

The zero point of the scale is set at the level where the atmospheric pressure is equal to that at sea level on Earth.

MAPPING NEPTUNE

The face of Neptune came as a surprise to Voyager mission scientists when the Voyager 2 probe passed the planet in 1989. No one had expected the detail visible in the planet's atmosphere. Uranus, the planet passed by Voyager some three years earlier, presented a plain face to observers. Neptune, even farther from the Sun and therefore presumably colder, was expected to be equally, if not more, inactive. Instead, the planet displayed the hallmarks of an energetic giant: cloud belts and zones, cyclonic storms, and furious winds—the fastest in the known Solar System, raging in some storm systems at over 2,200 feet per second (670 m/s). Still, Neptune's banding and large storm systems are not as unchanging as Jupiter's, and already some of the features discovered by Voyager 2 have gone while new ones have appeared. Clouds, similar to Earth's cirrus-type clouds, also continually move across the planet's disk, streaking its surface with white.

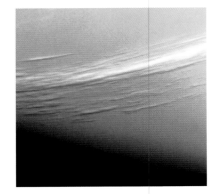

Echoes of Earthly skies (above)
This amazing Voyager 2 photo shows cirrus-like cloud formations high in the atmosphere of Neptune, casting shadows on the layers below them.

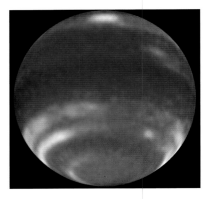

Springtime on Neptune (above)
In 2002, when the Hubble Space Telescope took this image of Neptune, the planet's south pole was facing the Sun more directly than during the Voyager 2 encounter. This change of season probably explains why bands of white clouds have become more common in Neptune's southern hemisphere.

Banded Neptune
As with Jupiter and Saturn, Neptune has alternating light zones and dark belts. These belts and zones indicate regions of atmospheric turbulence probably resulting from Neptune's internal heat source. As yet the cause of this internal heat source is undetermined.

Fierce winds
Neptune's fierce westerly winds are strongest at the equator, blowing at well over 1,000 feet per second (450 m/s). The wind drops uniformly at higher latitudes to become easterly winds near the poles.

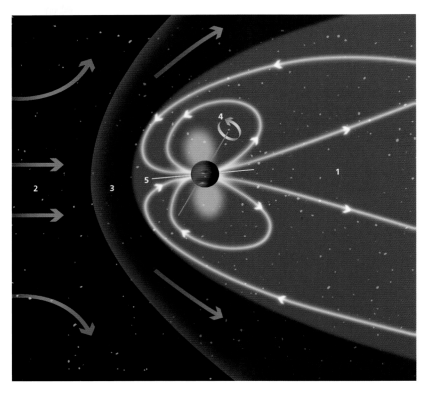

Tilted magnetism (above)
Neptune, like the other giants, has a sizable magnetic field, its intrinsic strength about 25 times Earth's. However, as with Uranus, the Neptunian field is tilted greatly with respect to the planet's spin axis and it is not centered on the core. The reason for this anomaly is unknown. In the illustration above, Neptune's magnetic field (1) deflects the solar wind (2), creating a region known as the bow shock (3). The planet's spin axis (4) is notably at odds with its magnetic axis (5).

Vanishing storms (above)
Voyager 2 took this image of Neptune's Great Dark Spot encircled by clouds in 1989. Though similar in make-up to Jupiter's long-enduring Great Red Spot, by 1994 the spot had gone.

White clouds over blue planet
In the same way that Uranus's methane-heavy atmosphere accounts for its blue-green color, Neptune's atmosphere, with its even higher concentrations of methane, absorbs red wavelengths of light and reflects blue. The planet appears deep blue as a result. About 30 to 60 miles (50–100 km) above the main cloud deck, Neptune's distinctive white clouds streak the planet, changing its face day to day. They are most likely composed of methane ice crystals. Neptune's rapid rotation means these clouds form parallel to the equator.

The rings of Neptune (left)
Neptune has five known rings, which, like those of Uranus, are all dark and are probably composed of icy boulders covered in carbon-rich substances. The rings are named after five scientists whose work influenced our understanding of Neptune.

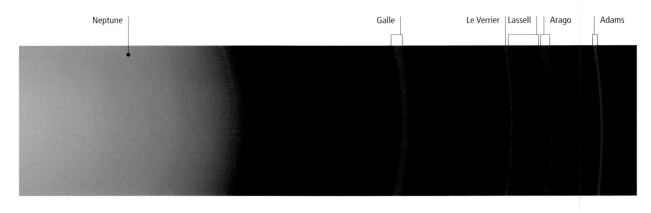

| Neptune | | Galle | Le Verrier | Lassell | Arago | Adams |

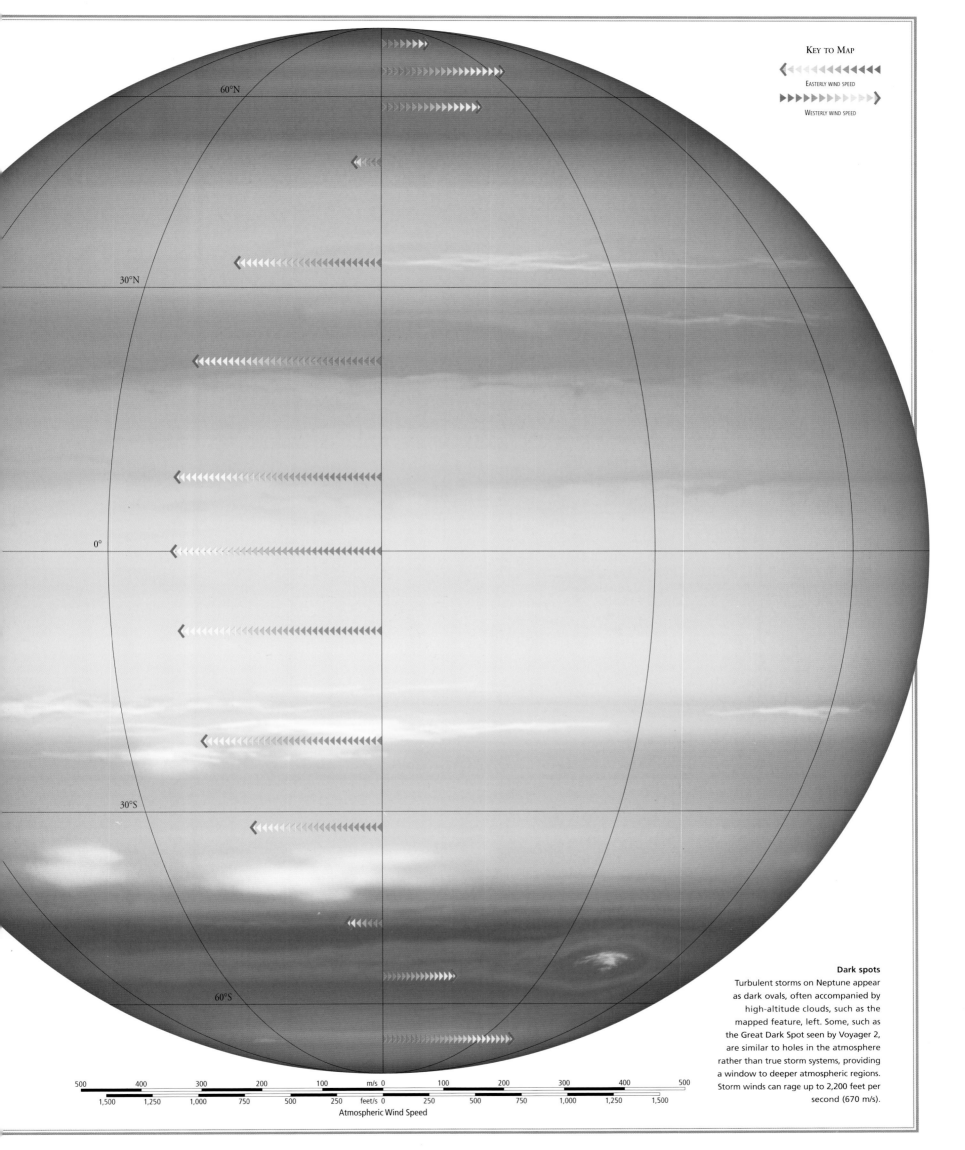

EASTERLY WIND SPEED

WESTERLY WIND SPEED

60°N

30°N

0°

30°S

60°S

Dark spots
Turbulent storms on Neptune appear
as dark ovals, often accompanied by
high-altitude clouds, such as the
mapped feature, left. Some, such as
the Great Dark Spot seen by Voyager 2,
are similar to holes in the atmosphere
rather than true storm systems, providing
a window to deeper atmospheric regions.
Storm winds can rage up to 2,200 feet per
second (670 m/s).

| 500 | 400 | 300 | 200 | 100 | m/s 0 | 100 | 200 | 300 | 400 | 500 |

| 1,500 | 1,250 | 1,000 | 750 | 500 | 250 | feet/s 0 | 250 | 500 | 750 | 1,000 | 1,250 | 1,500 |

Atmospheric Wind Speed

SATELLITES OF NEPTUNE

Neptune is encircled by a family of thirteen known satellites. Possibly Neptune has fewer moons than are found around the other gas and ice giants, but the low count could be due to the fact that the other planets are closer to Earth, and their moons easier to detect. Mighty Triton was the first moon to be found, in 1846, just a few weeks after the discovery of Neptune itself. Nereid came to light in 1949. Nereid is the third biggest but still only one-eighth the size of Triton. The Voyager 2 probe brought the moon count up to eight in 1989. Since then, four satellites were located in 2002, and one in 2003, none of which has yet been named.

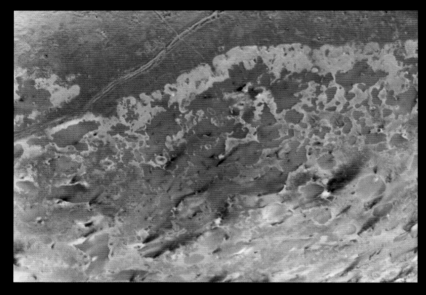

Icy geysers (above)
This Voyager 2 photo of the surface of Triton shows a remarkably active surface, considering the surface temperature of -391°F (-235°C) makes it the coldest measured object in the Solar System. The dark streaks are deposits of nitrogen frost left by cryogenic geyser activity.

Size comparison (below)
Triton is the only large satellite of Neptune. At 1,682 miles (2,707 km) in diameter it is the seventh-largest moon in the Solar System. Nereid, Larissa, and Proteus are only a fraction of Triton's size. All others are far smaller still.

Moon orbits

This diagram shows the orbits of three large satellites of Neptune: Larissa, Proteus, and Triton. If the other moons are taken into account, the entire Neptunian system has a huge radius of 29 million miles (46.7 million km)—or almost one-third the radius of Earth's orbit.

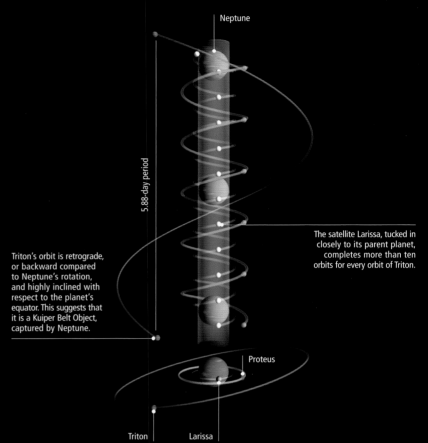

Triton's orbit is retrograde, or backward compared to Neptune's rotation, and highly inclined with respect to the planet's equator. This suggests that it is a Kuiper Belt Object, captured by Neptune.

The satellite Larissa, tucked in closely to its parent planet, completes more than ten orbits for every orbit of Triton.

Nereid's eccentric path (below)
The orbit of Nereid is more elongated than that of any other satellite, taking the moon from 800,000 to 6 million miles (1.3–9.5 million km) from the planet. Like Triton, it is most likely a captured Kuiper Belt Object.

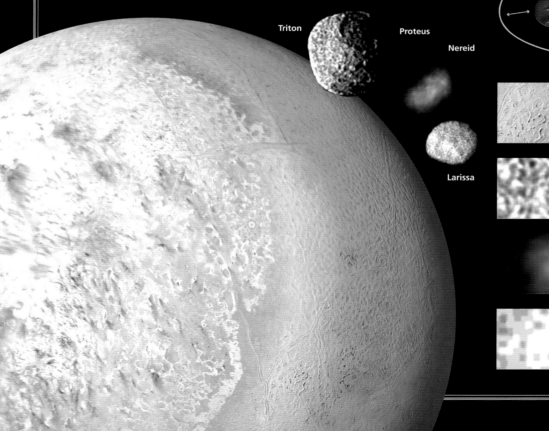

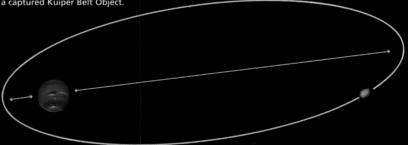

Triton
Discovered: 1846
Diameter: 1,682 miles (2,707 km)
Mean orbital radius: 220,438 miles (354,760 km)
Orbital period: 5.88 days

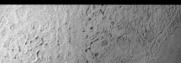

Proteus
Discovered: 1989
Diameter: 261 miles (420 km)
Mean orbital radius: 73,102 miles (117,647 km)
Orbital period: 1.12 days

Nereid
Discovered: 1949
Diameter: 211 miles (340 km)
Mean orbital radius: 3,425,870 miles (5,513,400 km)
Orbital period: 360.14 days

Larissa
Discovered: 1981
Diameter: 122 miles (196 km)
Mean orbital radius: 45,701 miles (73,548 km)
Orbital period: 13.31 hours

Mapping Triton

The only images of the surface of Triton are those taken by the Voyager 2 probe. While many of them are of excellent quality, the probe was only able to photograph about half the surface as it flew past, so nothing is known about the northern polar region. Triton's surface is bizarre, especially the so-called "cantaloupe" terrain of frozen nitrogen and methane, which is unique to Triton. Monad Regio is one such area with this terrain.

30°N

Tuonela
Planitia

Ruach
Planitia

Slidr Sulci

Bubembe Regio

Monad
Regio

Cipango
Planum

Kibu
Patera

Yasu Sulci

0°

Lo Sulci

Ob Sulci

Ho Sulci

Mangwe Cavus

Boynne Sulci

Abatos Planum

Vimur Sulci

Scale is correct for
latitude 30°S / longitude 0°

km   miles
0   0

250

250

500   250

500

Namazu
Macula

30°S

Doro Macula

Viviane
Macula

Zin
Maculae

Akupara
Maculae

Uhlanga Regio

Kikimora
Macula

60°S

Hili Plume

90°W

90°E

SP

Triton's south pole (left)
This Voyager 2 composite polar projection reveals Triton's scalloped cap of frozen nitrogen and methane that extends as far as 10 degrees north of the equator. Bright rays that radiate from the cap probably consist of fresh snow or frost blown by winds in Triton's thin atmosphere.

From the edge of the Solar System (right)
Voyager 2 obtained this image of Neptune and Triton, in crescent phase, following its closest approach to Neptune. This was among the last planetary images returned during the Voyager program.

DWARF PLANETS

In 2006, astronomers from the International Astronomical Union (IAU) had a historic meeting, at which they decided for the first time on a formal definition for a planet. Overnight, Pluto—considered since its discovery in 1930 to be the ninth planet—was stripped of its planethood. Now, Pluto and the large asteroid Ceres (found between Mars and Jupiter) are known as dwarf planets. A dwarf planet is a celestial object orbiting the Sun which is massive enough for its own gravity to make it almost spherical, but whose orbit criss-crosses those of other bodies. Ceres, for example, orbits among the asteroids, and Pluto orbits in the Kuiper belt beyond Neptune. We now know that Pluto is not unique, nor is it the largest dwarf planet (an honor presently belonging to Eris). Since 2006, the number of confirmed dwarf planets has grown to five. All except Ceres are found beyond the orbit of Neptune and are called plutoids. In addition to the five known dwarf planets, another nine or so large trans-Neptunian objects are currently being considered for inclusion among the dwarf planets, which would bring the total up to 14.

Mini worlds
This diagram shows all five dwarf planets compared to the Earth. From left to right, they are Ceres, Makemake, Haumea, Pluto and Eris. Even the largest two, Eris and Pluto, are less than one fifth the size of the Earth.

DWARF PLANET STATISTICS

	Ceres	Makemake	Haumea	Pluto	Eris
Discovered	1901	2005	2004	1930	2005
Average distance from Sun (AU)	2.77	45.79	43.34	39.48	67.67
Orbital period (yrs)	4.6	309.9	285.4	248.09	557
Axial rotation period (sidereal)	0.38	Not known	Not known	6.39	0.3
Diameter (Earth=1)	0.076	0.12	0.09	0.18	0.19
Diameter (km/miles)	975/605	1500/932	1150/715	2306/1433	2400/1491
Mass (Earth=1)	0.00015	0.00067	0.00067	0.0022	0.0028
Sunlight strength (% of Earth's)	13%	0.05%	0.05%	0.06%	0.02%
Escape velocity (km/s and miles)	0.51 / 0.32	0.80 / 0.50	0.84 / 0.52	1.20 / 0.75	1.3 / 0.81
Axial tilt from orbit	3°	Not known	Not known	119.59°	Not known
Orbital inclination	10.59°	28.96°	28.19°	17.14°	44.19°
Surface gravity (Earth=1)	0.027	0.05	0.045	0.059	0.082
Number of satellites	0	0	2	3	1
Orbital eccentricity	0.08	0.159	0.189	0.249	0.442
Location	Asteroid belt	Kuiper belt	Kuiper belt	Kuiper belt	Scattered disc
Surface temperature (C/F)	-106 / -159	-243 / -405	-241 / -402	-229 / -380	-231 / -384

Objects in orbit
Like comets, Pluto, Eris, and many Kuiper Belt Objects go around the Sun in long elliptical orbits, taking centuries to make one circuit of the Sun. By comparison, the orbits of the eight major planets are more like circles.

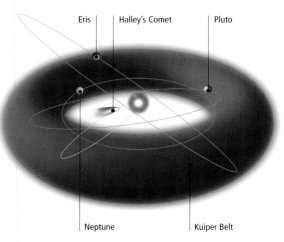

Eris   Halley's Comet   Pluto

Neptune   Kuiper Belt

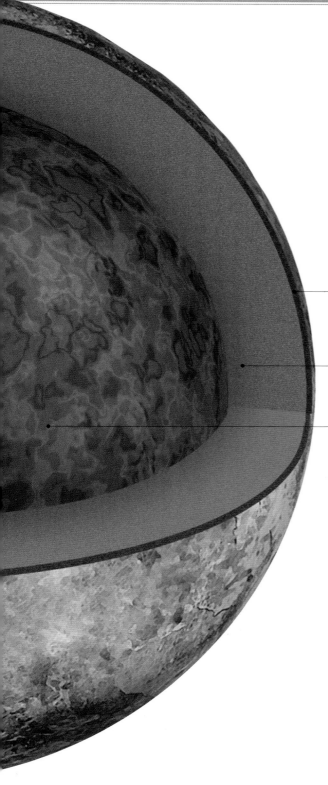

Structure of a typical plutoid

No probe has ever visited a dwarf planet, so we know comparatively little about them. The most well-studied of the trans-Neptunian dwarf planets, or plutoids, is Pluto, since it has been known much longer than all the others. Pluto is relatively heavy for its size. So our best guess is that this worldlet is made up of 70 percent rock, with ices making up the remainder. We also know from albedo (reflectivity) measurements that its surface is bright, and probably covered in nitrogen ice. Some astronomers suspect that Pluto resembles Neptune's largest moon, Triton. We can only speculate what the other plutoids might be like, both internally and externally. But given that they orbit far from the Sun, it's a good bet that they will be somewhat icy, similar to Pluto.

Crust
The extent of Pluto's crust is unknown. It is believed to be covered in patches of ice such as nitrogen, water, methane, and ethane. There are also dark areas, possibly harboring organic substances.

Mantle
Pluto's mantle is probably rich in ices, and may contain substantial amounts of frozen water.

Core
Below the mantle, most of Pluto's interior is taken up by its solid core. This is probably made mostly of rocky silicate materials.

Dwarf planet atmospheres

Pluto does have an atmosphere of sorts, but this thin envelope of nitrogen, methane, and carbon monoxide has a surface pressure of about one 10-millionth that of Earth's. That's equivalent to the pressure about 50 miles (80 km) above the surface of Earth, into the upper mesosphere where meteors burn up. It is thought that Pluto's atmosphere extends for about 370 miles (600 km) above the planet. It is also believed that the atmosphere is transient. As the planet's elliptical orbit takes it farther from the Sun, its atmosphere freezes out and falls as snow. The same may be true of Eris, whose surface is very bright. It is farther from the Sun than Pluto, so its atmosphere may already have frozen out. Little is known about the atmospheres, if any, of the other plutoids. Meanwhile, Ceres has no known atmosphere.

Atmospheric breakdown
Pluto's atmospheric composition has been determined from observations made when the planet passes in front of a reasonably bright star.

Dwarf planet in color
This is the clearest image we currently have of the surface of Pluto. Evidently the planet is quite brown, with a dark band of unknown substance and origin straddling its equator.

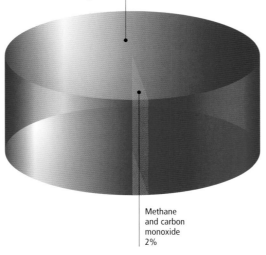

Nitrogen 98%

Methane and carbon monoxide 2%

New Horizons
Although no probe has ever visited a dwarf planet, that will change if NASA's New Horizons spacecraft is successful. The spacecraft is expected to reach Pluto in 2015, when it will map both the dwarf planet and its largest satellite, Charon.

Binary dwarf planet
This Hubble photo shows Pluto (left) compared to the largest of its three satellites, Charon (right). Pluto is the only dwarf planet so far known with a substantial moon, although some of the others do have smaller ones.

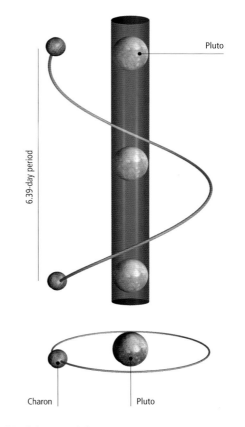

6.39-day period

Pluto

Charon   Pluto

Orbit of Charon and Pluto
A day on Pluto, Charon's rotation period, and Charon's orbital period are all identical: 6.39 days. Seen from Pluto, Charon would always show the same face and would remain fixed at exactly the same point in the sky.

THE KUIPER BELT

In 1992, two astronomers discovered an unknown icy body, 125 miles (200 km) in diameter, orbiting the Sun between 40.9 and 47.0 astronomical units (AU) with a period of 296 years. It was named 1992 QB1. Since this find, hundreds of similar objects have been uncovered, generally beyond the orbit of Neptune. Here at last was incontrovertible evidence of the Kuiper Belt, a long-suspected belt of icy planet-building leftovers surrounding the Sun at the fringes of the Solar System. The Kuiper Belt contains an estimated 10 million to 1 billion deep-frozen objects. While most remain in stable orbits beyond the planetary realm, from time to time one is disturbed by the gravitational influence of the outer planets and is put into a highly elliptical orbit into the inner Solar System where it becomes a short-period comet. Recently, astronomers found that the belt has an unexpected sharp outer edge at 50 AU.

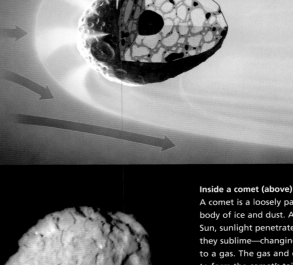

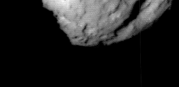

Inside a comet (above)
A comet is a loosely packed, non-uniform body of ice and dust. As it approaches the Sun, sunlight penetrates the surface ices and they sublime—changing directly from a solid to a gas. The gas and dust erupt into space to form the comet's tail.

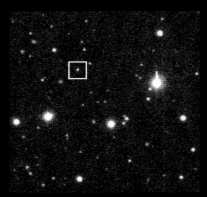

Far-flung speck (left)
Kuiper Belt Objects (KBOs) are so far away and so small and dark that none has ever been seen in any detail. This image, showing a KBO called 2004 DW (indicated by the white box), is one of the best photos we have of a KBO.

Distant giant (below)
One of the largest KBOs found to date is Quaoar (pronounced khwa-war), seen here in an artist's impression. Quaoar is currently being considered for inclusion as a dwarf planet, like Pluto and Eris.

Dirty snowball (above)
Comet Wild 2, seen here, was the subject of NASA's Stardust spacecraft, which flew past the comet on January 2, 2004, and collected dust from its coma. This is among the clearest ever photos taken of a cometary nucleus.

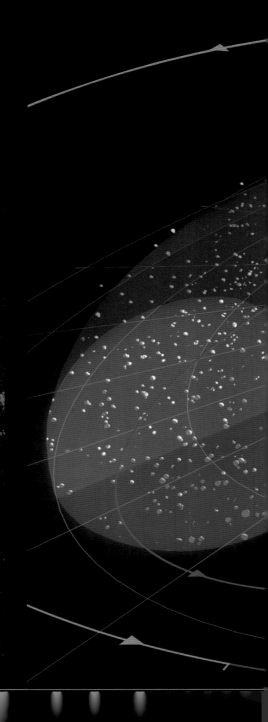

Classifying comets (right)

Comets are classified according to the length of their orbit and their orbital inclination. Short-period comets are divided into two subgroups: Jupiter-types and Halley-types. Jupiter-type comets have periods of less than twenty years and orbit at moderate inclinations to the plane of the Solar System. They have mean orbital radii that are less than or almost equal to that of Jupiter and many are strongly influenced in their orbits by that planet. Halley-type comets have intermediate orbital periods of 20 to 200 years. Long-period comets circle the Sun once every 200 to several million years. Long-period comets (and possibly Halley-types) originate in the Oort Cloud and come from random directions.

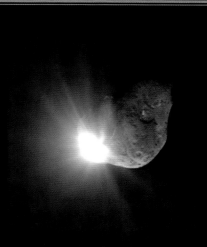

SOME REPRESENTATIVE COMETS

JUPITER-TYPE COMETS	ORBITAL PERIOD	PERIHELION DISTANCE	LAST SEEN
Encke	3.30 years	0.340 AU	2003
Wild 2	6.39 years	1.583 AU	2003
Borrelly	6.86 years	1.358 AU	2001
HALLEY-TYPE COMETS			
Tempel-Tuttle	32.91 years	0.982 AU	1998
Crommelin	27.89 years	0.743 AU	1984
Halley	76.1 years	0.587 AU	1986
LONG-PERIOD COMETS			
Hale-Bopp	2,320 years	1.315 AU	1997
Hyakutake	72,000 years	0.230 AU	1996

Charting the Kuiper Belt (below)

The Kuiper Belt, mostly contained within 30 to 50 AU, has three dynamical populations. The classical KBOs (yellow) occupy a zone between 40 and 50 AU. The resonant objects (blue) have orbits in harmony with Neptune's. Finally, there are the scattered KBOs (red), which have high inclinations. Each object crosses the plane of the ecliptic at junctions known as orbital nodes, shown as tick marks on the orbits below.

KEY TO SYMBOLS

♃ JUPITER — PLANETARY ORBIT — CLASSICAL KBO ORBIT ⊥ CLASSICAL KBO ORBITAL NODES

♆ NEPTUNE ●— APHELION — RESONANT KBO ORBIT ⊥ RESONANT KBO ORBITAL NODES

○— PERIHELION — SCATTERED KBO ORBIT ⊥ SCATTERED KBO ORBITAL NODES

⊥ PLANETARY ORBITAL NODES

Deep Impact (above)

On July 4, 2005 the nucleus of the short-period comet Tempel 1 was struck by the impactor segment of NASA's Deep Impact spacecraft at a speed of several miles per second. The flyby probe obtained this image 67 seconds after impact. It shows a plume of fine ejecta material illuminated by sunlight. Analysis of the impact sequence revealed information about the interior composition of the comet.

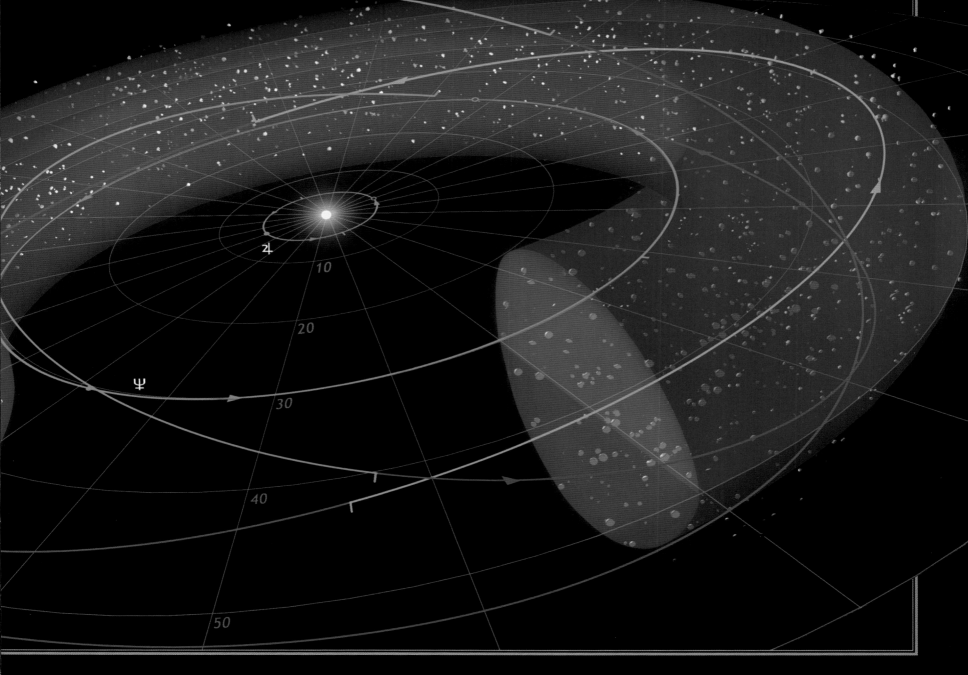

Beyond
the Kuiper Belt

Over a hundred astronomical units from our star, bounded by a shell called the heliopause, the edge of interstellar space begins—but not the end of the Sun's realm. The true edge of the Sun's kingdom lies a thousand times more distant still. Here, the Sun clings feebly to a spherical halo of icy fragments, trillions in number—a structure called the Oort Cloud. Like their relatives in the Kuiper Belt, the Oort Cloud occupants are potential cometary nuclei. But while the Kuiper Belt is the source of short-period comets, long-period comets originate in the Oort Cloud. Sedna (illustrated right with a hypothetical moon) is a member of the inner Oort Cloud and was discovered in 2003. It is perhaps two-thirds the size of Pluto, but most such objects are far smaller.

Charting the Oort Cloud (below right)
The Oort Cloud is roughly spherical but may be stretched due to tidal forces from the core of the Milky Way galaxy. It is about 200,000 AU across. On the scale of this illustration the orbit of Neptune would be about one-quarter the size of the period at the end of this sentence.

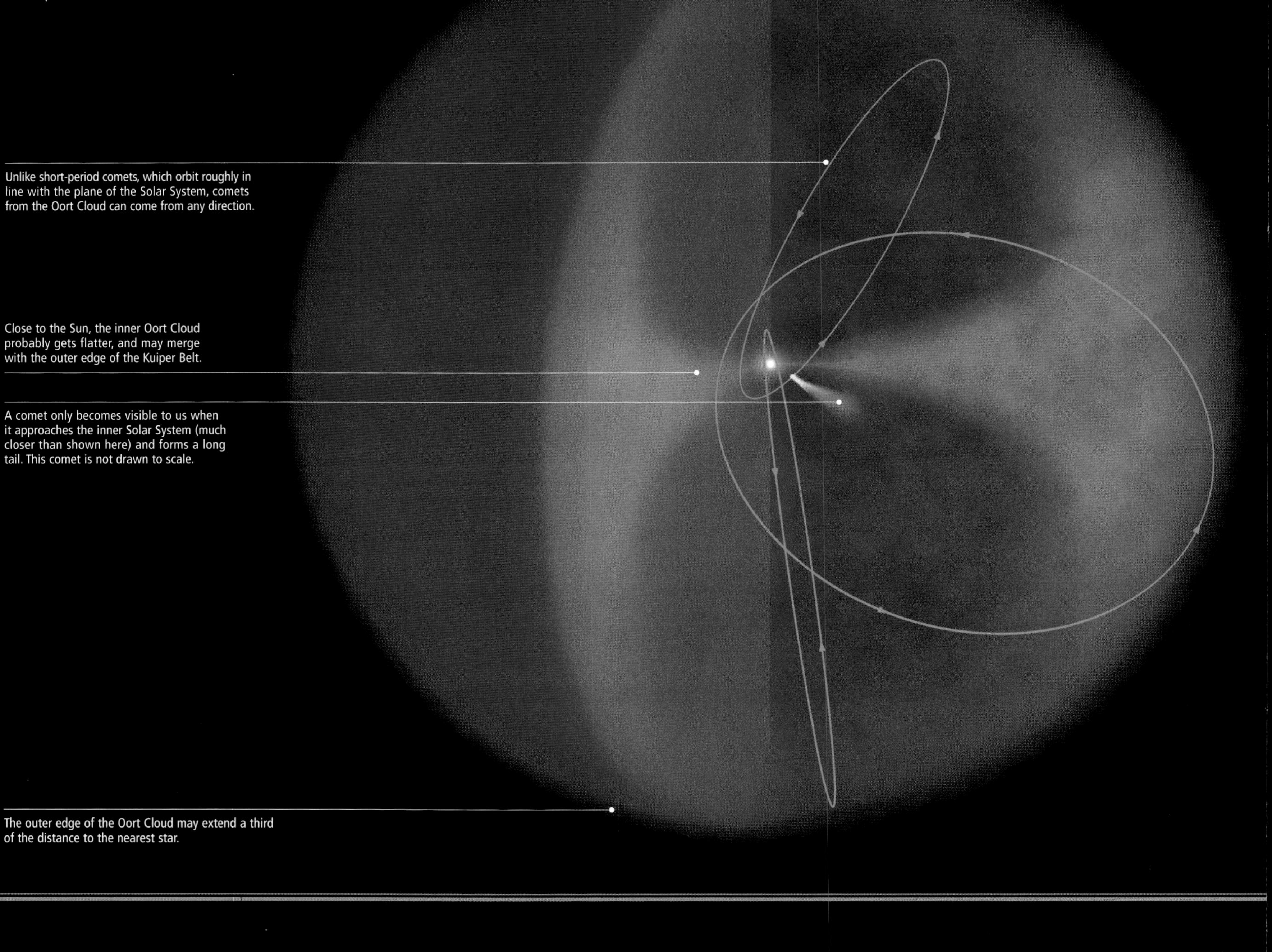

Unlike short-period comets, which orbit roughly in line with the plane of the Solar System, comets from the Oort Cloud can come from any direction.

Close to the Sun, the inner Oort Cloud probably gets flatter, and may merge with the outer edge of the Kuiper Belt.

A comet only becomes visible to us when it approaches the inner Solar System (much closer than shown here) and forms a long tail. This comet is not drawn to scale.

The outer edge of the Oort Cloud may extend a third of the distance to the nearest star.

The heliopshere

The Solar System is enclosed inside the heliosphere: a bubble blown by the Sun's steady flow of charged particles in the interstellar medium. Its inner boundary, where the solar wind first shows the effect of the interstellar medium by slowing down, is called the termination shock (1). Its outer boundary, where pressure from the solar wind is equaled by the pressure of the interstellar medium, is the heliopause (2). As the heliosphere moves through the interstellar medium, a zone of turbulence is created at the leading edge (3). This is known as the bow shock because it is analogous to the wave formed in front of a boat as it travels through water. Voyager 1 (the longer of the orange trajectory lines) is thought to have crossed the termination shock in December 2004 when the craft was about 94 AU from the Sun.

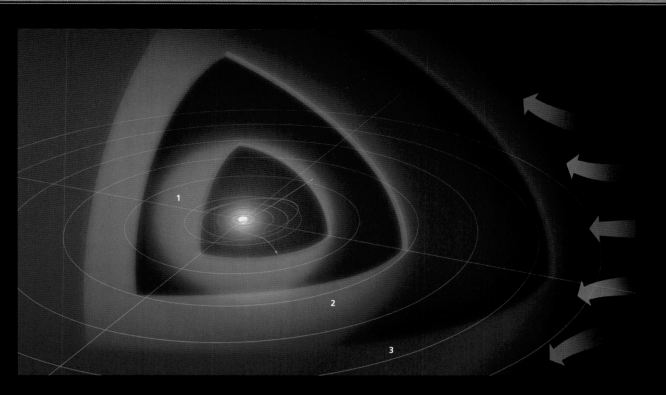

Long-distance caller (above)
Comet Hale-Bopp, seen in 1997, was one of the brightest comets of the 20th century. It was visible to the naked eye for a record-breaking 18 months. This is a long-period comet, having an orbit that takes 2,320 years to complete. It hails from the inner regions of the Oort Cloud. This photo shows Hale-Bopp's two tails: a white dust tail and a tail of glowing ionized gas

In a coma (right)
Comet Hyakutake, discovered in 1996 by the Japanese astronomer whose name it bears, is a long-period comet. On its recent visit, its orbital period was pushed from 15,000 to 72,000 years due to the gravitational influence of the giant planets. This Hubble photo is a close-up of the comet's coma. The field of view is about 9,000 miles (14,000 km) across.

LIFE OF THE SOLAR SYSTEM

As illustrated, right, our Solar System began within a dark cloud of interstellar gas and dust called a molecular cloud (1). Eddies within the cloud initiated its gravitational collapse, transforming it within about two million years into a disk (2). Immediately, the material in the disk started to agglomerate into solid lumps called planetesimals (3), which in turn coalesced into moon-sized building-blocks called planetoids (4). The Solar System was essentially complete after 30 to 50 million years (5), but debris continued to rain down on the planets during the heavy bombardment period, which persisted for well over a billion years (illustrated below). The Solar System has barely changed for billions of years now, but this state of equilibrium will not last forever. About seven billion years from now the Sun, its hydrogen spent, will swell to a red giant, engulfing some of the inner planets (6). Shortly after that it will shed its outer layers, creating a planetary nebula (7). Once that fades, all that will be left is a dim white dwarf and the remaining planets (8).

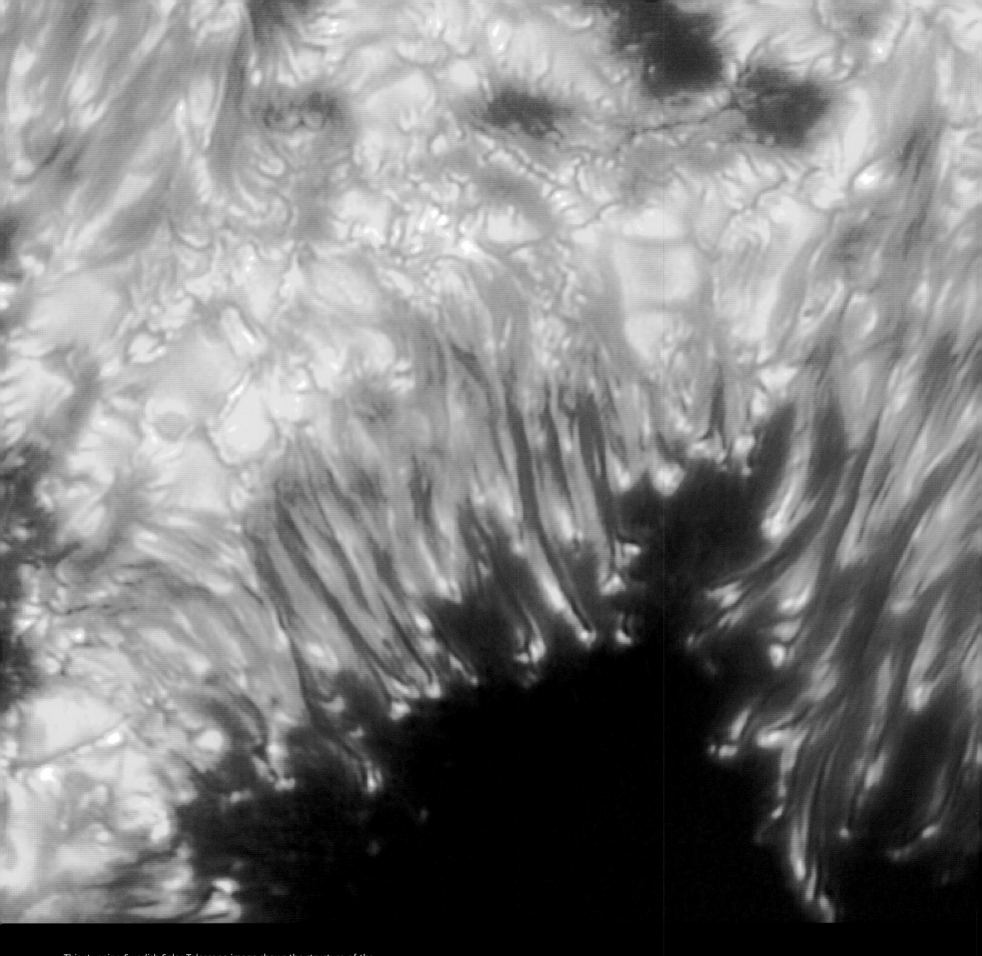

This stunning Swedish Solar Telescope image shows the structure of the
Sun's surface in the vicinity of a sunspot. The dark region is the umbra;
surrounding it is the brighter penumbra; and farther out, there is solar
granulation. The imaged area is about 19,000 miles (30,000 km) across.

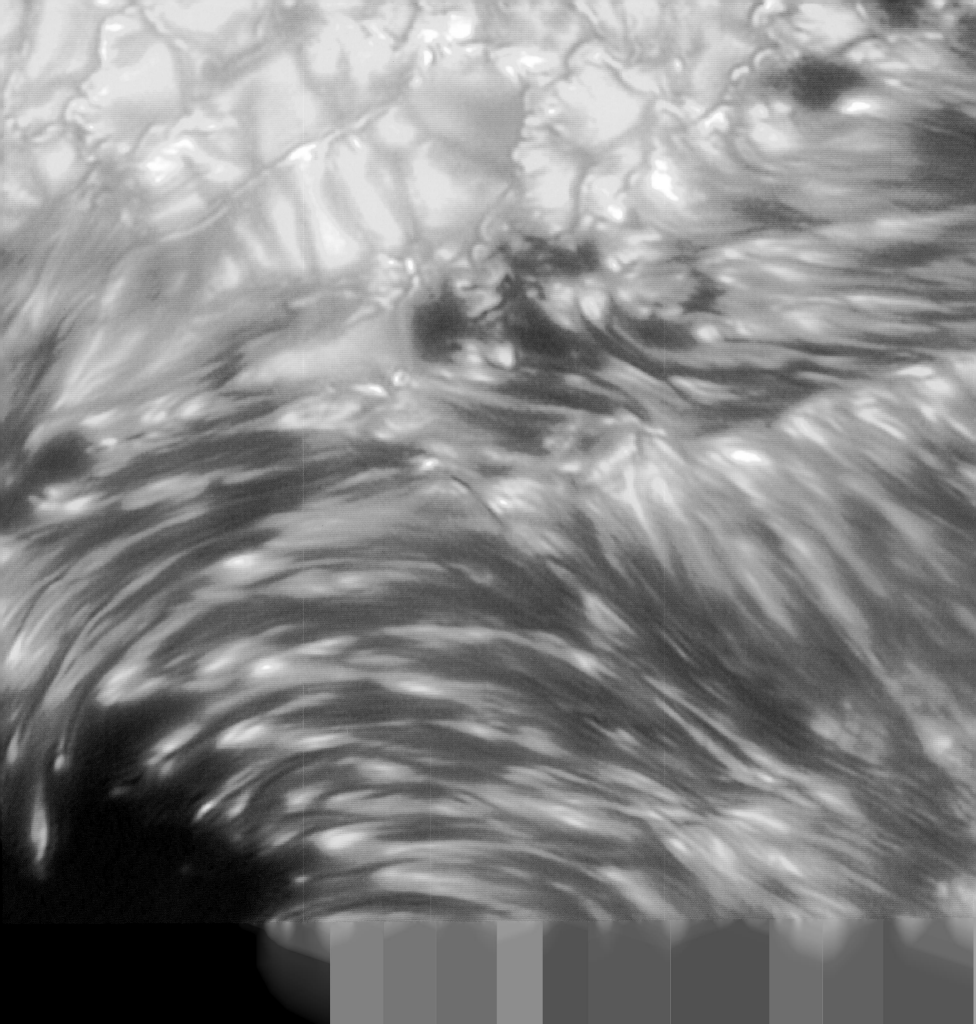

CHARTING THE NEAREST STARS

There is nothing particularly special about our Sun's place in the universe. It is positioned about two-thirds of the way from the center of the Milky Way Galaxy. Here the density of stars is moderate; in a volume of space spanning 24 light-years and centered on the Sun, there are 20 known star systems comprising a total of 30 stars. More than half of them are locked together in pairs or triplets. All of these stars, including the Sun, move around the center of the Milky Way on a vast orbit that takes 250 million years to complete. Most of our stellar neighbors are red dwarfs—about half the size of the Sun and somewhat cooler. The map on the right shows how they are distributed relative to the Solar System. The straight lines are the 24 hours of right ascension while the concentric circles mark distances in light-years. The Oort Cloud is also shown, warped due to the gravitational pull of the galactic core, positioned 26,000 light-years away in the direction indicated by the red lines on the smaller diagram.

OUR CLOSEST STELLAR NEIGHBORS

	SYSTEM	COMPONENT STARS	DIST. (LY)	V MAG	Mv	COLOR	SPECTRUM
1	Single	The Sun	--	−26.8	4.85	Yellow	G2V
2	Triple	Proxima Centauri	4.22	11.10	15.53	Red	M5.5V
		α CENTAURI A	4.39	−0.01	4.38	Yellow	G2V
		α CENTAURI B	4.39	1.35	5.70	Orange	K1V
3	Single	Barnard's Star	5.98	9.54	13.22	Red	M3.8V
4	Single	Wolf 359	7.78	13.46	16.55	Red	M6.5V
5	Single	Lalande 21185	8.26	7.48	10.44	Red	M2V
6	Binary	Sirius A	8.55	−1.46	1.47	Blue-white	A1V
		Sirius B	8.55	8.44	11.34	White	DA2
7	Binary	Luyten 726-8A	8.73	12.56	15.40	Red	M5.5V
		Luyten 726-8B	8.73	12.52	15.85	Red	M5.6V
8	Single	Ross 154	9.45	10.45	13.07	Red	M3.6V
9	Single	Ross 248	10.32	12.27	14.79	Red	M5.5V
10	Single	ε ERIDANI	10.50	3.73	6.19	Orange	K2V
11	Single	Ross 128	10.94	11.11	13.51	Red	M4.5V
12	Triple	Luyten 789-6 A	11.27	13.32	15.64	Red	M5-M7V
		Luyten 789-6 B	11.27	13.27	15.58	Red	
		Luyten 789-6 C	11.27	14.03	16.34	Red	
13	Binary	Procyon A	11.38	0.38	2.66	White	F5IV-V
		Procyon B	11.38	10.70	12.98	White	DA
14	Binary	61 Cygni A	11.40	5.21	7.49	Orange	K5V
		61 Cygni B	11.40	6.03	8.31	Orange	K7 V
15	Binary	Gliese 725 A	11.44	8.90	11.16	Red	M3.0V
		Gliese 725 B	11.44	9.69	11.95	Red	M3.5V
16	Binary	Groombridge 34 A	11.57	8.07	10.32	Red	M2V
		Groombridge 34 B	11.57	11.06	11.06	Red	M3.5V
17	Single	Lacaille 9352	11.73	7.34	9.75	Red	M2V
18	Single	ε INDUS	11.80	4.69	6.89	Orange	K3V
19	Single	τ CETUS	11.81	3.50	5.68	Yellow	G8V
20	Single	G 051-015	11.83	14.81	16.98	Red	M6.5V

Cataloging the nearest stars (left)
This table lists the 20 nearest star systems (30 stars) within a distance of 12 light-years from the Sun. In total there are twelve solitary stars, six binary, and two triple systems. Most are main-sequence stars powered by hydrogen "burning," while two (Sirius B and Procyon B) are very small, dense, dying stars known as white dwarfs. The visual magnitude (V Mag) of each star is listed, as well as the absolute visual magnitude (Mv), which is a measure of a star's intrinsic brightness, irrespective of its distance from Earth. Stellar spectrum is related to a star's color and temperature.

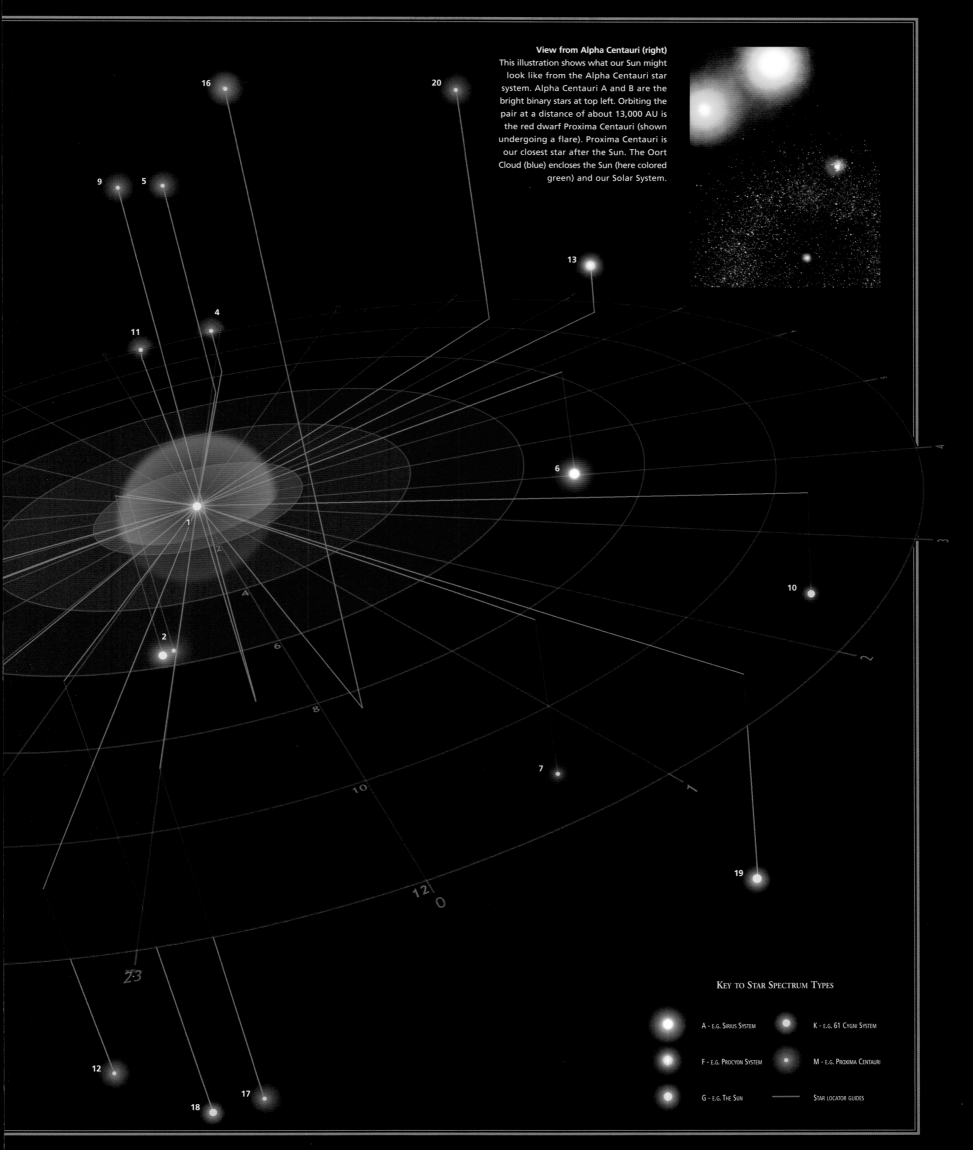

View from Alpha Centauri (right)
This illustration shows what our Sun might look like from the Alpha Centauri star system. Alpha Centauri A and B are the bright binary stars at top left. Orbiting the pair at a distance of about 13,000 AU is the red dwarf Proxima Centauri (shown undergoing a flare). Proxima Centauri is our closest star after the Sun. The Oort Cloud (blue) encloses the Sun (here colored green) and our Solar System.

KEY TO STAR SPECTRUM TYPES

A - E.G. SIRIUS SYSTEM

K - E.G. 61 CYGNI SYSTEM

F - E.G. PROCYON SYSTEM

M - E.G. PROXIMA CENTAURI

G - E.G. THE SUN

STAR LOCATOR GUIDES

THE SUN
SURFACE FEATURES

Strictly speaking the Sun does not have a surface, for it is a sphere
of ionized gas. Still, there does appear to be a sharp "edge,"
which astronomers refer to as the photosphere—a word that
means literally "sphere of light." When Italian astronomer
Galileo Galilei (1564–1642) first observed the photosphere,
projected through his telescope, he was dismayed to find
that it was not the pure and unblemished disk he expected.
Aside from the spots he saw, we now know that the Sun's
photosphere and lower atmosphere (known as the chromosphere
or "sphere of color") show remarkable details, including such
phenomena as granulation, faculae, and jet-like spicules, all
of which combine to give the Sun's surface its observed texture.

Sunspots and the solar cycle

Sunspots are regions where the Sun's magnetic field is concentrated, inhibiting the flow
of energy and rendering the surface somewhat cooler and therefore darker. At the center
of a typical spot is the darkest region, the umbra, which is around 2,900°F (1,600°C)
cooler than the rest of the photosphere. Meanwhile, in the more extensive penumbra,
the temperature is around 2,000°F (1,100°C) hotter than in the umbra, but still cooler
than the photosphere. Sunspot numbers are now known to vary according to a cycle that
takes about eleven years to complete. At the minimum of the cycle there may be few, if
any, spots on the Sun, but the number can increase to more than 100, with several large
spot groups, at solar maximum.

Solar cycle (above)
This sequence clearly shows the evolution of a solar cycle from 1991 (left foreground), when
the Sun was at the peak of its cycle, through to 1999 (right foreground) a year or so before
the next solar maximum. As expected, the mid-1990s were a quiet period for solar activity.
The ten images were captured by the Japanese Yohkoh satellite at regular intervals using
an X-ray telescope. The bright regions are highly magnetic.

Sunspot cross-section (above)
Sunspots are not flat, but are rather
depressions, shaped somewhat like
saucers. The slightly brighter penumbra
fibrils slope downward where they
merge with the central dark region,
the umbra. These depressions can
be up to 50,000 miles (80,500 km) in
diameter. They usually appear in pairs
or groups of opposite polarity moving
in unison across the Sun's surface,
linked by magnetic field lines.

1   2   3

Origins of the solar cycle (left)
At the beginning of a solar cycle
the Sun's internal magnetic field
is aligned from pole to pole (1).
However, because the Sun rotates
differentially, the magnetic field
at the equator rotates faster
than at the poles (2). Eventually
the magnetic field lines become
twisted, gain bouyancy, and
burst out of the surface to create
sunspots, loops, and flares (3).

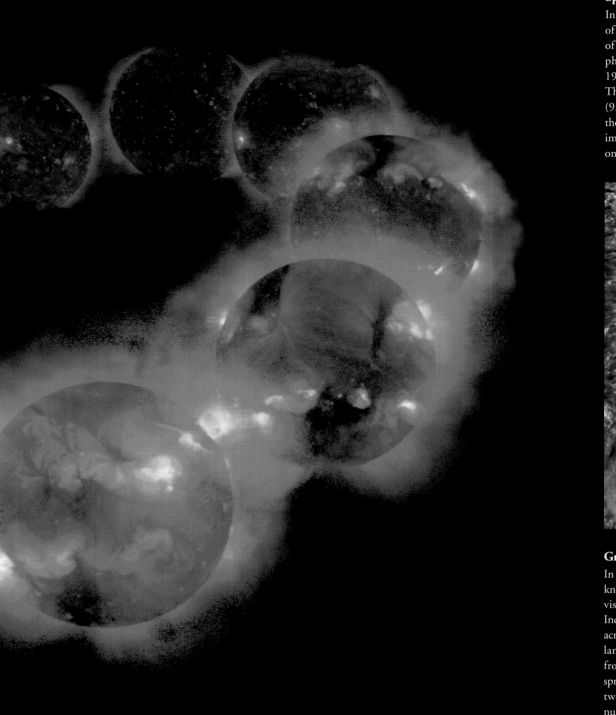

Spicules

In places, the Sun's surface has the appearance of a field of swaying grass. This effect is caused by spicules—jets of gas, generally in groups, that move upward from the photosphere into the lower chromosphere at about 19 miles per second (30 km/s) every five minutes or so. They can reach a maximum height of around 5,600 miles (9,000 km), fading after about fifteen minutes, and are thought to be formed by sound waves. The false-color image below was taken by the Swedish Solar Telescope on the island of La Palma.

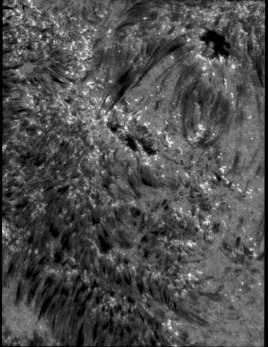

Granules and faculae

In close-up, the face of the Sun has a grainy appearance known fittingly as solar granulation. This effect is clearly visible in the Swedish Solar Telescope image below. Individual grains are typically about 600 miles (1,000 km) across, and are bounded by cooler, darker, "intergranular lanes." Solar granulation is the result of hot gas rising from the interior in giant convection cells and then spreading out and dispersing. Individual grains last around twenty minutes. Also visible in this photograph are numerous faculae—comparatively small bright patches that generally appear near sunspots and persist for weeks or months after the spots themselves have vanished.

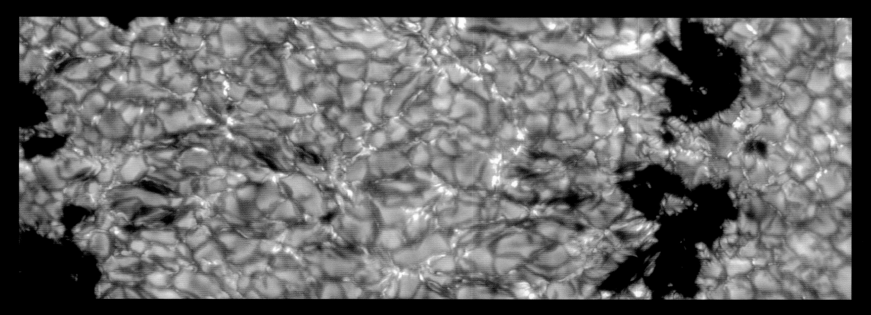

THE SUN: ATMOSPHERE

The Sun is a highly active object. Although it is stable as stars go, showing relatively little variability in its energy output, it is nevertheless prone to frequent eruptions of activity that can be witnessed in the turbulent solar atmosphere. The Sun's atmosphere is divided into two regions of different temperature and density. The chromosphere is the bottom layer, reaching 5,600 miles (9,000 km) above the photosphere, home to the jets of gas known as spicules. Above the chromosphere is the much more extensive outer atmosphere, the corona, a sparse veil of plasma with searing temperatures reaching 3,600,000°F (2,000,000°C). The corona is the stage upon which much violent activity is played out—in the form of flares, prominences, and Coronal Mass Ejections. The corona merges into the solar wind—the outflow of gas and particles from the Sun reaching to the outer edge of the Solar System.

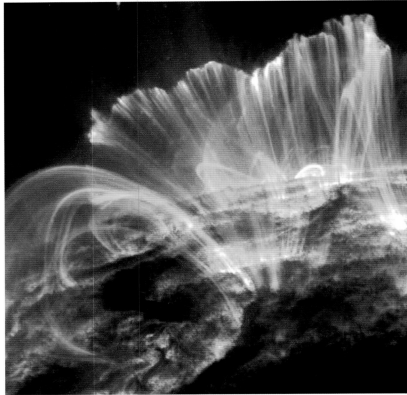

Coronal loops (above)
This TRACE (Transition Region and Coronal Explorer) image shows coronal loops—streamers of gas entrained in the solar magnetic field and held high above the photosphere.

Flaring up (left)
At left is an eight-hour photographic sequence showing a solar flare eruption. Some solar flares can extend well into the Sun's corona.

Solar prominence (below)
This SOHO (Solar and Heliospheric Observatory) satellite image of a huge solar prominence shows a cloud of charged gas erupting from the Sun into space. The false-color image was recorded in the ultraviolet region of the electromagnetic spectrum, and indicated a temperature within the prominence of around 100,000°F (60,000°C), cool, relative to the surrounding corona.

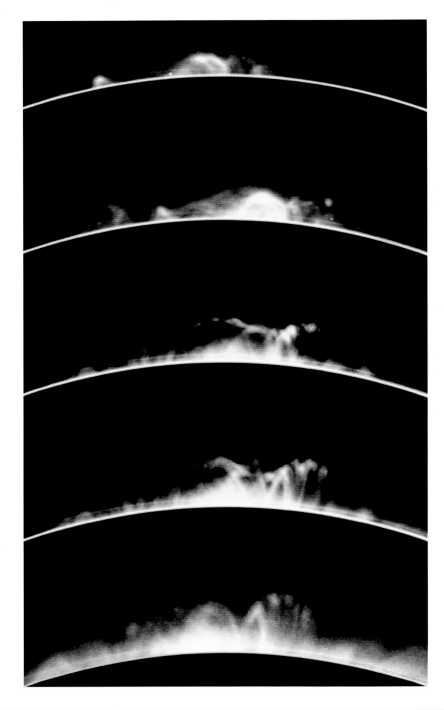

Flares, prominences, and loops

Flares, prominences, and coronal loops are all manifestations of our star's magnetic activity. Solar flares are vast eruptions of energy arising in an "active region" of the Sun, often associated with a sunspot group, typically lasting an hour. They emit radiation over a wide range of frequencies and can expel solar ions at speeds up to 70 percent that of light. Prominences are dense, loop-like structures embedded within but much cooler than the corona. When seen against the bright solar disk they appear as dark filaments. Coronal loops are ribbons of gas, again in the corona, that join two active regions on the solar surface, following magnetic field line paths.

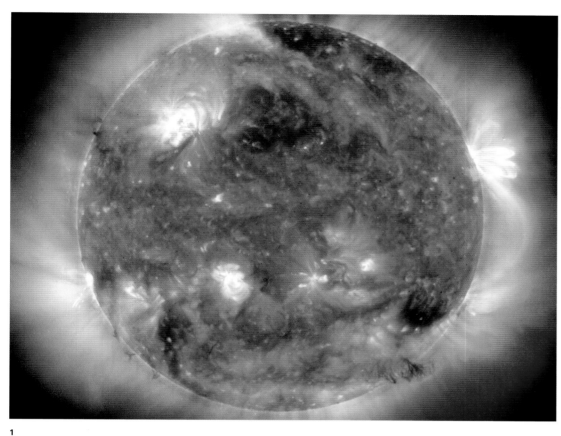

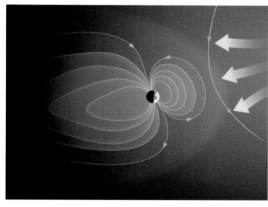

1

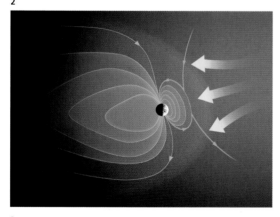

2

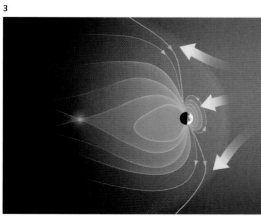

3

Coronal Mass Ejections

Coronal Mass Ejections (CMEs) involve the sudden expulsion of vast bubbles of solar material from the corona over a period of several hours. They are related to flares, but their connection is not well understood. During a CME, as much as 100 billion metric tons of plasma is ejected at speeds ranging from 6 to over 600 miles per second (10–1,000 km/s), much slower than during a flare but carrying significant momentum because of the increased mass. The energy of a powerful CME may approach that of a flare, and both events can often cause serious disruptions to communications satellites in orbit around Earth.

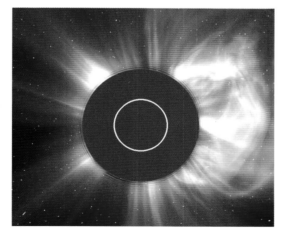

Solar eruption (above)
A Coronal Mass Ejection, a vast bubble of charged solar particles disgorged from the Sun's atmosphere, heads deeps into space in this image captured by the SOHO spacecraft. The white circle indicates the size and position of the Sun.

Earth strike (left)
As it approaches Earth (1), a Coronal Mass Ejection (CME) compresses our protective magnetic field (2), thus exposing satellites to dangerous solar radiation. If the CME has a magnetic field orientation of opposite polarity to that of our planet, it can cause magnetic field lines on the dark side of Earth to cross, which drives vast currents into our planet's atmosphere (3) to create even further havoc.

Corona

The corona is the outermost region of the Sun's atmosphere, extending several solar radii into space. Normally it cannot be seen because it is swamped by the much brighter disk of the Sun. However, the corona becomes visible during times of solar eclipse, when its structure of loops and prominences is revealed. The image on the left shows the corona as seen in ultraviolet light. The false colors indicate temperatures of 1,800,000°F (1,000,000°C) (blue); 2,700,000°F (1,500,000°C) (green); and 3,600,000°F (2,000,000°C) (red)—far hotter than is found in the chromosphere or photosphere.

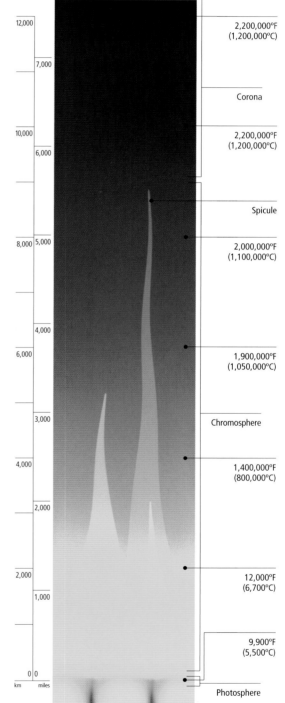

Chromosphere

The chromosphere is the lower atmosphere of the Sun. It is sandwiched between the photosphere and the corona and is about 5,600 miles (9,000 km) in depth. The temperature in the lower chromosphere is not much different to that in the photosphere, but above 1,500 miles (2,500 km) it rises abruptly, climbing to corona-like temperatures within a few thousand miles.

DISCOVERING THE SUN

The Sun is such a part of our daily lives that we can easily forget how utterly dependent we are on it. Our ancestors certainly recognized its importance, many cultures going to great lengths to study the Sun's movement through the year. The modern era of solar science began when the likes of Galileo, Kepler, and Copernicus helped establish that it was the Sun, not Earth, that lies at the center of the Solar System. It is the Sun's dazzling light that gives us life, but it has been perhaps the greatest obstacle to solar observation. However, unlike our forebears, we are no longer hindered by rudimentary instruments. Today's solar astronomer studies the Sun's light and magnetic field with observatories orbiting in space, along with unique solar tower telescopes raised above the turbulent air found at ground level.

Atmosphere revealed (below)
Until the development of the coronagraph, the Sun's active two-component atmosphere (chromosphere and corona) could be observed only during a total solar eclipse, when the bright solar disk is temporarily blocked by the Moon. Below is an eclipse from August 1999.

Shaft of gold (right)
On certain days of the year, as the Sun passes overhead, a vertical finger of sunlight penetrates a man-made shaft in the roof of this cave, known as the Solar Observatory of Xochicalco, Mexico. It was constructed sometime between AD 700 and 1000.

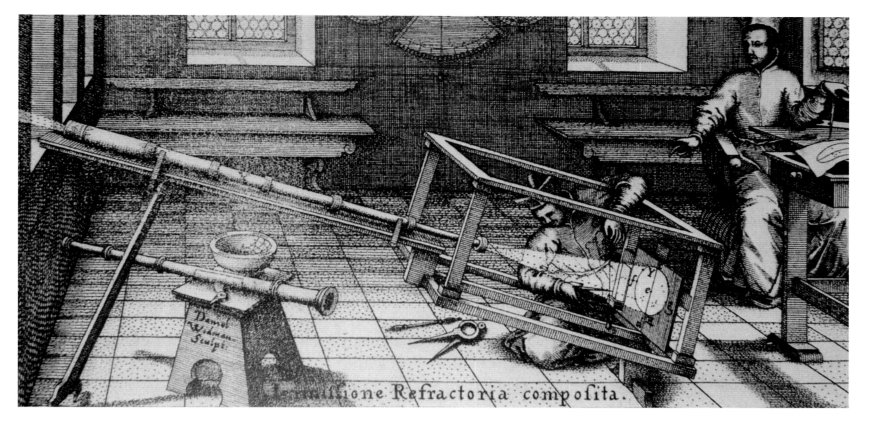

Studying sunspots (above)

Although the Italian astronomer Galileo Galilei (1564–1642) made the first telescopic observations of sunspots in 1611, two Germans —Christoph Scheiner (1575–1650) and Johannes Fabricius (1587–1615)—began their studies that same year. This sketch shows Scheiner and an assistant mapping the solar disk in 1611. Scheiner initially thought the spots were dark objects in transit across the Sun.

Solar wind echoes (below)

Spectacular polar aurorae, like this one below, along with comet tails, which always point away from the Sun, are the most visible manifestations of the solar wind. However, it was not until the 1950s that the wind's very existence was first proposed by the American astrophysicist Eugene Parker (born 1927). His theories were confirmed through direct satellite observations a decade later.

Sampling the Sun (left)

Launched in 2001, NASA's Genesis mission had a bold objective—to capture particles from the solar wind blustering out from the Sun, and to return them safely to Earth for study. Despite a high-speed crash landing in the Utah desert on its return to Earth in 2004, mission scientists were able to retrieve some of its precious cargo stored on ultra-pure wafers of silicon, gold, and sapphire.

Viewing the corona (left)

The Yohkoh satellite was a cooperative Japanese, United States, and United Kingdom solar observatory mission. Launched in 1991, Yohkoh's objective was to study the Sun's corona and solar flares. It functioned for more than ten years and greatly improved our understanding of solar activity.

SOHO observatory (right)

The joint ESA–NASA solar observatory called SOHO (Solar and Heliospheric Observatory) was launched in December 1995 to study the Sun at a distance of 930,000 miles (1.5 million km) from Earth, where it has an uninterrupted view of our local star.

Measuring Distances to the Stars

Until about 500 years ago, it was generally assumed the stars were fixed to a giant "celestial sphere," all at the same distance from Earth, which lay at the sphere's center. Beginning with the revolutionary theories of Nicolas Copernicus in the 16th century, we came in stages to understand, first, that it was Earth that revolved around the Sun, and that the Sun itself was but one of countless stars scattered through space at distances much greater than the human mind can truly comprehend. Still, that does not mean stellar distances are unknown. In fact, we know the distances to the Sun and the nearest stars to high precision, although measuring the distance to more distant stars is a difficult and imprecise science.

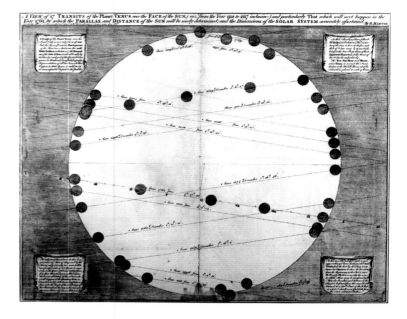

Charting the transits of Venus (above)
The transits of Venus across the Sun were of particular interest to the great maritime powers of the 18th century because an accurate measurement of the astronomical unit meant more accurate navigation for their fleets. This print, published in London in 1757, shows the paths of seventeen transits of Venus expected from the year 918 to 2117.

The "black drop effect" (above)
Due to Earth's turbulent atmosphere, Venus's edge, as it transits the Sun, appears stretched into a "black drop." This effect, illustrated here during the 1761 Venus transit, means that precise timings critical for this method of measurement are almost impossible to gauge.

Transit of Venus (below)
During a transit of Venus, illustrated below, the planet's exact position relative to the solar disk varies depending on the location of the observer on Earth, because of the effects of parallax. Critical events during the transit—such as the point when Venus is first viewed touching the Sun—from two different latitudes, are precisely timed. By comparing these measurements it is possible to derive the distance to Venus by triangulation. Once this distance is accurately calculated, an estimate of the astronomical unit, the distance between Earth and the Sun, and thus other distances within the Solar System can be determined.

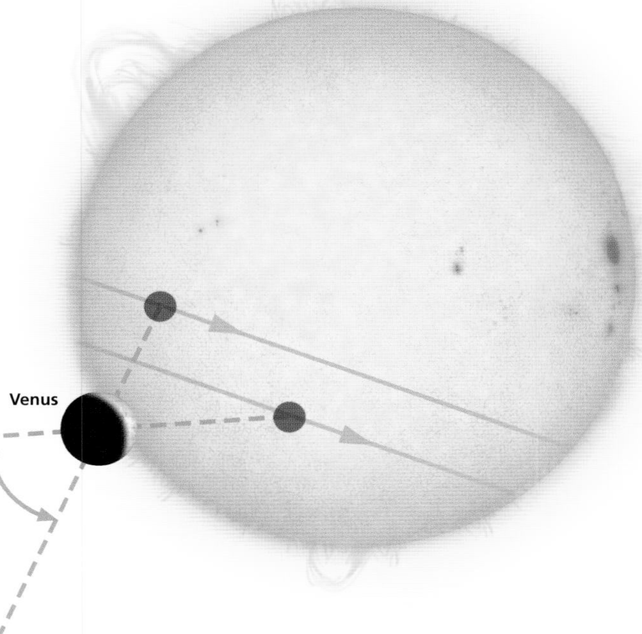

Venus

Angle required
for triangulation

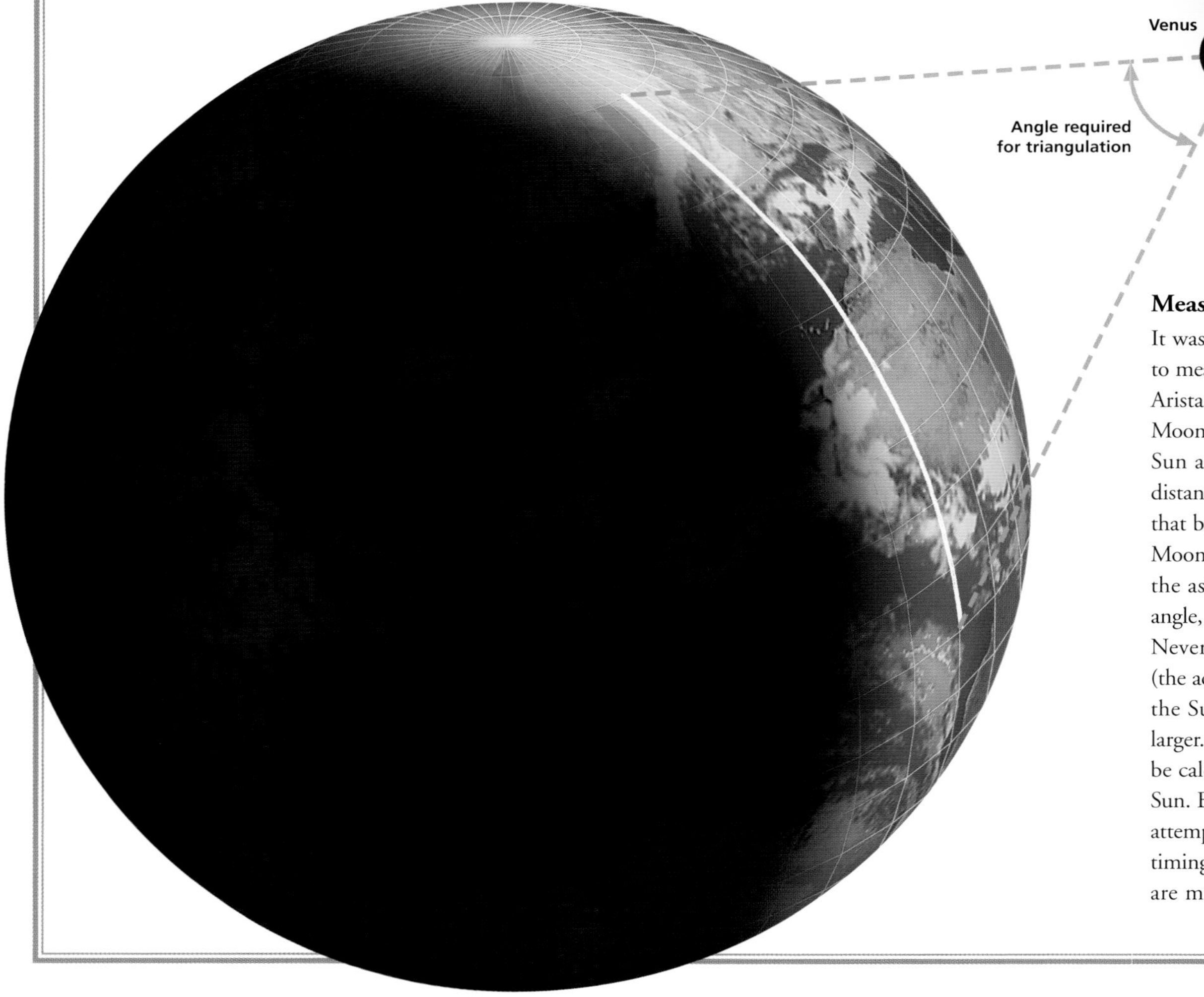

Measuring the astronomical unit

It was the ancient Greeks who made the first systematic attempts to measure the distance to the Sun (the astronomical unit or AU). Aristarchus of Samos (c. 320–250 BC) understood that when the Moon is at quarter phase, it forms a right-angle triangle with the Sun and Earth. Having previously reckoned the Earth–Moon distance from observations of a lunar eclipse, Aristarchus knew that by measuring the angle in the sky between the Sun and the Moon it was possible, using simple trigonometry, to estimate the astronomical unit. Sadly, a precise measurement of this angle, critical to the experiment, was beyond Greek technology. Nevertheless, Aristarchus's value of 20 Earth–Moon distances (the actual value is 389 Earth–Moon distances) established that the Sun was much farther than the Moon and substantially larger. By the 17th century, it was realized that the AU could be calculated by close observation of Venus's transit across the Sun. English astronomer Jeremiah Horrocks (c. 1618–41) first attempted this in 1639, but the "black drop effect" made precise timings very difficult. Nowadays, distances in the Solar System are measured routinely using satellite telemetry and radar.

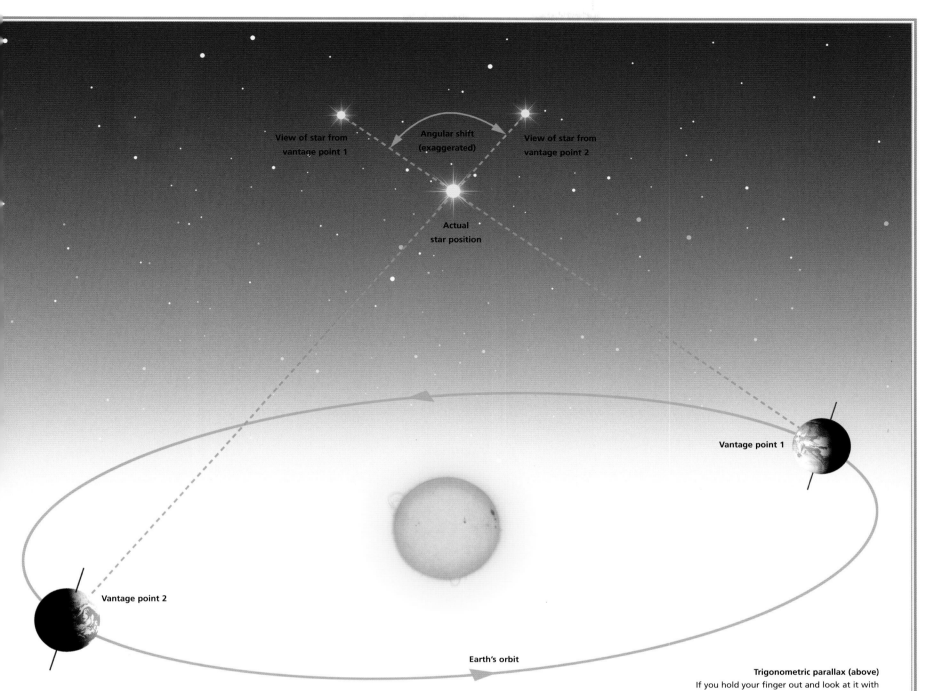

View of star from vantage point 1

Angular shift (exaggerated)

View of star from vantage point 2

Actual star position

Vantage point 1

Vantage point 2

Earth's orbit

Cataloging the stars (left)

The European spacecraft Hipparcos (illustrated left) was launched in 1989. Named after the Greek philosopher Hipparchus of Nicea, who first cataloged the stars, it measured, using trigonometric parallax, the distances to some 100,000 stars far more accurately than had been done before. The GAIA mission, due for launch in 2010, will provide even more precision and extend the range of parallax measurements 100 times farther than Hipparcos.

Trigonometric parallax (above)

If you hold your finger out and look at it with one eye closed and then the other, you will notice that it shifts relative to objects in the background. This effect, parallax, occurs because each eye observes your finger from a slightly different vantage point. Similarly, if you note the position of a nearby star relative to its more distant neighbors, then observe it again six months later when Earth is on the opposite side of its orbit, the star too will appear to shift by a tiny amount. If the exact angular shift can be measured, an accurate estimate of the star's distance using trigonometry can be made because the Earth–Sun distance is known to high precision.

Measuring the distance to the stars

For stars within a few hundred light-years, distances can be measured using trigonometric parallax—the apparent shifting of a nearby star relative to more distant stars when it is seen from different vantage points in Earth's orbit around the Sun. Friedrich Wilhelm Bessel (1784–1846) was the first to use this method to determine the distance to a star, 61 Cygni, in 1838. His calculation was within a few percent of the modern estimate. For more remote stars, though, astronomers rely on a variety of "standard candles"—stars of known brightness. Obviously the farther away a star is, the fainter it appears. So if you know how bright that star really is, its luminosity, you can compare this with its actual brightness in the sky and estimate how far it must be. People do the same thing everyday when they judge the distance to a car by the brightness of its headlights. The most important "standard candles" are the Cepheid variables—stars that vary their brightness with a period precisely related to their luminosity. By measuring the period, the star's luminosity can be determined.

CLASSIFYING STARS

Astronomers classify the stars according to their temperature and luminosity. The classification system has two main elements: the spectral type and the luminosity class. The spectral type is a letter followed by a number, indicating the star's surface temperature and hence its color. The hottest stars, blue-white in color, are type O. After that, getting progressively cooler, are types B, A, F, G, K, and M, the last four being quite cool. Three further types, R, N, and S, are similar to K- and M-type stars but have slightly different compositions. The numbers—which run from 0 (hottest) to 9 (coolest)—represent ten subclasses of the main seven groups. The luminosity class, meanwhile, is indicated by a roman numeral from I to V. Class I stars, the supergiants, are the most luminous; class II stars are called bright giants; class III stars are giants; class IV stars are subgiants; and class V, dwarfs. The illustration at right compares the relative sizes of six known stars of various spectral classification. Our nearest stars are predominantly M-type stars, of luminosity class V.

Proxima Centauri (right)
Proxima is of spectral type M5.5V, a red dwarf, the most common variety of star in the universe. Red dwarfs are small and faint, and Proxima is no exception. It is 20,000 times dimmer than the Sun, one-seventh its size, and requires a telescope to see it—despite being the closest known star to the Solar System, 4.22 light-years away.

Sirius B (right)
Sirius B, the binary partner to Sirius A, is a white dwarf, spectral class dA2, the dead core of a once-larger star. It is only 0.8 percent the diameter of the Sun, smaller even than Earth. Curiously, the more massive a white dwarf, the smaller it is, due to the crushing effects of higher gravity.

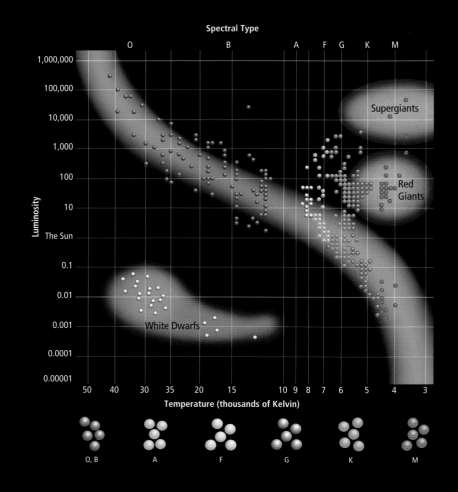

Hertzsprung-Russell diagram

When stars are plotted with their color or temperature against their luminosity—as in a Hertzsprung-Russell diagram (above)—a pattern emerges. Extending from the top left (hot and luminous) to the bottom right (cool and dim) is a curved line known as the main sequence, on which most stars lie. Stars here are known as dwarfs (luminosity class V), all shining by converting hydrogen into helium in their cores. As stars evolve, they grow cooler, moving to the right where the giants and supergiants are found. White dwarfs, the exposed cores of once Sun-like stars, are located at bottom left.

Rigel (right)
Rigel is a bright blue supergiant in Orion, of spectral type B8I. Despite being 770 light-years away, it is so luminous—40,000 times brighter than the Sun and 50 times its size—that it is the seventh brightest star in our skies. Rigel is dwarfed by the largest stars of all, red supergiants such as Antares in Scorpius, which is at least 400 times the size of the Sun.

Arcturus (far right)
This star, 37 light-years away in Boötes, is the brightest north of the celestial equator and fourth most conspicuous in the entire sky. Arcturus is an orange giant, spectral type K1.5III, about 2,700°F (1,500°C) cooler than the Sun but 25 times its size and, as a result, far more luminous.

The Sun (below and left)
The Sun is a mid-sized, yellow dwarf, spectral class G2V, with a surface temperature of about 9,900°F (5,500°C).

Sirius A (below)
Sirius, the brightest star in the sky as seen from Earth, is actually a binary. The brighter and larger of the pair, known as Sirius A, is an A1V dwarf star, meaning it is blue-white with a surface temperature of about 18,000°F (10,000°C). It is about 1.7 times the size of the Sun.

BINARY AND MULTIPLE STAR SYSTEMS

Solitary stars like the Sun are in a minority. Something like 60 percent of all stars are locked up in binary or higher-order systems, in which two or more members travel around a common center of mass. Binaries occur most frequently, triples slightly less commonly, and so on. Many well-known stars are actually binary or multiple systems, such as Alpha Centauri, Procyon, and Sirius, which are all nearby stars, and the six-star extraordinaire Castor, 52 light-years away in the constellation Gemini. Multiple star systems may form when formerly single stars come together. But as a rule, stars are at such distances from each other that such chance encounters very rarely occur. The vast majority of multiple stars are simply born that way.

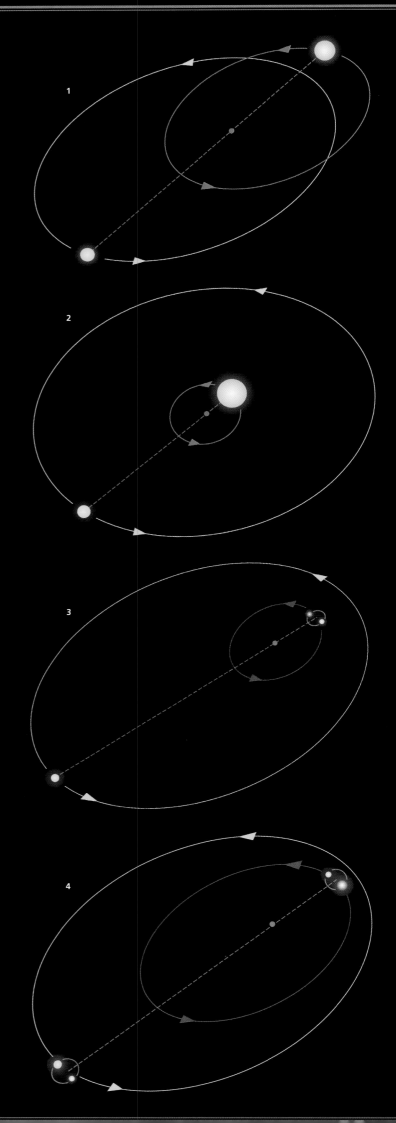

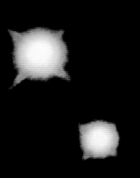

Two nearby binaries (above and left)
The photo above shows a close-up view of the sky's brightest star, Sirius—actually a binary consisting of a blue-white star and a much smaller, denser star called a white dwarf. The false-color image was obtained using the Chandra X-ray telescope. To the left are two stars from the Alpha Centauri system, the closest star system to the Sun. The two stars, Alpha Centauri A and B, are of similar classification to the Sun, and orbit each other once every 80 years. Given that the third star in this system, Proxima Centauri, orbits this pair only once every 0.5 to 2 million years, it is possible that it is not bound to this pair at all.

The dynamics of binary and multiple systems

The series of diagrams at right illustrate the orbital dynamics of binary and multiple systems. In a binary system each star moves in an elliptical path around the barycenter (the green dot), the balance point between them. They move such that the line between them always passes through this point, even though their distance from each other varies periodically (1). Binaries can also have more circular orbits (2). Second from the bottom is a hierarchical triple (3), where an outer star (yellow) moves around an inner pair as if they were a single star. The inner pair move in a tighter path around each other. At the bottom is a quadruple system (4)—two pairs of stars, each pair orbiting the other while the pairs in turn revolve around their own barycenter.

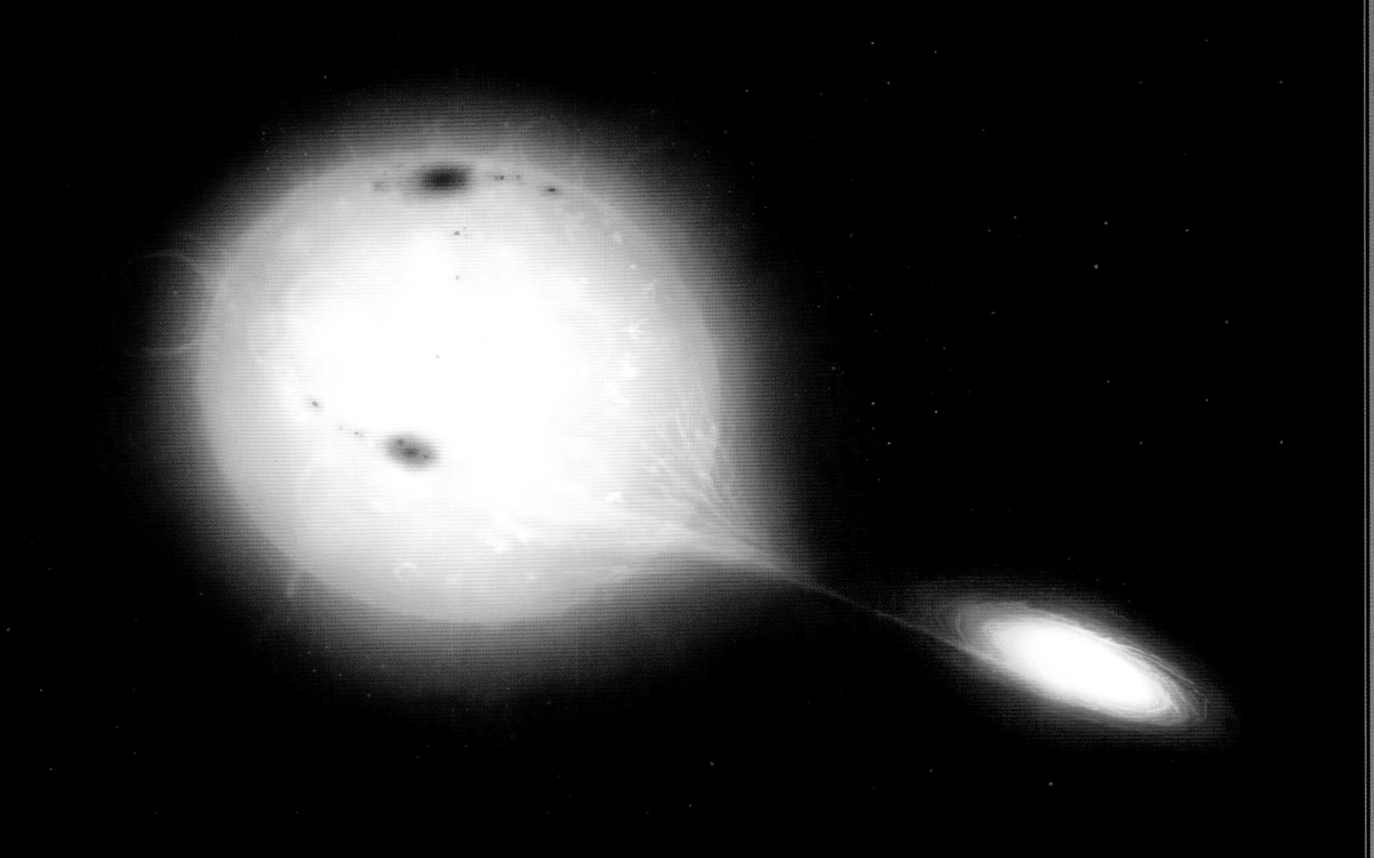

Proxima Centauri (above)
Proxima Centauri is a red dwarf
much fainter than the Sun and
only a fraction of its size. This
artist's impression shows Proxima
Centauri in the foreground with
a hypothetical planet in close
attendance. Off to the left are
Alpha Centauri A and B, a close
binary around which Proxima
Centauri may be in orbit.

Interacting binary (right)
In some binary systems the
individual components are
so close together that they
actually interact. Cataclysmic
variables, such as the one
shown here, are an example of
binary interaction. The larger
star is a red dwarf while, its
partner is a very dense white
dwarf, its gravity stretching its
partner into an egg shape. The
white dwarf steals matter from
its companion, forming a
flattened disk around itself
known as an accretion disk.

New Planetary Systems

A decade ago, one of the great questions of astronomy, "Are there planets beyond the Solar System?" was answered. Not only is the answer in the affirmative, but the rate at which planets continue to be found is accelerating as technology improves. Planets around Sun-like stars now appear to be the norm, not the exception. Since 1995, astronomers have uncovered well over a hundred of these "extrasolar" planetary systems. With several stars harboring more than one planet, the total number of extrasolar worlds is now approaching 200. The questions that follow now are whether these systems are typical, and do any harbor life. These questions so far remain unanswered.

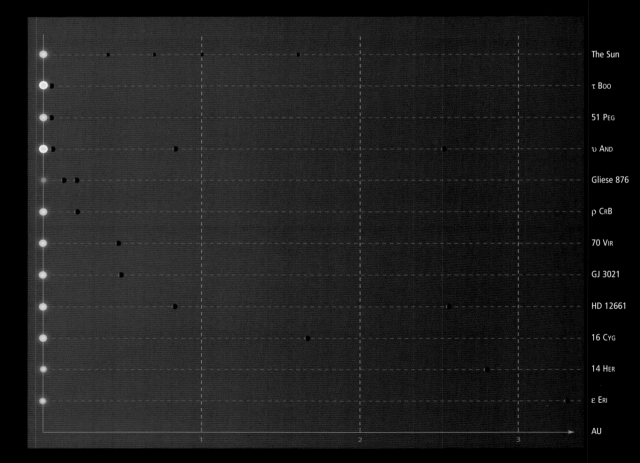

The Sun

τ Boo

51 Peg

υ And

Gliese 876

ρ CrB

70 Vir

GJ 3021

HD 12661

16 Cyg

14 Her

ε Eri

AU

Extrasolar planet (above left)
This European Southern Observatory photograph from 2004 was the first confirmed image of an extrasolar planet. The planet (red) is orbiting a very dim failed star, a brown dwarf named 2M1207 (which appears blue in this infrared photo). The planet (five times the mass of Jupiter) is almost twice as far from its parent as Neptune is from the Sun.

Alien asteroids (above)
Our Solar System is not the only one with a belt of asteroids. The Spitzer Space Telescope has found evidence of a similar but much more massive belt around a star called HD 69830, 41 light-years away in Puppis. This artist's impression shows the belt as it might be seen from the vicinity of a planet outside the belt.

Extrasolar systems (left)
This diagram compares the Solar System (top) with eleven extrasolar planetary systems, to a distance of 3.3 astronomical units (AU) in each system. Almost all known exoplanets are giants, somewhat like Jupiter. Surprisingly, while in our Solar System such planets orbit beyond 5 AU, in these new systems the giants are in tight orbits—often far closer to their star even than Mercury is to the Sun. However, the apparent lack of smaller worlds, or of larger worlds in distant orbits, could be deceptive. We may simply have not found these planets yet, because the current detection methods are sensitive only to massive planets in close orbits.

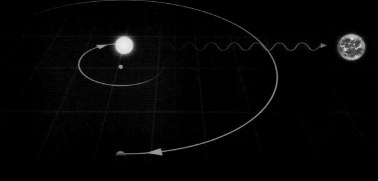

Planet hunting

Astronomers find planets not directly but by the effects they have on their parent stars. As the planet and star orbit their common center of mass (shown as a green dot in the illustrations above and below), the planet moves in a wide ellipse while the star executes a much smaller motion, exaggerated here. If the orbital plane of the planetary system is edge-on to Earth, then the planet will be moving away from us while its star is approaching. Light from this star will be blueshifted to shorter wavelengths (above). Half an orbit later, when the star is moving away, its light will be redshifted (below). This variation between red- and blueshifted states enables the presence of a planet to be inferred.

The search for Earth-like worlds

NASA's Terrestrial Planet Finder (TPF) and ESA's Darwin are two proposed missions to look for extrasolar planets. The aims of these missions (which may become a single collaborative project) are indeed bold: not only to locate planets no larger than Earth, but to analyze their atmospheres for signs of gases that might indicate life. The Darwin mission proposes a flotilla of perhaps six satellite telescopes, each at least 5 feet (1.5 m) across, in communication with a central hub and a satellite, as illustrated above. Using a technique known as interferometry, the signals from the telescopes can be combined to produce a single, sharp image with unprecedented resolution. It will also be possible using this method to cancel out the glare of the star, revealing the dim glow from any planets that might be orbiting it. However, the technology for all this is a little way off: neither Darwin or TPF will launch before 2015 at the earliest.

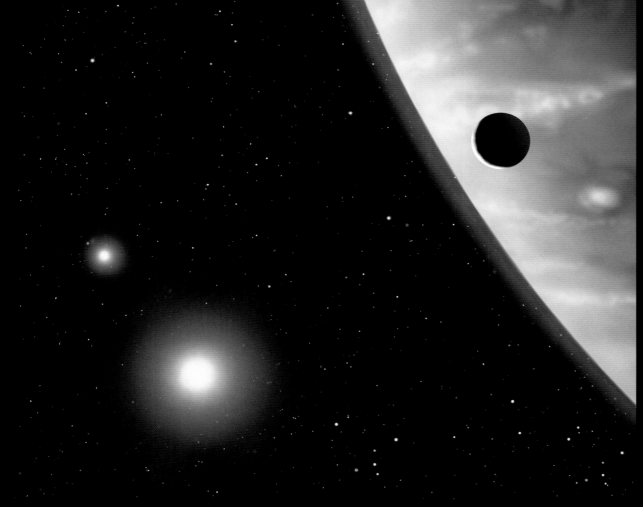

Extrasolar giant (left)

16 Cygni B is an orange star somewhat like the Sun. It was one of the first stars known to harbor an extrasolar planet. The planet, which is about 1.5 times the mass of Jupiter, swings around 16 Cygni B in 798.9 days at a distance of just 1.67 AU. The planet is depicted as a blue gas giant in this artist's interpretation, which also shows a purely speculative moon in close attendance. The parent star, 16 Cygni B (lower left), is actually part of a binary system. Its distant partner (more than 700 AU away) is shown above it and to the left.

Worlds in creation (below)

Astronomers are discovering planets not only around other stars but planetary systems in the making. This illustration is of a disk of dust surrounding a surprisingly low-mass brown dwarf star discovered using the Spitzer Space Telescope. There is probably enough mass in the disk to form one gas giant and a few Earth-sized rocky planets.

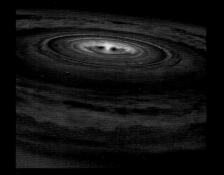

DISCOVERING THE STARS

Our knowledge of the stars has improved dramatically since the Italian philosopher Giordano Bruno (1548–1600) was burnt at the stake for suggesting (among other heresies) that the Sun was simply a nearby star. However, it was not until the 19th century, with the development of techniques such as spectroscopy and the use of parallax in measuring stellar distances, that this proposition was confirmed. Because the Sun is so nearby, cosmically speaking, we have been able to learn a great deal about the stars simply by studying our own at close quarter. And by looking to the stars, each at a different stage in its evolution, astronomers have been able to piece together their life cycles, and hence the eventual fate of the Sun and the Solar System. Now we know what the stars are made of, how hot they are, and how they move through space. But as the recent discoveries of brown dwarf stars and extrasolar planets indicate, there are still many stellar mysteries remaining.

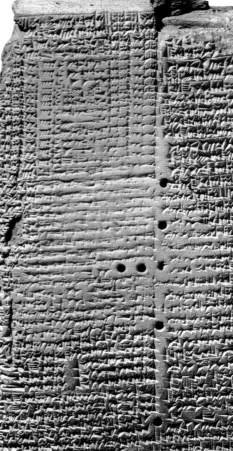

Egyptian astronomy (below)
Astronomy was important to the ancient Egyptians, but it was more of a religion than a science. The constellation Orion, for example, represented Osiris, the god of the dead. This image from a mummy case depicts the deity Shu (god of the atmosphere) separating his daughter Nuit (goddess of the sky) from Earth.

Babylonian astronomy (right)
This Babylonian tablet, dating from around 500 BC, is covered with inscriptions describing the motions of the stars and planets. The Babylonians were keen astronomers and astrologers who learned how to predict eclipses; invented the angular degree, still used to measure angular distances; and devised an efficient form of numerical notation.

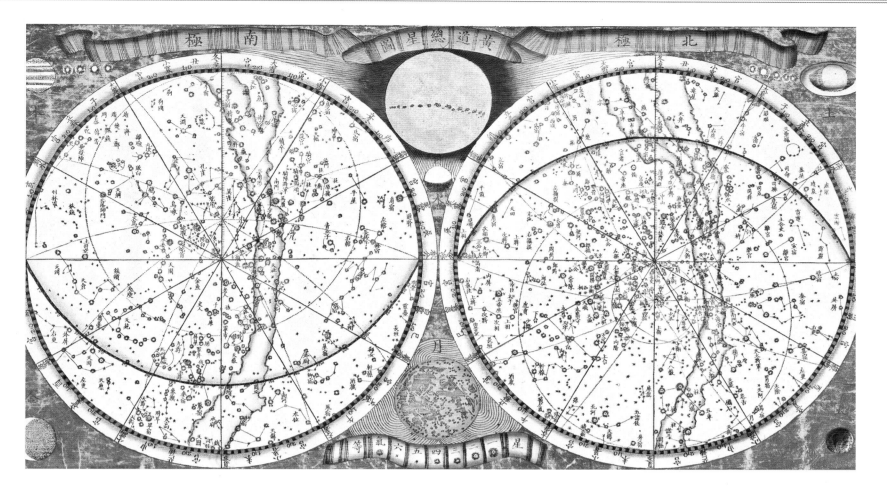

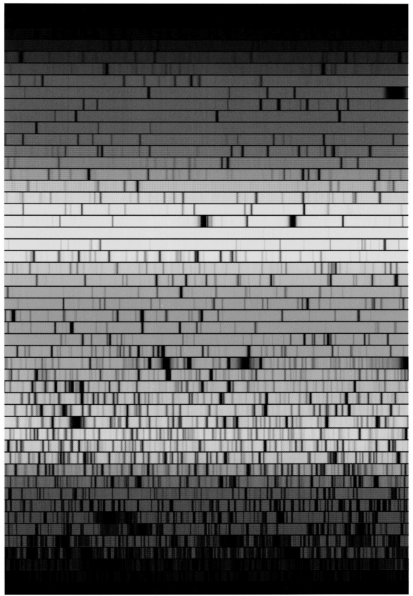

Spectroscopy

Astronomy took a great leap forward in the 1860s with the development of spectroscopy. By passing starlight through a kind of grid known as a grating, a spectrum is revealed—a map showing the intensity of the light as a function of wavelength. Curiously, as well as revealing a rainbow of light, dark lines are also present, as seen in this image of the spectrum of Arcturus at left. Each set of dark lines uniquely identifies an atomic species: hydrogen lines appear at certain wavelengths, helium lines at a different set, and so on. So spectroscopy provides a means to find out what stars (and other objects) are actually made of. It can also reveal their speed relative to the Solar System.

Doppler tomography (below)

Some stars have huge spots covering vast areas on their surface. Since the 1980s, astronomers have indirectly imaged the surfaces of these stars using a technique known as Doppler tomography, similar in some ways to the various medical imaging techniques doctors use to see inside the body.

Chinese celestial spheres (above)

The Chinese have long been keen astronomers and their records go back centuries. There are clues that they may have discovered sunspots long before the currently accepted date of 1611, and their recording of the supernova of 1054 that resulted in the Crab Nebula (M1), is well established. This 18th-century map shows 1,464 stars arranged into 283 constellations.

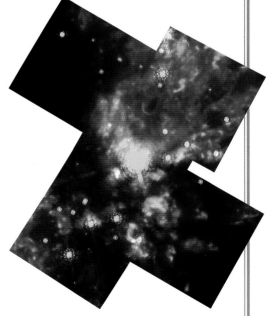

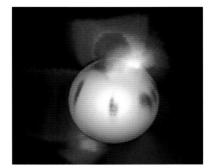

Becklin-Neugebauer Object (above)

While many astronomical objects are visible only in the infrared spectrum, it is necessary to get above as much of the atmosphere as possible to make more detailed observations. This Hubble Space Telescope image shows the Becklin-Neugebauer Object, a massive star and vibrant source of infrared radiation deep inside the Orion Nebula. Discovered in 1966, this was the first major discovery of infrared astronomy.

OBSERVING THE SKY

We humans have been observing the sky for as far back in history as we care to look. But things stepped up a gear 400 years ago, when the Italian astronomer Galileo Galilei (1564–1642) turned his telescope to the heavens. Since then, the telescope has become the most staple astronomical instrument, and it has evolved enormously. Today's telescopes are monsters with huge apertures—the current record holders are the Keck telescopes in Hawaii with apertures of 33 feet (10 m). Last century, optical telescopes were joined by instruments designed to observe space at the radio and microwave wavelengths. We have also learned to put telescopes into space, opening up new branches of astronomy in regions of the electromagnetic spectrum (infrared, ultraviolet, and X-ray) that are difficult or impossible to carry out from the ground due to the absorbing effects of our protective atmosphere.

Galileo's telescope (above)
Observations by the Italian astronomer Galileo Galilei demonstrated the power of the telescope in astronomy, and in so doing he revolutionized the subject. In this illustration he is seen (right of the telescope) demonstrating his device in Venice.

Eye on the sky (left)
Optical telescopes have grown steadily larger over the centuries as the search for ever-more magnification and light-collecting power has intensified. Sitting atop Mauna Kea, Hawaii, at an altitude of 13,700 feet (4,200 m), are two of the island's many telescopes, the Canada-France-Hawaii Telescope (seen to the left in this image) and the Gemini North Telescope (to the right). Around the globe, hundreds of telescopes like these, their "eyes" trained skyward, make it possible for us to peer ever-deeper into the heavens.

Radio telescopes

Radio astronomy had its origins in the 1930s, when American engineer Karl Jansky (1905–50) discovered a radio "hum" emanating from the sky in the direction of Sagittarius—near the center of our own Milky Way. Many astronomical objects emit these waves and radio telescopes are now a central tool in astronomy. Radio astronomy has two big advantages: one does not have to wait for the Sun to set; and clouds do not pose a problem, for radio waves arrive from space all day, every day, regardless of the weather. Radio telescopes are usually much larger than optical telescopes, because the longer wavelengths involved require bigger apertures to maximize resolution. The photo at right shows the Very Large Array of radio telescopes in New Mexico.

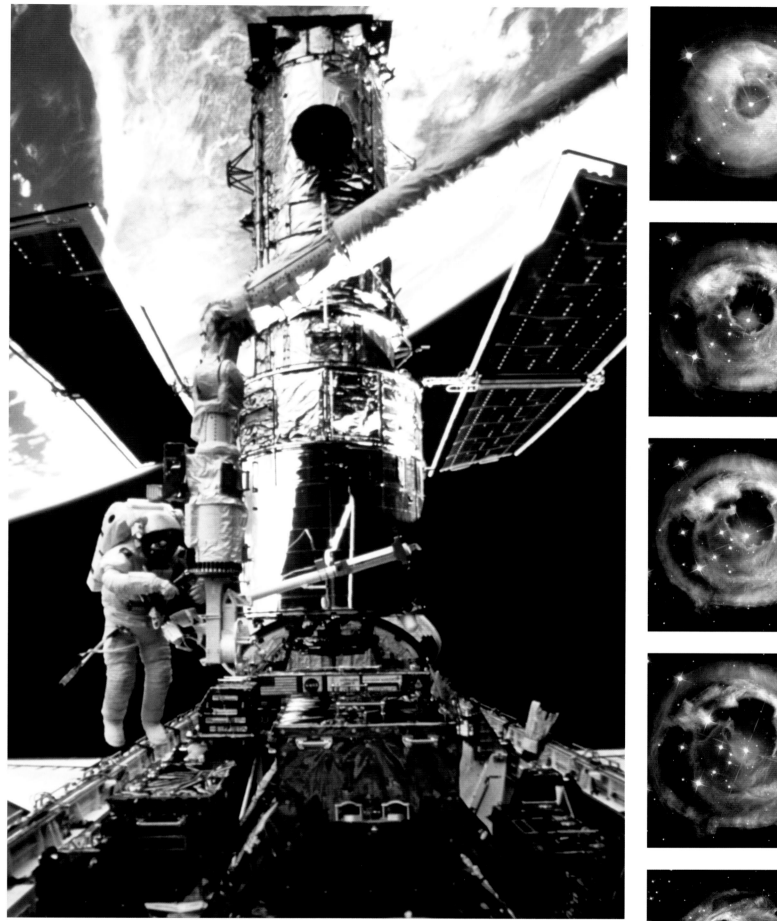

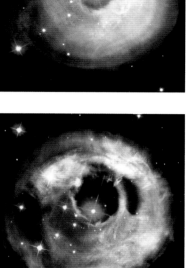

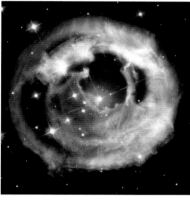

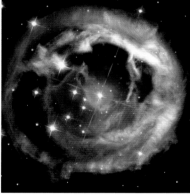

Hubble serviced (above)

The Hubble Space Telescope, launched in 1990, is the world's most famous telescope. It orbits Earth at an altitude of 350 miles (570 km) and can make observations in the visible, ultraviolet, and near-infared wavelengths. Hubble has greatly advanced our understanding of the universe. In this image, an astronaut is servicing the telescope during the STS-82 mission in February 1997.

Space telescopes

The best way to see the heavens is to be there—above the blurring effects of our planet's atmosphere. Indeed, in many cases this is the only way to do it, for our atmosphere, while transparent to optical light, is opaque to ultraviolet light, X-rays, and most infrared light. Although many people have heard of the Hubble Space Telescope—which shot this sequence (right) showing the red supergiant V838 Monocerotis as its shroud of dust was illuminated by a sudden stellar brightening—it is just one among several other observatories, peering into the depths of space over a wide range of wavelengths.

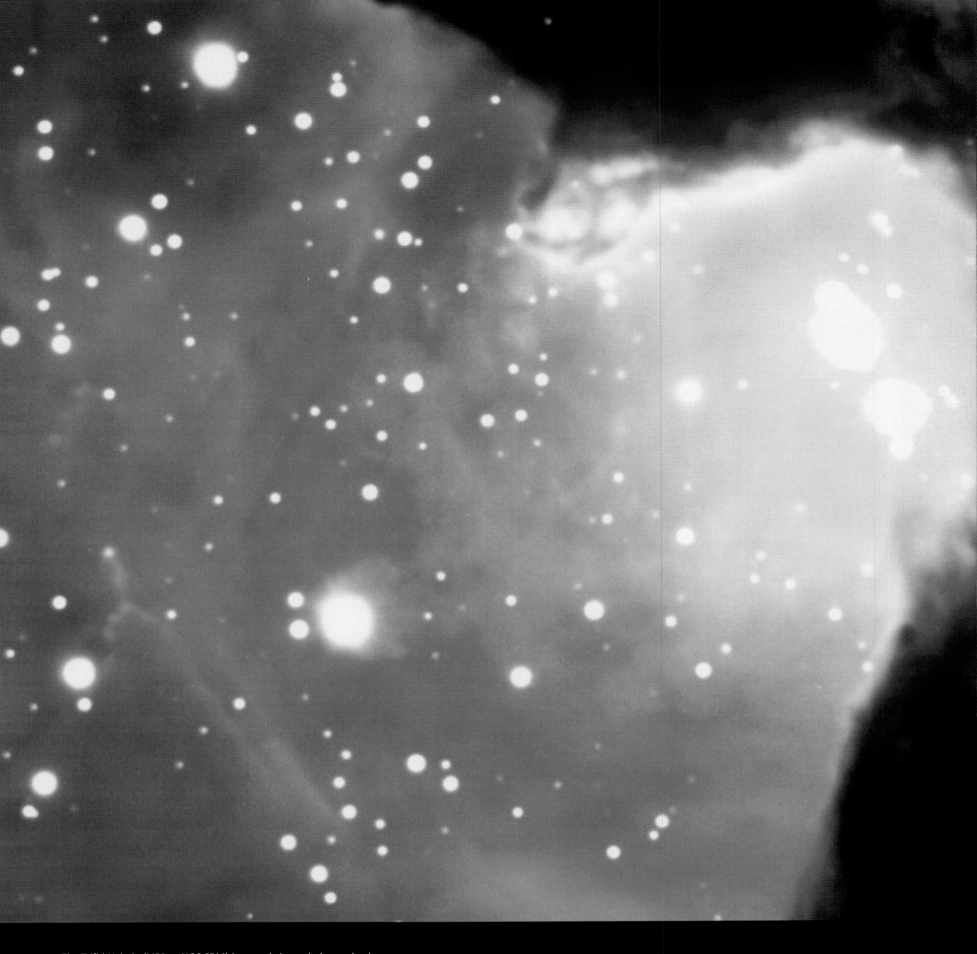

The Trifid Nebula (M20 or NGC 6514) is an emission nebula—a glowing cloud of gas and dust inside which stars are being born—located within the Local Neighborhood. The bright center of this nebula harbors a clutch of newborn stars just 100,000 years old.

THE LOCAL
NEIGHBORHOOD

CHARTING THE LOCAL NEIGHBORHOOD

In the previous chapter we focused on our stellar doorstep, encountering the few dozen stars that surround the Sun. Now we take a look at the bigger picture, extending our view to a radius of 5,000 light-years from our Solar System. This is still only a fraction of the entire Milky Way, which is more than ten times larger. But within this region, which we call the Local Neighborhood, celestial riches abound. Huge clouds of gas and dust known as molecular clouds are found here, and indeed right across the Galaxy. Nestling within these clouds are vast stellar nurseries, backlighting exquisite nebulas and interstellar medium, and gilding the Milky Way's galactic arms with vibrant color. And where there is star birth, there is also death: explosive supernovas and blooming planetary nebulas that herald the end of the stellar lifecycle; once mighty stars leaving behind white dwarfs, neutron stars, pulsars, and black holes.

The Local Neighborhood

The Local Neighborhood, a region some 10,000 light-years across and 3,000 light-years deep, is mapped in detail here. The entire Galaxy, at this scale, would be about 15 feet (4.5 m) across. Clusters and nebulas are shown here larger than true scale, and the disk has been flattened for the purpose of mapping. Sections of our closest galactic spiral arms form three distinct bands across the map, the local Orion Arm at center. The gas that fills these arms has a structure somewhat like that of Swiss cheese, populated by bubbles blown in the interstellar medium by stellar explosions.

Stellar newborns
This false-color infrared image is a close-up showing a cluster of newborn stars in the Orion Nebula. These stars, located about 1,500 light-years away in the constellation Orion, illuminate the gas and dust that surround and gave birth to them. The pink color is a vast outflow of gas streaming away from a newly forming star in the background.

Orion Arm
Also known as the Local Arm, this is our Solar System's immediate region.

Gaseous hourglass
This object, 2,000 light-years distant, is known by the prosaic name of Sharpless 106 (Sh2-106). It contains a young star just 100,000 years old, surrounded by a nebula of material thrown off by the star. At the center of this false-color infrared photo, a vast pancake of gas and dust

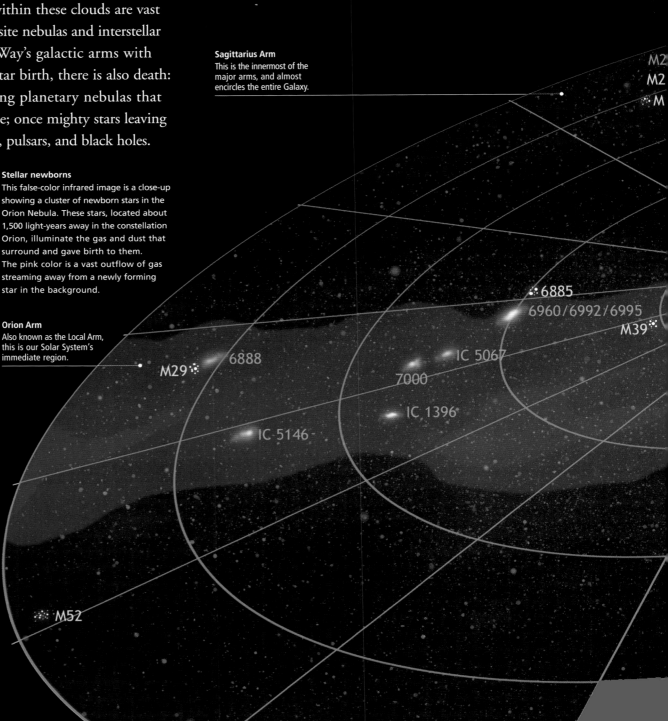

Sagittarius Arm
This is the innermost of the major arms, and almost encircles the entire Galaxy.

M2
M2
M

6885
6960/6992/6995
M39

M29
6888
IC 5067
7000
IC 1396
IC 5146
M52

Perseus Arm
This broad, fraying band forms the main outer arm

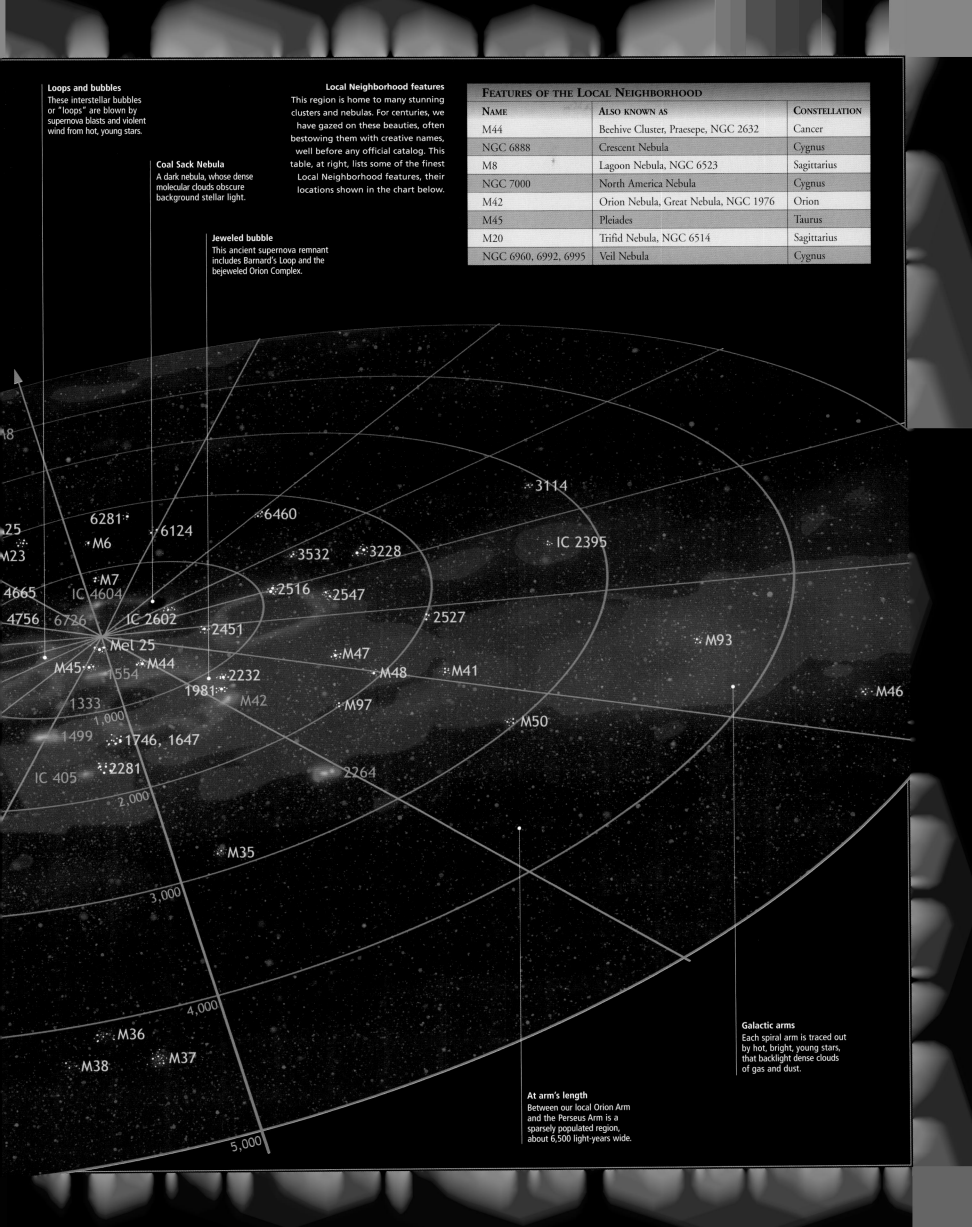

Loops and bubbles
These interstellar bubbles or "loops" are blown by supernova blasts and violent wind from hot, young stars.

Coal Sack Nebula
A dark nebula, whose dense molecular clouds obscure background stellar light.

Jeweled bubble
This ancient supernova remnant includes Barnard's Loop and the bejeweled Orion Complex.

Local Neighborhood features
This region is home to many stunning clusters and nebulas. For centuries, we have gazed on these beauties, often bestowing them with creative names, well before any official catalog. This table, at right, lists some of the finest Local Neighborhood features, their locations shown in the chart below.

FEATURES OF THE LOCAL NEIGHBORHOOD		
NAME	**ALSO KNOWN AS**	**CONSTELLATION**
M44	Beehive Cluster, Praesepe, NGC 2632	Cancer
NGC 6888	Crescent Nebula	Cygnus
M8	Lagoon Nebula, NGC 6523	Sagittarius
NGC 7000	North America Nebula	Cygnus
M42	Orion Nebula, Great Nebula, NGC 1976	Orion
M45	Pleiades	Taurus
M20	Trifid Nebula, NGC 6514	Sagittarius
NGC 6960, 6992, 6995	Veil Nebula	Cygnus

Galactic arms
Each spiral arm is traced out by hot, bright, young stars, that backlight dense clouds of gas and dust.

At arm's length
Between our local Orion Arm and the Perseus Arm is a sparsely populated region, about 6,500 light-years wide.

INTERSTELLAR MEDIUM

We think of space as just that—a vast sea of nothing, punctuated by the occasional star. But in fact this seeming void is filled with an extremely sparse but measurable scattering of material known as the interstellar medium (ISM). The ISM, the fabric from which stars are formed and into which they expire, makes up about one-tenth of the visible mass of our Galaxy, and is found mostly in a thin sheet some 300 light-years deep within the thicker disk of stars surrounding the Galactic hub. More than 90 percent of the ISM by mass is gas, chiefly hydrogen gas, but with significant quantities of helium too. The remainder is composed of so-called dust—minute particles of carbon, silicon, and other compounds, far smaller than household dust motes. The ISM is not always readily visible, but, in its absorption and distortion of stellar light, creates many stunning celestial sights—the swirling reds of emission nebulas and the black depths of dark nebulas.

The Local Bubble (above)
Our Sun (at the center of the illustration above) lies in a region of space that is comparatively empty of interstellar medium. This void, known as the Local Bubble, is several hundred light-years across, and was created around 1 to 2 million years ago when a star near the Sun exploded. Like a plow through snow, shockwaves from this blast cleared out a hole in the surrounding interstellar medium.

Space dust (right)
Some particles of the gas and dust cloud that became the Solar System survived the process and are preserved within primitive meteorites. By isolating and studying these tiny "presolar grains," scientists can learn much about the content of the ISM and the long-dead stars that created these particles. This grain is made of carbon, but particles made of a variety of minerals have been found that predate the Sun.

Interstellar dust

Between one and ten percent of the mass of the interstellar medium is in the form of tiny particles of dust. They are created in the outer atmospheres of red giant stars, and also during supernova explosions. Their exact composition is uncertain, but they are thought to contain silicate materials as well as carbon-laden substances such as graphite. Interstellar dust grains are very small—between 10 and 100 nanometers across—and they are spread very thinly through the Galaxy. Nevertheless they are extremely good at absorbing starlight, which is why clouds rich in interstellar dust often appear dark and solid seen in front of stars and brighter nebulas. Dust clouds can also be conspicuous even if there is no bright background, because absorbed starlight heats up the dust, creating emissions that can be detected at infrared wavelengths. And the presence of this cosmic dust can also be inferred—even if it cannot be seen—because starlight becomes polarized as it passes through.

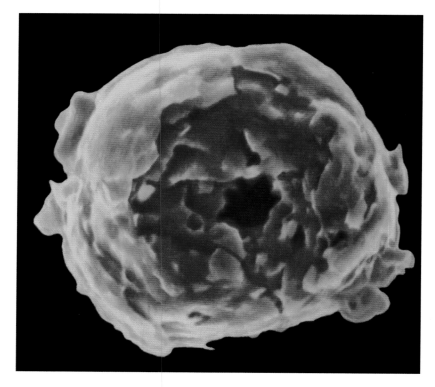

Churning cirrus (above)
These wispy clouds of hydrogen gas, laden with grains of interstellar dust, are known as infrared cirrus. These filaments appear as churning cirrus-like clouds across all parts of the sky, and are detected at infrared wavelengths because the dust particles within the cooler hydrogen are heated by ultraviolet radiation from nearby stars.

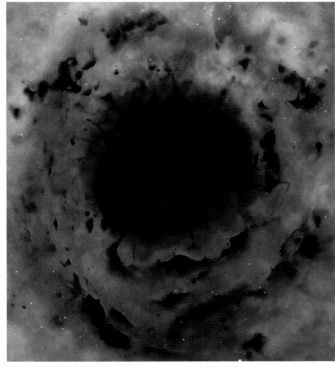

Busy globules (left)
Some gas clouds are comparatively small. This illustration shows a small blob of gas and dark dust known as a globule, or Bok globule after the astronomer who first studied them. As their name suggests, globules are usually fairly spherical. They are no larger than a light-year across, and may be much smaller still, and are generally in the process of forming new stars.

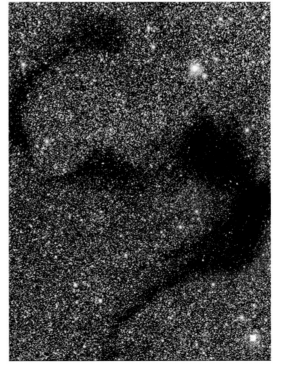

Serpentine dust clouds (right)
This dark nebula, named the Snake Nebula (or Barnard 72), in the constellation Ophiuchus, is formed from a series of dust-rich interstellar clouds about four light-years across. These obscure background stars create a distinctive sinuous path across a small patch of sky.

MOLECULAR CLOUDS

Molecular clouds account for half of the entire mass of the interstellar material in the Milky Way. They come in a wide variety of sizes—from globules less than a light-year across to gigantic blankets more than a hundred times larger, containing enough material to make millions of stars. As their name suggests, molecular clouds are rich in molecules. The most common molecule—accounting for three-quarters of the mass of a typical molecular cloud—is molecular hydrogen, or H_2, in which atoms of hydrogen have been bonded together in pairs. Single helium atoms are prominent as well (about one-quarter by mass), along with normal (atomic) hydrogen. More complex molecules such as ammonia can also be present but are much rarer. Molecular clouds are very cold with temperatures of around –420°F (–250°C), which allows molecules to form and survive. And as they contain significant amounts of starlight-absorbing interstellar dust, they frequently appear dark, visible if they block the light of more distant stars or when highlighted by stars within.

HII regions

Often, dark molecular clouds have parts lit up as bright, vibrant nebulas by stars formed within them. These dazzling patches are known as HII (aitch-two) regions. HII is ionized hydrogen, not to be confused with H_2 or molecular hydrogen. Whereas a normal hydrogen atom consists of a proton at its center with an electron bound to it, in ionized hydrogen the electron is missing, leaving the proton by itself. HII regions are created inside molecular clouds where stars form. When the new stars "turn on," they begin to emit floods of energetic ultraviolet radiation, ionizing the surroundings and causing them to glow. The Orion Nebula (M42) is perhaps the most famous HII region known. An HII region can grow around a cluster of stars before radiation pressure from the young stars blows away its gases.

Ionizing sources (below)
This image shows the bright young star S Monocerotis, one of several in the Christmas Tree Cluster (NGC 2264), which is ionizing the interstellar clouds that surround it. S Mon is the bright star in the top left corner. The clouds are red where they are excited by ultraviolet starlight and made to glow, forming an HII region. The blue, meanwhile, is starlight reflected by dust in the clouds.

Orion's light (below right)
The famous Orion Nebula (M42), in the constellation Orion, is seen in this photo, as captured at infrared wavelengths by the United Kingdom Infrared Telescope on Mauna Kea, Hawaii. The bright region we know as the Orion Nebula is merely a small part of a more extensive structure. It is situated on the edge of, and in front of, a much larger but darker giant molecular cloud.

Giants of the Galaxy

Molecular clouds come in a bewildering variety of sizes. The largest of all are known as giant molecular clouds (GMCs)—and it is a name well deserved. Our Galaxy contains about 3,000 of these colossal formations, and they constitute its largest discrete objects. GMCs are typically 100 to 150 light-years across, but they can be almost twice that size and include an incredible ten million solar masses—packed with enough raw material to create millions of stars. GMCs are more than 1,000 times denser than other interstellar clouds and, being crammed with significant quantities of dust, they are also opaque. The nearest GMC is a vast cloud of gas and dust covering much of the constellation Orion in our sky. The famous Orion Nebula (M42) is just the latest site of star formation within this much larger cloud.

The Omega Nebula (main image)
The Omega Nebula (also known as M17, the Swan Nebula, or the Horseshoe Nebula), 5,000 light-years from the Solar System, is shown in this near-infrared image. The bright section is an HII region, illuminated by young stars. The darker portions on the right are rich in interstellar dust, hiding the stars behind them and providing a dark canvas for the nebula's glowing gas. M17 is associated with a much larger giant molecular cloud.

The Dark River (above)
The bright orange star, at center left in this image, is Antares in the constellation of Scorpius, its glow illuminating a surrounding dust cloud. Above it, and to the far right, can be seen a dark "river" of obscuring dust and gas which is a small part of a much larger complex known as the Dark River. South is to the left.

Pipe Nebula (left)
This is a photo of a dark cloud of gas and dust known as the Pipe Nebula or LDN 1773, in the constellation Ophiuchus. The Pipe Nebula is about 100 light-years long and, extending for several degrees, is one of the largest dark clouds in the entire sky, forming part of the Dark River seen in the image above.

Star Formation

Star formation is a miracle of nature, and it happens—in astronomical terms—in the blink of an eye. The Sun, for example, took about 30 to 50 million years to form, and more massive stars develop much more quickly. Molecular clouds provide the raw material for star creation, and gravity the driving force. A dense knot of interstellar gas and dust, subject to stronger gravitational forces than its surroundings, by virtue of its higher mass, will collapse in on itself, heating up as it does so until, at its core, millions of years later, a new star emerges. Some molecular clouds are so huge that they give rise to entire clusters of stars at once. But smaller fragments of clouds, called globules, may nurture only a single star, or none at all if they are insufficiently massive.

Jet collision (below)
Herbig-Haro objects, named after the two astronomers who first studied them, are emission nebulas associated with young stellar objects. When a star is forming, it often emits a jet of charged particles into space. Where this jet hits the surrounding interstellar medium, it glows conspicuously, forming streaks as seen in this image of HH 34 in Orion.

From stellar death to stellar birth (right)
Often, star formation is triggered by a supernova—the cataclysmic death of a massive star: At the end of its life, this red giant (1) supernovas, sending shockwaves through the interstellar medium (2). These compress the surrounding gases, causing them to undergo gravitational collapse (3). Over time, the result is a glowing stellar nursery like Henize 206 (4).

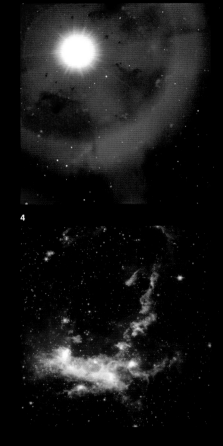

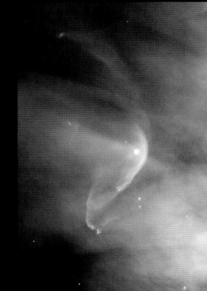

Fiery birth (above and below)
Young stars often emerge in dramatic fashion. The image above of LL Orionis within a gaseous bow shock, like an interstellar wake, shows one such dramatic beginning. Another is seen in the image below, which shows plumes of gas ejected from a Herbig-Haro object HH 32 glowing in the light of energized hydrogen (green) and sulfur (blue) atoms.

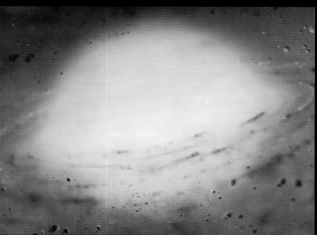

Star birth 1: Protostar (above)

No interstellar cloud is uniformly dense. There are always certain "knots" or "cores" that are slightly denser and more opaque than others. These regions tend to have a somewhat stronger gravitational pull and, if conditions are right, will suck in surrounding material and initiate a slow collapse. Gradually, what began as a knot grows denser, its gravity increasing all the time and drawing in more material. After a million or so years the core develops into a stellar cocoon known as a globule—a thick, dark blob, roughly spherical, about 60,000 AU across. At the center of the globule is a warm mass about the size of the Solar System, spinning and emitting strong infrared radiation. This is known as a protostar. The illustration above shows an impression of a protostar at a late stage of development, when it is hot enough to emit optical light.

Star birth 2: Proplyd (left)

As material continues to be drawn in toward the center of the globule from farther out, it begins to flatten out, somewhat like pizza dough spun in the air. About 100,000 years after the formation of the protostar, it has shrunk to about 1 AU in diameter, and is now surrounded by a gigantic, bloated pancake of gas and dust known as a protoplanetary disk or proplyd, more than 100 AU across. Proplyds are thought to be infant planetary systems, the gas and dust eventually becoming planets orbiting the central star. They are strong infrared sources, hot and busy in their centers but gradually cooling off and becoming fatter toward their extremities.

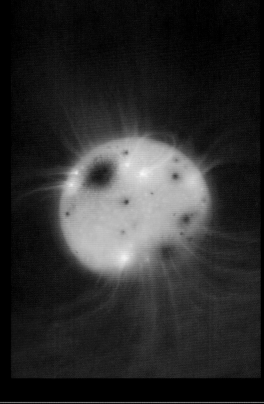

Star birth 3: T Tauri star (left)

After another million years or so the protostar at the center of the proplyd, having shrunk now to only a few times the diameter of the Sun, becomes an object known as a T Tauri star. T Tauri stars spin very rapidly and have intensely powerful magnetic fields. As a T Tauri star spins, its powerful magnetism attracts nearby gas and sucks it in along magnetic field lines, causing massive flares which are the hallmark of T Tauri stars. This intensive magnetic activity also creates large spots, similar to sunspots but covering far greater areas on the surface.

Star birth 4: Bipolar molecular outflow (right)

As a T Tauri star snatches gas from its surrounding disk, it flings it outward. The ejected material cannot escape along the plane of the disk and is instead deflected perpendicularly, along the star's spin axis, forming two particle beam jets known as a bipolar molecular outflow. Where these beam jets hit the surrounding interstellar gases, they cause them to light up, forming bright nebulas called Herbig-Haro objects. The outflow stage in the formation of a star is very brief, lasting only 10,000 years or so. After that, it takes another few tens of millions of years of steady gravitational contraction before the T Tauri star is able to initiate hydrogen fusion in its core. It is at this point that the infant star's life begins.

THE ORION STAR FACTORY

Some 1,500 light-years away in the constellation Orion lies one of the largest known star factories—and certainly the closest. The most celebrated portion of this gigantic complex is the famous Orion Nebula or Great Nebula (M42). M42 has the highest surface brightness of any nebula, which makes it distinctive to the naked eye, even from a city. Deep within its dusty mists, stars and planetary systems are in the process of formation. The relative proximity of this stellar nursery has given astronomers insight into the mechanics of how giant clouds of gas collapse in on themselves to form stars. Here we take a look at the Orion Nebula and its surroundings to witness the miracle of star birth.

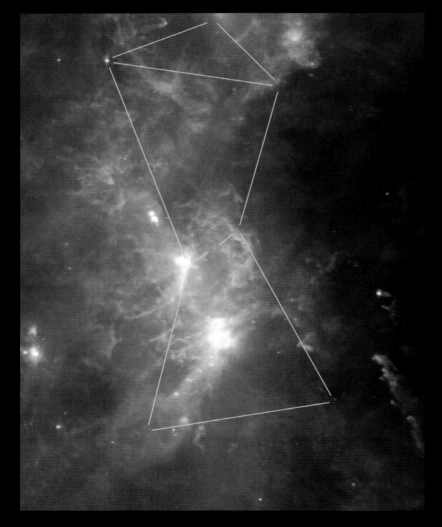

Orion: more than meets the eye
The Orion Nebula is merely a small part of a much larger interstellar molecular cloud complex called the Orion Complex, with dense patches of interstellar gas and dust, rich in molecules of hydrogen. Each of the clouds in this complex is around 1,500 light-years away, 100 light-years across, and has the mass of about 100,000 times that of our Sun. The image above shows the entire constellation of Orion as seen at infrared wavelengths. The Orion Nebula is clearly visible as the bright patch in the lower middle of the image, but in fact the entire region is crammed with gas and dust. The photo on the right shows the constellation Orion and its surroundings at optical wavelengths for comparison. The pink arc to the left of Orion's Belt is an expanding shell of material from an ancient supernova explosion. It is known as Barnard's Loop. The white rectangle indicates the area covered by the large image of Orion's Sword on the facing page.

Orion's Trapezium (below)
Within the center of the Orion Nebula is a clutch of about one thousand newborn stars, each around a million years old. Many of these infant stars can be seen in this European Southern Observatory infrared photo. The four bright stars near the center form the Trapezium.

New planetary systems (below)
This striking Hubble photo of the region near the Trapezium shows what are, in all likelihood, planetary systems in formation, deep in the heart of the Orion Nebula. They are known as proplyds, short for protoplanetary disks. They are the small blobs predominantly to the left of this image.

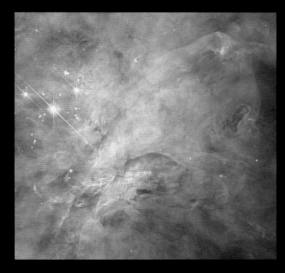

Closing in on proplyds (below)
Four young stars in the Orion Nebula feature in this close-up, which spans just under 0.14 light-years. The two light-colored disks at center are proplyds illuminated by hot nearby stars; the dark dot is also a proplyd, but is farther away, out of reach of the starlight. Proplyds may, in time, form new planetary systems.

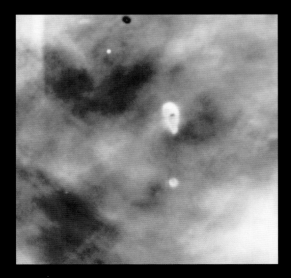

Orion's Sword

Orion's Sword gets its name from its position in the sky, immediately below the three stars that form Orion's Belt. This photo is a close-up of the region, showing the Orion Nebula (M42) and de Mairan's Nebula (M43) at the bottom, separated by a dark lane of gas and dust. The southern and brightest half of the nebula, M42, is centered around the star Theta Orionis, which is a multiple-star system also known as the Trapezium. (The white square corresponds to the image at top left, which zooms in on the Trapezium area.) The Orion Nebula is about 20 light-years across and covers a patch of sky about four times the area of a full Moon. It contains enough material to make several hundred stars like our Sun. At the top of this image is an adjacent gas cloud complex in blue, with components cataloged under the names NGC 1973, 1975, and 1977.

Open Clusters

Often when stars form, they do so en masse. The giant molecular clouds that give birth to them can be so massive that they disgorge entire assemblies of stars at the same time. These are known as open clusters. In our Local Neighborhood and adjacent areas of the Galaxy we can see about 1,000 open clusters. Like molecular clouds they are distributed around the Milky Way's spiral arms. Some clusters may harbor just a few dozen stars in a region of space a few light-years across. But others are far more impressive, their stars crammed together hundreds of times tighter than the stars in the neighborhood of the Sun. However, most clusters do not last very long—usually a few hundred million years at most. As these open clusters travel around the Galaxy, the cluster stars are pulled by the gravity from other stars and gas clouds that they encounter and are, one by one, wrenched free.

Jewels of nature (left)
This cluster of about 100 stars is known as the Jewel Box, after the strikingly diverse colors of its principal members. The Jewel Box, also known as NGC 4755 or Kappa Crucis, is about 20 light-years across and lies 7,500 light-years away in the southern constellation Crux, the Southern Cross.

The Christmas Tree Cluster (right)
This cluster takes its popular name from its resemblance to a Christmas tree. The tree, on its side here, has the star V427 Mon as its crown. The related Cone Nebula points at the tree's apex, at the left of the image.

Short-lived associations

Some stars group together in loose structures known as stellar associations. Unlike clusters, these groups are not strongly bound by gravity, breaking up within about 10 million years as they experience tidal forces from passing stars and gas clouds. Associations contain dozens of very hot, young stars and are concentrated along the Galaxy's spiral arms. High-mass star groups, spectral types O and B, are identified as OB associations. Medium-mass and lower-mass star groups are R and T associations, respectively.

Sharpless 140 (above)
This infrared Spitzer Space Telescope image shows a star cluster and the nebula that gave it life. The cloud, Sharpless 140, is about 3,000 light-years away in Cepheus, and has a small cluster of very hot stars at its heart—the bright region in this image. The bow shape defines the outer edge of the cloud, illuminated by a star outside the image.

Elephant Trunk Nebula (right)
The concentration of interstellar gas and dust in this optical Canada-France-Hawaii Telescope image is known as the Elephant Trunk Nebula or IC 1396. It is the birthplace of stars, and harbors a small cluster of stellar newborns.

M35 (NGC 2168), Trumpler classification: III 3 r

Butterfly Cluster (M6), Trumpler classification: II 3 m

NGC 2516, Trumpler classification: I 3 r

Pleiades (M45), Trumpler classification: II 3 r n

Classification of open clusters

Astronomers love classifying things, and star clusters are not immune. They use the system known as Trumpler classification, after the astronomer who developed it. Clusters are classified with three codes based on their appearance. First is a Roman number (I to IV) indicating the degree of concentration, I being the tightest. After that is a number (1 to 3) to denote the range of brightness among the stars, 1 indicating a small range. Then a letter is added to indicate the "richness" of the cluster or the number of members—p for poor, m for moderate, and r for rich. Lastly, if nebulosity is associated with the cluster, a suffix n is included. The clusters M35, Butterfly, NGC 2516, and Pleiades are shown above and left with their Trumpler classifications indicated.

Variable Stars

The stars may look constant and unchanging, but in fact a great many of them are variable—that is, they change their light output with time. Some variables are extrinsic, meaning the stars appear to change their brightness because of such factors as rotation or orbital motion. Eclipsing binaries are an example. Then there are intrinsic variables, which modulate their actual physical luminosity. Sometimes the brightness of an intrinsic variable changes periodically, as with Miras, Cepheids, and RR Lyrae stars. But sometimes the variation is aperiodic and unpredictable, as when a star suddenly brightens due perhaps to flaring or other activity. Below are two false-color images showing a Cepheid's variable brightness—note the perceptible difference in size between the dots at the center of each image.

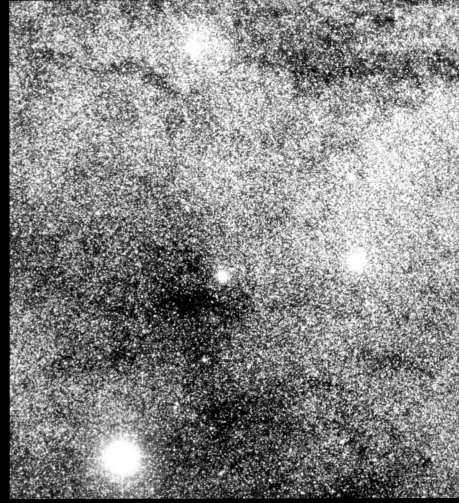

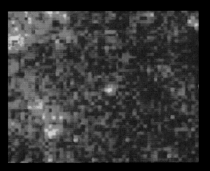 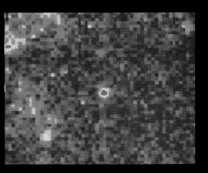

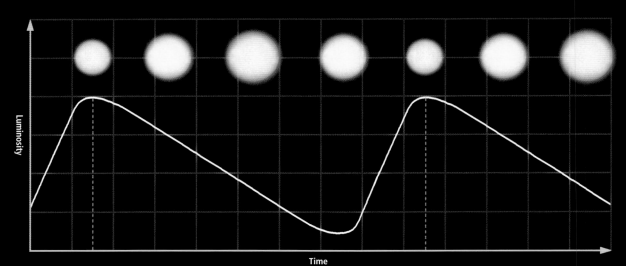

Cepheids

The Cepheid variables, named after the prototype Delta Cephei in Cepheus, are supergiants that expand and contract, varying their luminosity as they do so. The diagram, left, shows how, as they vary their diameter, their color and brightness change in sympathy. The period with which a given example varies—easily measurable by observing the star over several days—is directly related to its intrinsic brightness. By comparing its known intrinsic brightness with its apparent brightness in the sky, astronomers are able to determine its distance. It's like judging the distance to a car by how bright its headlights are.

Eclipsing binaries

Some stars that appear to vary their light output are not actually intrinsically variable. One such class of stars are the eclipsing binary stars. Just as the Moon will occasionally pass in front of the Sun to produce an eclipse, so the two stars in a binary star system can pass in front of each other, causing the light level to dip with periodic regularity. Prototype eclipsing binary stars are Algol (Beta (β) Persei); Beta (β) Lyrae; and W Ursae Majoris; all of which famously exhibit this phenomenon, though at different periodic intensities. The illustration to the right is of W Ursae Majoris, a binary that consists of two stars very much like our Sun.

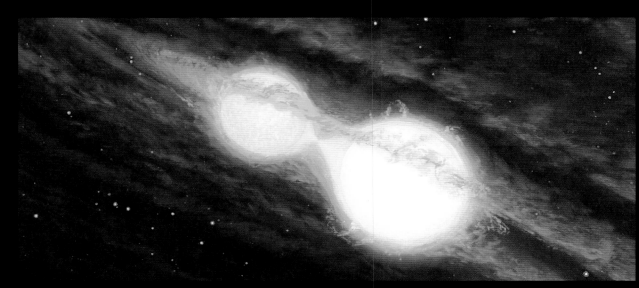

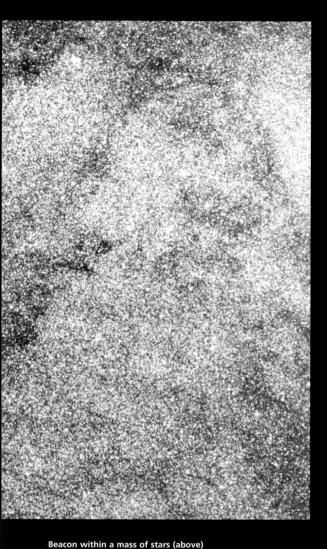

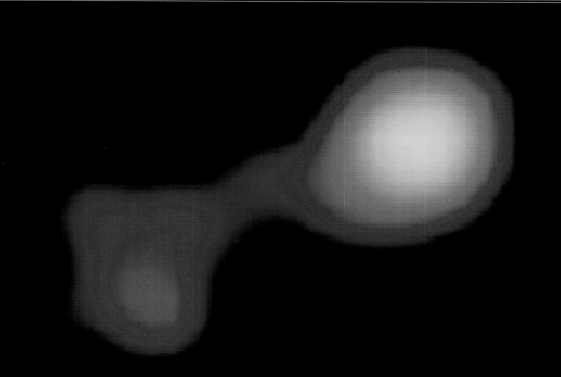

Mira variables

Mira stars are the most commonly seen stellar variable. They are red giants or supergiants whose visible light output can vary by factors of up to several thousand. They are named after the prototype star Mira (Omicron (o) Ceti)—the right-most star in the images above and right. Mira's size and instability cause stellar wind to pour from its upper atmosphere. The gas, shown in blue above, accretes around companion star Mira B (left).

Beacon within a mass of stars (above)
Set against thick star clouds in a heavily populated region of the Milky Way is the Cepheid variable W Sagittarii (the bright star at top left in this image). This dying star's beacon of light pulsates between magnitudes 4.3 and 5.1 over a period of 7.59 days—a pattern of variability that suggests that it lies about 1,500 light-years away. If this is so, W Sagittarii could be pouring out about 2,500 times our Sun's luminosity.

Distant Cepheids (below)
This Hubble Space Telescope image of the majestic spiral galaxy NGC 4603 captures in its frame some 36 Cepheid variable stars, which have indicated in their pulse rates that this galaxy is about 108 million light-years away. This galaxy was one of the farthest whose distance was determined by Hubble's detection of Cepheid variables, assisting scientists in their quest to measure the scale and expansion rate of the universe.

RR Lyrae stars

Another important class of variable stars are the RR Lyrae stars. Like Cepheids, these are pulsating yellow-white giants, and are used as cosmic yardsticks. Most RR Lyrae stars have about the same absolute magnitude. Therefore, by comparing two such stars, astronomers can easily work out their relative distances. RR Lyrae stars, though, are fainter than Cepheids, and can, therefore, only be used to determine relatively modest distances. Below is M3, a globular cluster in Canes Venatici whose rich population of RR Lyrae stars (seen as blue in this composite image) have enabled astronomers to determine that it lies 33,900 light-years away.

STELLAR EVOLUTION

Just like living creatures on Earth, stars are born, change as they age, and die. There are so many stars in space, each at a different stage of development, that astronomers have been able to piece together how a star ages. As illustrated right, stars evolve differently depending on their intial mass. Most will spend about 90 percent of their lives on the main sequence, burning hydrogen. Sedate, low-mass stars such as the Sun (middle track) will grow little over about ten billion years or more, before moving off the main sequence and swelling to become red giants. Massive stars (left track) burn their fuel quickly, and evolve into even larger and more luminous stars—red supergiants—within a few million years. And very low-mass stars called red dwarfs (top track) shine for trillions of years—longer than the current age of the universe—before they gradually shrink and fade.

Ticking supergiant (above)
Eta (ε) Carinae, captured here by the Hubble Space Telescope, is a massive star (actually most probably a binary pair) which, in 1843, flared briefly to become the second brightest star in the sky, after Sirius. It is a phenomenal five million times as bright as the Sun, and is destined to explode as a supernova.

Betelgeuse (below)
This series of computer-simulated images of the surface of the red supergiant Betelgeuse predicts a variable surface of bright spots and giant convection cells that change rapidly over the course of a few days. Betelgeuse is the only star, aside from the Sun, whose surface can be directly imaged, albeit not very well.

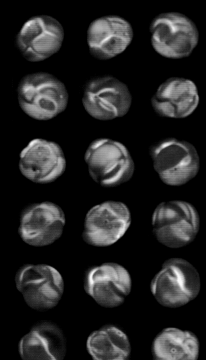

Rivaling Mars (above)
This photo shows the red supergiant star Antares (center)—meaning "rival of Mars"—in the constellation Scorpius. Antares shines with immense power—to our eyes, more than 10,000 times as bright as the Sun—and if placed at the center our Solar System would stretch beyond the orbit of the planet that is its namesake.

STAR DEATH: LOW-MASS STARS

Low-mass stars such as the Sun evolve slowly, taking billions of years to run low in hydrogen fuel in their core and swell into red giants. Some hydrogen remains, burning at the outer edge of the red giant's inner core, but inside the pressure builds so that the star begins to fuse helium. This red giant state lasts only until all the helium is gone, at which point the star, as if puffing one last breath, throws off its outer layers in spectacular plumes known as a planetary nebula. These gas clouds have nothing to do with planets, but get their name from the tiny disks they often present in small telescopes. Lit from within by the dying star, now a white dwarf, and sculpted by the star's environs, these stunning but brief death throes last only 50,000 years or so. The gas clears, and the white dwarf, its fuel spent, cools and fades from the sky.

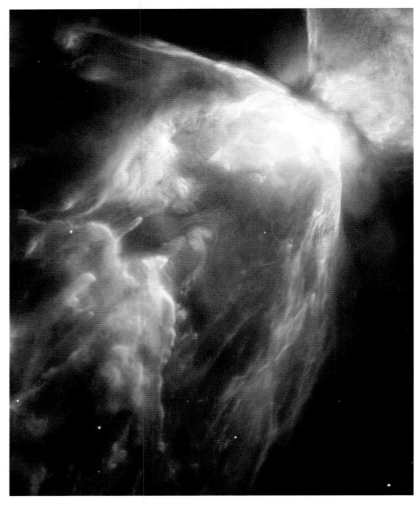

Draco's eye (below)
The striking planetary nebula known as the Cat's Eye (NGC 6543), in the constellation of Draco, takes its name from the shape of its central portions, which are shown blue in this false-color image. The tenuous, green, gaseous halo seen here spans about 3 light-years.

Space bug (right)
This spectacular Hubble image shows vibrant gas flows pouring from a dying star in Scorpius. Known as the Bug Nebula (NGC 6302), this is an energetic planetary nebula rich with churning strands of gas. It is one of the brightest known examples of this class of object.

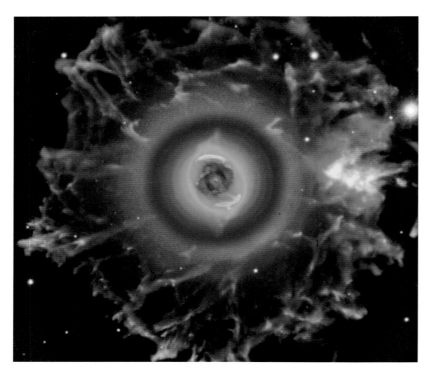

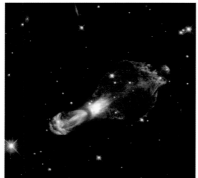

Protoplanetary nebula (left)
This photo shows a protoplanetary nebula, destined to become a full planetary nebula in around 1,000 years or so. The main blue lobe is a shell of expanding gas thrown off by the progenitor star, glowing brightly as it hits the surrounding interstellar medium.

Cosmic ant (right)
This is a classic example of a so-called bipolar planetary nebula, where the dying star has thrown off not a single, spherical, shell of gas but rather two jet-like lobes. Its curious shape has earned it the name Ant Nebula.

Diamond core (immediate left)
Mature white dwarfs may have cores of crystallized carbon—just like a gigantic diamond—surrounded by a shell of hydrogen and helium.

Massive dwarfs (left)
Here a white dwarf of one solar mass is compared with Earth. More massive white dwarfs have higher gravity, but are physically smaller. White dwarfs can only ever have a mass up to 1.4 times that of the Sun; at larger masses the star collapses to form a neutron star or a black hole.

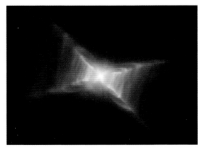

Protoplanetary nebulas (above and left)
The photo above captures the Boomerang Nebula, 5,000 light-years away in the constellation Centaurus, puffing out gas at about 370,000 miles per hour (600,000 km/h). On the left is the similarly shaped Red Rectangle Nebula. In both cases the central stars may be surrounded by doughnut-shaped rings of dust that prevent the stars's ejecta shells from expanding spherically, constraining the gas into cones along the spin axes.

STAR DEATH: HIGH-MASS STARS

When a massive star dies, it does so in a spectacular cosmic light show known as a supernova. Having swollen into a supergiant—larger and far brighter than the red giants that typify the ends of low-mass stars—there comes a point when the doomed star runs out of fuel in its core. In less than a second, the core implodes, no longer able to support itself against gravity's crush. Suddenly, shockwaves propagate outward from the shrinking core to rip the star's outer envelope to shreds, accompanied by a flood of neutrinos and powerful radiation. Supernovas routinely outshine entire galaxies, blazing for a brief 100 seconds or so, with the light of tens or even hundreds of billions of stars. But while destructive, they also serve a greater purpose, replenishing the interstellar medium with material for later generations of stars.

Elusive neutrinos (above)
Neutrinos, a byproduct of supernovas, are difficult to detect. Detectors usually comprise a giant bath of water (such as the Japanese Super-Kamiokande here). As the neutrinos pass through, some interact with the molecules in the liquid and leave tell-tale puffs of radiation.

Light shows (right and center)
In its last moments, a massive star becomes destabilized, its outer layers blasted off in a bright, catastrophic death throe known as a supernova (illustrated, center). What remains from these explosions are nebulas of tangled gas, like the Vela Supernova Remnant (right), and either a neutron star or a black hole.

Core of a red supergiant (below)
Stars over eight times the mass of the Sun develop a layered internal structure as they consume the ashes from previous generations of thermonuclear reactions. The discrete layers of iron (7), silicon (6), oxygen (5), neon (4), carbon (3), helium (2), and hydrogen (1) are, by red supergiant stage, densely compressed—the core just larger than Earth, while the star itself spans several AU. While most elements give out energy as they burn, supporting the star against gravity—iron fusion does not. Once enough iron accumulates, the core implodes in a fraction of a second, shock waves shattering the star and flaring into a supernova.

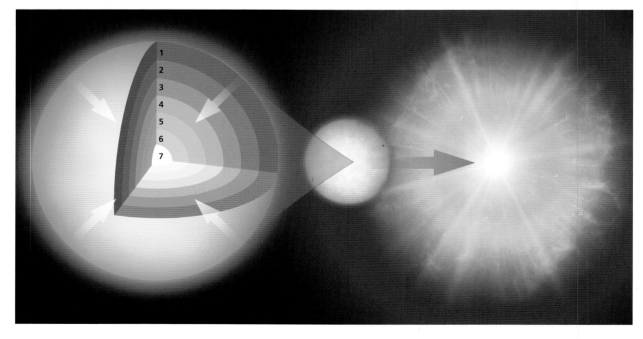

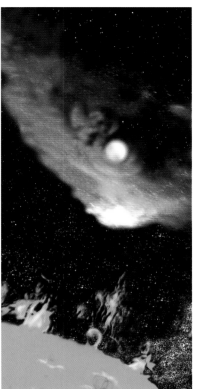

Stellar giants

A tiny minority of stars are so massive, so powerful, that they literally rip themselves apart. These are the Wolf-Rayet (WR) stars, which bear the names of the two French astronomers who discovered them in 1867. WR stars are blue supergiants, of spectral class W, a type that is similar to the massive O spectra stars. Each harbors enough material to make perhaps 50 or more stars like the Sun, and has a surface temperature in the region of 45,000 to 90,000°F (25,000–50,000°C). So bright are these stars that the power of their own radiation blows off their outer layers of hydrogen, significantly shortening their lives. The mass loss manifests itself as a potent stellar wind, a gaseous outflow that rushes away from the star's surface at speeds of up to 1,300 miles per second (2,000 km/s), burying the central star in a debris shell somewhat like a planetary nebula. The infrared image below shows a WR star acting like a hose pipe, spraying dust into space as it rotates, creating a spiral pattern. The image above is an artist's impression of a WR star (blue) in a binary system, its material forming a glowing bow shock (red) as it wraps around its stellar partner.

STELLAR REMNANTS

When a massive, solitary star goes supernova, leaving behind the gaseous filaments of a supernova remnant, the stage is set for some truly exotic science. Depending on the mass of the original star, either a neutron star or a black hole will result. A neutron star is not really a star anymore. It is an extremely hot, highly magnetic, spinning ball of subatomic particles called neutrons. Neutron stars are the densest known material objects in existence, no larger than a city. Just a marble-sized chunk from one of these stars would weigh about as much as an entire mountain of solid rock. Black holes, for their part, are even more bizarre. They are stellar remnants where the mass has been compressed to a single point by gravitational contraction. They are called black holes because they are a region of space from which nothing can ever escape—not even light.

Jet set (above)
Some black holes are truly phenomenal in scale. The elliptical galaxy M87 is believed to harbor a supermassive black hole in its heart—with the mass of about two billion of our Suns. This Hubble image shows a jet of subatomic particles blasting out of the galaxy, powered in some unknown way by the central black hole.

Glowing stellar remains (right)
This web-like membrane of glowing gas, known as IC 443, is a supernova remnant left behind by a supernova about 8,000 years ago in our Milky Way Galaxy. Supernova remnants can remain visible for hundreds of thousands of years, their lifetime dependent on the amount of material ejected by the star's final blast.

Black holes

Black holes are perhaps the most enigmatic astrophysical objects of all. They are believed to form from those stellar cores that, having run out of nuclear fuel and blasted off most of the mass of the star, still contain more than about three solar masses of material. With that much matter all in one place and no central engine pushing outward, there is no known force that can prevent the star from collapsing to a single point. Its gravity consumes it utterly, and it becomes a black hole. Black holes, by definition, emit no light, no radiation of any kind. Nevertheless, astronomers are certain they have found some stellar mass black holes indirectly, usually in binary star systems where they are seen sucking material from their luckless companions. The blue supergiant called Cygnus X-1 is almost certainly orbiting a black hole.

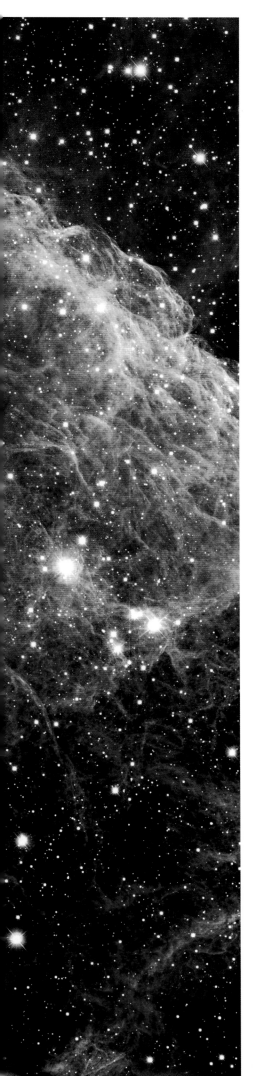

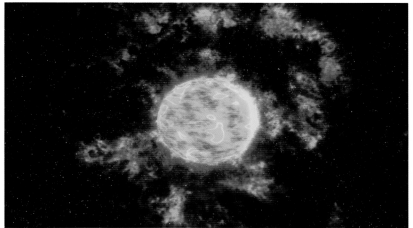

Wolf-Rayet star—final hours (1)

Black hole birth (left and below)
A Wolf-Rayet star, hours before its demise (1), begins to run catastrophically short on fuel within its layered core (2). With no energy to support its mass, the core collapses, giving birth to a black hole (3). Greedily, the black hole sucks in the outer stellar layers, flattening them to form a disk, but a small amount of energy escapes through the polar regions, possibly powered by the spin of the newborn black hole (4). Piercing the stellar surface, the material belches out into space (5). Internal collisions within this energized stellar debris create a powerful jet of particles and radiation, which is seen from Earth as a spectacular gamma-ray burst (6).

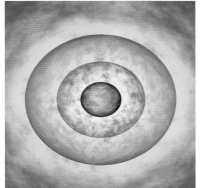

Fuel shortage (2)

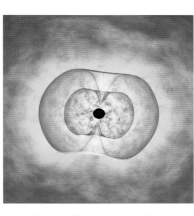

Core collapse and black hole birth (3)

Escaping the black hole (4)

Piercing the stellar surface (5)

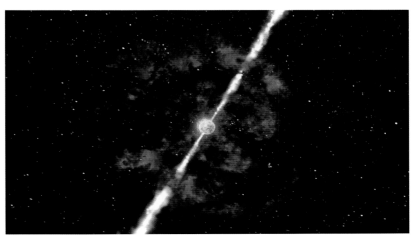

Gamma-ray burst (6)

Neutron stars

Most giant stars do not end up as black holes. After they have "gone supernova," a remnant core, between 1.4 and 3 times the mass of the Sun, forms a solid ball composed entirely of subatomic particles called neutrons. These stellar "cinders" are known as neutron stars. Neutron stars, like the one pictured below, are exceedingly compact—a teaspoonful of its material weighs an incredible billion metric tons.

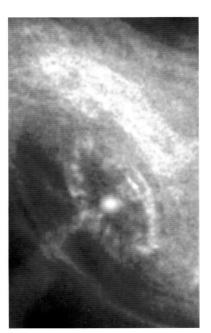

Pulsars

Neutron stars are left spinning extremely rapidly after they form. This rotation is what enables astronomers to detect them, and is, in fact, what led to their discovery in the 1960s. Some neutron stars emit beams of radio waves and sometimes higher energy radiation from their magnetic poles. As they spin, these beams rotate like cosmic lighthouses. If Earth happens to lie within the sweep of the beam, the radio emission will be seen to blink on and off with precise regularity. These neutron stars are known as pulsars. It's a misnomer, in that no pulsating is involved, only rotation. But the name has stuck. The Chandra X-ray image, left, shows the pulsar at the heart of the Crab Nebula, 6,300 light-years away in Taurus.

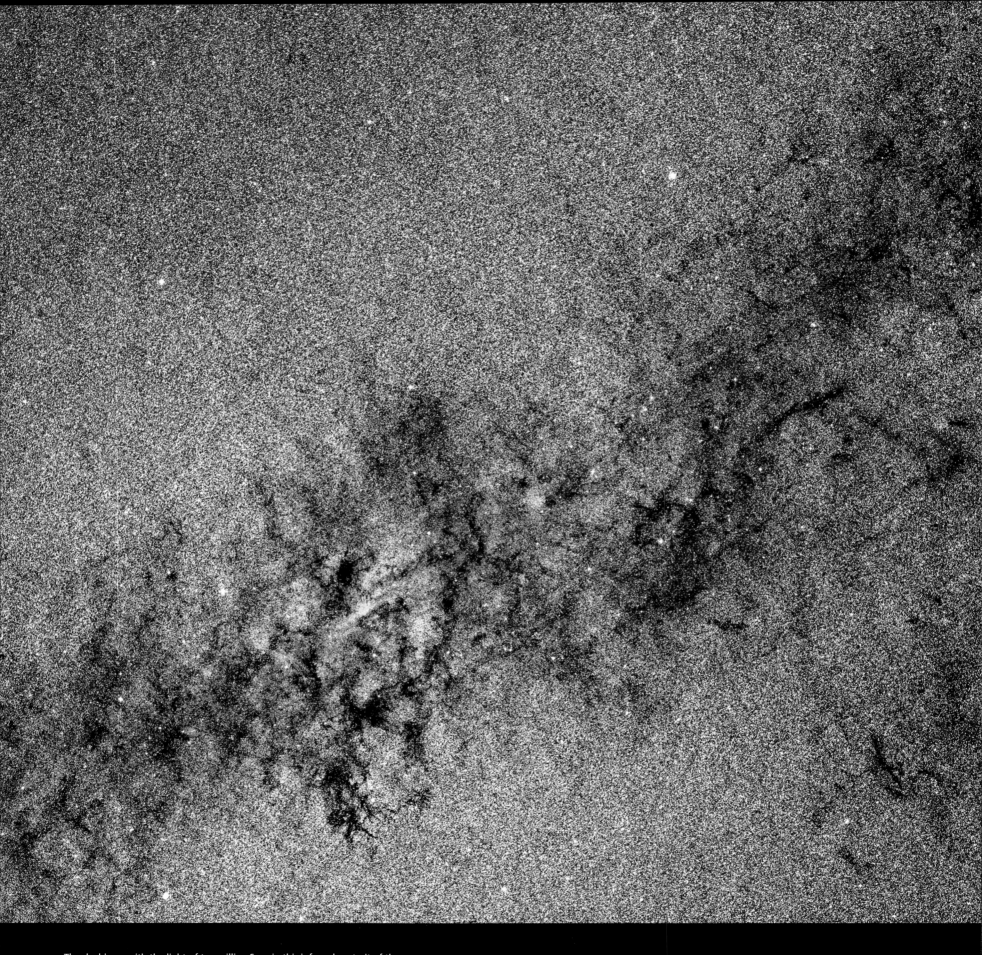

The sky blazes with the light of ten million Suns in this infrared portrait of the Milky Way Galaxy. The Galactic core, thought to harbor a supermassive black hole, is at the lower left of the image. The stars here and along the Galactic plane appear reddened because their light is scattered by thick dust.

CHARTING THE MILKY WAY

Zooming out from the Local Neighborhood by a factor of ten, the true nature and structure of our home in extragalactic space becomes apparent. This is the Milky Way, a disk-shaped island of 200 billion stars measuring at least 100,000 light-years in diameter. The Solar System lies in the thick of its disk, about 25,000 light-years from the center. If we could somehow project ourselves above the Galactic plane and then to the side of the disk, the Milky Way would look something like the illustration below. A bulge of stars 15,000 light-years thick dominates the center, tapering to a disk of stars about one–fifth that depth in the vicinity of the Local Neighborhood. Stars are not distributed evenly. The spiral arms, rich in interstellar gas and dust, are stellar birthplaces, so these tend to be populated with young blue stars. The bulge is older, giving it a yellow-orange hue characteristic of evolved stars.

The Milky Way (below and right)
On a dark night at the right time of year, a thick band of stars crisscrosses the heavens, as seen in the photo on the right. We see this band because we are within, and looking along, a giant disk of stars—a spiral galaxy. However, mapping our Galaxy's spiral arms is not easy. Astronomers must survey the sky at radio wavelengths. The velocity of gas clouds orbiting the Galactic center can be measured using spectroscopic analysis of the radio waves they emit. Because the velocity of a given cloud determines its place in the Galaxy, astronomers can then build up an idea of the actual spiral pattern. The map below shows the arms as we believe them to be arranged, along with the central bulge which has a thick bar of stars running through its middle.

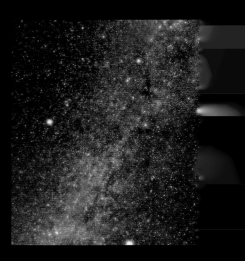

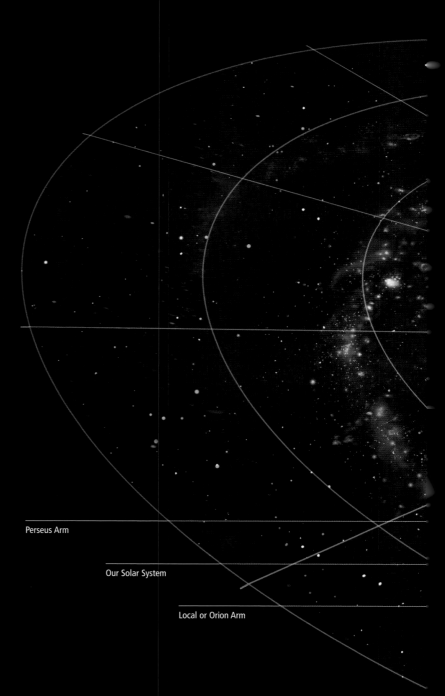

Perseus Arm

Our Solar System

Local or Orion Arm

The Galaxy in cross-section (left)
When the contents of the Galaxy are charted in cross-section, we can see that it is more than a thin disk of stars and dust. Surrounding the central bulge is a vast spherical region known as the Galactic halo. This is the realm of dense stellar orbs called globular clusters that orbit around and through the plane of the Milky Way.

Cygnus Arm

Carina-Sagittarius Arm

Molecular ring

Central bulge | Central bar

Galaxy in the garden (right)
The Milky Way gets its name for the faint band of "milky" light that stretches across the sky on a dark night. This photo shows the sky looking toward Sagittarius. The Milky Way is particularly bright in this direction because it marks the location of the center of the Galaxy. However it would be much brighter were it not for thick veils of obscuring dust.

Norma Arm

Crux-Scutum Arm

10 000

20 000

30 000

40 000

50 000

THE DISK

In common with other spiral galaxies, the Milky Way's disk has a bluish hue. This is because its spiral arms are traced by young stars, which tend to be blue. The predominance of young stars here is partly explained by the concentration in the disk of interstellar gas and dust—the raw material for new stars. However, the trigger for lots of new star creation (as well as an explanation for the spiral patterns in the disk) is density waves: zones of enhanced compression that rotate at slower speeds compared to the orbits of the stars themselves. Stars and other material are only part of a spiral arm for a while and then move out, somewhat like cars entering and leaving a bottleneck of traffic on a busy road. The brightest stars that are sparked into life by a density wave die out before they have traveled very far, which is why the spiral arms are traced by these stellar beacons.

Glowing disk (right)
This all-sky infrared photo of the Milky Way is made from the captured light of more than half a billion stars. The dark lane running through the middle is interstellar gas and dust, which is confined to the disk. The Magellanic Clouds are also captured at bottom right.

Milky Way twin (left)
Astronomers believe that the Milky Way is a type of galaxy called a barred spiral, similar to the galaxy M83 seen here. As in our Galaxy, a thick bar-like structure of old stars passes through the middle, with the spiral arms attached to its ends.

Radio continuum (408 MHz)

Atomic hydrogen

Radio continuum (2.5 GHz)

Molecular hydrogen

Infrared

Mid-infrared

Near-infrared

Optical

X-ray

Gamma-ray

Observing the Milky Way

Although we can clearly see the spiral structures of galaxies external to our own, determining the structure of the Milky Way is very difficult because we are embedded within its disk. It is rather like trying to determine the shape of a large forest while standing among the trees. Still, astronomers have the entire range of the electromagnetic spectrum at their disposal to help them in their quest. The series of images on the left shows the disk of our Galaxy at a range of different wavelengths, each of which helps make up a complete picture of our Galactic home. Radio wavelengths are particularly suited to tracing hot ionized gas and energetic electrons moving through the interstellar medium, which are often associated with supernova explosions. Infrared observations allow us to detect thermal emissions and to "see" through clouds of dust. Finally, energy from exotic objects such as neutron stars and black holes is best observed in the X-ray and gamma-ray end of the electromagnetic spectrum.

Beacon in the dust (below)
This is the view toward the center of the Milky Way in the region of the zodiacal constellation Scorpius, whose bright orange star, Antares, shines at center right.

Disk nurseries (left and below)
The Milky Way's disk is thick with star-forming nebulas and dust clouds. To the left we can see into the heart of a typical nebula known as the Butterfly (IC 1318), 1,500 light-years away in Cygnus. The red color is from hydrogen, glowing as it absorbs the light of nearby stars (such as Sadr [γ Cygni], top left), while the dark lanes are filaments of interstellar dust. Below, a whole string of nebulas can be seen in the constellation Sagittarius, the brightest of which is the red Lagoon Nebula (M8), at center.

THE CENTER OF THE GALAXY

The center of the Milky Way—its nucleus or central bulge—is the hub about which the rest of the Galaxy revolves. It is a dense ball, roughly spherical, comprised mostly of evolved red stars, ancient in the extreme. There is almost certainly a bar, about 5,000 light-years across and at least 20,000 light-years long, running through the center, which connects to the inner edges of a vast circle of stars called the molecular ring. The nucleus is impossible to observe at "normal" or optical wavelengths, being hidden behind 25,000 light-years of gas and interstellar dust. However it is still possible to peer into the Galaxy's heart in other wavelengths and learn something about its contents. To the right is an artist's impression of the Arches Cluster, a massive gathering of around 2,000 stars near the center. Some of the stars are more than a hundred times the mass of our humble Sun.

Star cemetery (above)
This X-ray image, which covers about three degrees of sky, reveals white dwarfs, black holes, and neutron stars near the Galactic core, which lies within the white patch at the center.

Infrared core (below)
The core and disk of the Milky Way glows brightly at infrared energies, as seen in this high-resolution image. The imaged area is about 500 light-years across.

Revealing the Galactic center

From Earth, the Milky Way's center is hidden behind thousands of light-years of gas and dust. However, astronomers have made great progress in their study of this very dense and active region. The first sign that something unusual lies at the heart of the Galaxy came with the advent of radio astronomy in 1932 and the detection of a strong radio emission in Sagittarius. It has been a primary target of radio telescopes ever since. More recently, orbiting X-ray and gamma-ray observatories have uncovered more secrets of the enigmatic nucleus. On the larger scale, a survey of 30 million stars carried out by NASA's Spitzer infrared telescope and completed in 2005, has finally enabled astronomers to get a good idea of the structure of the inner Galactic region. It indicated a central bar of old stars at least 20,000 light-years long.

Sagittarius A

At the center of the Milky Way is a strong radio wave source known as Sagittarius A (Sgr A). It is about 50 light-years across and is threaded with much longer filaments of gas, entrained along magnetic field lines hundreds of light-years long. Deep within Sagittarius A is a compact central core called Sagittarius A* (pronounced, "A-star"), which pinpoints the physical center of the Milky Way Galaxy. Sagittarius A* measures about 120 AU across and is crammed with 3.7 million solar masses of material, and yet emits very little radiation. Sagittarius A* is most probably a supermassive black hole, a somewhat smaller version of those detected at the heart of active galaxies.

Core uncovered (below)

This Very Large Array radio image shows the center of the Milky Way. The bright yellow glow is Sagittarius A. The fainter emissions in its vicinity hail from active star-forming regions and some supernova remnants—the remains of once mighty stars. The imaged area is about 12,000 light-years across.

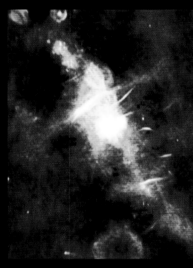

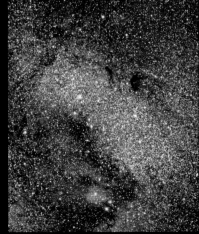

View to the Galactic heart (above)

The Sagittarius Star Cloud—a treasure trove of mostly ancient stars near the heart of the Milky Way—is the focus of this image from the Hubble Space Telescope. Some of the red stars here are among the Galaxy's oldest. Scientists hope to learn about our Galaxy's history by studying these stellar relics.

GLOBULAR CLUSTERS

By far the vast majority of the Milky Way's stars live out their lives in the disk or the nucleus. However, hundreds of millions more can be found orbiting the Galaxy, in so-called globular clusters. Globular clusters, as their name suggests, are roughly spherical swarms of stars (far more extensive than open clusters) usually measuring 100 to 300 light-years across and containing between several tens of thousands and a few million stars each. Almost all of these stars are ancient, having surpassed 10 billion years of life. Globular clusters orbit the Milky Way on highly elliptical paths that are steeply inclined to the Galactic plane, passing through that plane as they move. Our Milky Way hosts an estimated 150 to 200 globulars, but they are not unique to our Galaxy—they are readily observed in orbit around other galaxies, both elliptical and spiral.

Nearby blue stragglers (left)
At a distance of 7,200 light-years, NGC 6397 is the second closest globular cluster to the Sun. The extreme proximity of stars in its core has resulted in the formation of numerous blue straggler stars and oddities such as a suspected neutron star orbiting a red giant.

Omega Centauri (above)
Omega Centauri, located 16,000 light-years away in the constellation Centaurus, is the largest and brightest of the Milky Way's globular clusters. It is made up of well over a million stars and measures over 600 light-years from one extreme to the other. This is a true-color Anglo–Australian Observatory photo.

Looking for the invisible (below)
The Hubble Space Telescope has been used to search for low-mass objects—perhaps part of the Milky Way's "missing mass"—within the globular cluster M22. As illustrated below, Hubble looked through the cluster to search for any brightening of the background stars due to an effect known as gravitational lensing.

Charting globular clusters

The diagram above plots the distribution of most of the Galaxy's globular clusters. Large numbers of these globular clusters are in orbits that bring them high above the Galactic plane, which is probably a consequence of the way that the Milky Way developed. It is thought that globular clusters condensed from individual clouds of gas and dust and were then captured by the Milky Way. Evidence for this comes from the ages of the stars in globular clusters. These stellar geriatric wards contain some of the Milky Way's most ancient stars, some even predating the Galaxy's formation. However, many clusters do contain anomalous younger stars, which are called blue stragglers. Blue stragglers may form when two low-mass red stars collide within the cluster, or they could result from interactions between two closely orbiting stars. In the 1930s, astronomers estimated the position of our Sun (shown at right in the illustration above, but not to scale) within the Milky Way by determining the distribution of globular clusters around the Galaxy.

Ultraviolet Omega Centauri (left)
The Ultraviolet Imaging Telescope captured
this ultraviolet image of Omega Centauri
during a Space Shuttle mission in 1990. This
was the first clear image of Omega Centauri
produced at these wavelengths. Many of the
stars here are not visible in land-based,
optical images.

Lost planets in M22 (right)
This photo of the heart of M22 was captured
by Hubble during its examination of this
globular cluster in 1999. During this search
Hubble detected—by means of gravitational
lensing—objects about 80 times the mass of
Earth that could possibly be planets wrenched
from parent stars within the cluster.

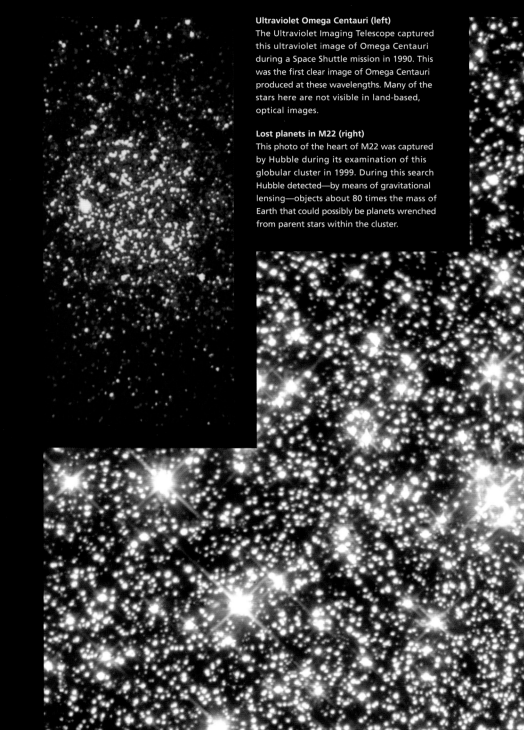

Stellar sphere (left)
M3, photographed here, is a globular cluster
located about 100,000 light-years away in
the constellation Canes Venatici. This vast
ball of half a million stars, which measures
150 light-years across, can be clearly seen
using binoculars.

Globular extraterrestrials? (right)
M13, also known as the Hercules Globular
Cluster, is the most prominent globular
cluster of the northern celestial hemisphere.
In 1974, M13 was selected as the target of
one of the first radio messages addressed to
intelligent extraterrestrial life. We cannot
expect a reply for at least 30,000 years.

THE HALO AND DARK MATTER

We think of our Galaxy largely as a flattened disk, for that is how it and other spirals appear to our eyes. But there is more to the Milky Way—a great deal more. In fact the Milky Way lies at the center of a vast "halo" with two distinctly different components. The inner or visible halo extends out to about 65,000 light-years from the Galactic bulge. This halo is the realm of the globular clusters, which swarm around our Galaxy on highly inclined elliptical orbits. Reaching beyond this is a much darker and more massive halo called the Galactic corona. This is composed of invisible "dark matter" and extremely hot gas at temperatures that are measured in millions of degrees. It reaches perhaps 200,000 to 300,000 light-years into space, or one-tenth of the distance to the Andromeda galaxy.

Gamma-ray halo (above)
The Milky Way's halo is a significant source of gamma radiation. Taken at gamma-ray wavelengths, this all-sky view reveals the extent and position of the halo (shown in blue) above and below the Galactic plane.

Other halos (below)
Our Galaxy is not the only spiral with a halo. This image shows a similar feature around the galaxy NGC 4613. The halo is seen in blue at X-ray wavelengths, while the orange part shows the underlying galaxy in optical light.

The halo

The illustration above shows the Milky Way (center) and its inner, visible halo, which has a radius of about 65,000 light-years. The inner halo is a dynamic place with globular clusters swarming around the Galaxy in large eccentric orbits, but there is more. Astronomers recently found a tiny elliptical galaxy called the Sagittarius Dwarf Elliptical (SagDEG) (1), which is in orbit around the Milky Way, closer in than the Magellanic Clouds. During its motion around the Milky Way on an inclined orbit, a great trail of stars is wrenched out of SagDEG by the gravity of the Milky Way, forming the so-called Sagittarius stream (2). The inner regions of the halo are also home to galactic fountains (3) and high-velocity clouds (4). The latter are clouds of hydrogen gas moving around above the plane of the Galaxy at speeds faster than the underlying Galaxy itself. Their origin is uncertain, but they may be related to galactic fountains. Galactic fountains act as vents for the hot, ionized gas that forms when supernovas in the Galactic disk erupt in a small area at the same time. They send vast bubbles of expanding gas tens of thousands of light-years into the halo. There, the gas eventually cools down and falls back to the disk as "galactic rain."

Dark matter

Observations have shown that, measured from the center, the speed of rotation in the Milky Way begins to drop off with radius but then remains essentially constant. The same is true of other disk galaxies. However this is not the rotation that would be expected of the disks of stars, gas, and dust that we can observe. The only explanation is that there is a lot of material which we cannot see, surrounding and within all galaxies, that affects the way they rotate. This material has been termed "dark matter," and it is thought to outweigh normal matter by a factor of ten, possibly much more. Some dark matter may be made of ordinary material which simply emits little or no light, such as black holes, brown dwarfs or MACHOs. Alternatively, the matter is particulate, composed of particles that do not interact strongly with normal matter, such as neutrinos.

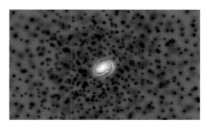

Extragalactic MACHOs (above)
This is a conceptual depiction of MACHOs (Massive Compact Halo Objects) embedded within the Galactic halo. These hypothetical forms of dark matter consist of ordinary matter that emits little or no radiation, yet add significantly to the mass of the galaxy.

Dark matter trap (below left)
This mysterious-looking contraption is part of a dark matter detector installed deep underground in Yorkshire, England. It is designed to detect elusive dark matter particles as they interact with normal atoms.

Intangible enclosure (below)
This X-ray image shows a hot gas cloud embedded within a cluster of galaxies. The presence of this cloud is an indication of the existence of dark matter because the gravity of the observable matter would not be capable of containing the gas without it.

The Andromeda Galaxy (M31) is the largest galaxy in the Local Group—the galaxy cluster that includes our Milky Way. This sprawling spiral of stars, visible to the naked eye as a fuzzy cloud, was first recorded in AD 905. Two of M31's satellite galaxies—M32 and M110—can also be seen in this image.

THE LOCAL GROUP

CHARTING THE LOCAL GROUP

The Local Group is the name given to the small cluster of galaxies to which the Milky Way belongs. Spanning a volume of space about 6 to 8 million light-years across, this sprinkling of stellar islands contains about 40 or so members with a combined mass of some 2 trillion Suns. Its largest members are the Andromeda Galaxy (M31), the Milky Way, and the Pinwheel Galaxy (M33). Andromeda and the Milky Way, in particular, dominate the cluster. And it is likely that these galaxies will eventually pull the whole group together to form a supergalaxy. However, most members are small and faint. These include irregular galaxies such as the Magellanic Clouds and dwarf elliptical galaxies—easily the most common type in the universe. Dwarf ellipticals, however, are so small and faint that they cannot easily be detected beyond Andromeda. As a result, a precise gauge of the Local Group's size has proved difficult to establish.

The Local Group
The map below charts the Local Group within a radius of 3 million light-years of the Milky Way. In total, 32 galaxies are plotted, though the Local Group contains others farther afield and one too close to the Milky Way to show clearly. The total number may be 40 or more. The map shows how the Milky Way and M31 dominate the cluster. Both of them are surrounded by their own satellites, such as the Large Magellanic Cloud (part of which is pictured right). Only the three spirals—the Milky Way, M31, and M33—are shown to scale. The others have been greatly enlarged for clarity. The nearest galaxies outside the Local Group are about 10 million light-years away.

GALAXIES WITHIN 3 MILLION LIGHT-YEARS			
	NAME	TYPE OF GALAXY	DISTANCE (10^6 LY)
1	The Milky Way	Spiral	--
2	Sagittarius Dwarf (SagDEG)	Dwarf elliptical/spheroidal	0.09
3	Large Magellanic Cloud (LMC)	Irregular	0.18
4	Small Magellanic Cloud (SMC)	Irregular	0.21
5	Ursa Minor Dwarf	Dwarf spheroidal	0.24
6	Draco Dwarf	Dwarf spheroidal	0.28
7	Sculptor Dwarf	Dwarf spheroidal	0.30
8	Sextans Dwarf	Dwarf spheroidal	0.32
9	Carina Dwarf	Dwarf spheroidal	0.36
10	Fornax Dwarf	Dwarf spheroidal	0.50
11	Leo II (Leo B)	Dwarf spheroidal	0.75
12	Leo I	Dwarf spheroidal	0.90
13	Phoenix Dwarf	Dwarf irregular/spheroidal	1.6
14	Barnard's Galaxy (NGC 6822)	Irregular	1.8
15	NGC 185	Dwarf elliptical	2.3
16	NGC 147	Dwarf elliptical	2.4
17	Leo A (Leo III)	Irregular	2.5
18	Andromeda VII (Cassiopeia Dwarf)	Dwarf spheroidal	2.6
19	Andromeda VIII	Dwarf spheroidal	2.7
20	Cetus Dwarf	Dwarf spheroidal	2.8
21	Andromeda VI (Pegasus II)	Dwarf spheroidal	2.8
22	Andromeda III	Dwarf spheroidal	2.9
23	M110 (NGC 205)	Dwarf elliptical/spheroidal	2.9
24	M32 (NGC 221)	Dwarf elliptical	2.9
25	Andromeda Galaxy (M31)	Spiral	2.9
26	Andromeda I	Dwarf spheroidal	2.9
27	IC 1613	Irregular	2.9
28	Andromeda V	Dwarf spheroidal	2.9
29	Andromeda II	Dwarf spheroidal	2.9
30	Pisces Dwarf (LGS 3)	Dwarf irregular/spheroidal	3.0
31	Pinwheel Galaxy (M33)	Spiral	3.0
32	Pegasus Dwarf	Irregular	3.0

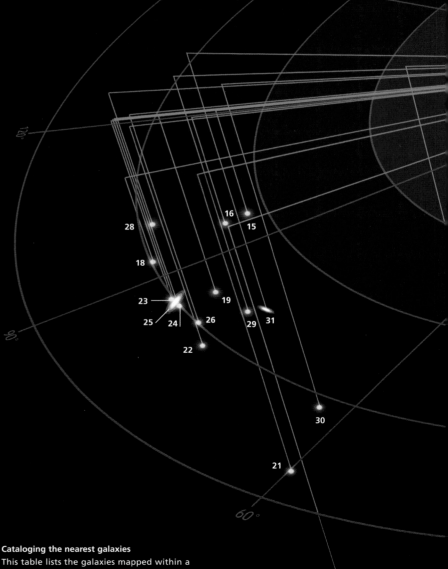

Cataloging the nearest galaxies
This table lists the galaxies mapped within a radius of 3 million light-years of the Milky Way. Although the distances to the very closest galaxies are known fairly accurately, the same is not true of the more distant members of the Local Group. Dwarf spheroidal galaxies are a subclass of dwarf elliptical galaxies distinguished by low luminosity.

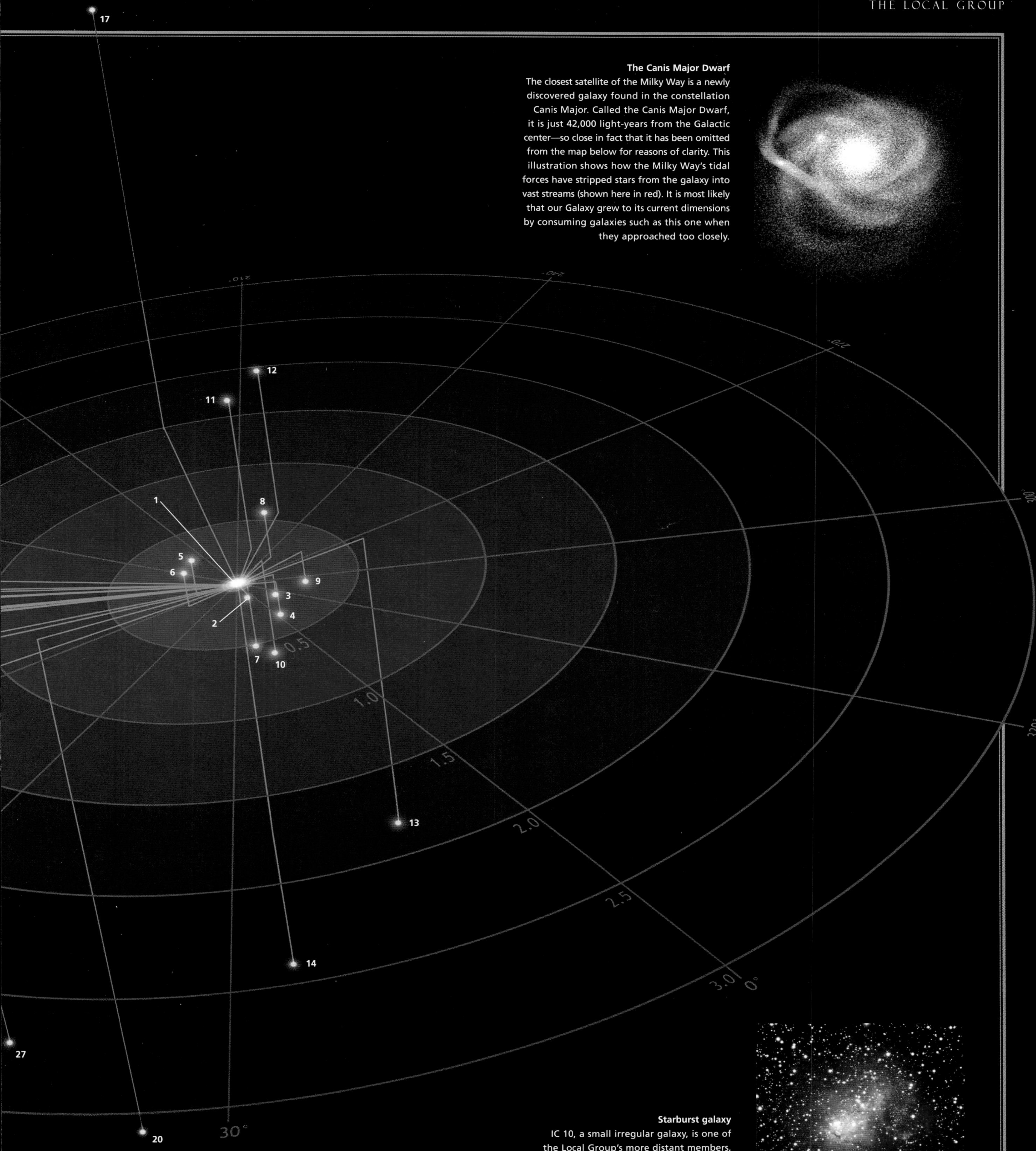

The Canis Major Dwarf
The closest satellite of the Milky Way is a newly discovered galaxy found in the constellation Canis Major. Called the Canis Major Dwarf, it is just 42,000 light-years from the Galactic center—so close in fact that it has been omitted from the map below for reasons of clarity. This illustration shows how the Milky Way's tidal forces have stripped stars from the galaxy into vast streams (shown here in red). It is most likely that our Galaxy grew to its current dimensions by consuming galaxies such as this one when they approached too closely.

Starburst galaxy
IC 10, a small irregular galaxy, is one of the Local Group's more distant members, situated about 4.2 million light-years from the Milky Way. It is known as a "starburst galaxy," meaning its rate of star formation is exceptionally high. Astronomers are uncertain as to what might have triggered this activity.

SATELLITE GALAXIES

Just as gravity keeps Earth encircling the Sun, so it invisibly tethers small satellite galaxies to the Milky Way. The Large Magellanic Cloud (LMC) and its more compact companion, the Small Magellanic Cloud (SMC), are irregularly shaped mini galaxies, and the largest of our Galaxy's satellites. They are easily visible in the southern hemisphere, looking somewhat like detached fragments of the Milky Way. The LMC is the closer of the two, 160,000 light-years away and 20,000 light-years across. The SMC is a little less than half this size and about 40,000 light-years farther away. There are eleven other satellites, some only recently discovered, hidden behind the Milky Way's interstellar dust clouds. The two closest, within 90,000 light-years, are the Canis Major Dwarf and Sagittarius Dwarfs Elliptical (SagDEG). The smallest are only 500 light-years across.

Galactic companions (above left and left)
These two photos capture the LMC (above left) and the SMC (left) at optical or visible wavelengths. The pink glow at the right in the LMC is the enormous Tarantula Nebula (see images on facing page, top right). The sparkling orb in the lower image is the globular cluster 47 Tucanae. At 15,000 light-years away it is much closer than the SMC which lies behind it.

Infant stars in the SMC (right)
This Hubble Space Telescope image shows a star cluster in the heart of the SMC called NGC 346. Some stars, detected by Hubble strung along the dark, intersecting dust lanes, are extremely young and have not yet begun converting hydrogen into helium in their cores via thermonuclear reactions. Fragmentary galaxies like the Magellanic Clouds are thought to closely resemble the galaxies that populated the early universe, so star birth within them is of particular interest to astronomers and cosmologists.

Diving into the Tarantula (right and far right)
The Tarantula Nebula or NGC 2070 (right) is a truly monstrous star factory within the LMC, well over 800 light-years in diameter. If it were in the location of the nearby Orion Nebula, it would span one-quarter of the sky and be visible in daylight. The image at far right shows Hodge 301, a star cluster within the Tarantula. Many of the cluster's most massive stars have exploded as supernovas, compressing the surrounding gas into sheets and filaments visible at the upper part of the image.

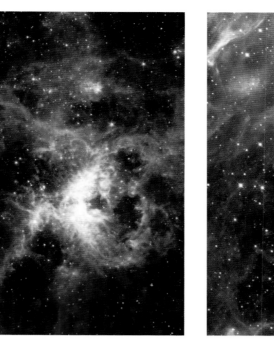

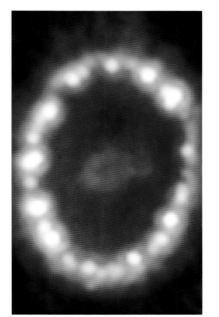

The Magellanic Stream (above)
In the 1970s, it was discovered that the LMC and SMC are embedded within a diffuse ribbon of hydrogen gas which stretches for more than 120 degrees across the sky, passing close to the southern pole of the Milky Way. This is known as the Magellanic Stream, illustrated above with the leading arm to the right of the Clouds and the stream to the left. It is probably the result of material ripped out of the Clouds or the Milky Way (or both) some 200 million years ago during a tidal interaction between the three galaxies.

Ring of fire (left)
In 1987, the LMC was the site of the brightest supernova to be recorded in the last 400 years when a 20-solar-mass star exploded. This photo of SN 1987A, as the supernova was officially named, was taken sixteen years later. Clearly visible is a ring of gas, about one light-year across, heated to millions of degrees by blast waves spreading out from the supernova.

Spiral Galaxies

Spirals are the most easily recognizable and beautiful of all galaxies, yet they account for fewer than one-third of the galaxies found in the universe. Spirals are composed of flattened disks that surround central bulges, but their most prominent features are of course their spectacular spiral arms. These majestic accoutrements are the result of compression waves that propagate around a galaxy's disk, condensing gas and initiating star formation. Thus star birth and death in these spiral disks is a continuing process and the galaxies, as a result, are seeded with star-forming clouds of interstellar gas and dust. The newer stars that populate the arms and disk give these regions their distinctive blue hues; while the older stars, yellowing with age, are concentrated in the central bulge and in the globular clusters that encircle spiral galaxies in long elliptical orbits.

Classifying spiral galaxies

Astronomers classify spiral galaxies according to the size of their central bulges and the degree to which their spiral arms are wound. Tightly wound spirals with large nuclei are classified Sa; if the arms are more open the galaxy is classed Sb; and Sc is reserved for those galaxies with very loose spiral arms and small nuclei. Some spirals have central bulges with a slightly different structure—a thick, central bar of stars that runs through the nucleus. These are known as barred spirals, and are classified SBa, SBb, or SBc. Examples of normal and barred spirals can be seen above (NGC 4622, classed Sb, on the left; NGC 1300, classed SBb, center). Meanwhile, some galaxies, while disk-shaped like spirals, have no apparent spiral structure. These are known as lenticular galaxies and are classed S0. An example is NGC 2787, above right.

Perfect spirals (top and opposite page)
The Triangulum Galaxy, also known as the Pinwheel or M33 (above), is one of the Local Group's three spiral galaxies, but it is not very large, only half the size of the Milky Way. This photo shows M33 as captured by a large ground-based telescope. The facing page shows a much larger and more stately spiral. This is M51, also known as the Whirlpool for obvious reasons. This galaxy, some 25 million light-years away, is not in the Local Group though it is a superb example of a spiral. In this Hubble image hot young stars show up as blue while regions of star birth are red.

Whirlpool nursery (right)
This close-up of the Whirlpool Galaxy (M51) shows in detail a section of one of the galaxy's spiral arms. Star-forming regions are shown red in this image, illuminated by young stars embedded within them. The Whirlpool Galaxy is a particularly rich site of star creation due to its interaction with a much smaller galaxy, NGC 5195, which has been gliding past in close proximity for several hundred million years. Gravitational interaction with this interloper has, over time, compressed interstellar dust and gas, sparking star formation.

Edge-on spiral and companion (left)
This photo reveals a spiral galaxy (NGC 1532 in Eridanus) seen here almost edge-on. As in our Milky Way, the galactic disk is run through with lanes of light-obscuring dust clouds. NGC 1532 is engaged in a gravitational tug-of-war with a smaller, irregular galaxy (NGC 1531, at top left). The two galaxies are interacting with each other in the same way that the Milky Way influences the Large and Small Magellanic clouds. As the two galaxies move around each other, they pull diffuse streams of stars and gas from their neighbor, spreading them across intergalactic space.

Dusty spiral (right)
Bode's Galaxy (M81) is a prominent, well-formed spiral galaxy located about 12 million light-years away in the constellation of Ursa Major. It gives its name to the small galaxy cluster adjacent to the Local Group—the M81 group—to which it belongs. This infrared image maps in red the generous distribution of dust and gas through the spiral arms of the galaxy.

ELLIPTICAL AND IRREGULAR GALAXIES

Most members of the Local Group are either elliptical or irregular galaxies. Elliptical galaxies are the most common type in the universe, accounting for around 60 percent of the total, while irregulars make up about 10 percent. The Local Group's examples of these galaxies are mostly very small, known as dwarf ellipticals and dwarf irregulars. They measure only a few thousand light-years across and often contain no more stars than globular clusters. As their names suggest, ellipticals are spheroidal, while irregulars have no easily recognizable structure and differ from one galaxy to another. Like spirals, irregulars contain both young and old stars and have active stellar nurseries within them, but ellipticals are usually populated only by ancient, red stars. Not all ellipticals are small. The largest galaxies of all are the giant ellipticals, whose stars number in their trillions. None is represented in the Local Group.

Satellites of Andromeda (above)
The Andromeda Galaxy plays host to a wealth of satellite galaxies. Two of the largest are M110 (above) and M32 (below). Both are dwarf elliptical galaxies several thousand light-years across. However, M110 is often called a dwarf spheroidal galaxy—similar to an elliptical but having a looser concentration.

Barnard's Galaxy in Sagittarius (right)
Barnard's Galaxy, or NGC 6822, is a Local Group dwarf irregular with a modest stellar contingent of about 10 million members. Like others of its type, Barnard's Galaxy boasts several sites of active star formation, as well as nebula bubbles, pink in this image, blown by stellar wind from intensely hot Wolf-Rayet stars within.

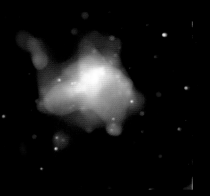

Supernova action (above)

The dwarf irregular galaxy NGC 1569, 7 million light-years away in Camelopardalis, sits just outside the realm of the Local Group. This X-ray image shows bubbles of gas heated by the action of dramatic supernova explosions erupting out of the galaxy.

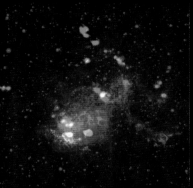

Irregular gas (above)

This is a composite optical and radio portrait of the irregular Local Group member IC 10. The optical image is in blue, while ionized hydrogen is shown as red and carbon monoxide as green. Such observations reveal that the distribution of gas in irregular galaxies is more irregular than once thought.

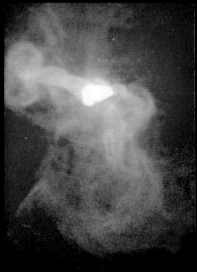

Star shredder (above)

M87 in Virgo is one of the largest known giant elliptical galaxies. At its heart there is thought to be a supermassive black hole, 2.6 billion times the mass of the Sun, consuming stars that approach too close. This composite X-ray and radio image reveals jets of subatomic particles, powered by the core, extending into extragalactic space.

Interacting Galaxies

Galaxy clusters are crowded places. While the stars within individual galaxies are exceptionally distant from each other—tens of millions of stellar diameters apart—galaxies in the densest clusters are separated from their neighbors by only ten to twenty galactic diameters. Galaxies in a cluster can be likened to balls on a snooker table, while for stars it is more like a grain of sand every few tens of miles. For this reason, interactions between galaxies are common; and yet when they occur, hardly any of the stars within will come close to colliding. The two galaxies flow together and merge but their stars rarely touch. Galactic interaction plays a major role in the evolution of galaxies and galaxy clusters. The Milky Way, for example, is approaching the Andromeda Galaxy, and the two are expected to merge to form a single, larger entity that will dominate the Local Group.

Stellar wheel (left)
This enigmatic galaxy is known as Hoag's Object, named after the astronomer who discovered it in 1950. Hoag's Object is a so-called ring galaxy with a bright nucleus that is surrounded by a ring of comparatively young stars. It is located about 600 million light-years away in the constellation Fornax. Ring galaxies are normally formed when a small galaxy passes right through the core of a spiral, sending out shockwaves to ignite new stars in its wake. Strangely, Hoag's Object shows no other signs of collision and the ring structure is more likely the remains of a galaxy that passed too close.

Merging galaxies

When we look deeper and deeper into space, we are peering farther back into time, for it has taken longer for light to reach us from these distant objects. One observation that astronomers have made is that the farther back they look, the more common spiral galaxies become, whereas in the more immediate universe it is the ellipticals that reign. Why is this? The answer, very probably, is that as time has progressed, more and more spiral galaxies have merged to form ellipticals. Not only does this explain why spirals are now in the minority, it also neatly accounts for the lack of interstellar gas in ellipticals because gas is generally stripped out when galaxies collide, left stranded in intergalactic space. Ellipticals are not the only possible outcome of galactic mergers; many different forms, both beautiful and strange, have been observed.

Galactic cannibalism

Galactic cannibalism is the process by which a smaller galaxy is entirely consumed by a larger one. Often there is no trace left of the smaller galaxy, but sometimes telltale signs remain. NGC 1316, 53 million light-years away in the Fornax galaxy cluster, is typical of a galaxy that has grown by consuming others. It is pictured at left, captured by the Hubble Space Telescope. Normally, giant ellipticals are devoid of interstellar gas and dust, but this example is not. The wispy material readily seen right across the galaxy, strung into dark filaments and loops, is thought to be the remains of one or more spiral galaxies swallowed by NGC 1316 in the past 100 million years.

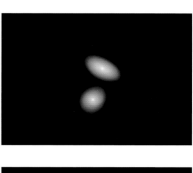

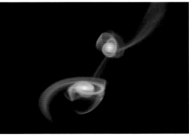

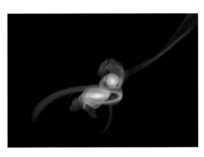

Ripples in the cosmic pond (above)
The galaxy on the right in the image above is cataloged AM 0644-741 and is found in the small southern constellation Volans. It was probably once a normal spiral. However, at some point in the distant past, another, smaller galaxy (which is out of the frame) collided with AM 0644-741 face-on and plunged right through it, sending out a shockwave which has triggered the blue ring of star formation captured here.

Galactic unraveling (right)
Galaxies do not have to collide in order to affect each other. This galaxy is UGC 10214, better known as the Tadpole Galaxy. In this case, a close encounter with a much smaller neighbor has pulled a long stream of stars and gas out of the Tadpole and splashed them across the canvas of extragalactic space. The Tadpole's "tail" can be traced for some 280,000 light-years. The Tadpole can be found 420 million light-years away in Draco.

The future of the Milky Way

The gap between the Milky Way and Andromeda galaxies is closing at about 300,000 miles per hour (500,000 km/h). In about 3 billion years (long before the Sun has become a red giant) the galaxies will collide. The series of images to the right is from a computer simulation of the resulting gravitational dance that will end, after about a billion years, with the birth of a new elliptical galaxy. From the vantage point of Earth, Andromeda will grow ever larger in the night sky until the familiar stars of the Milky Way are joined by a second, intersecting arch of stars. Then, one of two fates awaits the Sun and its planets: either it will be flung into the depths of extragalactic space or drawn into the new galaxy.

This image, constructed from extensive Hubble observations, is a unique "mass map," which charts the distribution of material in a galaxy cluster 4.5 billion light-years away. Each bright, reddish blob is a galaxy, held gravitationally within the cluster by normally invisible dark matter, mapped in blue.

Universe of Galaxies

CHARTING THE UNIVERSE

So far in this book we have considered the universe from our home planet right out to the group of galaxies to which our Milky Way belongs. We can now take one final step farther out to look at the cosmos in its entirety. Astronomers place the distances of some protogalaxies at over ten billion light-years, which indicates that the visible universe is at least twice that in its expanse. In this chapter we take a look at the universe on this vast scale to reveal clusters of galaxies; clusters of clusters (or superclusters); ominous-sounding cosmic voids; and young, active galaxies and quasars perched near the edge of visible space. When we look deep into space we also look deep into the past, witnessing the aftermath of the Big Bang that gave birth to the universe. Here we will examine the universe's evolution to its current state and investigate how it might evolve in the deep future.

Universe of superclusters (below)
Mapping the universe on the largest scale is a challenge because the necessary observations are so difficult to make. The map here, which shows the distribution of material out to a distance of one billion light-years from the Milky Way (at center), is representative rather than precise. On this mind-bogglingly vast scale, which is about one-fourteenth the size of the visible universe, the "clumpiness" of the cosmos is already clearly evident. Individual galaxies have vanished, to be replaced by vast structures, hundred of millions of light-years across, called superclusters—cosmic swarms of galaxy clusters, containing tens of thousands of galaxies, and thousands of trillions of stars. The concentric circles mark distances in steps of 200 million light-years from the Milky Way.

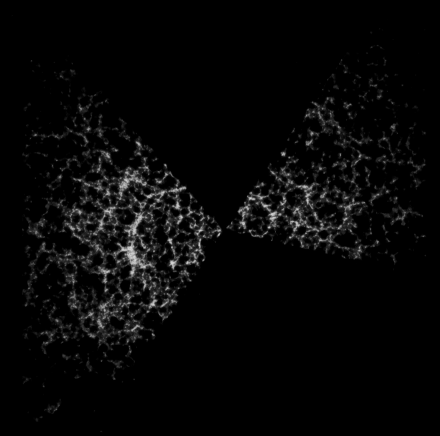

Mapping the universe (above and left)
The Sloan Digital Sky Survey is an ambitious project to observe one-quarter of the entire sky at high resolution, noting the positions of 100 million celestial objects and measuring the distances to about a million galaxies and 100,000 quasars, which are some of the most distant objects known. The aim of this collaborative project is to produce a detailed map of the three-dimensional distribution of matter to the edge of the visible universe. The image above shows a partial view of the universe as reconstructed from data obtained so far. The survey telescope in New Mexico is shown at left.

13

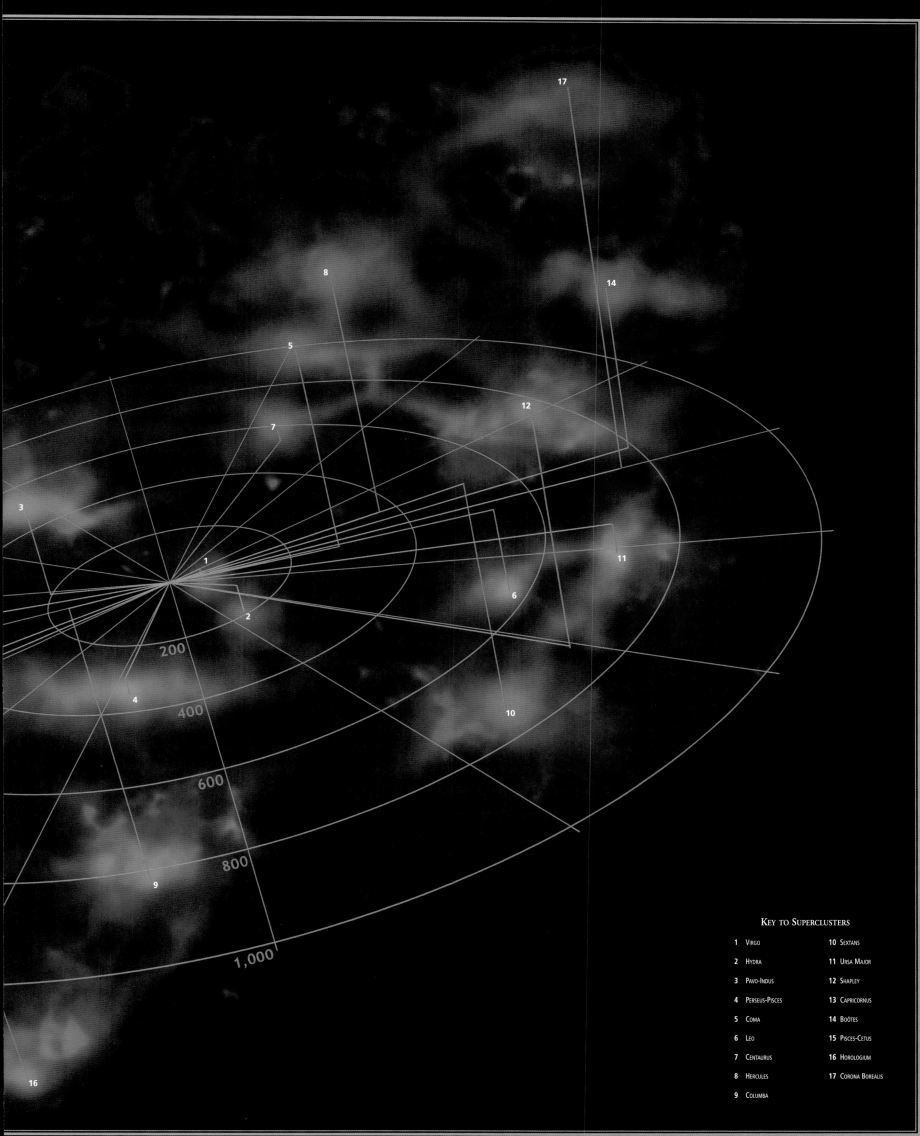

200

400

600

800

1,000

KEY TO SUPERCLUSTERS

1	VIRGO	10	SEXTANS
2	HYDRA	11	URSA MAJOR
3	PAVO-INDUS	12	SHAPLEY
4	PERSEUS-PISCES	13	CAPRICORNUS
5	COMA	14	BOÖTES
6	LEO	15	PISCES-CETUS
7	CENTAURUS	16	HOROLOGIUM
8	HERCULES	17	CORONA BOREALIS
9	COLUMBA		

Expansion of the Universe

In the 1920s, astronomers made a most startling couple of discoveries. The first was that the universe was far larger than they had previously imagined. What were once known as "spiral nebulas," such as the Whirlpool Galaxy (M51), were found to be in fact entire galaxies in their own right; external to, and similar to our own. An even bigger surprise emerged at about the same time: this huge cosmos, so recently assumed to be static and unchanging, was found to be expanding, taking the Milky Way and all other galaxies along with it for the ride. (This was also the first observational evidence to show that the universe may once have had a beginning.) Nowadays, the expansion of the universe is a well-established fact. Furthermore, as we will see a little later, current thinking is that this expansion is actually accelerating. The universe, it seems, is racing away from us, in every direction.

Redshift and expansion

An American astronomer named Edwin Hubble (1889–1953), having captured spectra from more than twenty galaxies, concluded in the late 1920s that they were all moving away from us. The spectrum of a galaxy, like that of a star, contains dark lines that enable astronomers to tell which elements the galaxy is made from. However these spectral lines were not where Hubble expected to find them. By comparing the spectra of these galaxies with a standard spectrum, it was clear that the lines were shifted toward the red which meant the galaxies were moving away—as space expands, the light is stretched, to longer (redder) wavelengths—an effect known as cosmological redshift. Hubble also observed that the farther away the galaxy, the faster it appeared to be receding. This relationship between distance and redshift is now known as Hubble's Law and provides crucial evidence for the expanding universe model.

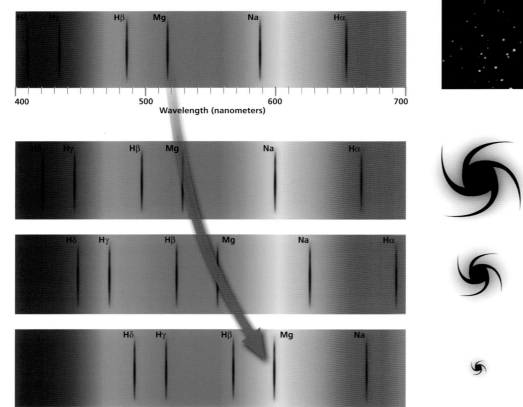

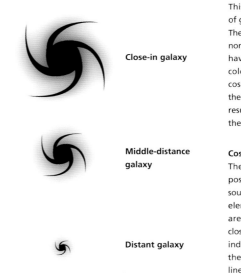

Close-in galaxy

Middle-distance galaxy

Distant galaxy

Galactic distances (above)
This illustration represents the change in spectra of galaxies according to their distribution in space. The foreground galaxies, at close distances, appear normal. However, the galaxies at farther distances have their light redshifted as indicated by their color. Although this phenomenon is known as cosmological redshift, wavelengths right across the electromagnetic spectrum are stretched as a result of the expansion of the universe, not just the light that we can see.

Cosmological redshift (left)
The top spectrum in this illustration shows the position of several spectral lines from a nearby source. These lines are fingerprints of the various elements within the light source. Underneath are spectra from galaxies at various distances: closest at the top and farthest at the bottom, as indicated by the galaxy symbols to the right of the spectra. The spectra show how the spectral lines shift to redder wavelengths as the distance to a galaxy increases.

Measuring expansion

Since stumbling upon the realization that the universe is expanding, cosmologists have been concerned with pinning down a number known as the Hubble Constant. This number describes the rate at which the universe is expanding and provides a crucial step toward determining the age of the universe. Measuring the distance to galaxies is essential in the search for an accurate Hubble Constant. This requires "standard candles" in order to calibrate cosmological redshift observations. Cepheid variables—stars whose variation allows for easy distance calculations—are an example. Using this method, the galaxy M100 (pictured below), containing more than twenty Cepheid stars, was found to be 60 million light-years away. Distances to more remote galaxies require brighter standard candles such as Type 1a supernova flares. These supernovas have the same intrinsic maximum brightness, allowing for fairly straightforward distance estimates. Another method is to compare the fluctuations of brightness between pixels in a digital image—the farther away the galaxy, the smoother its light appears. This method works best with elliptical galaxies.

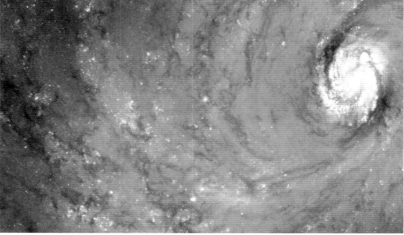

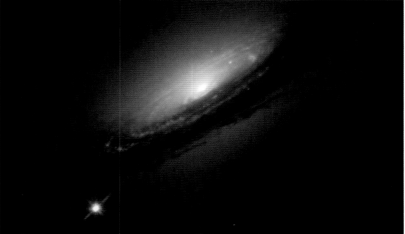

Cosmic expansion (below)
Though the universe is expanding, individual galaxies remain constant in size, the distance between them increasing at a rate that depends on their initial separation, as illustrated below. The galaxies themselves do not enlarge because their gravity is stronger than the force of expansion. Over time, wavelengths of light are stretched by the expansion, moving toward the red end of the visible spectrum and beyond.

Flare in the distance (right)
In 1994 a star on the outskirts of the galaxy NGC 4526 flared up to become a Type 1a supernova (lower left). All such supernovas are thought to have the same intrinsic maximum brightness and therefore are valuable markers when measuring the expansion rate and geometry of the universe.

GALAXY CLUSTERS

Just as stars bunch up together to form clusters and galaxies, so entire galaxies, in turn, tend to gather in vast assemblages known as galaxy clusters. These clusters are the largest structures in the universe bound together by gravity. Some clusters are almost as old as the universe itself. Astronomers classify galaxy clusters according to the density (or "richness") and number of their members. The Local Group, of which the Milky Way is a part, is an example of a small cluster, containing only a few dozen members. At the other extreme are gigantic, rich structures such as the Virgo and Coma clusters, tens of millions of light-years across and home to thousands of galaxies.

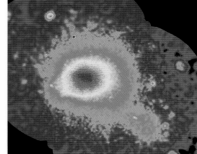

Coma Cluster (top left)
The Coma Cluster (Abell 1656), named for its location in the northern constellation Coma Berenices, is an example of a large galaxy cluster, with as many as 3,000 individual members concentrated toward the center. The cluster is located about 300 million light-years away and is about 20 million light years across.

Coma collision (above)
This ROSAT X-ray satellite observatory view of the Coma Cluster clearly shows its central core (red and yellow) merging with another, smaller concentration of galaxies—the green extension on the lower right.

Giant on the doorstep (left)
Another large galaxy cluster is the Virgo Cluster, situated in the zodiacal constellation of the same name. Containing some 2,000 galaxies and sprawling 9 million light-years across, Virgo is the closest massive cluster to the Milky Way, located only 60 million light-years away. At the center of this photo is M87, a huge elliptical galaxy thought to be the dominant member of the cluster. Many of the brightest galaxies in the Virgo Cluster are easily observable in amateur telescopes.

Clusters of dark matter

The presence of large amounts of invisible material, or "dark matter," appears to be both the explanation for individual galaxy dynamics as well as for the existence of the universe's largest known structures, galaxy clusters. In 1933, Swiss astrophysicist Fritz Zwicky (1898–1974) found that the orbital motions of galaxies within the Coma Cluster indicated a total mass that was far too low for it to remain bound as a cluster. Without dark matter providing the gravitational pull, member galaxies would break free and the cluster would rapidly disintegrate. This dark matter has never been directly observed but may be present in several forms throughout the universe. Brown dwarfs (failed stars) and black holes are "normal matter" candidates for some of this mass but much more must be exotic particles such as weakly interacting massive particles (WIMPS).

Galactic magnifier (above)
The galaxy cluster in this striking Hubble photo, Abell 2218, lies in the constellation Draco. Located some 2 billion light-years away, it is exceptionally distant. However, the curious arcs of light, seemingly within the cluster, are distorted galaxies at least five times more distant and would be invisible if not for the presence of Abell 2218. The gravity of this cluster amplifies and distorts the light from these background galaxies like a gigantic cosmic magnifying lens, pulling them into focus to produce the multiple arcs that we see. This phenomenon is known as gravitational lensing, and was predicted by Einstein's general theory of relativity.

Distant giant (above right)
This composite image is of the young, massive galaxy cluster known as RDCS 1252.9-2927. The mauve splash is extremely hot, X-ray emitting, intracluster gas detected by the Chandra X-ray satellite. Optical emissions captured by the Very Large Telescope are shown red, yellow, and green. This cluster is so far away that we see it as it was when the universe was just 5 billion years old, or about 35 percent of its present age. The merging process, believed to be crucial for cluster formation, takes a long time. Until recently, it was not thought possible for massive galaxy clusters like this one to have formed so early on.

Recent cluster (right)
This false-color infrared image of the galaxy cluster 1ES 0657-558 in the constellation Carina was obtained by the ground-based Very Large Telescope in Chile. This cluster is a source of strong X-ray emission and is asymmetrically distributed, indicating that it has only recently formed. The arc at top right is a distant galaxy gravitationally lensed by this young cluster.

ACTIVE GALAXIES

While galaxies come in many different shapes and sizes, some are profoundly out of the ordinary. These "active galaxies" emit a huge amount of energy across the electromagnetic spectrum. Depending on the type of galaxy, this can be in the form of visible light, infrared, radio waves, ultraviolet, X-ray, or gamma rays. Active galaxies include radio galaxies, quasars, blazars, and Seyfert galaxies. They often boast jets of plasma blasted millions of light-years into space. Exactly how these jets are produced is not well understood. But one thing that is generally agreed is that all active galaxies are powered by the same central engine: probably a supermassive black hole, weighing millions or possibly billions of solar masses. These black holes are surrounded by vast disks of shredded stars and other matter, as illustrated on the right. The disks are encircled by gaseous, doughnut-shaped rings, as shown in the illustration below. All such structures are known as active galactic nuclei, or AGN.

Radio galaxies

Soon after the advent of radio astronomy, it was discovered that some galaxies are exceptionally strong sources of radio waves. In many cases the sources are compact, covering an area comparable in size to the optical dimensions of the underlying galaxy. But in so-called extended sources, the radio waves come from vast stretches of space, many times larger than the galaxies themselves. In a typical extended source, jets of charged particles emanate from the underlying AGN. These jets collide with the gas surrounding the galaxy—the intracluster medium—to produce vast lobe-shaped chambers of energized gas far larger than the galaxy. These lobes are powerful sources of radio energy generated by particles moving through the magnetic fields.

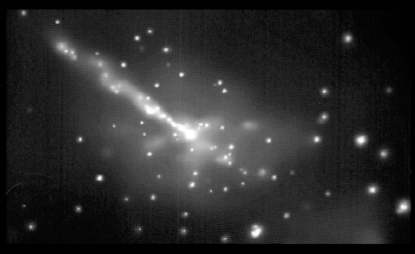

The unified model

Astronomers think that blazars, quasars, and radio galaxies are all essentially the same thing—they only appear different to us because of their orientation in space. According to this so-called unified model, all active galaxies have exactly the same ingredients: an active nucleus powered by a supermassive black hole, a surrounding torus of gas, and particle jets. If the galaxy is oriented so that from Earth we look straight down the jet, we call that galaxy a blazar (1). If we see the galaxy more from the side, we observe a quasar (2). And if we happen to be looking almost perpendicularly at the jets, we see a radio galaxy (3).

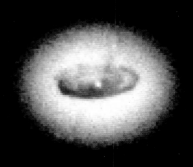

Weighing a black hole (left)
This remarkable Hubble Space Telescope image reveals a whirlpool of gas and dust at the center of the elliptical galaxy NGC 4261 in the Virgo Cluster. The disk is probably the remnant of a smaller galaxy that fell into the core of NGC 4261 and is being consumed by the black hole within. By measuring the speed of the gas swirling around the black hole, astronomers were able to estimate its mass as 1.2 billion times that of the Sun, yet crammed into a space not much larger than the Solar System.

Centaurus A (top, above, and left)
Centaurus A is a well-known radio galaxy located just eleven million light-years away. At the top is the galaxy seen in visible light. Here we can see that Centaurus A is the result of a collision between an elliptical galaxy and a spiral galaxy (which contributes the dark bisecting lanes of dust). Above is the galaxy as seen by the Chandra X-ray satellite. It reveals a jet emanating from the core. The other bright sources are probably X-ray binaries in which a neutron star or small black hole is accreting matter from a nearby companion star. At left is a radio image of the galaxy. The visible galaxy is tiny in relation to the two lobes of energized gas on either side of it—which span more than a million light-years each.

Quasars

Quasars are the most enigmatic of all active galaxies. The name is a contraction of "quasi-stellar," the name given to them by their discoverers because they look almost identical to stars. The reason for this resemblance is that quasars, while the brightest objects in the universe, are typically several billion light-years away—so remote that they appear as singular points of light, just as stars do. Only supermassive black holes are capable of powering such stupendously luminous objects. Quasars appear to have been most common about ten billion years ago. None are found nearby.

SUPERCLUSTERS AND VOIDS

We saw earlier how galaxies are grouped together to form clusters, often containing up to several thousand members. But the universe's predilection for camaraderie does not stop there. For on the very largest scales of all, entire groups of galaxies are themselves bunched up to form unimaginably vast "clusters of clusters"—structures known as superclusters. It follows that because much of the universe's matter is concentrated like this, there must be other regions between superclusters which are by comparison fairly empty. These are known as cosmic voids, or just voids. Voids are roughly spherical and typically 200 million light-years in diameter. The average void is only one-tenth as dense as the rest of the universe, and some of them contain very few galaxies.

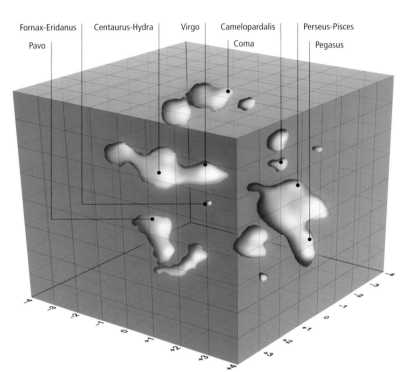

Fornax-Eridanus | Centaurus-Hydra | Virgo | Camelopardalis | Perseus-Pisces

Pavo | Coma | Pegasus

Local superclusters (left)
This illustration shows the distribution of superclusters within 400 million light-years of the Milky Way (indicated by a red dot). The numbers represent steps of 100 million light-years. The dominant superclusters are the Centaurus-Hydra supercluster and the Perseus-Pisces supercluster, which are locked in a gravitational tug of war.

The "Great Attractor" (below left)
This image shows a region of the sky rich with galaxies belonging to the cluster Abell 3627. The "Great Attractor"—a suspected massive concentration of galaxies—is thought to lie in this portion of the sky, pulling the Milky Way and other galaxies toward it.

Filaments and voids (below)
This image from the Max Planck Institute for Astrophysics is a supercomputer simulation of matter distribution within the local universe. Such simulations match observed structures very well. Dark voids bordered by long filamentary superclusters are clearly apparent.

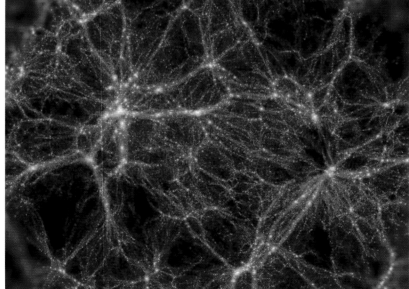

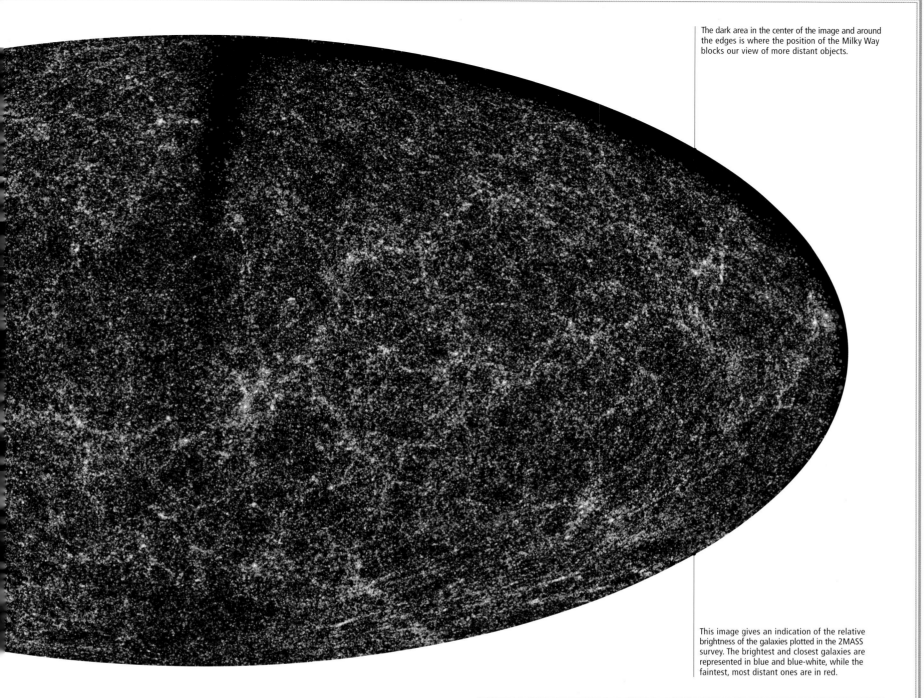

The dark area in the center of the image and around the edges is where the position of the Milky Way blocks our view of more distant objects.

This image gives an indication of the relative brightness of the galaxies plotted in the 2MASS survey. The brightest and closest galaxies are represented in blue and blue-white, while the faintest, most distant ones are in red.

Surveying the universe

In recent decades several research groups have been dedicated to detecting and mapping the large-scale structures of the universe by analyzing the redshift of thousands or even millions of galaxies to plot their position in space. The illustration at right shows how a typical survey operates (in this case the 2dFGRS survey conducted from the Anglo–Australian Observatory). Usually, only narrow sections of the sky are surveyed to economize on valuable telescope time. Often, two surveys are made in opposite or near-opposite directions to test the assumption that, on the largest scales, the universe looks the same in any direction. An alternative means of getting an impression of the structure of the universe is to create entirely computer-generated models. In these simulations an extremely powerful computer is fed data representing an initial distribution of matter and a set of physical laws. The computer then runs the scenario forward in time to see how the distribution of matter "evolves" under the action of gravity.

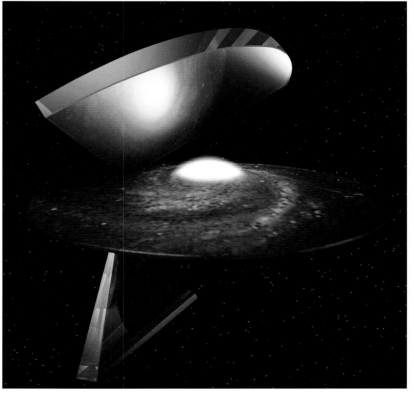

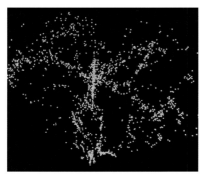

Universal man (left)

This distribution of galaxy clusters in a slice of sky is known endearingly as the "stick man" for its resemblance to a human figure. The image comes from the first attempt to survey the large-scale structure of matter in deep space. Known as the Center for Astrophysics Redshift Survey, it was completed in 1982. This survey also led to the discovery of the "Great Wall," a sheet of galaxies about 600 million light-years long by 250 million light-years wide, making it the largest known structure in the universe.

COSMIC MICROWAVE BACKGROUND

In 1965, two physicists, Arno Penzias (born 1933) and Robert Wilson (born 1936), using a sensitive radio antenna, inadvertently picked up a hiss emanating from the entire sky. They had stumbled upon something that had been predicted theoretically. The "hiss" is the cosmic microwave background (CMB) or cosmic background radiation—a sea of radiation in the microwave region of the spectrum. The radiation hails from a time 380,000 years after the Big Bang, when the universe had a temperature similar to that on the surface of the Sun. Since then, the expansion of space has stretched the wavelength of that radiation from optical to microwave, and it has cooled down to just 4.91°F (2.73°C) above absolute zero.

Cosmic evolution

In 1992, the NASA satellite COBE (the COsmic Background Explorer) made a landmark discovery: background radiation varies in temperature by the tiny amount of one part in 100,000, exactly as expected by Big Bang theory. This temperature variation has been mapped by the recent NASA mission Wilkinson Microwave Anisotropy Probe (WMAP), which can detect variations of a few millionths of a degree. These tiny differences in temperature are believed to have arisen from slight fluctuations in the density of matter in the infant universe. The series of images at left illustrate how these slight differences evolved into the galaxy-rich filamentary structure of the cosmos we observe today (bottom).

Tuning in to the cosmos (right)
This highly detailed all-sky picture constructed from WMAP satellite data, maps slight temperatures differences in the background radiation by color. Warmer temperatures are shown red, cooler temperatures, green and blue.

Detecting the CMB (below)
The WMAP satellite, illustrated here, was launched on June 30, 2001, and orbits Earth at a distance of 930,000 miles (1.5 million km). Like COBE before it, it has mapped the entire microwave sky but at a far higher resolution. The detailed data about the young universe obtained so far appears to confirm the Big Bang hypothesis.

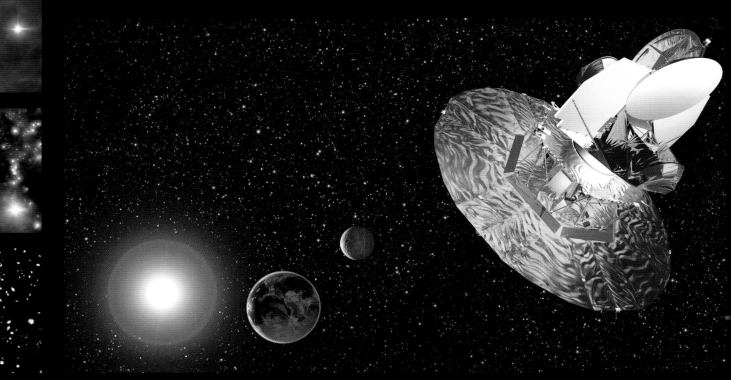

Cosmic light horizon

As astronomers take longer and longer exposures of the sky, they sample ever-fainter objects which are ever-farther away. Because light travels at a finite speed, we see these distant structures not as they are now, but as they were when their light left them, billions of years ago. Light from the farthest detected protogalaxies has taken more than 13 billion years to reach us. However, there is a limit to how far back we can see. Electrons and protons in the early universe had yet to form into atoms and the universe was opaque, a fog of particles and light. Then, at a time now reckoned to be 380,000 years after the Big Bang, atoms first formed and photons were free to travel through space. This time is as far back as we can hope to see. The "cosmic light horizon" (illustrated right) is a sphere centered on Earth with a radius of approximately 13.7 billion light years. It is what COBE and WMAP have in effect tuned into.

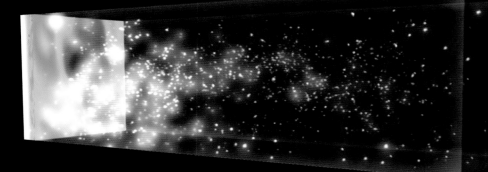

Cosmic time machine (left)
This illustration shows the WMAP satellite observatory looking back through space and time to scan the cosmic light horizon at the far left. This is the equivalent of taking a photo of an 80-year-old person on the day of their birth.

BIG BANG AND THE FIRST THREE MINUTES

The realization early last century that the universe is expanding had profound implications. For if the universe is growing, it must once have been smaller, and there must have existed a time when the entire cosmos occupied a single point. For reasons that may never be fully understood, this initial cosmic seed expanded in an event known as the Big Bang. Everything we now see around us—from subatomic particles to galaxies—all of it evolved from material spewed forth in this initial fireball of creation 13.7 billion years ago. Much of this happened very quickly. Just three minutes after time zero, the temperature had cooled to the degree that protons and neutrons were moving slowly enough to stick when they collided, creating the nuclei of the universe's hydrogen and helium atoms.

Time

0 seconds

Inflation era

10⁻⁴³ seconds

10⁻³⁵ seconds

10⁻¹² seconds

Quarks
By this time the universe consisted of fairly heavy particles called quarks and anti-quarks. Here we show only the so-called "up quark" and the "down quark" but four other species were also forged. At the end of this phase the temperature of the universe was 10^{15} K.

Time zero: Big Bang
The Big Bang itself occurred, according to latest estimates, 13.7 billion years ago. It was the moment of creation for not only matter, but space and time itself. There was nothing "outside" or "before" the Big Bang, because the Big Bang was all that there was or had ever been.

Exotic particles
We can only guess what particles were created in the first instants of the Big Bang. Here we simply call them "exotic particles," fashioned alongside "particles" of radiation called photons.

Cosmic inflation
When it was 10^{-35} seconds old, the universe we see today underwent an exponential increase in expansion known as inflation. It was smaller than an atom but swelled to the size of a grapefruit, then resumed its slower growth. By 10^{-32} seconds, inflation had ended and the temperature had dropped to about 10^{35} K.

Bubble chamber (above)
To recreate and study the kinds of particles that might have been created in the extremely hot and energetic conditions of the universe's first moments, particle physicists smash particles together at nearly the speed of light in gigantic particle accelerators. This false-color image shows the trails left by charged particles moving in superheated liquid inside a so-called "bubble chamber." An applied magnetic field pulls the particles into characteristic spirals.

The particle zoo (right)
The number and diversity of particles created in the Big Bang is staggering. Just a few are illustrated here. Generally there are two families of truly elementary particles—those that are not made up of others. These are leptons (electrons being one species) and quarks. Protons and neutrons are not elementary, in that they are made up of quarks. All particles in the known universe probably have antimatter counterparts, but antimatter now is exceptionally rare.

KEY TO SYMBOLS

EXOTIC PARTICLES	RADIATION	NEUTRON
UP QUARK	ELECTRON	ANTI-NEUTRON
ANTI-UP QUARK	ANTI-ELECTRON (POSITRON)	DEUTERIUM NUCLEUS
DOWN QUARK	PROTON (HYDROGEN NUCLEUS)	HELIUM NUCLEUS
ANTI-DOWN QUARK	ANTI-PROTON	LITHIUM NUCLEUS

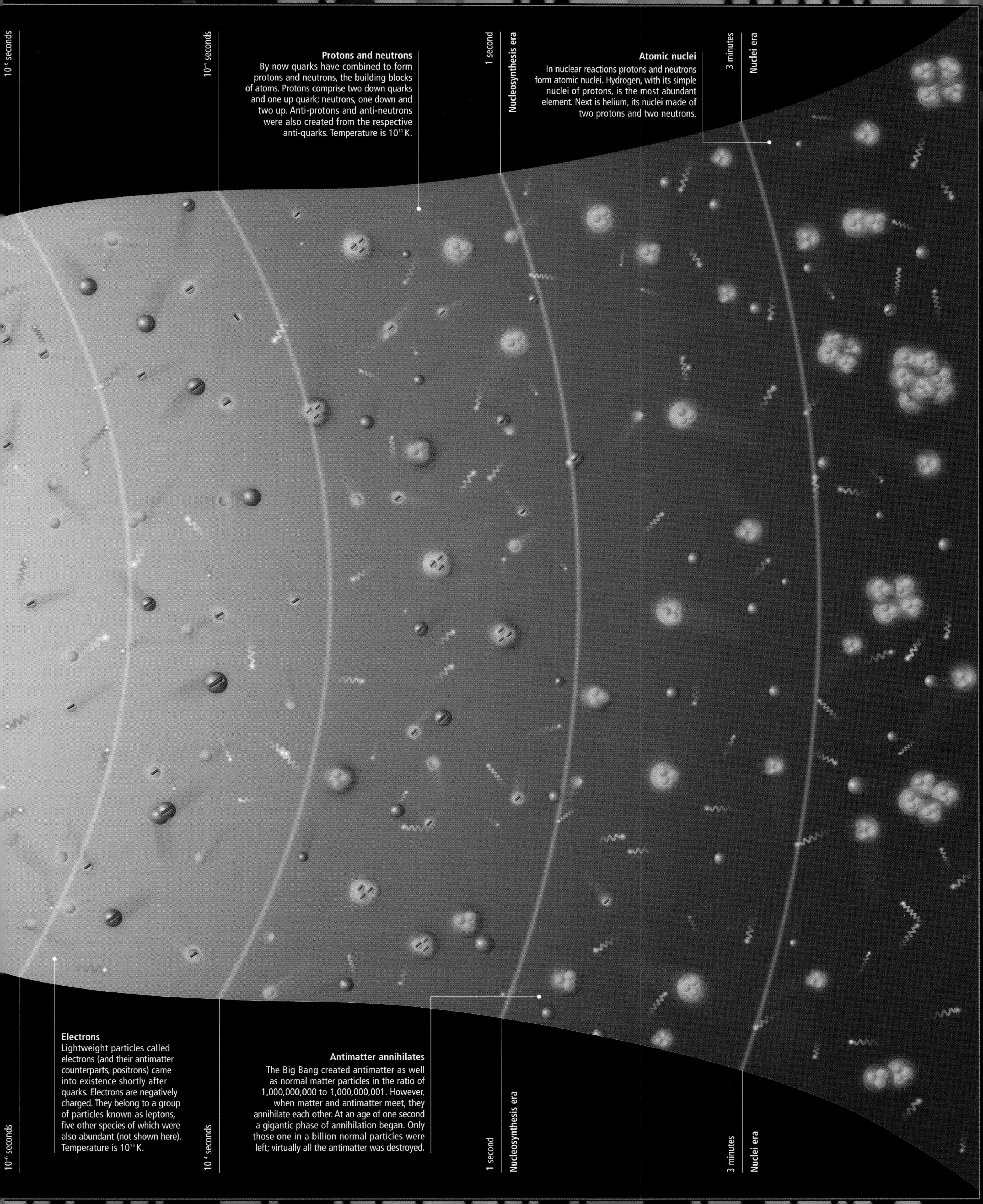

10⁻⁶ seconds

10⁻⁴ seconds

10⁻¹ seconds

1 second

Nucleosynthesis era

3 minutes

Nuclei era

Protons and neutrons
By now quarks have combined to form
protons and neutrons, the building blocks
of atoms. Protons comprise two down quarks
and one up quark; neutrons, one down and
two up. Anti-protons and anti-neutrons
were also created from the respective
anti-quarks. Temperature is 10^{11} K.

Atomic nuclei
In nuclear reactions protons and neutrons
form atomic nuclei. Hydrogen, with its simple
nuclei of protons, is the most abundant
element. Next is helium, its nuclei made of
two protons and two neutrons.

Electrons
Lightweight particles called
electrons (and their antimatter
counterparts, positrons) came
into existence shortly after
quarks. Electrons are negatively
charged. They belong to a group
of particles known as leptons,
five other species of which were
also abundant (not shown here).
Temperature is 10^{13} K.

Antimatter annihilates
The Big Bang created antimatter as well
as normal matter particles in the ratio of
1,000,000,000 to 1,000,000,001. However,
when matter and antimatter meet, they
annihilate each other. At an age of one second
a gigantic phase of annihilation began. Only
those one in a billion normal particles were
left; virtually all the antimatter was destroyed.

10⁻⁶ seconds

10⁻⁴ seconds

1 second

Nucleosynthesis era

3 minutes

Nuclei era

A Brief History of the Universe

Astronomers have a good idea of how the contents of the universe have evolved with time. They know this because they can literally see back in time. Powerful telescopes combined with very long exposures of the sky (such as the Hubble Deep Fields, which had exposures measured in days) reveal exquisitely faint—and therefore distant—objects. And because distant objects are older, simply because their light has taken longer to reach us, deep exposures give us unprecedented views of the cosmos in its infancy. We now think that the first galaxies—called protogalaxies—probably formed between 200 to 600 million years after the Big Bang, along with the first stars. The illustration on the right follows the evolution of the universe and its contents from its fiery birth to the present day.

Supernova seeds (right)
This image is a supercomputer simulation of protogalaxy filaments in the universe some 200 million years after the Big Bang. At this time the universe was alive with supernova explosions that signaled the end of the first generation of stars. These massive, short-lived stars were the first to forge elements such as carbon, oxygen, and iron, and their explosive deaths spread material into space that formed subsequent generations of stars.

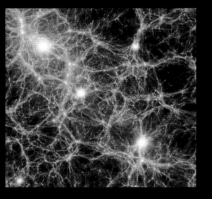

At an age of about 380,000 years, the first whole atoms began to form and the universe became transparent to photons for the first time. This epoch is known as the "decoupling" stage.

Within a million years of the Big Bang, the new universe's supply of hydrogen and helium organized itself into gigantic gas clouds.

Nobody is entirely sure when the first stars and protogalaxies came into existence, but around 200 to 600 million years after the Big Bang is a good estimate.

Large-scale structure (below)
These frames show a computer simulation of the evolution of the universe from an initially smooth fog of gas (left) to the clumpy and filamentary structure we observe today (right).

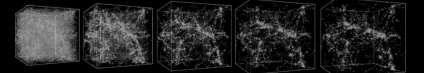

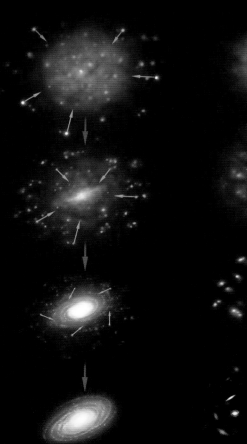

Birth of galaxies

There are two theories to explain how the first galaxies formed, both of which are illustrated left. The first is termed the "bottom-up" scenario (left stream). The early universe was filled with relatively small clouds of gas. Stars formed within these clouds, and then these giant globular clusters agglomerated to form increasingly larger masses, becoming the first galaxies. These galaxies were ellipticals, but spiral galaxies were formed when two or more ellipticals interacted. An alternative explanation—the fragmentation or "top-down" scenario (right stream)—proposes that the initial gas clouds were much larger than galaxies. They gradually broke up under gravitational eddies and each smaller cloud then condensed to form an individual galaxy. If the cloud was spinning fast enough it would become a spiral, otherwise an elliptical galaxy was formed.

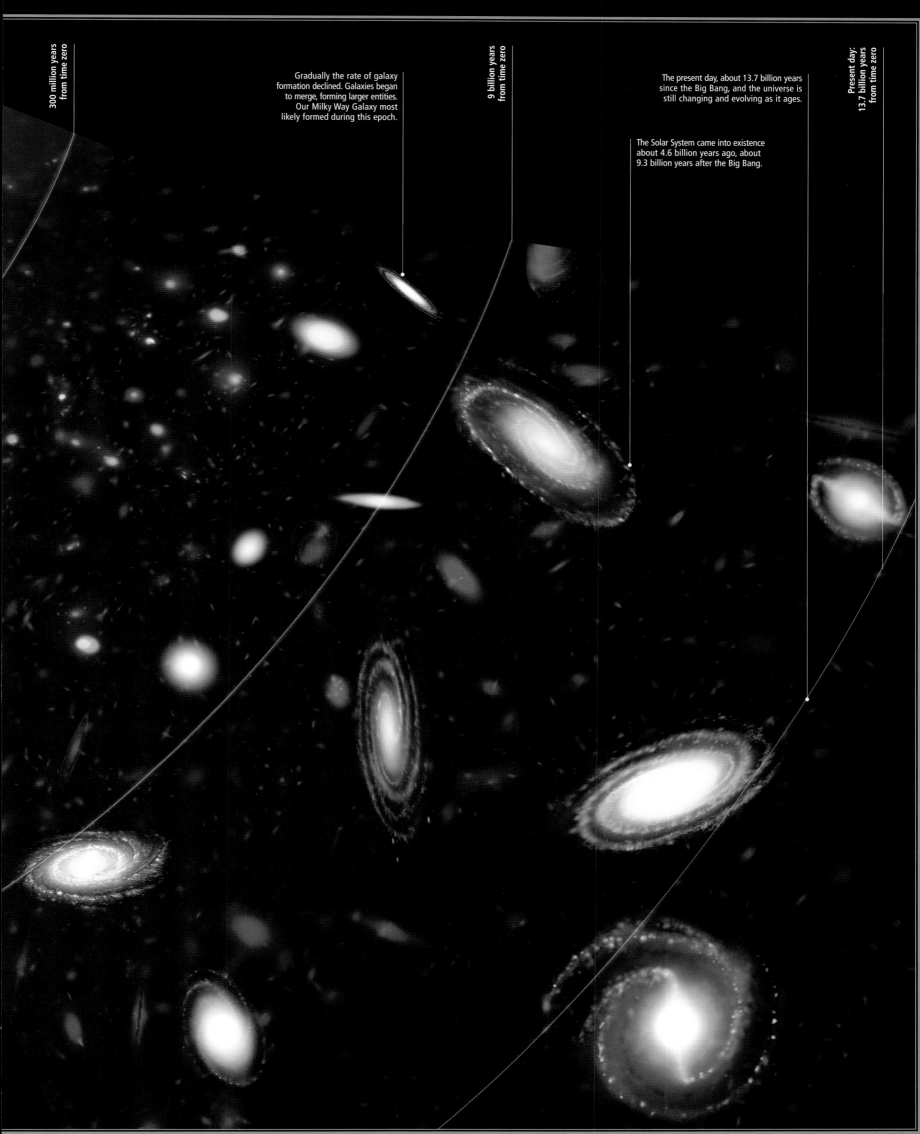

300 million years
from time zero

Gradually the rate of galaxy
formation declined. Galaxies began
to merge, forming larger entities.
Our Milky Way Galaxy most
likely formed during this epoch.

9 billion years
from time zero

The present day, about 13.7 billion years
since the Big Bang, and the universe is
still changing and evolving as it ages.

The Solar System came into existence
about 4.6 billion years ago, about
9.3 billion years after the Big Bang.

Present day:
13.7 billion years
from time zero

FUTURE OF THE UNIVERSE

Broadly speaking there are two possible futures for the universe. Either the universe will eventually collapse in on itself, or expand forever. Until recently, cosmologists believed that the amount of matter in the universe—visible and dark—would determine the result. If there was a critical density of matter, gravity would eventually slow the expansion of the universe, stopping it only after an infinite amount of time. Too much matter, and the expansion would eventually reverse. Too little, and the expansion would slow but nonetheless continue without end. It now seems that matter is not the only player in determining the future of the universe. Recent discoveries suggest that continued expansion seems to be our fate, but at an accelerating rate. This is possible because of the repulsive effect of what is known as "dark energy."

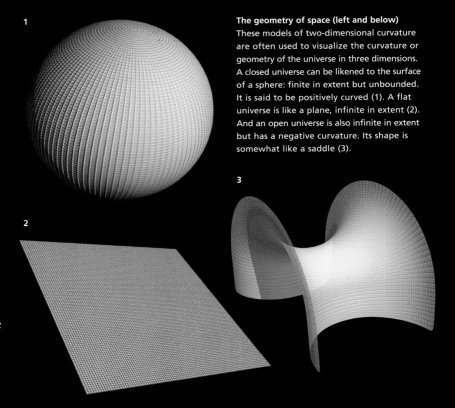

The geometry of space (left and below)
These models of two-dimensional curvature are often used to visualize the curvature or geometry of the universe in three dimensions. A closed universe can be likened to the surface of a sphere: finite in extent but unbounded. It is said to be positively curved (1). A flat universe is like a plane, infinite in extent (2). And an open universe is also infinite in extent but has a negative curvature. Its shape is somewhat like a saddle (3).

The attraction of dark energy

In 1998, astronomers trying to determine the Hubble Constant made an astonishing discovery: the universe's expansion is accelerating. This discovery forced cosmologists to refine their understanding of the future of the universe. A type of mass-energy, called "dark energy," that has density but acts as an anti-gravitational or repulsive force, has been theorized to explain continued expansion with acceleration. Dark energy is believed to account for 73 percent of the contents of the cosmos, as illustrated in the pie chart below.

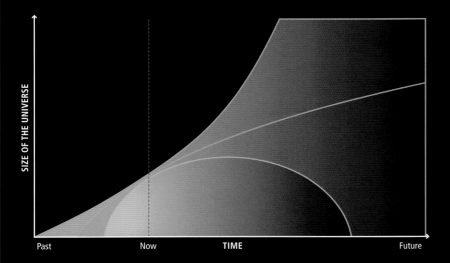

SIZE OF THE UNIVERSE

Past · Now · TIME · Future

Tracking the future (left)
The future of a universe of critical density is tracked by the green line. The orange line indicates the fate of those with too much matter. The preferred model, an infinitely expanding yet accelerating universe, is shown by the blue line.

| Dark energy 73% | Ordinary matter 4% | Cold dark matter 23% |

A multitude of universes

Some theorists speculate that we live in a "multiverse" or "metauniverse"—ours being just one cosmos among an infinite number (illustrated left). While seemingly within the realms of science fiction, these theories are based on actual mathematical modeling and existing physical laws. A number of hypothesized multiverses are possible. For instance, bubbles from the "foam" of a parent universe might form brief small universes; wormholes in space-time; or more prolonged universes like our own. Various interpretations of quantum mechanics permit other "parallel universes," either identical to ours or with different sets of physical laws. It is not believed that these universes could communicate, however.

Accelerating universe (right)
These diagrams represent the three possible futures of the universe. This is the favored model, an accelerating universe. Here the universe will expand forever while at the same time speeding up as it does so. This means that all but the nearest galaxies will recede into the distance, eventually dying as particles decay.

Present time
Universe expands rapidly and becomes increasingly empty.

The Big Rip (right)
Some cosmologists speculate that the accelerating expansion of the universe will eventually overwhelm gravity and the universe will end in a "Big Rip," as galaxies, stars, and eventually all matter is torn apart.

Present time
Universe expands rapidly until matter breaks apart.

Asymptotic universe (below)
An asymptotic universe expands forever, slowing all the time but never quite stopping.

Closed universe (below)
In a closed universe there is enough matter to eventually stop expansion. It then recollapses back to zero size in an event known as the "Big Crunch."

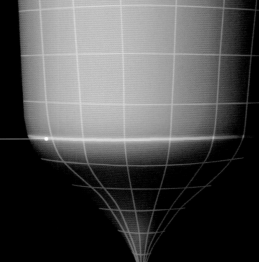

Present time
Critical expansion rate

Present time
Universe expands then collapses

↑
Direction of time

Understanding the Night Sky

Use these pages to familiarize yourself with the way celestial objects are mapped, how they move as Earth rotates, and how they change over long timescales. The magnitude scale is also useful to help you understand how bright objects appear in the sky.

Precession

Earth's rotational axis is not fixed in space. Instead, like a spinning toy top, the axis slowly wobbles, sweeping out a conical section of space. A single rotation takes 25,800 years. This phenomenon is called precession and it means our view of the stars changes with time. At this time in history, Polaris marks the north celestial pole but this has not always been the case. During the time of the ancient Egyptians, that honor went to Thuban in Draco.

The celestial sphere

We long ago realized that there is no celestial sphere above Earth, but it is still useful to think of a sphere when it comes to mapping the position of celestial objects. Astronomers plot the position of stars and other objects using the celestial coordinates right ascension and declination on this sphere, which are analogous to the more familiar longitude and latitude on Earth.

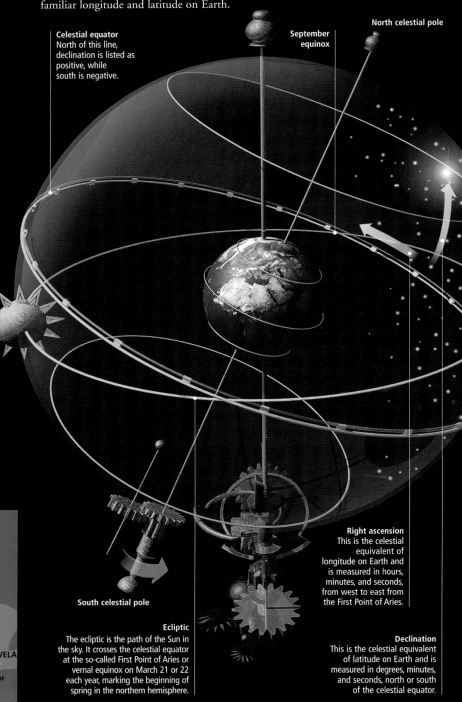

Celestial equator
North of this line, declination is listed as positive, while south is negative.

September equinox

North celestial pole

South celestial pole

Ecliptic
The ecliptic is the path of the Sun in the sky. It crosses the celestial equator at the so-called First Point of Aries or vernal equinox on March 21 or 22 each year, marking the beginning of spring in the northern hemisphere.

Right ascension
This is the celestial equivalent of longitude on Earth and is measured in hours, minutes, and seconds, from west to east from the First Point of Aries.

Declination
This is the celestial equivalent of latitude on Earth and is measured in degrees, minutes, and seconds, north or south of the celestial equator.

Deneb

CEPHEUS   CASSIOPEIA

Polaris
North celestial pole (NCP)

URSA MINOR

URSA MAJOR

NORTH

CENTAURUS

Hadar
Rigil Kent   CRUX
Acrux

South celestial pole (SCP)

VELA

CARINA
Avior

Large Magellanic Cloud (LMC)   Canopus

Small Magellanic Cloud (SMC)

SOUTH

Relative movement of the stars

Depending on where you are on Earth, the stars describe different motions across the heavens. On the equator, they rise vertically due east and set due west. As you move away from the equator, stars rise and set at an angle to the horizon and some will remain permanently hidden from view. At the poles, they neither rise nor set, but move sideways in the sky as Earth rotates.

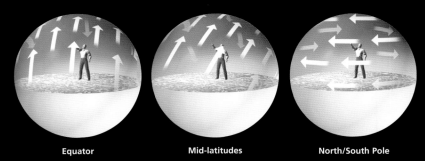

Equator   **Mid-latitudes**   **North/South Pole**

Finding north

Finding the north polar star, Polaris, is easy. First, locate the famous pattern of stars known as the Plough or the Big Dipper in Ursa Major. Then mentally draw a line joining the two stars at the end of the Dipper's "bowl," extend it five times and you arrive at Polaris, the brightest star in the constellation Ursa Minor.

Finding south

To approximately locate the celestial south pole, simply extend the long axis of Crux, the Southern Cross, four and a half times. This places you about where a line bisecting that joining the bright stars Rigil Kent and Hadar crosses your original line. The intersection of these two imaginary guides marks the south celestial pole.

Magnitude scale

The larger the magnitude of an object, the fainter it is. The scale is logarithmic, not linear. Each magnitude difference of 1 corresponds to a change in brightness of a multiple of 2.5.

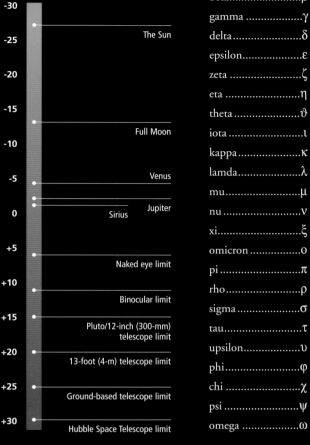

-30
-25 The Sun
-20
-15
-10 Full Moon
-5 Venus
0 Sirius | Jupiter
+5 Naked eye limit
+10 Binocular limit
+15 Pluto/12-inch (300-mm) telescope limit
+20 13-foot (4-m) telescope limit
+25 Ground-based telescope limit
+30 Hubble Space Telescope limit

Lower-case Greek alphabet

alpha .... α
beta........................ β
gamma .... γ
delta...................... δ
epsilon................... ε
zeta .... ζ
eta .... η
theta...................... ϑ
iota .... ι
kappa..................... κ
lamda.................... λ
mu......................... μ
nu .... ν
xi............................ ξ
omicron .... o
pi .... π
rho......................... ρ
sigma .... σ
tau.......................... τ
upsilon................... υ
phi.......................... φ
chi .... χ
psi .... ψ
omega .... ω

Stars

The main stars in each constellation are labeled with a lower-case letter of the Greek alphabet, usually, though not always, in order of brightness starting with α (alpha). These labels were introduced by the German astronomer Johann Bayer (1572–1625) in his star atlas published in 1603 and are sometimes known as Bayer letters. The brightest and most prominent stars are often referred to by their common names which are often corrupted forms of Arabic names: for instance Alpha Orionis, "alpha of Orion," is better known as Betelgeuse. Flamsteed numbers are often used for somewhat fainter stars. First appearing in the French edition of English astronomer John Flamsteed's (1646–1719) star catalog, these numbers are applied to the stars of a constellation in order from west to east. Variable stars are usually assigned a single upper-case Roman letter from R through to Z or a combination of two upper-case Roman letters followed by the name of the constellation.

ABBREVIATIONS FOR NON-STELLAR OBJECTS USED IN THIS ATLAS

PREFIX	TYPE	ASTRONOMER, WORK, OR OBSERVATORY
(none)	Various	*New General Catalog* (NGC)
Cr	Open cluster	Per Collinder (1890–1974)
IC	Various	*Index Catalog* (IC)
K	Open cluster	Ivan King (born 1927)
M	Various	Charles Messier (1730–1817)
St	Open cluster	Jürgen Stock (1923–2004)
Tr	Open cluster	Robert J. Trumpler (1886–1956)
U	Galaxy	*Uppsala General Catalog* (UGC)
Mel	Open cluster	Philibert Melotte (1880–1961)
PK	Planetary nebulas	Lubos Perek (born 1919) & Lubos Kohoutek (born 1935)

Non-stellar objects

Many different systems have been developed to catalog celestial objects; the better known include the *New General Catalog* (NGC), the *Index Catalog* (IC), and the Messier (M) catalog of nebulas, star clusters, and galaxies. In the maps that follow, *New General Catalog* numbers are given without a prefix while Messier object numbers and *Index Catalog* numbers are given M and IC prefixes respectively.

Refer to the description for highlights of the brightest stars and constellations in that season's night sky.

The Milky Way is indicated by a stream of light blue stretching across the sky.

These tables show the times and dates at which the season's sky may be viewed.

The map shows the location of stars for observers located within latitude ranges 10° to 15° north or south of the position indicated here during the season shown.

True star color is indicated in this key.

Deep-sky objects are identified by this key.

Star sizes correspond to their apparent visual magnitude—the brightness of stars as seen from Earth.

NORTHERN WINTER: LOOKING NORTH

Looking north in the winter, the sky still belongs to several bright constellations. These include Ursa Major, Cassiopeia, Perseus, Andromeda, and Auriga. During early winter, Ursa Major is ascending in the northeast, while Cassiopeia's W sinks in sympathy in the northwest. Auriga is very high overhead come early December, with its bright yellow star Capella marking the zenith for those observing from latitudes close to 45 degrees north. By the end of winter, Capella is still well established at high altitudes and Ursa Major is upside down.

Northern Spring: Looking North

The Great Bear (Ursa Major) is well placed during the spring months. In March it appears perpendicular to the horizon, with the inverted handle of the Big Dipper pointed straight at Boötes. As the season unfolds, it climbs higher, finally achieving its peak position close to the zenith (depending on your latitude) around early May. The bright yellow Capella in Auriga is also noteworthy during springtime, as is the thick band of the Milky Way, but both sink closer to the northwestern horizon as summer approaches.

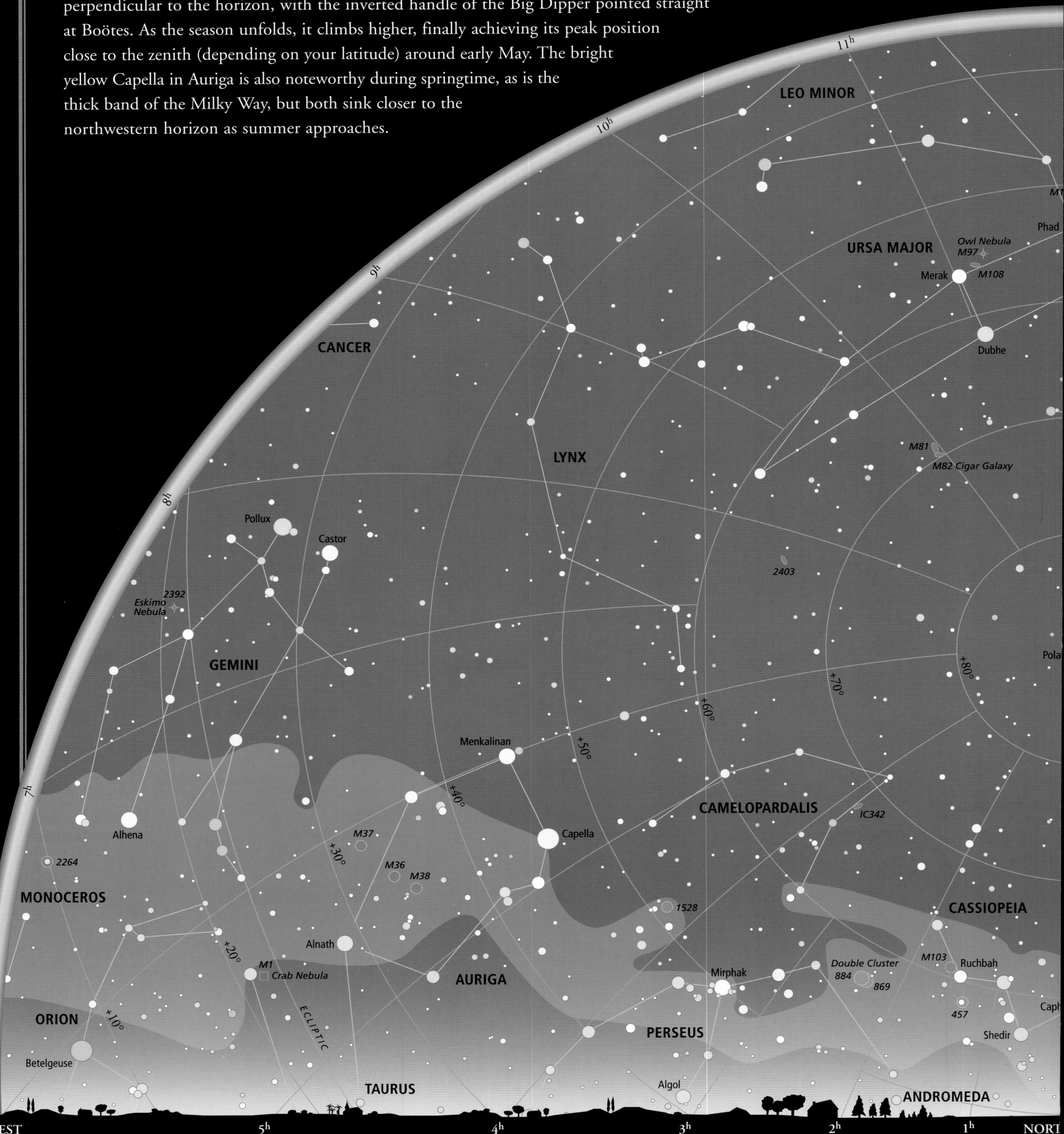

LEO MINOR

URSA MAJOR

Owl Nebula
M97

Phad

Merak
M108

Dubhe

CANCER

LYNX

M81

M82 Cigar Galaxy

2403

Pollux

Castor

2392
Eskimo
Nebula

+80°

Pola

GEMINI

+70°

Menkalinan

+60°

+50°

CAMELOPARDALIS

IC342

Alhena

+40°

2264

+30°

M37

M36
M38

Capella

1528

CASSIOPEIA

MONOCEROS

+20°

Alnath

M1
Crab Nebula

AURIGA

Double Cluster
884
869

Mirphak

M103

Ruchbah

457

ORION

+10°

Betelgeuse

ECLIPTIC

PERSEUS

Algol

Shedir

Caph

TAURUS

ANDROMEDA

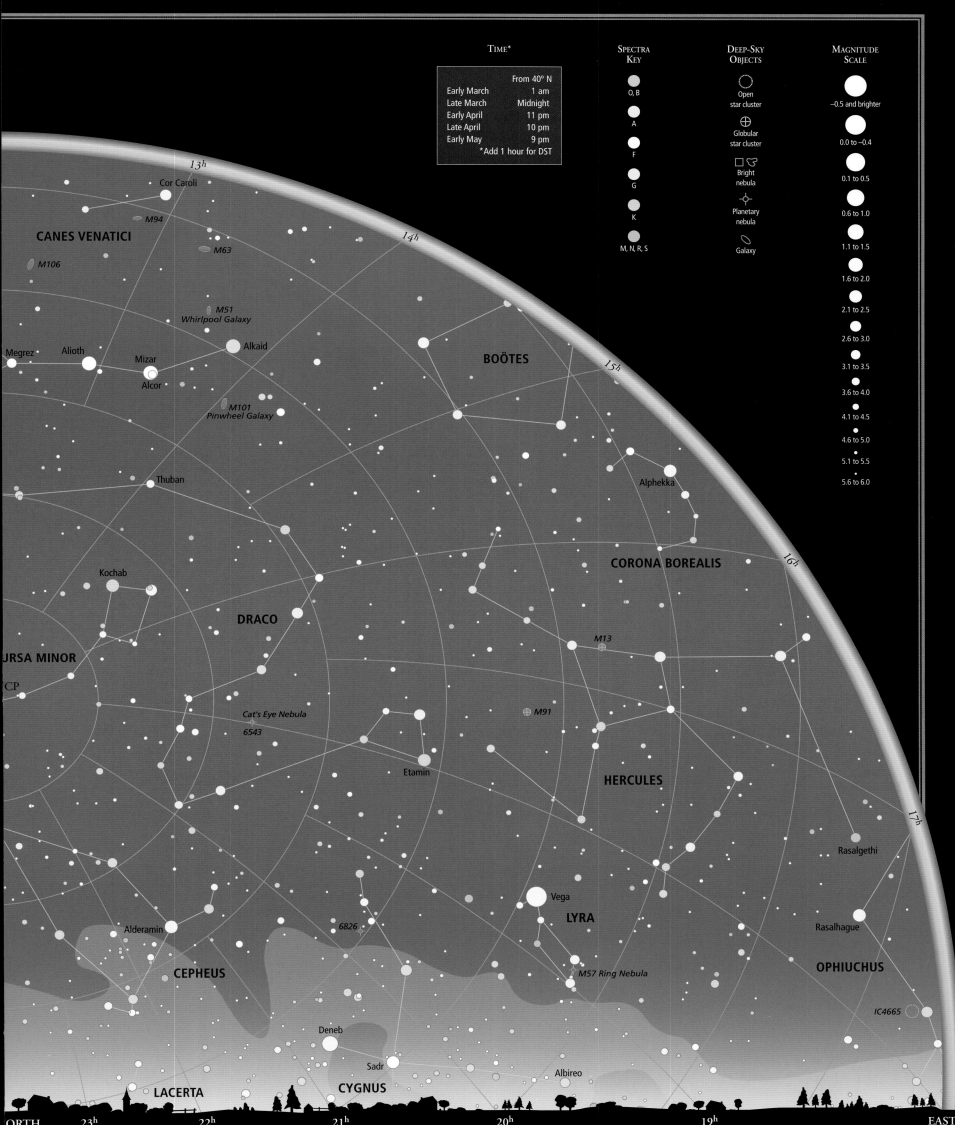

TIME*

	From 40° N
Early March	1 am
Late March	Midnight
Early April	11 pm
Late April	10 pm
Early May	9 pm
	*Add 1 hour for DST

SPECTRA KEY

O, B
A
F
G
K
M, N, R, S

DEEP-SKY OBJECTS

Open star cluster
Globular star cluster
Bright nebula
Planetary nebula
Galaxy

MAGNITUDE SCALE

−0.5 and brighter
0.0 to −0.4
0.1 to 0.5
0.6 to 1.0
1.1 to 1.5
1.6 to 2.0
2.1 to 2.5
2.6 to 3.0
3.1 to 3.5
3.6 to 4.0
4.1 to 4.5
4.6 to 5.0
5.1 to 5.5
5.6 to 6.0

13ʰ
14ʰ
15ʰ
16ʰ
17ʰ

Cor Caroli
M94
CANES VENATICI
M63
M106
M51 Whirlpool Galaxy
Alkaid
BOÖTES
Megrez
Alioth
Mizar
Alcor
M101 Pinwheel Galaxy
Thuban
Alphekka
Kochab
CORONA BOREALIS
DRACO
M13
URSA MINOR
CP
Cat's Eye Nebula
6543
M91
HERCULES
Etamin
Rasalgethi
Vega
LYRA
Rasalhague
Alderamin
6826
M57 Ring Nebula
OPHIUCHUS
CEPHEUS
IC4665
Deneb
Sadr
Albireo
LACERTA
CYGNUS

23ʰ
22ʰ
21ʰ
20ʰ
19ʰ

NORTH
EAST

NORTHERN SPRING: LOOKING SOUTH

Spring is in the air, and the southern sky is studded with several bright stars and constellations. Brightest of all is Arcturus in Boötes, high in the southeast. Virgo is also prominent, its brightest star Spica halfway up the sky. Leo marches boldly across the celestial sphere from east to west—its front paw marked by the bright blue star Regulus and the tail by Denebola. Also on show are second-magnitude Alphard in Hydra and Procyon in Canis Minor. This is a good season for telescope owners to go galaxy hunting in the Virgo Cluster.

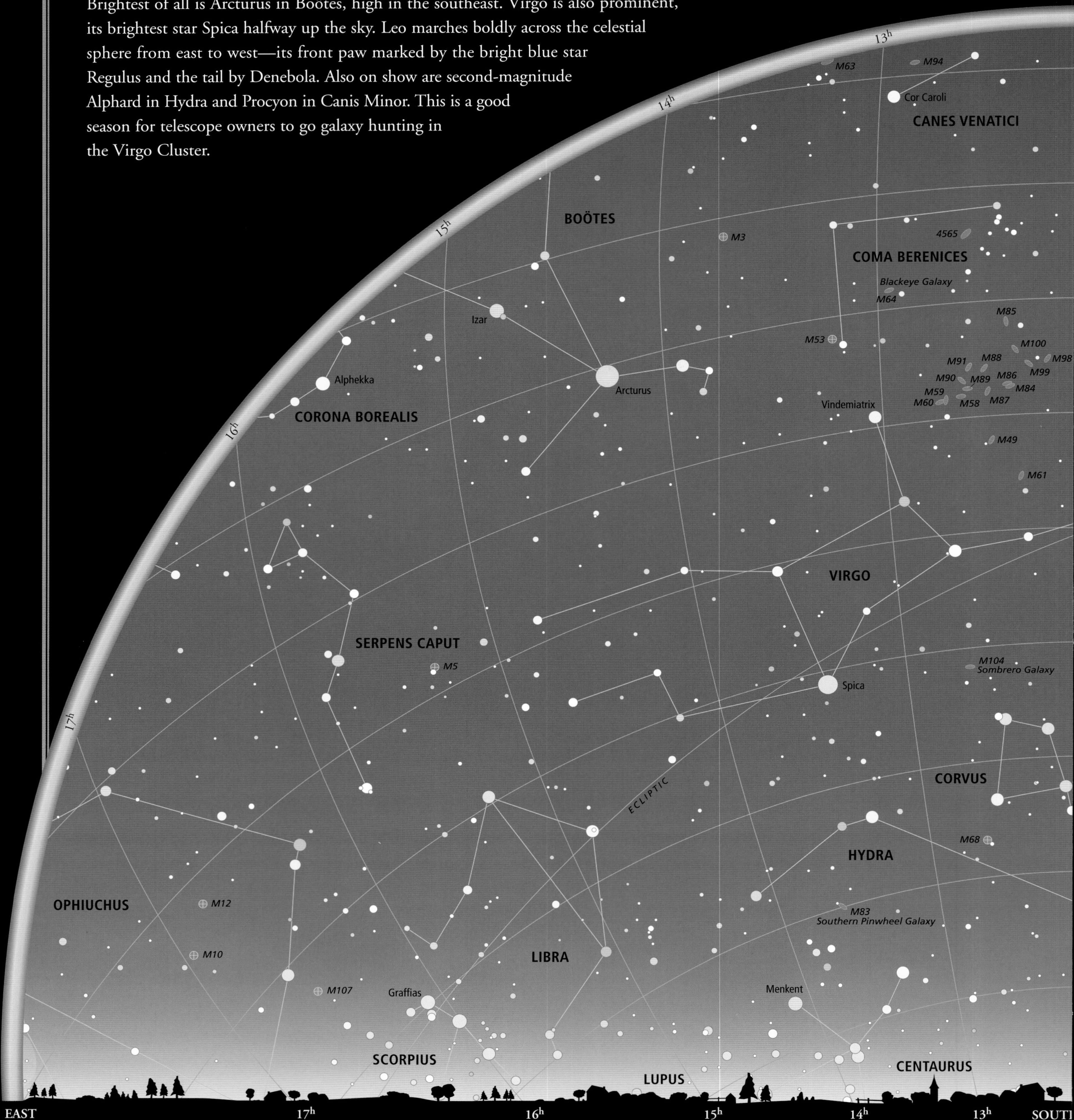

13ʰ

M63

M94

Cor Caroli

CANES VENATICI

14ʰ

BOÖTES

⊕ M3

4565

COMA BERENICES

Blackeye Galaxy

M64

15ʰ

M85

Izar

M53 ⊕

M100

M91 M88 M98

Alphekka

M90 M89 M86 M99

M59 M84

Arcturus

Vindemiatrix M60 M58 M87

CORONA BOREALIS

16ʰ

M49

M61

VIRGO

SERPENS CAPUT

M104
Sombrero Galaxy

⊕ M5

Spica

CORVUS

ECLIPTIC

M68 ⊕

HYDRA

17ʰ

OPHIUCHUS

⊕ M12

M83
Southern Pinwheel Galaxy

⊕ M10

LIBRA

⊕ M107   Graffias

Menkent

SCORPIUS

CENTAURUS

LUPUS

EAST   17ʰ   16ʰ   15ʰ   14ʰ   13ʰ   SOUTH

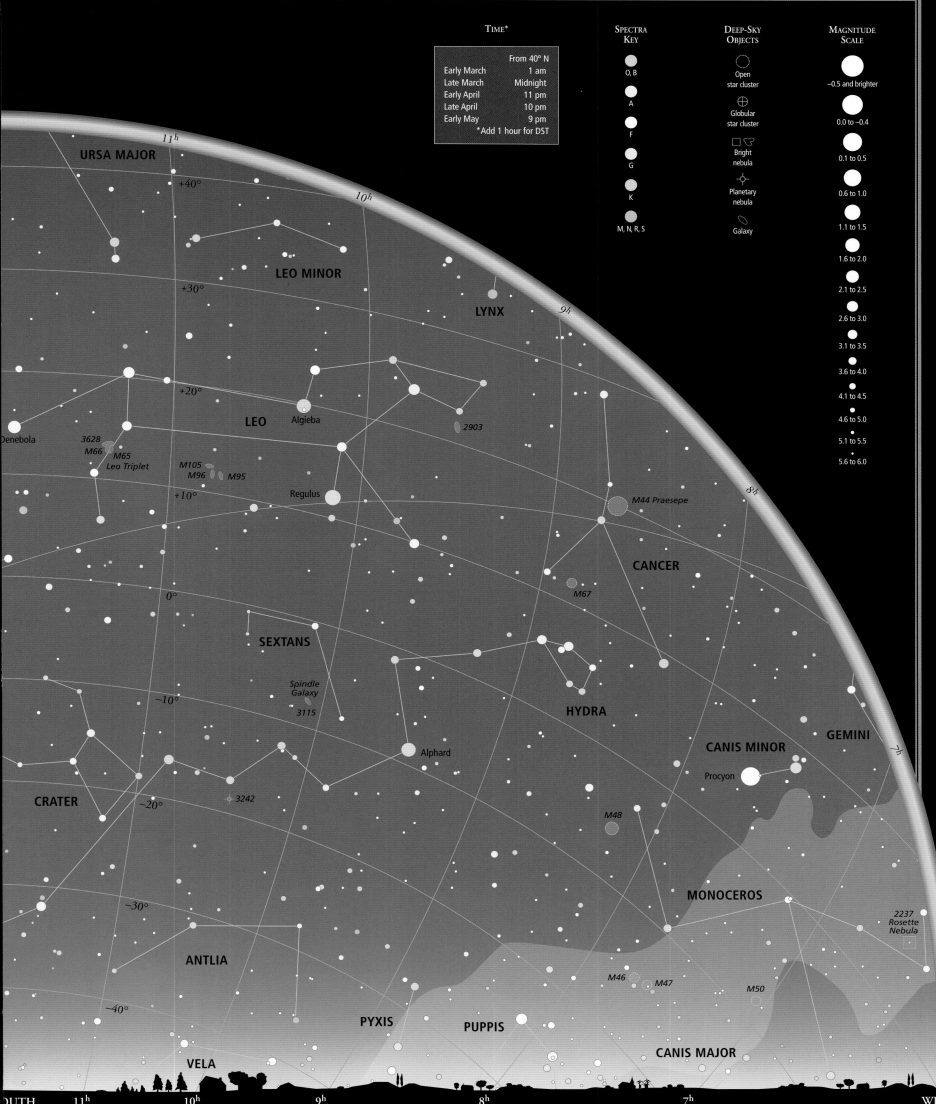

TIME*

	From 40° N
Early March	1 am
Late March	Midnight
Early April	11 pm
Late April	10 pm
Early May	9 pm
	*Add 1 hour for DST

SPECTRA KEY

O, B
A
F
G
K
M, N, R, S

DEEP-SKY OBJECTS

Open star cluster

Globular star cluster

Bright nebula

Planetary nebula

Galaxy

MAGNITUDE SCALE

−0.5 and brighter
0.0 to −0.4
0.1 to 0.5
0.6 to 1.0
1.1 to 1.5
1.6 to 2.0
2.1 to 2.5
2.6 to 3.0
3.1 to 3.5
3.6 to 4.0
4.1 to 4.5
4.6 to 5.0
5.1 to 5.5
5.6 to 6.0

URSA MAJOR

LEO MINOR

LYNX

Denebola

LEO

Algieba

2903

3628
M66
M65
Leo Triplet
M105
M96 M95

Regulus

M44 Praesepe

CANCER

M67

SEXTANS

Spindle
Galaxy
3115

HYDRA

CANIS MINOR

GEMINI

Alphard

Procyon

CRATER

3242

M48

MONOCEROS

2237
Rosette
Nebula

ANTLIA

M46 M47 M50

PYXIS

PUPPIS

CANIS MAJOR

VELA

SOUTH 11ʰ 10ʰ 9ʰ 8ʰ 7ʰ WEST

11ʰ
10ʰ
9ʰ
8ʰ
7ʰ

+40°
+30°
+20°
+10°
0°
−10°
−20°
−30°
−40°

NORTHERN SUMMER: LOOKING NORTH

As spring turns to summer, the inverted Great Bear (Ursa Major) is still unmistakable, close to the zenith. Lower down, Cassiopeia's distinctive W skirts down to the northern horizon and then begins to climb once again in the east as summer deepens. By early August, Cassiopeia is high in the sky and on her side. She is embedded in the Milky Way, which now emerges perpendicularly from the northeastern horizon, carrying Perseus along with it. As summer draws to a close, the Great Bear is still fairly high in the northwest, particularly at higher northern latitudes.

HERCULES

M13 ⊕

M92 ⊕

Etam

CORONA BOREALIS

17ʰ

16ʰ

654
Cat's Ey
Nebu

15ʰ

Izar

BOÖTES

DRACO

Thuban

Kochab

14ʰ

Pinwhel Galaxy
M101

URSA MINOR

M3 ⊕

Alkaid

Whirlpool Galaxy
M51

NO

Alcor

Mizar

Alioth

+70°

+80°

M63

M94

Cor Caroli

CANES VENATICI

Megrez

+60°

M106

M109

+50°

M53 ⊕

13ʰ

Vindemiatrix

M64   Blackeye
Galaxy

COMA
BERENICES

4565

+40°

Phad

Dubhe

Cigar Galaxy   M82

M97   M108
Owl Nebula   M81
Merak

M60 M59
M90 M91
M88   M85
M58   M89
M87 M86   M100

M84

M99
M98

+30°

URSA MAJOR

2403

M49

+20°

+10°

Denebola

LEO

LEO MINOR

LYNX

VIRGO

WEST   11ʰ   10ʰ   9ʰ   8ʰ   7ʰ   NORT

TIME*

From 40° N
Early June	1 am
Late June	Midnight
Early July	11 pm
Late July	10 pm
Early August	9 pm

*Add 1 hour for DST

SPECTRA KEY

O, B
A
F
G
K
M, N, R, S

DEEP-SKY OBJECTS

Open star cluster
Globular star cluster
Bright nebula
Planetary nebula
Galaxy

MAGNITUDE SCALE

−0.5 and brighter
0.0 to −0.4
0.1 to 0.5
0.6 to 1.0
1.1 to 1.5
1.6 to 2.0
2.1 to 2.5
2.6 to 3.0
3.1 to 3.5
3.6 to 4.0
4.1 to 4.5
4.6 to 5.0
5.1 to 5.5
5.6 to 6.0

Vega

LYRA

19h

20h

CYGNUS

Sadr

6826

6960

Veil Nebula

6992, 6995

21h

Deneb

7000

North America Nebula

7026

M39

Alderamin

22h

LACERTA

CEPHEUS

Polaris

CASSIOPEIA

Caph

Scheat

Shedir

Ruchbah

457

M103

23h

PEGASUS

CAMELOPARDALIS

Markab

IC342

M110
Andromeda Galaxy
M31   M32

M76

884   869
Double Cluster

Alpheratz

Mirach

PERSEUS

Almaak

ANDROMEDA

Algenib

Mirphak

PISCES

PISCES

TRIANGULUM

NORTH   5h   4h   3h   2h   1h   EAST

NORTHERN SUMMER: LOOKING SOUTH

As summer begins, Arcturus of Boötes is the dominant star in the southern skies. It gradually moves west as the season progresses. Scorpius, with its fiery red Antares, is a vivid constellation during the summer months, but you ideally need to be at low latitudes to see it, otherwise it is lost in the denser skies toward the horizon. Summer is, of course, also the time of the Summer Triangle, formed by the three bright stars Vega (in Lyra), Altair (in Aquila), and Deneb (in Cygnus, previous map). This asterism is now well established in the northern summer skies and very high overhead.

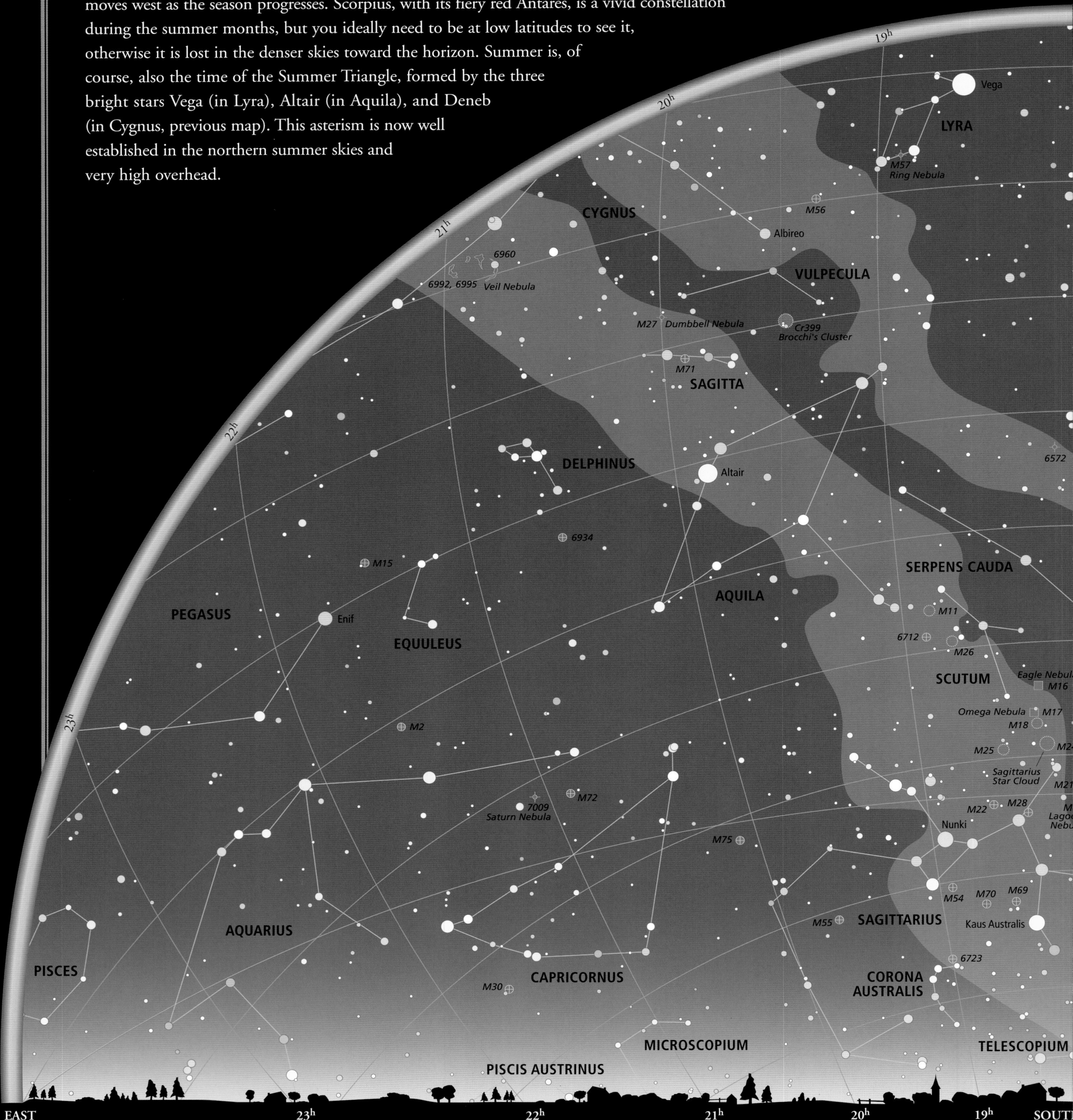

19^h

Vega

LYRA

20^h

$M57$
Ring Nebula

$M56$

CYGNUS

Albireo

21^h

6960

VULPECULA

6992, 6995 Veil Nebula

$M27$ Dumbbell Nebula

Cr399
Brocchi's Cluster

$M71$

SAGITTA

22^h

DELPHINUS

6572

Altair

6934

$M15$

SERPENS CAUDA

PEGASUS

Enif

AQUILA

$M11$

EQUULEUS

6712

$M26$

SCUTUM

Eagle Nebula
$M16$

Omega Nebula $M17$
$M18$

23^h

$M2$

$M25$ $M2$

Sagittarius
Star Cloud

$M72$

$M21$

7009
Saturn Nebula

$M22$ $M28$

Lago
Nebu

Nunki

$M75$

$M54$ $M70$ $M69$

$M55$ SAGITTARIUS

Kaus Australis

AQUARIUS

PISCES

6723

CAPRICORNUS

CORONA
AUSTRALIS

$M30$

MICROSCOPIUM

TELESCOPIUM

PISCIS AUSTRINUS

EAST

23^h

22^h

21^h

20^h

19^h SOUTH

TIME*

From 40° N
Early June	1 am
Late June	Midnight
Early July	11 pm
Late July	10 pm
Early August	9 pm

*Add 1 hour for DST

SPECTRA KEY

O, B
A
F
G
K
M, N, R, S

DEEP-SKY OBJECTS

Open star cluster
Globular star cluster
Bright nebula
Planetary nebula
Galaxy

MAGNITUDE SCALE

−0.5 and brighter
0.0 to −0.4
0.1 to 0.5
0.6 to 1.0
1.1 to 1.5
1.6 to 2.0
2.1 to 2.5
2.6 to 3.0
3.1 to 3.5
3.6 to 4.0
4.1 to 4.5
4.6 to 5.0
5.1 to 5.5
5.6 to 6.0

17^h
16^h
15^h
14^h
13^h

+40°
+30°
+20°
+10°
0°
−10°
−20°
−30°
−40°

M92
M13

HERCULES

CORONA BOREALIS
Alphekka

Izar

BOÖTES

Rasalgethi

Rasalhague

Arcturus

OPHIUCHUS

IC4665

SERPENS CAPUT

M14
M12
M10
M5

M107

Sabik

M23
M9

Vindemiatrix

20
ifid Nebula

Graffias

VIRGO

M19
M80

Antares
M62
M4

LIBRA

ECLIPTIC

M6

SCORPIUS

M7
Shaula

6231
5986

LUPUS

HYDRA

Spica

SOUTH
17^h
16^h
15^h
14^h
13^h

WEST

NORTHERN FALL: LOOKING NORTH

Fall in the northern hemisphere sees the Great Bear (Ursa Major) low down on the northern horizon, while Cassiopeia, now a heavenly M, lies opposite, high above it on the other side of the pole star, Polaris. The Milky Way now bisects the sky, spilling out of the northeast, up to the zenith and down to the southwest. As winter approaches, the Summer Triangle—Vega, Deneb, and Aquila's Altair (following map)—sinks ever farther, with Vega slipping behind the northwestern horizon some time in November. Meanwhile, in the northeast, the Gemini twins Castor and Pollux are conspicuous by mid-fall, preceded by Capella in Auriga.

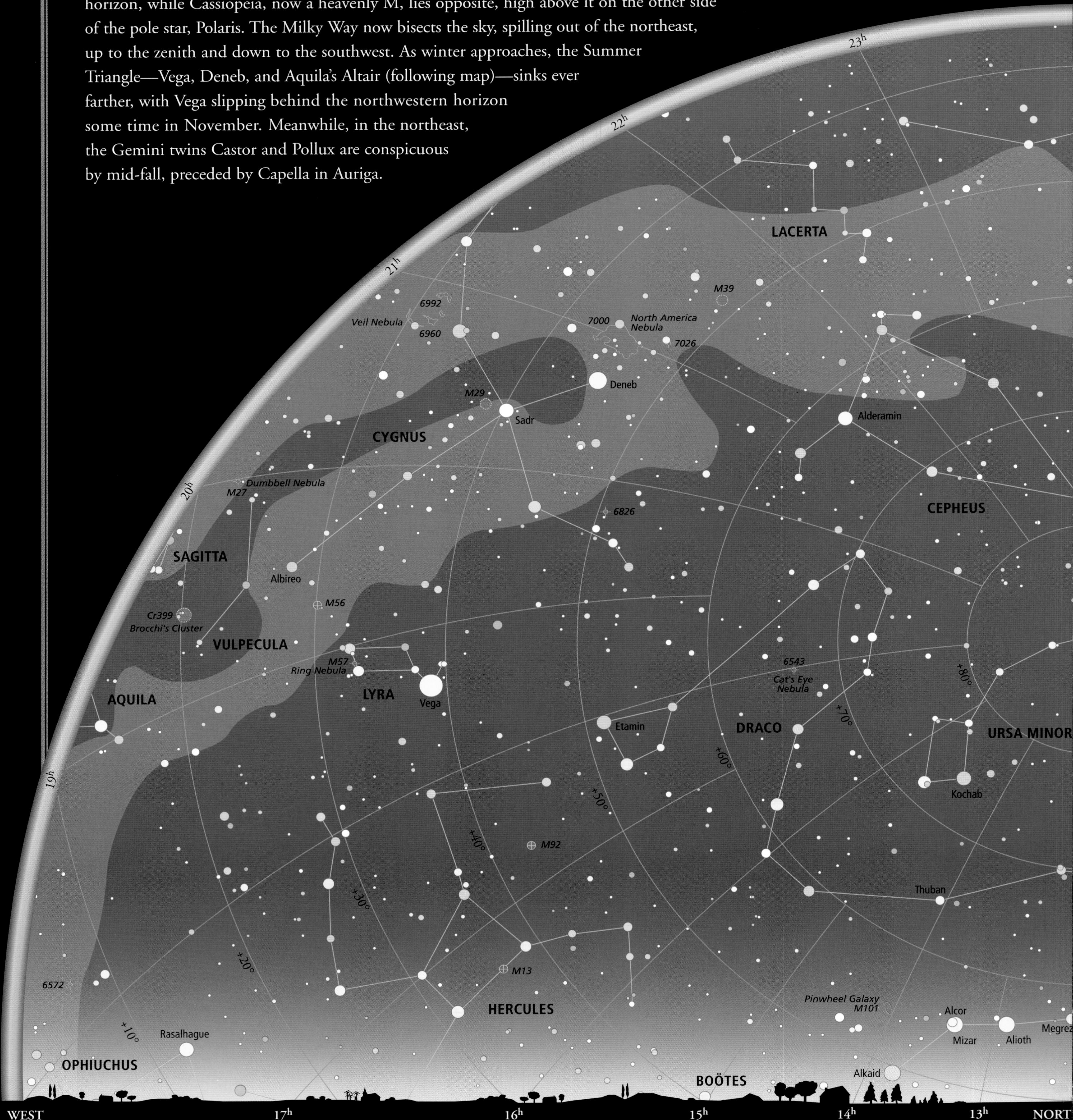

23ʰ

22ʰ

LACERTA

M39

21ʰ

6992

7000   North America Nebula

Veil Nebula

6960   7026

Deneb   Alderamin

M29

Sadr

CYGNUS

20ʰ   Dumbbell Nebula   6826   **CEPHEUS**

M27

SAGITTA

Albireo

Cr399   M56
Brocchi's Cluster

VULPECULA   6543
                  Cat's Eye
M57   Nebula   +80°
Ring Nebula

AQUILA   **LYRA**   Etamin   **DRACO**   +70°   **URSA MINOR**

19ʰ   Vega

+60°

+50°   Kochab

+40°   M92

+30°   Thuban

6572   +20°

+10°   M13   Pinwheel Galaxy
                      M101   Alcor

Rasalhague   **HERCULES**   Mizar   Alioth   Megrez

OPHIUCHUS   **BOÖTES**   Alkaid

WEST   17ʰ   16ʰ   15ʰ   14ʰ   13ʰ   NORTH

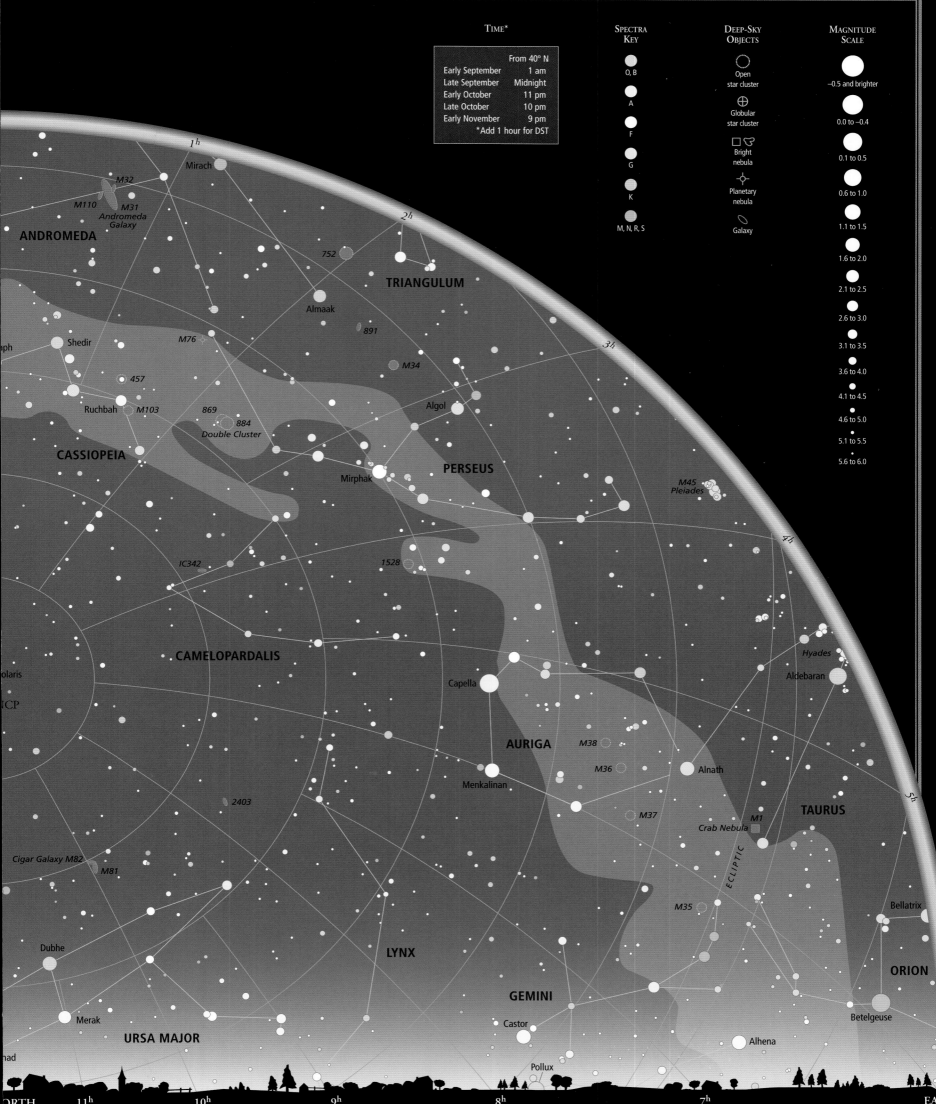

ANDROMEDA

M32
M110 M31
Andromeda
Galaxy

Mirach

1ʰ

2ʰ

752

TRIANGULUM

Almaak

891

M34

3ʰ

aph Shedir
M76
457
Ruchbah M103
CASSIOPEIA
869
884
Double Cluster

Algol

Mirphak

PERSEUS

M45
Pleiades

4ʰ

IC342

1528

CAMELOPARDALIS

olaris

ICP

Hyades

Aldebaran

Capella

2403

AURIGA

M38

M36

Menkalinan

Alnath

TAURUS

M37

M1
Crab Nebula

5ʰ

Cigar Galaxy M82

M81

ECLIPTIC

M35

Bellatrix

Dubhe

LYNX

ORION

Merak

GEMINI

Betelgeuse

URSA MAJOR

Castor

Alhena

nad

Pollux

NORTHERN FALL: LOOKING SOUTH

Looking south, the Great Square of Pegasus is high overhead. The summer is over and the Summer Triangle has gone with it—although Altair in Aquila remains as a reminder. Now, the sky due south is largely devoid of bright constellations, but a few bright to medium-bright stars persist. These include Fomalhaut in Piscis Austrinus (albeit not far above the horizon), Deneb Kaitos in Cetus, Hamal in Aries, and Aldebaran in Taurus farther to the southeast. With winter ever nearer, Taurus will become more prominent, along with the sparkling star clusters of the Pleiades and Hyades.

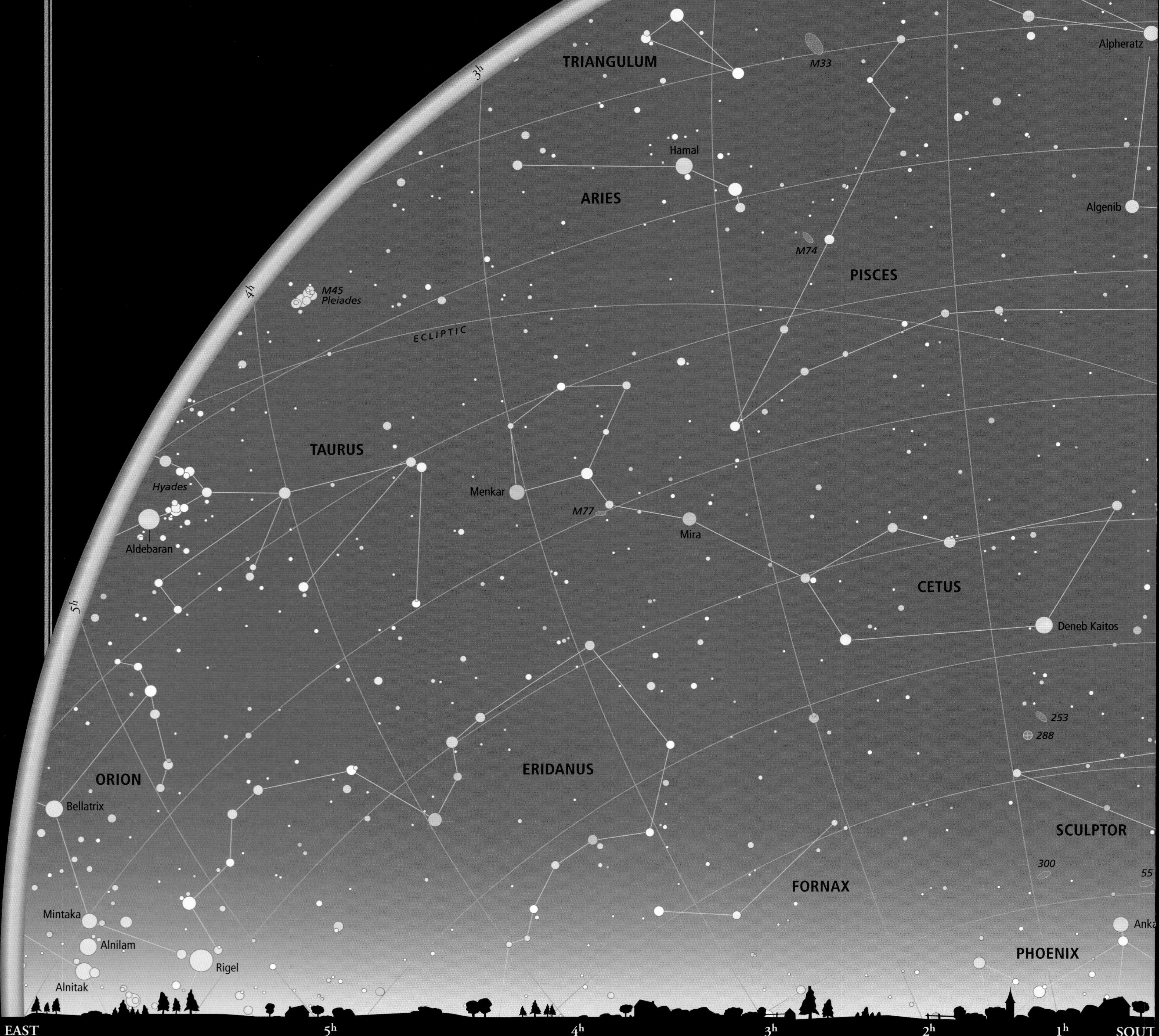

M110

M32

M31
Andromeda
Galaxy

ANDROMEDA

1ʰ

M33

2ʰ

752

Mirach

Alpheratz

3ʰ

TRIANGULUM

Hamal

Algenib

ARIES

M74

PISCES

M45
Pleiades

4ʰ

ECLIPTIC

TAURUS

Menkar

Hyades

M77

CETUS

Mira

Aldebaran

Deneb Kaitos

5ʰ

ERIDANUS

253

288

ORION

SCULPTOR

Bellatrix

300

55

FORNAX

Mintaka

Anka

Alnilam

PHOENIX

Rigel

Alnitak

EAST   5ʰ   4ʰ   3ʰ   2ʰ   1ʰ   SOUT

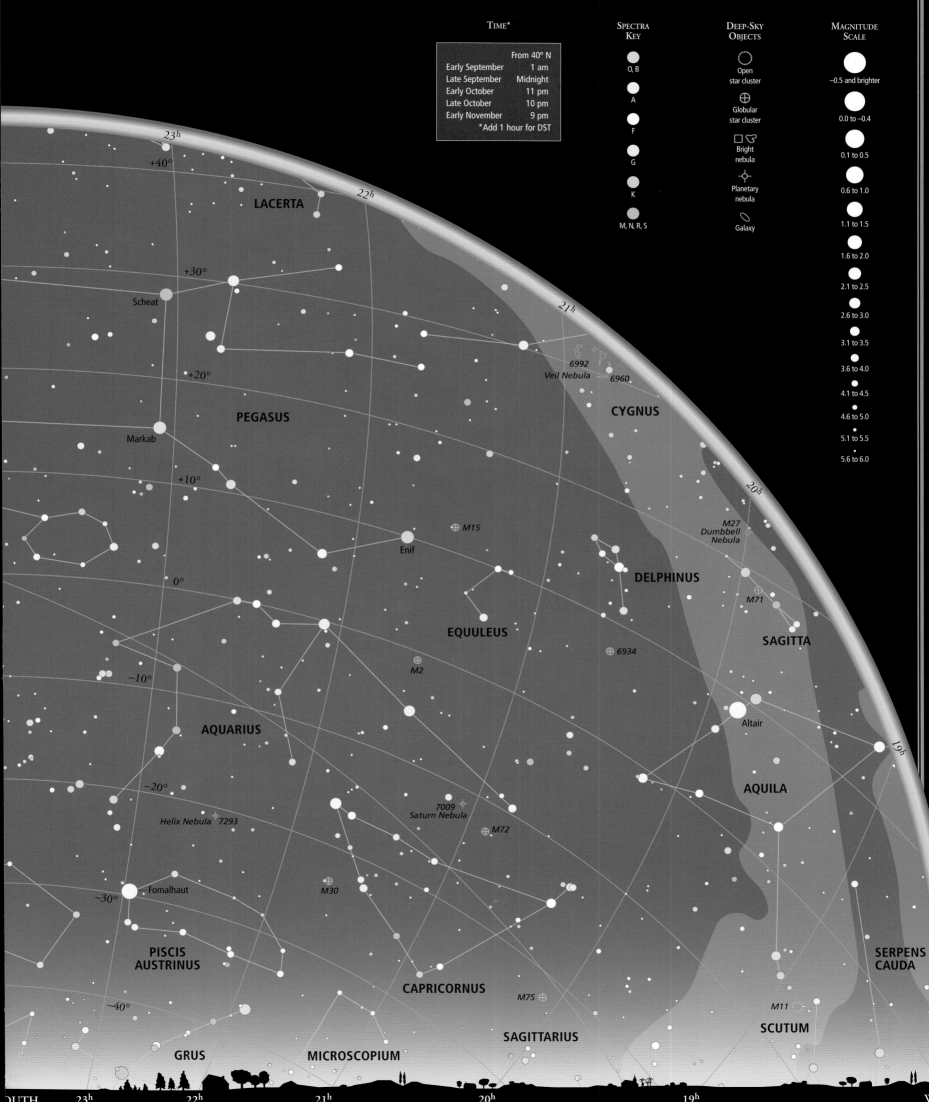

TIME*

From 40° N
Early September   1 am
Late September   Midnight
Early October   11 pm
Late October   10 pm
Early November   9 pm
*Add 1 hour for DST

SPECTRA
KEY

O, B
A
F
G
K
M, N, R, S

DEEP-SKY
OBJECTS

Open
star cluster

Globular
star cluster

Bright
nebula

Planetary
nebula

Galaxy

MAGNITUDE
SCALE

−0.5 and brighter
0.0 to −0.4
0.1 to 0.5
0.6 to 1.0
1.1 to 1.5
1.6 to 2.0
2.1 to 2.5
2.6 to 3.0
3.1 to 3.5
3.6 to 4.0
4.1 to 4.5
4.6 to 5.0
5.1 to 5.5
5.6 to 6.0

23h
+40°
LACERTA
22h
+30°
Scheat
21h
+20°
6992
Veil Nebula
6960
CYGNUS
PEGASUS
Markab
+10°
M15
Enif
M27
Dumbbell
Nebula
DELPHINUS
20h
M71
0°
EQUULEUS
SAGITTA
6934
−10°
M2
Altair
AQUARIUS
−20°
AQUILA
19h
7009
Saturn Nebula
M72
Helix Nebula 7293
M30
−30° Fomalhaut
PISCIS
AUSTRINUS
SERPENS
CAUDA
CAPRICORNUS
M75
M11
−40°
SCUTUM
SAGITTARIUS
GRUS   MICROSCOPIUM

SOUTH   23h   22h   21h   20h   19h   WEST

Northern Winter: Looking North

Looking north in the winter, the sky still belongs to several bright constellations. These include Ursa Major, Cassiopeia, Perseus, Andromeda, and Auriga. During early winter, Ursa Major is ascending in the northeast, while Cassiopeia's W sinks in sympathy in the northwest. Auriga is very high overhead come early December, with its bright yellow star Capella marking the zenith for those observing from latitudes close to 45 degrees north. By the end of winter, Capella is still well established at high altitudes and Ursa Major is upside down.

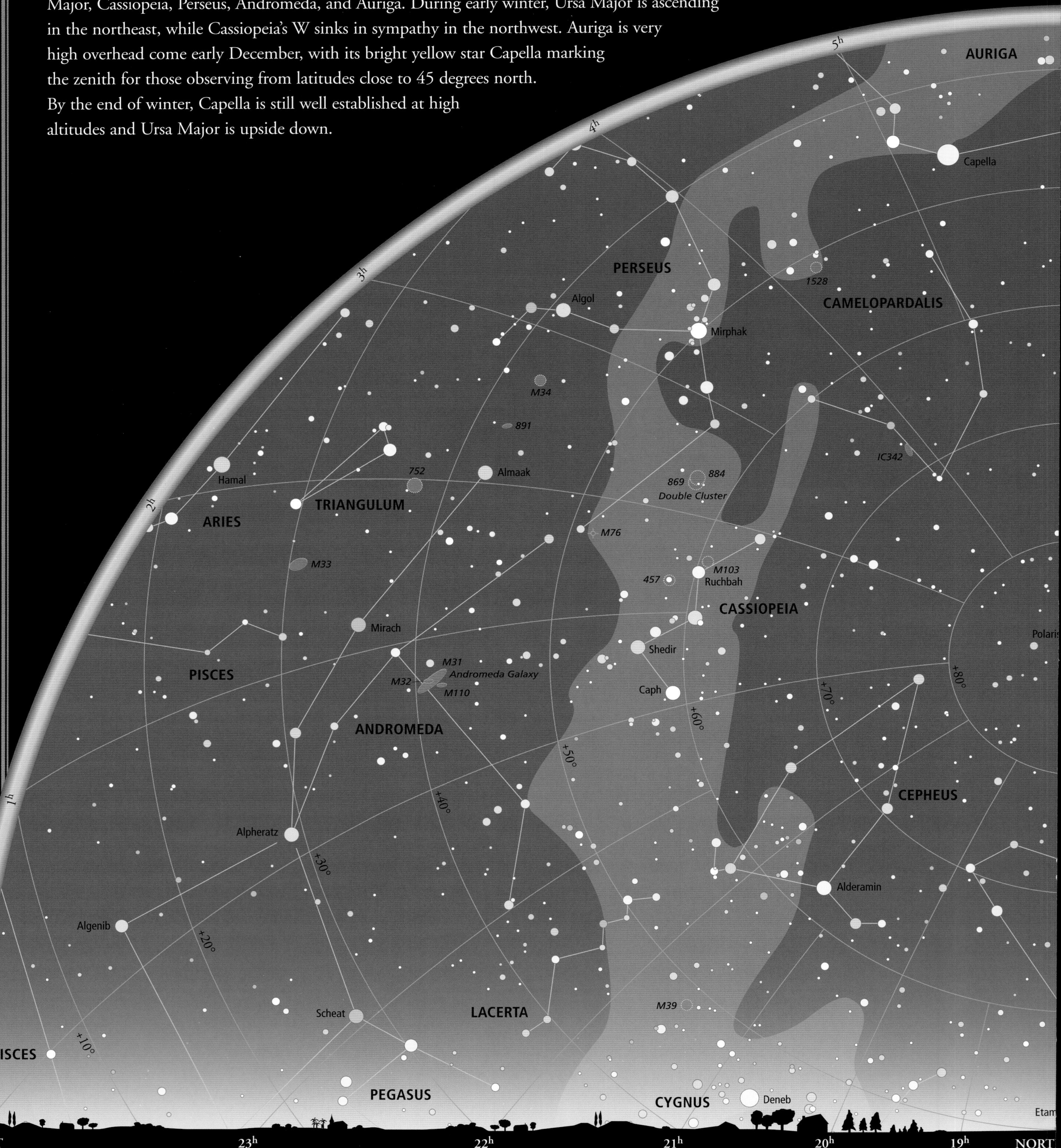

AURIGA

Capella

5ʰ

4ʰ

PERSEUS

1528

CAMELOPARDALIS

Algol

Mirphak

M34

891

IC342

752 Almaak

869 884
Double Cluster

3ʰ

Hamal

TRIANGULUM

M76

2ʰ

ARIES

M103
Ruchbah

457

M33

CASSIOPEIA

Mirach

Shedir

PISCES

M31
Andromeda Galaxy

M32

M110

Caph

+80°

Polaris

ANDROMEDA

+70°

+60°

CEPHEUS

1ʰ

+50°

Alpheratz

+40°

Alderamin

+30°

Algenib

+20°

Scheat

LACERTA

M39

+10°

PISCES

PEGASUS

CYGNUS Deneb

Etam

WEST   23ʰ   22ʰ   21ʰ   20ʰ   19ʰ   NORTH

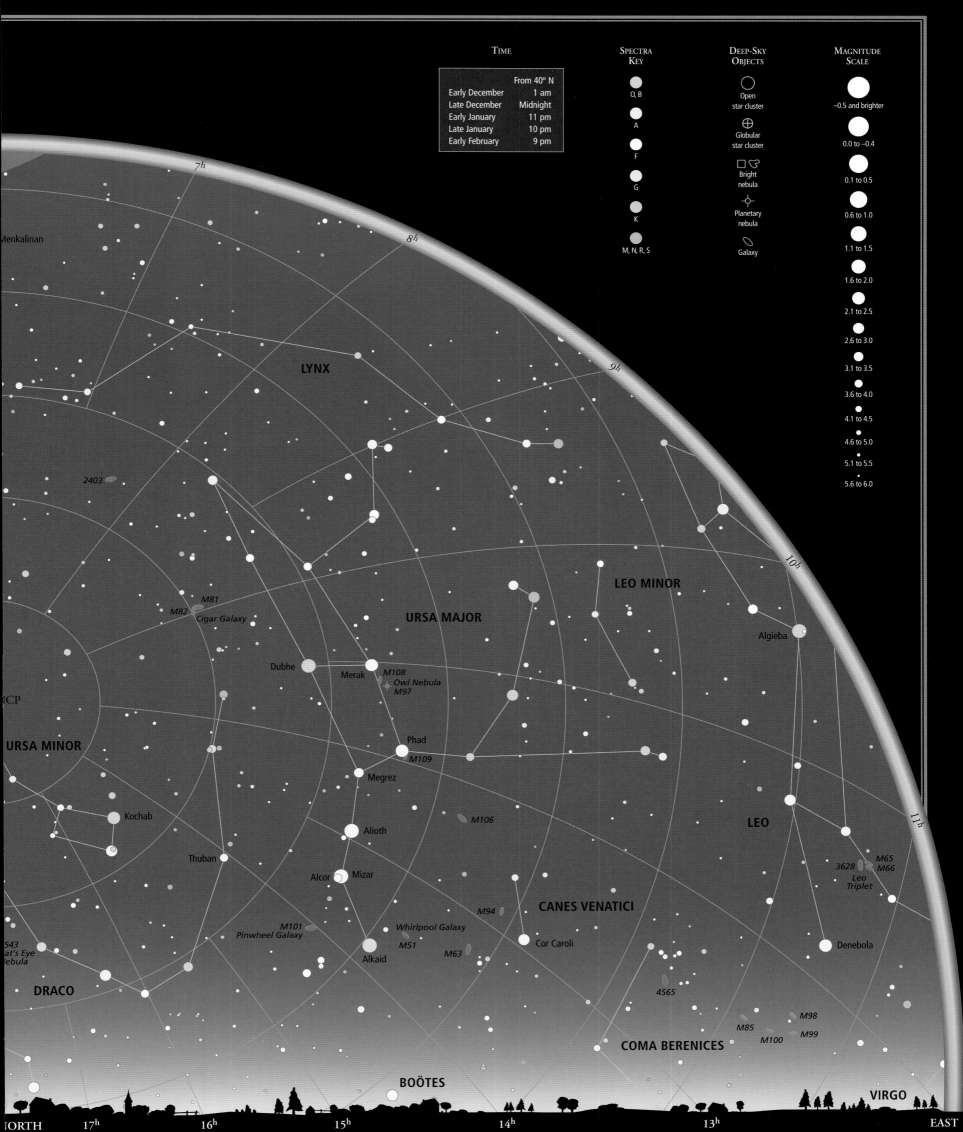

TIME

From 40° N	
Early December	1 am
Late December	Midnight
Early January	11 pm
Late January	10 pm
Early February	9 pm

SPECTRA KEY

O, B

A

F

G

K

M, N, R, S

DEEP-SKY OBJECTS

Open star cluster

Globular star cluster

Bright nebula

Planetary nebula

Galaxy

MAGNITUDE SCALE

−0.5 and brighter

0.0 to −0.4

0.1 to 0.5

0.6 to 1.0

1.1 to 1.5

1.6 to 2.0

2.1 to 2.5

2.6 to 3.0

3.1 to 3.5

3.6 to 4.0

4.1 to 4.5

4.6 to 5.0

5.1 to 5.5

5.6 to 6.0

7h

8h

9h

10h

11h

Menkalinan

LYNX

2403

M81

M82
Cigar Galaxy

URSA MAJOR

LEO MINOR

Algieba

Dubhe

Merak

M108
Owl Nebula
M97

NCP

URSA MINOR

Phad

M109

Megrez

Kochab

M106

LEO

Thuban

Alioth

M65
3628
M66
Leo Triplet

Alcor
Mizar

CANES VENATICI

M94

M101
Pinwheel Galaxy

Whirlpool Galaxy
M51

Cor Caroli

Denebola

543
at's Eye
ebula

Alkaid

M63

4565

DRACO

M98
M85
M100
M99

COMA BERENICES

BOÖTES

VIRGO

NORTH

17h

16h

15h

14h

13h

EAST

NORTHERN WINTER: LOOKING SOUTH

While the northern half of the winter sky contains many famous constellations, it is the south that features the real action. Here, the heavens are ablaze with bright stars: Betelgeuse and Rigel in Orion; Aldebaran and the Pleiades in Taurus; Sirius in Canis Major; Procyon in Canis Minor; and the twins Castor and Pollux in Gemini. The Milky Way also puts on a great show for the entire season. Meanwhile, look to the east for Leo the Lion with his bright star Regulus, and—at the end of winter—the winding constellation of Hydra, with its bright star Alphard.

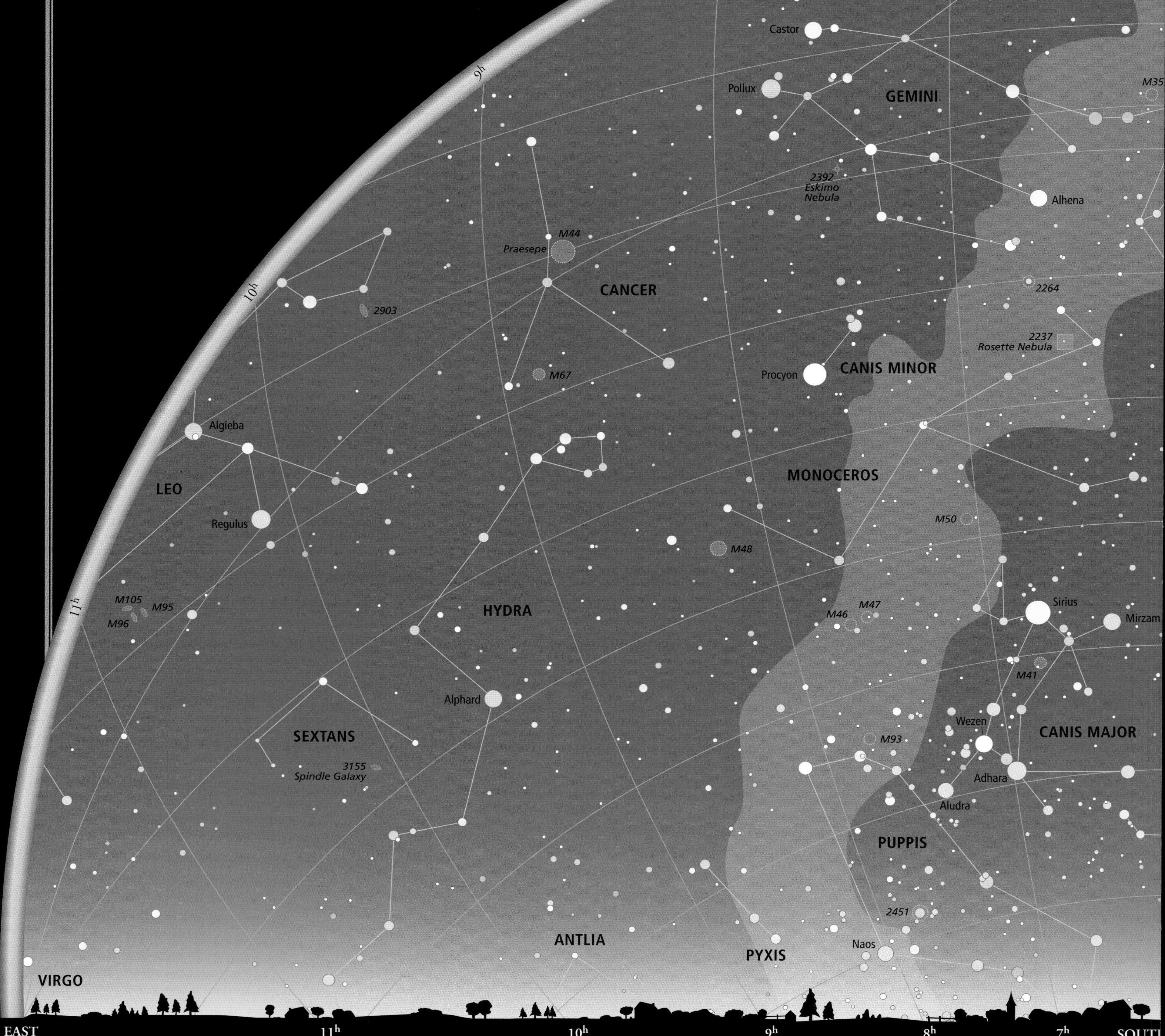

7ʰ

8ʰ

9ʰ

Castor

10ʰ

Pollux

GEMINI

M35

2392
Eskimo
Nebula

Alhena

Praesepe   M44

2903

CANCER

2264

2237
Rosette Nebula

M67

Procyon

CANIS MINOR

Algieba

MONOCEROS

LEO

M50

Regulus

M48

M105   M95

11ʰ

M96

HYDRA

M47

M46

Sirius

Mirzam

M41

Alphard

SEXTANS

Wezen

CANIS MAJOR

M93

3155
Spindle Galaxy

Adhara

Aludra

PUPPIS

2451

ANTLIA

Naos

PYXIS

VIRGO

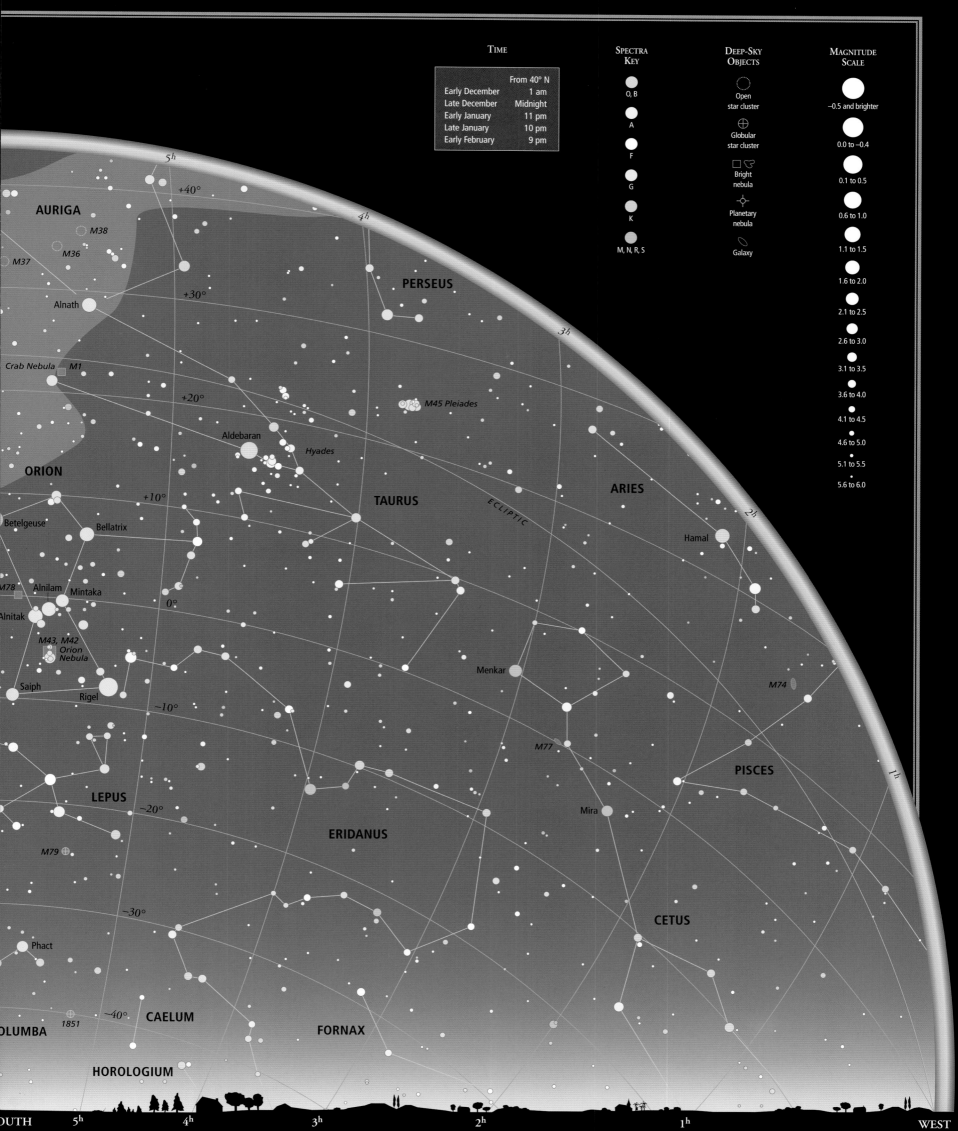

TIME

From 40° N	
Early December	1 am
Late December	Midnight
Early January	11 pm
Late January	10 pm
Early February	9 pm

SPECTRA KEY

O, B
A
F
G
K
M, N, R, S

DEEP-SKY OBJECTS

Open star cluster
Globular star cluster
Bright nebula
Planetary nebula
Galaxy

MAGNITUDE SCALE

−0.5 and brighter
0.0 to −0.4
0.1 to 0.5
0.6 to 1.0
1.1 to 1.5
1.6 to 2.0
2.1 to 2.5
2.6 to 3.0
3.1 to 3.5
3.6 to 4.0
4.1 to 4.5
4.6 to 5.0
5.1 to 5.5
5.6 to 6.0

AURIGA

M38
M36
M37

Alnath

5ʰ
+40°
+30°
+20°
+10°
0°
−10°
−20°
−30°
−40°

4ʰ

PERSEUS

3ʰ

Crab Nebula M1

ORION

M45 Pleiades

Aldebaran

Hyades

TAURUS

ECLIPTIC

ARIES

Hamal

2ʰ

Betelgeuse
Bellatrix

M78
Alnilam Mintaka
Alnitak

M43, M42
Orion
Nebula

Saiph
Rigel

Menkar

M74

Mira

M77

LEPUS

ERIDANUS

PISCES

CETUS

M79

M79

Phact

CAELUM

FORNAX

1851

HOROLOGIUM

COLUMBA

SOUTH
5ʰ
4ʰ
3ʰ
2ʰ
1ʰ

WEST

Southern Spring: Looking North

As spring begins in the southern hemisphere Altair, the brightest star in Aquila the Eagle, is prominent in the north. In fact the northern hemisphere's Summer Triangle—formed by Altair, Vega in Lyra (not shown), and Deneb in Cygnus—is also visible during early spring or late winter from the southern hemisphere. By the end of spring, the Milky Way is low down on the horizon, Pegasus and Andromeda are at moderate altitudes to the north, and Taurus is conspicuous in the northeast along with the Pleiades star cluster.

SCULPTOR

Fomalhaut

PISCIS AUSTRINUS

Helix Nebula
7293

23ʰ

22ʰ

M30

21ʰ

AQUARIUS

CAPRICORNUS

20ʰ

7009
M72
Saturn Nebula

M2

Markab

EQUULEUS

PEGASUS

Enif

M15

PEGASUS

6934

AQUILA

Scheat

19ʰ

DELPHINUS

6712

SAGITTA

6992, 6995
Veil Nebula

M11

M71

6960

SCUTUM

M27
Dumbbell Nebula

LACERTA

Altair

SERPENS CAUDA

Cr399
Brocchi's Cluster

CYGNUS

VULPECULA

Albireo

Deneb

WEST   19ʰ   20ʰ   21ʰ   22ʰ   23ʰ   NORTH

TIME*

	From 30° S
Early September	1 am
Late September	Midnight
Early October	11 pm
Late October	10 pm
Early November	9 pm

*Add 1 hour for DST

SPECTRA KEY

O, B
A
F
G
K
M, N, R, S

DEEP-SKY OBJECTS

Open star cluster
Globular star cluster
Bright nebula
Planetary nebula
Galaxy

MAGNITUDE SCALE

−0.5 and brighter
0.0 to −0.4
0.1 to 0.5
0.6 to 1.0
1.1 to 1.5
1.6 to 2.0
2.1 to 2.5
2.6 to 3.0
3.1 to 3.5
3.6 to 4.0
4.1 to 4.5
4.6 to 5.0
5.1 to 5.5
5.6 to 6.0

CASSIOPEIA

Caph
Shedir

ANDROMEDA

M32
M110 M31
Andromeda Galaxy

Alpheratz

Algenib

Mirach
Almaak

TRIANGULUM

M33
752
891
M34

Algol

PERSEUS

PISCES

Deneb Kaitos

CETUS

253
⊕ 288

ECLIPTIC

Hamal

ARIES

Mira

M74

M77

Menkar

M45
Pleiades

Hyades

TAURUS

Aldebaran

ERIDANUS

ORION

Mintaka

Bellatrix

Alnilam
Alnitak

+50°
+40°
+30°
+20°
+10°
0°
−10°
−20°
−30°

1ʰ
2ʰ
3ʰ
4ʰ
5ʰ

NORTH
1ʰ
2ʰ
3ʰ
4ʰ
5ʰ
EAST

Southern Spring: Looking South

The northerly direction during spring is worthwhile, but it is only by facing south that you can truly appreciate the real wonders of the sky at this time. The Magellanic Clouds are well placed throughout spring. The Milky Way is eye-catching early on, when the typical southern groups of Crux and Centaurus are also visible. But as spring draws to a close, the Milky Way, Crux, and Centaurus are lost in the haze of the southern horizon, leaving Canopus of Carina, Achernar of Eridanus, and Fomalhaut of Piscis Austrinus as the dominant southerly stars.

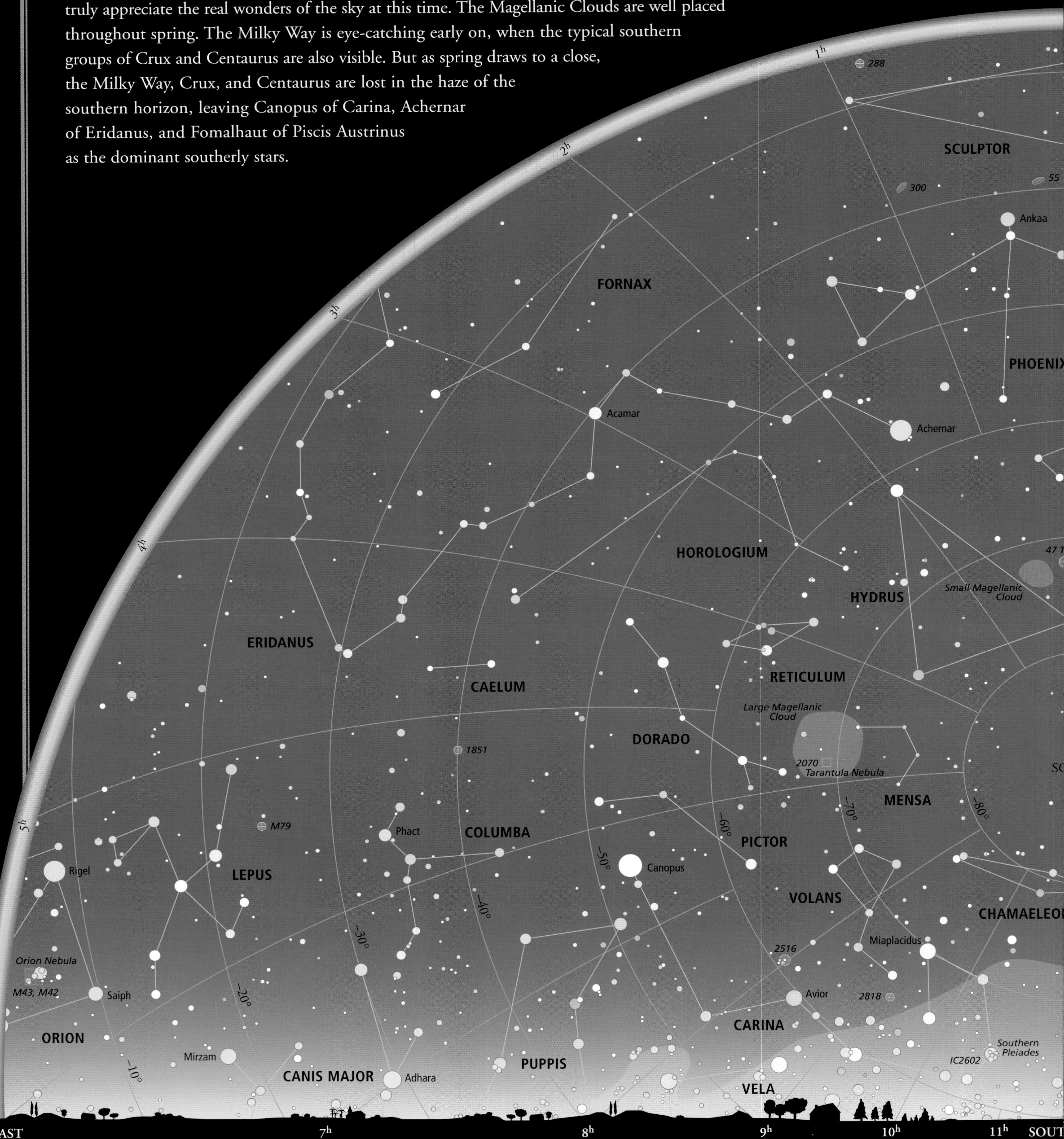

⊕ 288

SCULPTOR

⊘ 300

⊘ 55

Ankaa

2ʰ

1ʰ

FORNAX

PHOENIX

Acamar

Achernar

HOROLOGIUM

47 T

HYDRUS

Small Magellanic Cloud

3ʰ

ERIDANUS

RETICULUM

CAELUM

Large Magellanic Cloud

DORADO

⊕ 1851

2070 ◻
Tarantula Nebula

SC

4ʰ

MENSA

−70°

−60°

−80°

COLUMBA

PICTOR

⊕ M79

Phact

−50°

Canopus

VOLANS

−40°

5ʰ

Rigel

LEPUS

CHAMAELEO

Miaplacidus

−30°

2516

Orion Nebula

2818 ⊕

M43, M42

Saiph

−20°

Avior

CARINA

ORION

Southern
Pleiades

Mirzam

−10°

PUPPIS

IC2602

CANIS MAJOR

Adhara

VELA

EAST

7ʰ

8ʰ

9ʰ

10ʰ

11ʰ   SOUT

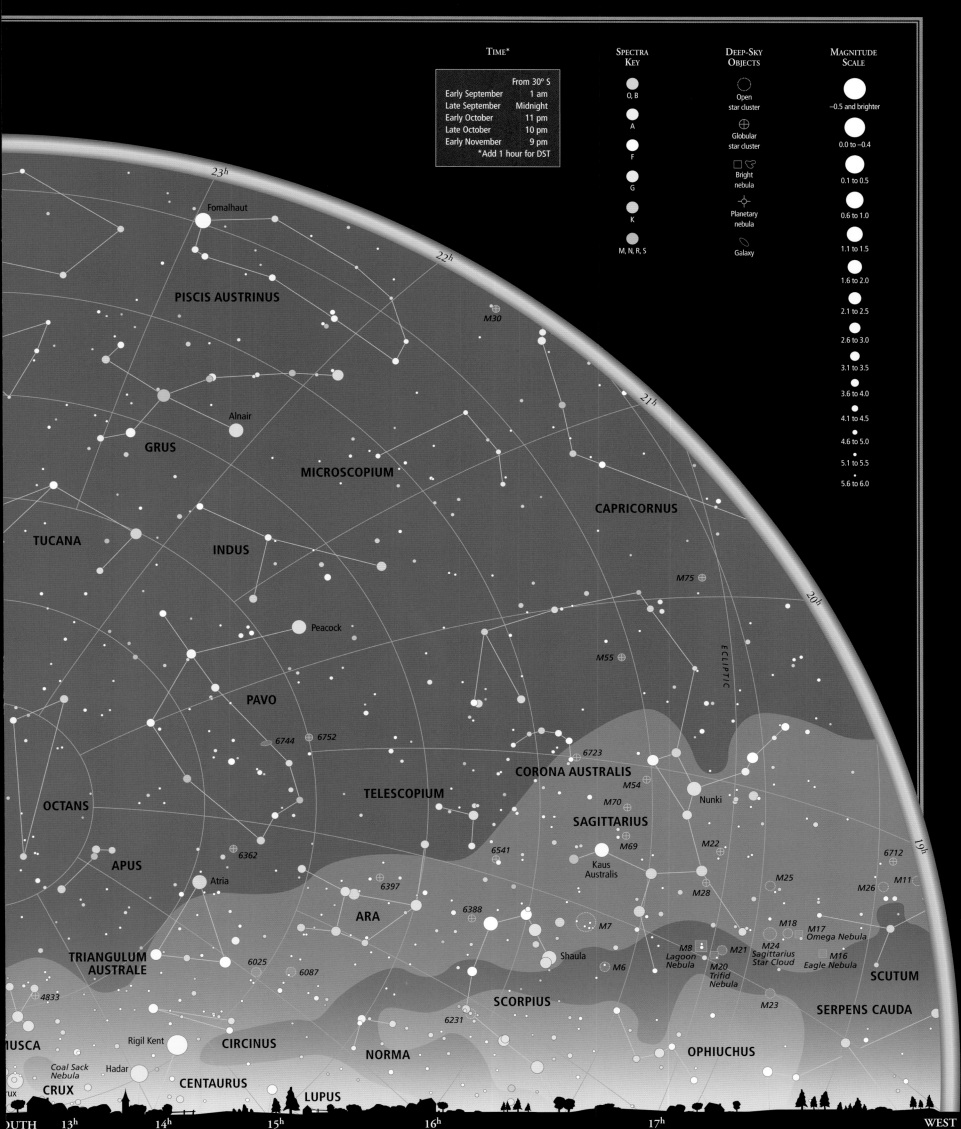

TIME*

From 30° S
Early September   1 am
Late September   Midnight
Early October   11 pm
Late October   10 pm
Early November   9 pm
*Add 1 hour for DST

SPECTRA KEY

O, B
A
F
G
K
M, N, R, S

DEEP-SKY OBJECTS

Open star cluster
Globular star cluster
Bright nebula
Planetary nebula
Galaxy

MAGNITUDE SCALE

−0.5 and brighter
0.0 to −0.4
0.1 to 0.5
0.6 to 1.0
1.1 to 1.5
1.6 to 2.0
2.1 to 2.5
2.6 to 3.0
3.1 to 3.5
3.6 to 4.0
4.1 to 4.5
4.6 to 5.0
5.1 to 5.5
5.6 to 6.0

23ʰ
22ʰ
21ʰ
20ʰ
19ʰ

Fomalhaut

PISCIS AUSTRINUS

M30

Alnair

GRUS

MICROSCOPIUM

CAPRICORNUS

TUCANA

INDUS

M75

Peacock

M55

ECLIPTIC

PAVO

6744   6752

6723

CORONA AUSTRALIS

M54

OCTANS

TELESCOPIUM

M70

Nunki

SAGITTARIUS

APUS

6362

6541

M69   M22

Atria

6397

Kaus Australis

M28   M25

6712

M26   M11

ARA

6388

M18   M17
Omega Nebula

TRIANGULUM AUSTRALE

6025

6087

M7

Shaula

M8
Lagoon Nebula

M21   M24
Sagittarius Star Cloud

M16
Eagle Nebula

SCUTUM

M20
Trifid Nebula

M6

4833

M23

SERPENS CAUDA

6231

SCORPIUS

MUSCA

Rigil Kent

CIRCINUS

NORMA

OPHIUCHUS

Coal Sack Nebula   Hadar

CENTAURUS

LUPUS

CRUX

13ʰ   14ʰ   15ʰ   16ʰ   17ʰ

SOUTH

WEST

Southern Summer: Looking North

Face north during the summer night, and the skies will be replete with sparkling constellations of bright stars. Taurus the Bull, Auriga the Charioteer, and Orion the Hunter encroach from the northeast around mid-December. By January, Orion is high in the heavens, with Procyon in Canis Minor to the east, and Sirius in Canis Major higher up. The Milky Way is also prominent throughout the summer. By summer's end, Regulus in Leo and the twins of Gemini also put in a show, but they remain fairly low down toward the horizon.

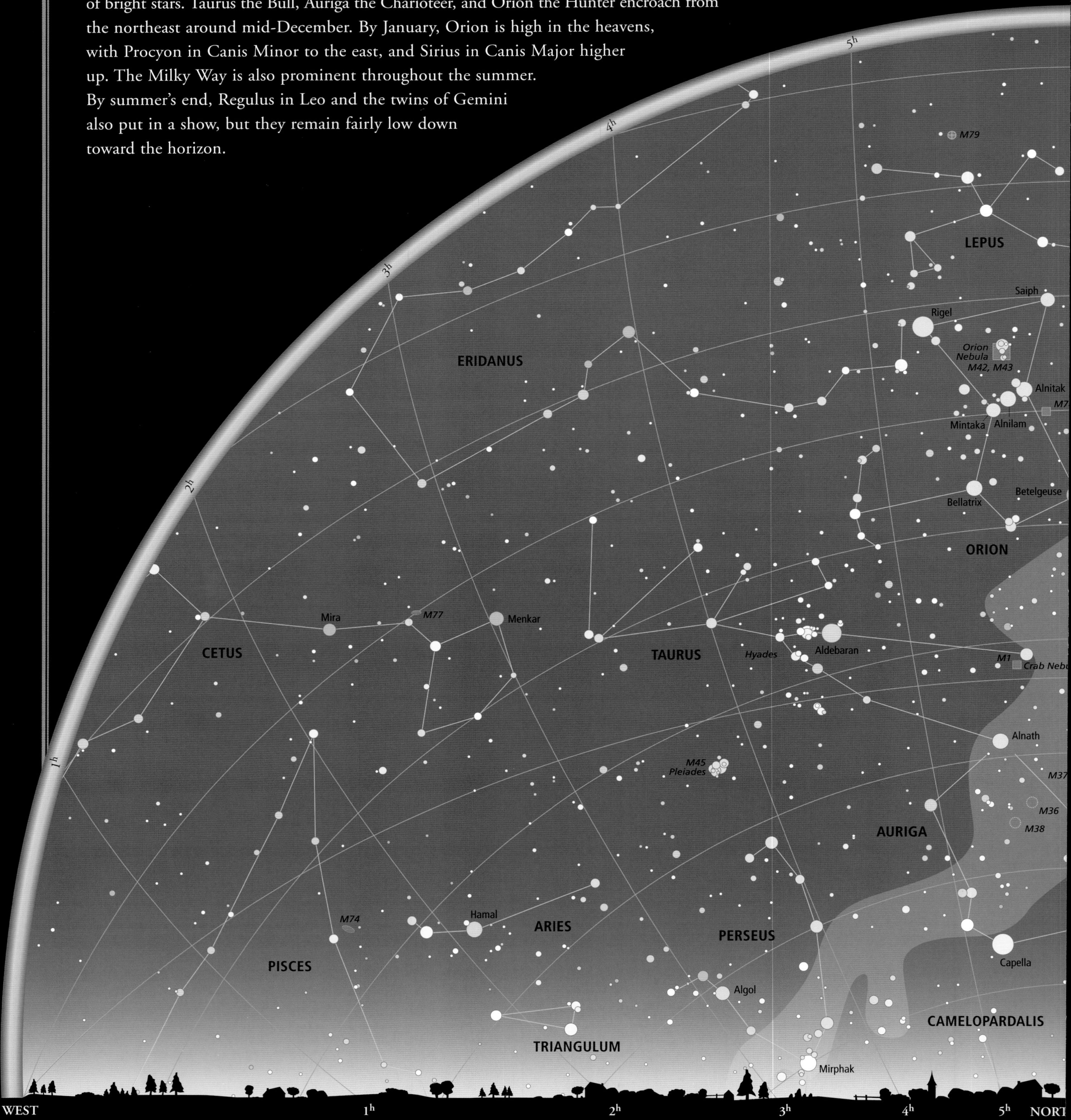

M79

LEPUS

5ʰ

4ʰ

3ʰ

2ʰ

1ʰ

Saiph

Rigel

ERIDANUS

Orion Nebula
M42, M43

Alnitak

M7

Mintaka Alnilam

Bellatrix

Betelgeuse

ORION

Mira M77 Menkar

CETUS

TAURUS Hyades Aldebaran

M1 Crab Nebula

Alnath

M37

M45
Pleiades

M36

M38

AURIGA

M74 Hamal

ARIES

PERSEUS

Capella

PISCES

Algol

CAMELOPARDALIS

TRIANGULUM

Mirphak

WEST 1ʰ 2ʰ 3ʰ 4ʰ 5ʰ NORTH

TIME*

	From 30° S
Early December	1 am
Late December	Midnight
Early January	11 pm
Late January	10 pm
Early February	9 pm

*Add 1 hour for DST

SPECTRA KEY

O, B
A
F
G
K
M, N, R, S

DEEP-SKY OBJECTS

Open star cluster

Globular star cluster

Bright nebula

Planetary nebula

Galaxy

MAGNITUDE SCALE

-0.5 and brighter
0.0 to -0.4
0.1 to 0.5
0.6 to 1.0
1.1 to 1.5
1.6 to 2.0
2.1 to 2.5
2.6 to 3.0
3.1 to 3.5
3.6 to 4.0
4.1 to 4.5
4.6 to 5.0
5.1 to 5.5
5.6 to 6.0

NORTH

EAST

7ʰ
8ʰ
9ʰ
10ʰ
11ʰ

CANIS MAJOR
Adhara
Wezen
Aludra
M41
Mirzam
Sirius
−30°
−20°
−10°
0°

PUPPIS
M93
M46
M47
M50

MONOCEROS
M48
2237
Rosette Nebula
Procyon
CANIS MINOR
2264
+10°
Alhena

HYDRA
Alphard

3115
Spindle Galaxy

SEXTANS

Eskimo Nebula 2392
+20°
M67
M44 Praesepe

CANCER
+30°
Pollux
Castor

GEMINI
+40°
LYNX

2903

Regulus

Algieba
M95
M96
M105

+50°
LEO

LEO MINOR

VIRGO

SOUTHERN SUMMER: LOOKING SOUTH

Facing south, the early summer sees Canopus in Carina and Achernar in Eridanus drawing the attention, with Canis Major and Puppis soaring in the southeast. The Magellanic Clouds are also very high up. As the weeks pass, the Milky Way once again begins to rise out of the southeast, bringing with it the brilliant stars of the Southern Cross (Crux) as well as Rigil Kent and Hadar (Alpha and Beta Centauri). By the end of the summer, the Milky Way cuts the sky in two, emerging from the south-southeast, spilling up close to the zenith, and then pouring back down to vanish below the northwestern horizon.

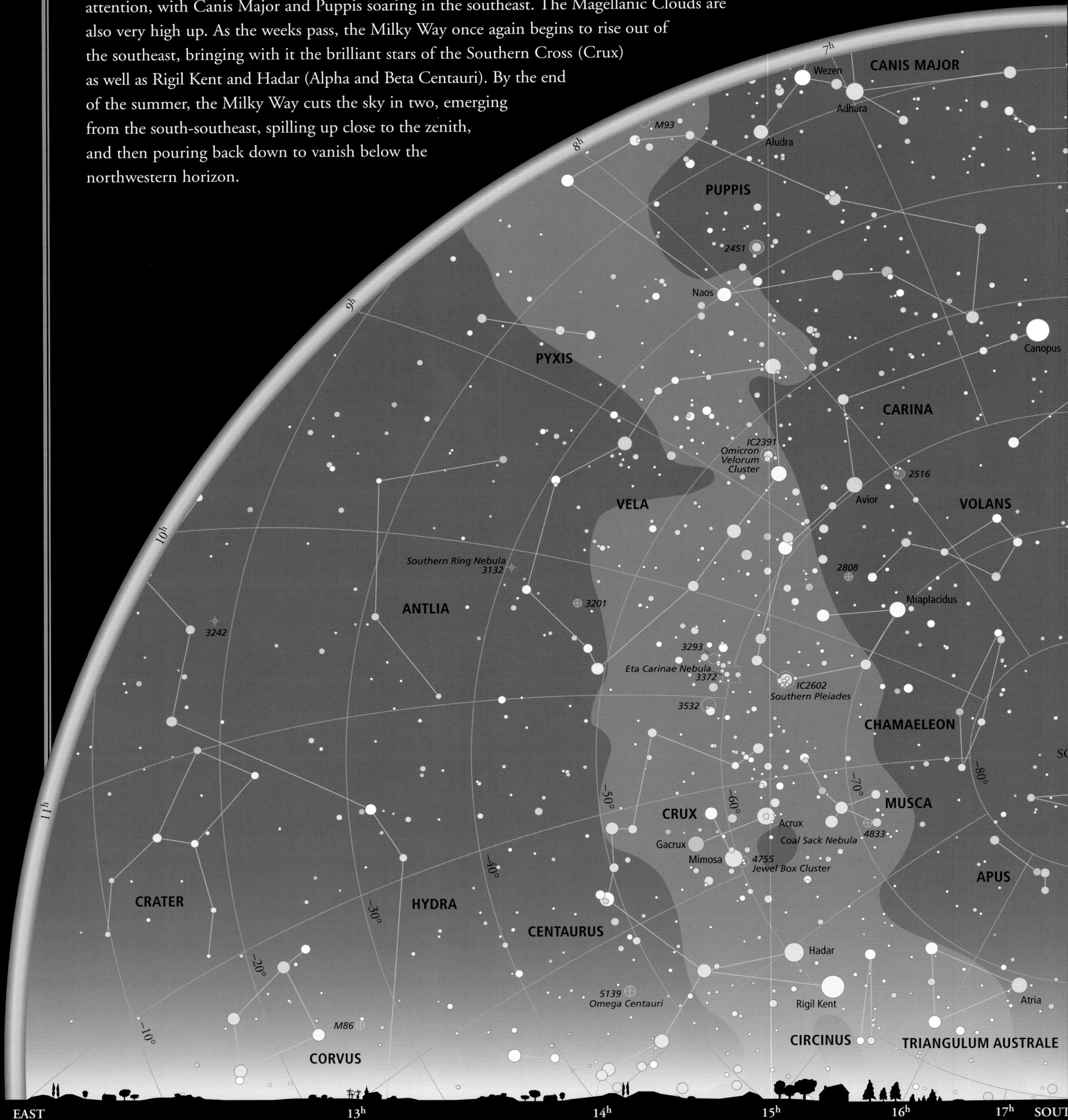

CANIS MAJOR

Wezen

Adhara

Aludra

M93

PUPPIS

2451

Naos

PYXIS

Canopus

CARINA

IC2391
Omicron
Velorum
Cluster

2516

Avior

VOLANS

VELA

Southern Ring Nebula
3132

2808

3201

Miaplacidus

ANTLIA

3242

3293

Eta Carinae Nebula
3372

IC2602
Southern Pleiades

CHAMAELEON

3532

−50°

−70°

−80°

−60°

MUSCA

CRUX

Acrux

Coal Sack Nebula

4833

Gacrux

−40°

Mimosa

4755
Jewel Box Cluster

APUS

CRATER

HYDRA

−30°

CENTAURUS

−20°

Hadar

5139
Omega Centauri

Rigil Kent

Atria

−10°

M86

CIRCINUS

TRIANGULUM AUSTRALE

CORVUS

EAST   13ʰ   14ʰ   15ʰ   16ʰ   17ʰ   SOUTH

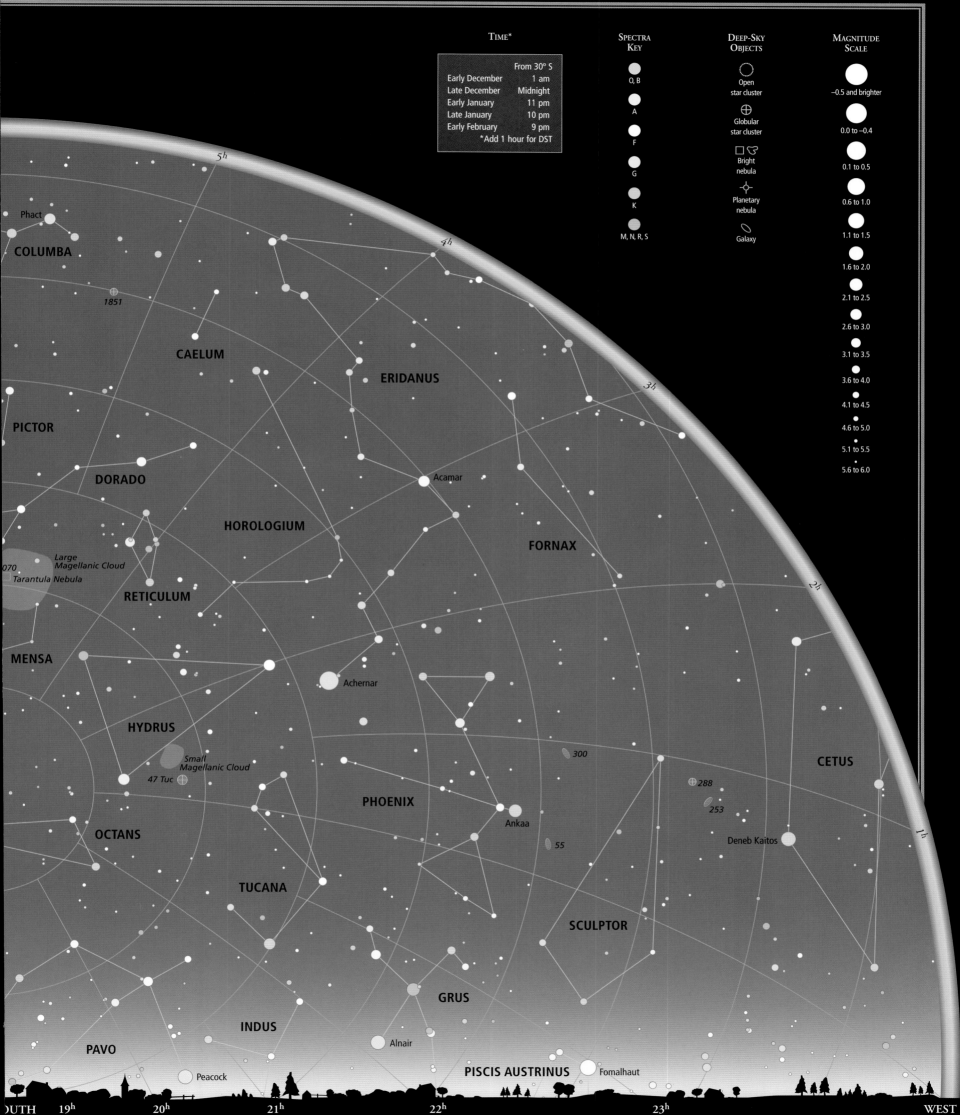

SOUTHERN FALL: LOOKING NORTH

Once the bright constellations of summer have sunk in the west, the fall sky looking north is not particularly dazzling, but there are still a few bright stars. Most notable are the orange Arcturus in Boötes, Spica in Virgo, Regulus in Leo, and Procyon in Canis Minor. Arcturus reaches its highest elevation in May, by which time Leo is sinking in the northwest and Hercules is rising in the northeast. This is a good time to go galaxy hunting, for the giant Virgo cluster of galaxies is well placed from March to May.

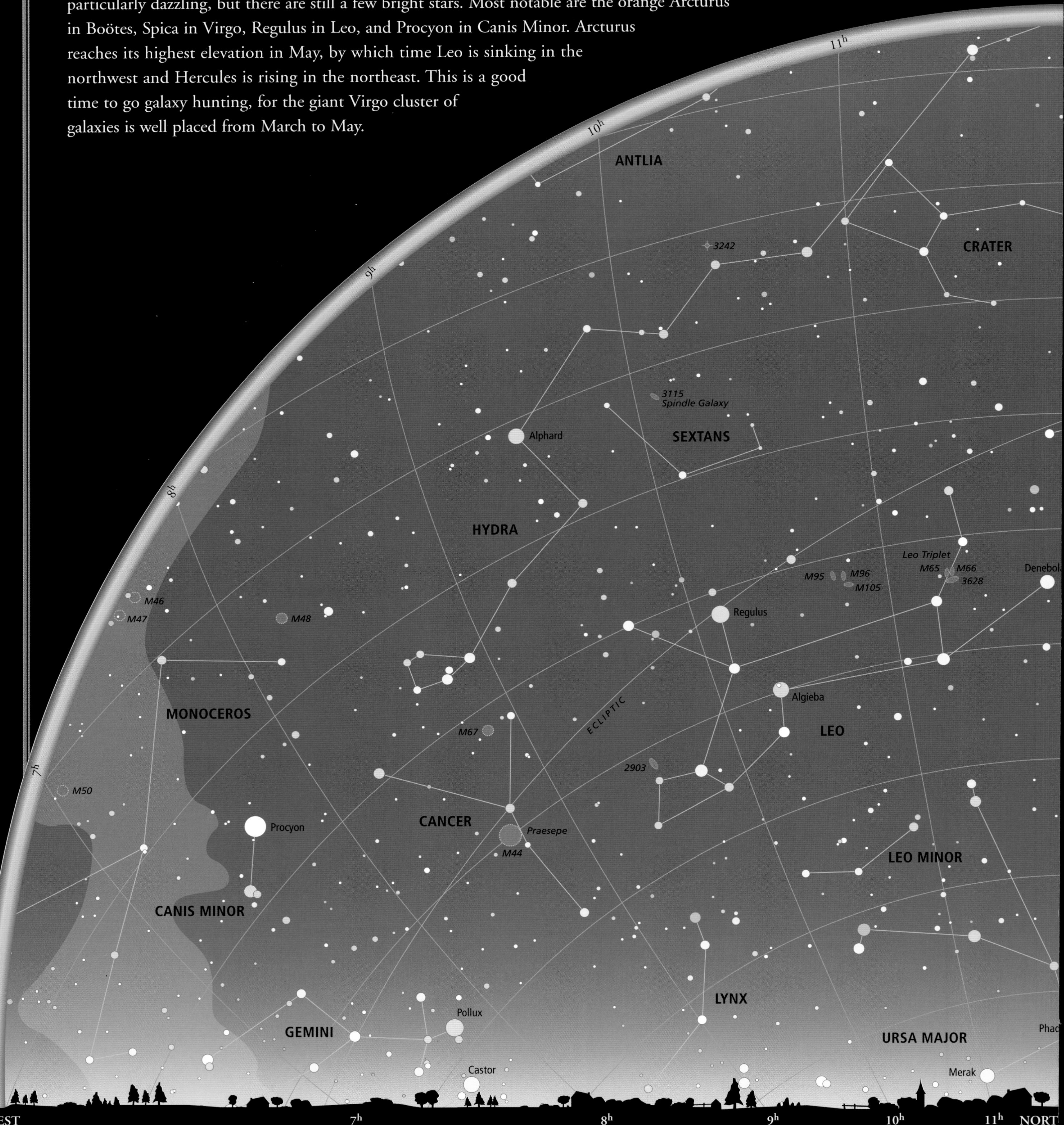

11^h

10^h

9^h

8^h

7^h

ANTLIA

CRATER

3242

3115
Spindle Galaxy

Alphard

SEXTANS

HYDRA

Leo Triplet
M65   M66
3628

Denebola

M95   M96
M105

M46

Regulus

M47

M48

Algieba

MONOCEROS

M67

LEO

ECLIPTIC

2903

M50

Procyon

CANCER

Praesepe

LEO MINOR

M44

CANIS MINOR

LYNX

Pollux

GEMINI

URSA MAJOR

Phad

Castor

Merak

WEST

7^h

8^h

9^h

10^h

11^h NORTH

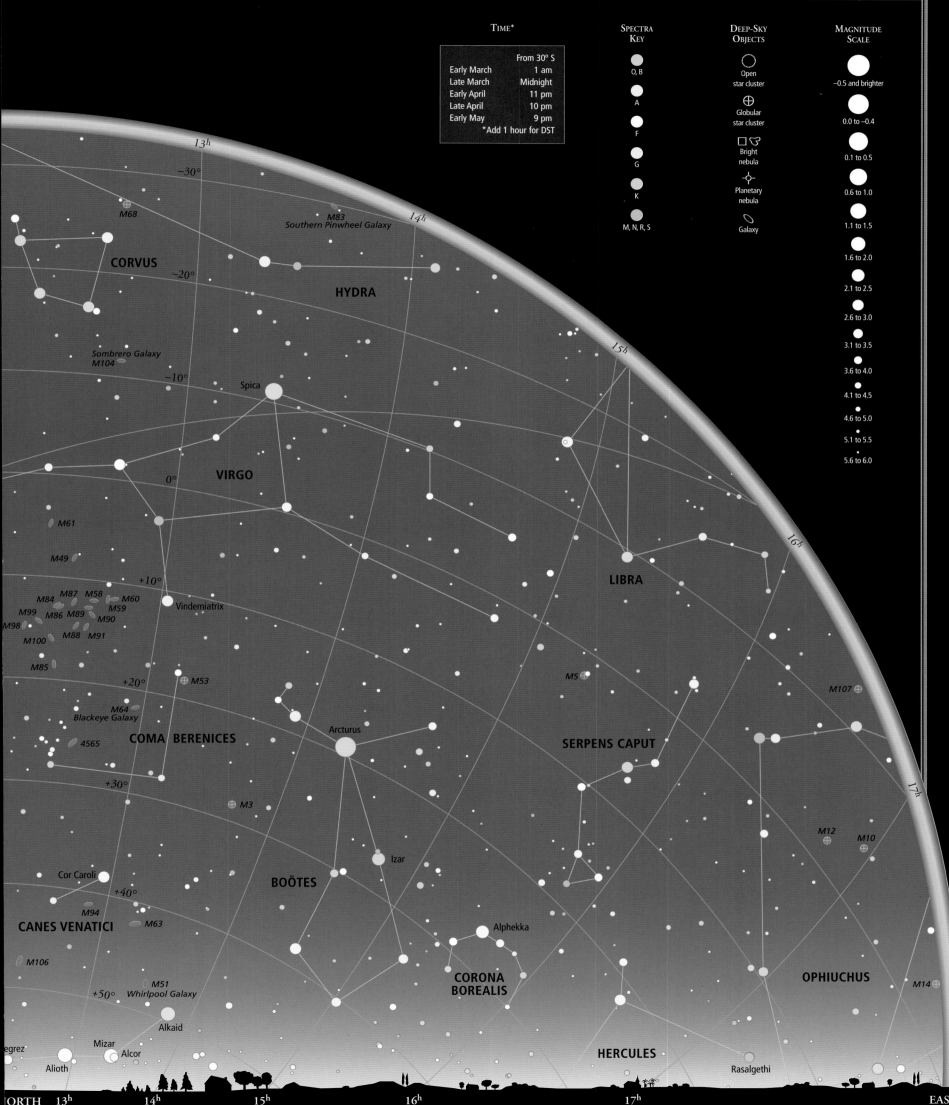

TIME*

	From 30° S
Early March	1 am
Late March	Midnight
Early April	11 pm
Late April	10 pm
Early May	9 pm

*Add 1 hour for DST

SPECTRA KEY

O, B
A
F
G
K
M, N, R, S

DEEP-SKY OBJECTS

Open star cluster
Globular star cluster
Bright nebula
Planetary nebula
Galaxy

MAGNITUDE SCALE

−0.5 and brighter
0.0 to −0.4
0.1 to 0.5
0.6 to 1.0
1.1 to 1.5
1.6 to 2.0
2.1 to 2.5
2.6 to 3.0
3.1 to 3.5
3.6 to 4.0
4.1 to 4.5
4.6 to 5.0
5.1 to 5.5
5.6 to 6.0

13ʰ
−30°
M68
−20°
M83
Southern Pinwheel Galaxy
14ʰ
CORVUS
HYDRA
Sombrero Galaxy
M104
−10°
Spica
15ʰ
0°
VIRGO
M61
M49
+10°
M84 M87 M58
M99 M86 M89 M90 M60
M98 M100 M88 M91 M59
Vindemiatrix
LIBRA
16ʰ
M85
+20° M53
M5
M107
M64
Blackeye Galaxy
4565
COMA BERENICES
Arcturus
SERPENS CAPUT
+30°
M3
M12 M10
Izar
Cor Caroli
BOÖTES
+40°
M94
M63
CANES VENATICI
Alphekka
M106
CORONA BOREALIS
OPHIUCHUS
M14
M51
+50° Whirlpool Galaxy
Alkaid
HERCULES
Negrez
Mizar Alcor
Alioth
Rasalgethi

NORTH 13ʰ 14ʰ 15ʰ 16ʰ 17ʰ EAST

SOUTHERN FALL: LOOKING SOUTH

Compared to the dim view facing north, the view looking south is a celestial treasure trove. The dominant feature here is the Milky Way, which arches across the sky like a celestial, star-studded rainbow. Beneath it, the Magellanic Clouds are hovering close to the horizon. Beautiful Crux, Carina, and Centaurus all remain prominent this season, with the Southern Cross (Crux) gaining maximum altitude in April. Do not confuse the Southern Cross with the False Cross whose upright ends in Avior of Carina, which is also in view during fall. Another star worthy of note this season is the vibrant red Antares in Scorpius, looking southeast.

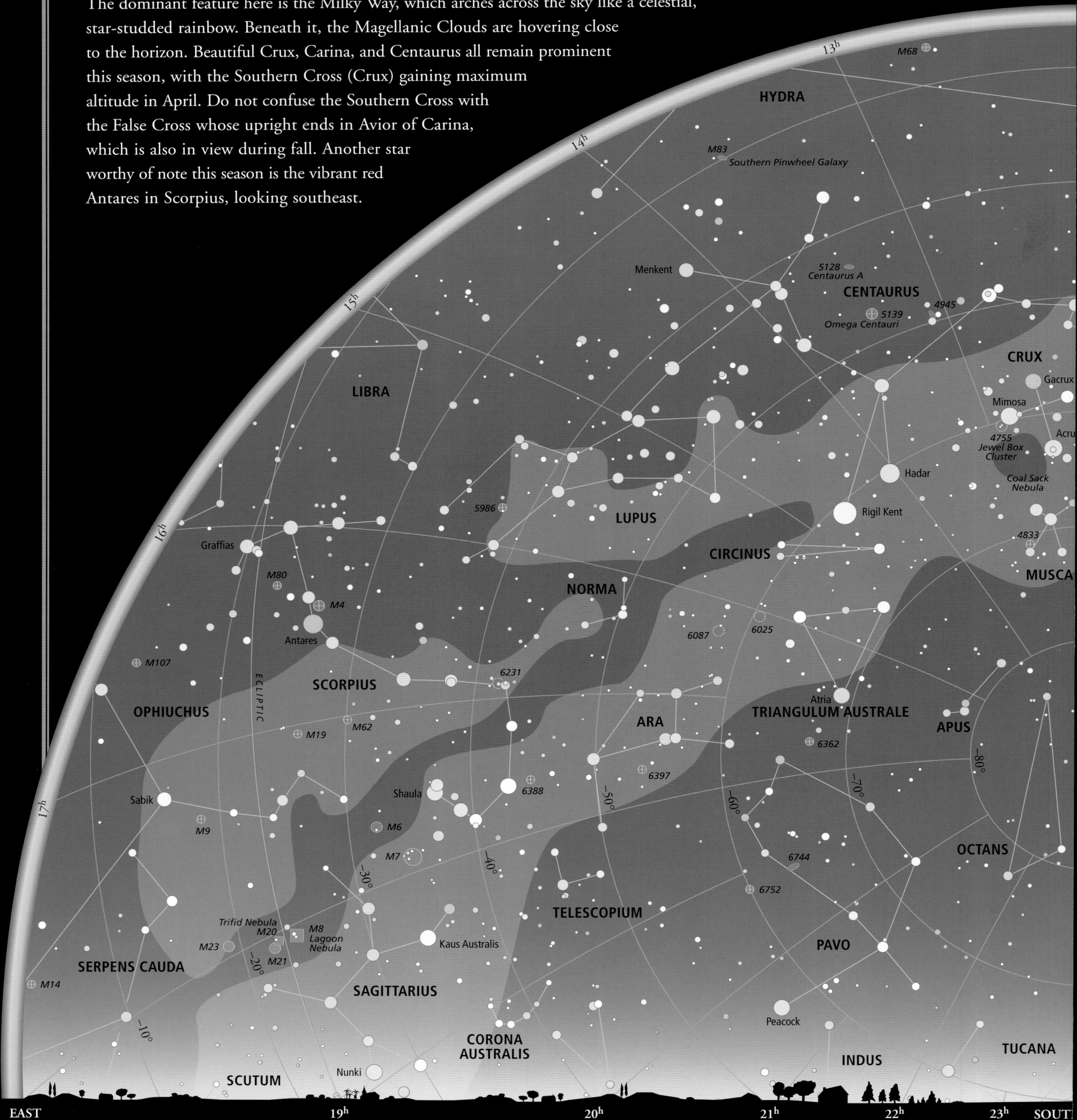

HYDRA

13^h

M68

14^h

M83
Southern Pinwheel Galaxy

Menkent

5128
Centaurus A

CENTAURUS

4945

15^h

5139
Omega Centauri

CRUX

Gacrux

Mimosa

LIBRA

4755
Jewel Box
Cluster

Acru

Coal Sack
Nebula

16^h

5986

LUPUS

Hadar

Rigil Kent

4833

Graffias

CIRCINUS

MUSCA

M80

NORMA

6087

6025

M4

Antares

6231

M107

SCORPIUS

ARA

Atria

TRIANGULUM AUSTRALE

APUS

M19

M62

6362

OPHIUCHUS

ECLIPTIC

-80°

-50°

6397

-70°

Sabik

Shaula

6388

-60°

OCTANS

M9

-40°

6744

M6

-30°

6752

M7

Trifid Nebula
M20

M8
Lagoon
Nebula

TELESCOPIUM

17^h

M23

-20°

M21

Kaus Australis

PAVO

SERPENS CAUDA

M14

SAGITTARIUS

Peacock

-10°

CORONA
AUSTRALIS

INDUS

TUCANA

Nunki

SCUTUM

EAST

19^h

20^h

21^h

22^h

23^h

SOUTH

TIME*

	From 30° S
Early March	1 am
Late March	Midnight
Early April	11 pm
Late April	10 pm
Early May	9 pm
	*Add 1 hour for DST

SPECTRA
KEY

O, B
A
F
G
K
M, N, R, S

DEEP-SKY
OBJECTS

Open
star cluster

Globular
star cluster

Bright
nebula

Planetary
nebula

Galaxy

MAGNITUDE
SCALE

−0.5 and brighter
0.0 to −0.4
0.1 to 0.5
0.6 to 1.0
1.1 to 1.5
1.6 to 2.0
2.1 to 2.5
2.6 to 3.0
3.1 to 3.5
3.6 to 4.0
4.1 to 4.5
4.6 to 5.0
5.1 to 5.5
5.6 to 6.0

11ʰ
10ʰ
9ʰ
8·ʰ
7ʰ

ANTLIA

Southern Ring
Nebula
3132

3201

VELA

3532
3293
3372
Eta Carinae Nebula

IC2602
Southern
Pleiades

PYXIS

IC2391
Omicron
Velorum Cluster

Naos

2451

M93

M46

2808

Avior

M47

Miaplacidus

2516

CHAMAELEON

CARINA

PUPPIS

Aludra

Wezen

VOLANS

Adhara

M41

M50

PICTOR

CP

Canopus

Sirius

Tarantula Nebula
2070

MENSA

Large Magellanic
Cloud

DORADO

COLUMBA

CANIS MAJOR

MONOCEROS

Mirzam

Small Magellanic
Cloud

RETICULUM

Phact

1851

47 Tuc

CAELUM

LEPUS

HYDRUS

HOROLOGIUM

Saiph

ORION

Southern Winter: Looking North

At the break of winter facing north, Boötes and Virgo are both high, their bright stars Arcturus and Spica governing the heavens. As the season progresses, these drift to the west while Scorpius and Sagittarius move into position very high overhead. The northern hemisphere's Summer Triangle—formed by Vega in Lyra, Deneb in Cygnus, and Altair in Aquila—doubles as the south's Winter Triangle if you are not too far south, straddling the bright Milky Way. These distinctive stars vanish as winter draws to a close, with the relatively faint Pegasus taking their place in the north.

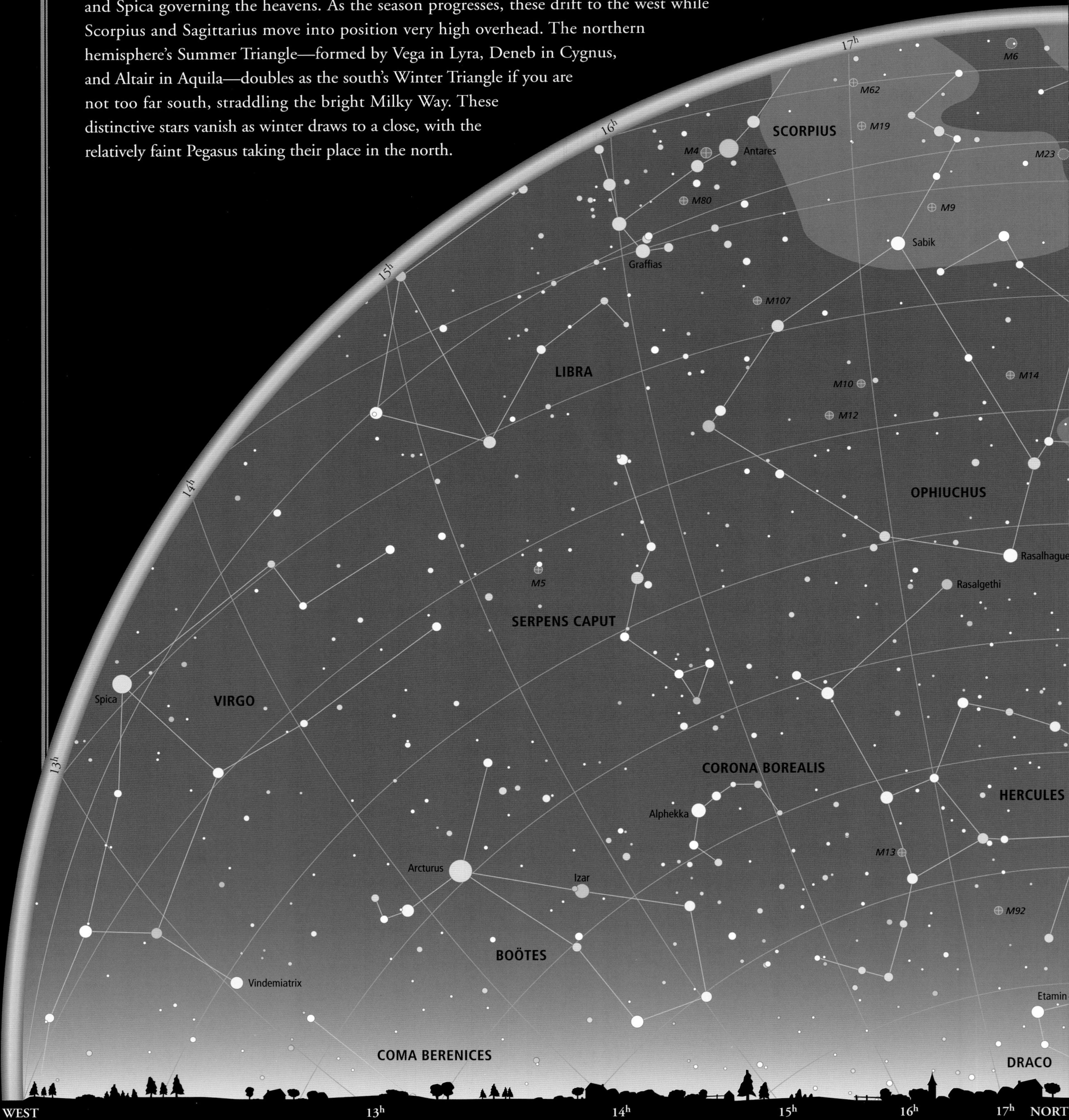

M6

M62

SCORPIUS

M19

M23

17h

M4

Antares

M80

M9

Sabik

16h

Graffias

M107

15h

LIBRA

M10

M14

M12

14h

OPHIUCHUS

Rasalhague

M5

Rasalgethi

SERPENS CAPUT

13h

VIRGO

Spica

CORONA BOREALIS

HERCULES

Alphekka

M13

Arcturus

Izar

M92

BOÖTES

Vindemiatrix

Etamin

COMA BERENICES

DRACO

TIME

	From 30° S
Early June	1 am
Late June	Midnight
Early July	11 pm
Late July	10 pm
Early August	9 pm

SPECTRA KEY

- O, B
- A
- F
- G
- K
- M, N, R, S

DEEP-SKY OBJECTS

- Open star cluster
- Globular star cluster
- Bright nebula
- Planetary nebula
- Galaxy

MAGNITUDE SCALE

- −0.5 and brighter
- 0.0 to −0.4
- 0.1 to 0.5
- 0.6 to 1.0
- 1.1 to 1.5
- 1.6 to 2.0
- 2.1 to 2.5
- 2.6 to 3.0
- 3.1 to 3.5
- 3.6 to 4.0
- 4.1 to 4.5
- 4.6 to 5.0
- 5.1 to 5.5
- 5.6 to 6.0

SAGITTARIUS
M69
M70
M54
−30°
M55
20h
3 Lagoon Nebula
M28
M22
Nunki
M21
M20 Trifid Nebula
−20°
M25
Sagittarius Star Cloud
M24
M18
M75
ECLIPTIC
M17 Omega Nebula
SCUTUM
M16 Eagle Nebula
−10°
21h
CAPRICORNUS
0°
M72
Saturn Nebula 7009
SERPENS CAUDA
6572
22h
+10°
AQUILA
Altair
6934
M2
+20°
Brocchi's Cluster
Cr399
M71
SAGITTA
EQUULEUS
VULPECULA
DELPHINUS
AQUARIUS
M27 Dumbbell Nebula
Ring Nebula
+30°
Albireo
M57
M56
M15
Enif
LYRA
Vega
6960
Veil Nebula 6992, 6995
+40°
M29
23h
+50°
CYGNUS
Deneb
PEGASUS
Markab
PISCES

SOUTHERN WINTER: LOOKING SOUTH

Facing south at the start of the southern winter, the Magellanic Clouds are both visible but quite low above the horizon. Carina is also low down in the southwest, but Crux and Centaurus still have pride of place. Later, Crux and Centaurus sink toward the southwest as the Magellanic Clouds ascend in sympathy, rounding the southern celestial pole. By winter's end, Carina is below the horizon (depending on your latitude) and Crux is not far above it. Centaurus is a little higher, though, and Achernar in Eridanus is a prominent beacon in the southeast.

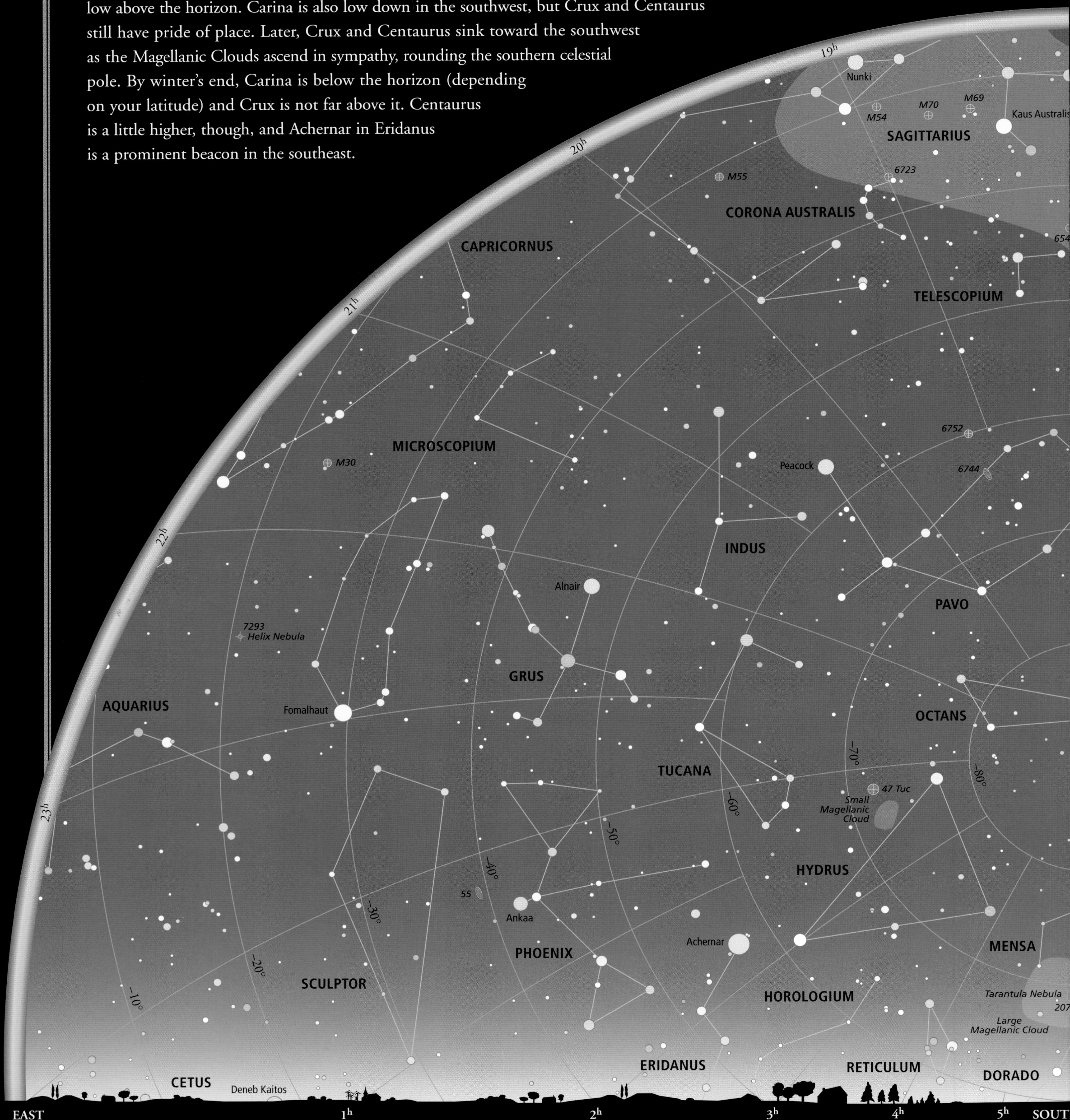

19ʰ

Nunki

M69
M70
M54

Kaus Australis

SAGITTARIUS

6723

20ʰ

M55

CORONA AUSTRALIS

CAPRICORNUS

654

TELESCOPIUM

21ʰ

6752

6744

MICROSCOPIUM

M30

Peacock

22ʰ

INDUS

PAVO

Alnair

7293
Helix Nebula

GRUS

OCTANS

AQUARIUS

Fomalhaut

–70°

–80°

47 Tuc

TUCANA

Small
Magellanic
Cloud

–60°

23ʰ

–50°

HYDRUS

–40°

55

Ankaa

MENSA

–30°

Achernar

PHOENIX

Tarantula Nebula

207

–20°

SCULPTOR

HOROLOGIUM

Large
Magellanic Cloud

–10°

CETUS   Deneb Kaitos

ERIDANUS

RETICULUM

DORADO

EAST   1ʰ   2ʰ   3ʰ   4ʰ   5ʰ   SOUTH

This view of a dazzling stretch of the Milky Way is centered on the distinctive constellation Crux. Also known as the Southern Cross, Crux is the smallest of the 88 constellations recognized today. The dark patch visible above Crux is the Coal Sack Nebula, an interstellar cloud of dust that obscures the light of stars beyond it.

THE CONSTELLATIONS

CHARTING THE CONSTELLATIONS

While some of the constellations we know today are truly ancient,
it was not until the 18th century that the last patches of sky were
named and not until 1930 that the International Astronomical
Union agreed on the boundaries of the 88 constellations we
recognize today. In the following pages each constellation is
mapped in detail along with photographs of some of the night
sky's most interesting features.

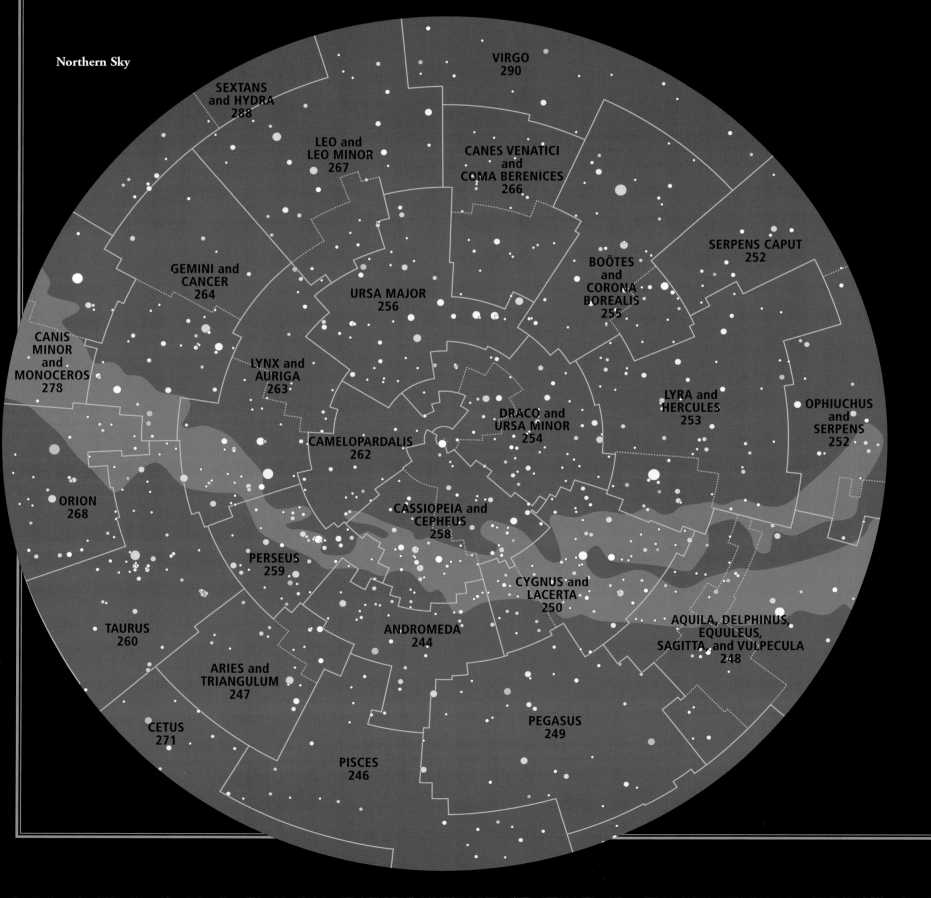

Northern Sky

VIRGO 290

SEXTANS and HYDRA 288

LEO and LEO MINOR 267

CANES VENATICI and COMA BERENICES 266

SERPENS CAPUT 252

BOÖTES and CORONA BOREALIS 255

GEMINI and CANCER 264

URSA MAJOR 256

CANIS MINOR and MONOCEROS 278

LYNX and AURIGA 263

LYRA and HERCULES 253

OPHIUCHUS and SERPENS 252

DRACO and URSA MINOR 254

CAMELOPARDALIS 262

ORION 268

CASSIOPEIA and CEPHEUS 258

PERSEUS 259

CYGNUS and LACERTA 250

TAURUS 260

ANDROMEDA 244

AQUILA, DELPHINUS, EQUULEUS, SAGITTA, and VULPECULA 248

ARIES and TRIANGULUM 247

CETUS 271

PEGASUS 249

PISCES 246

SPECTRA KEY

O, B
A
F
G
K
M, N, R, S

MAGNITUDE SCALE

0.0 and brighter
0.1 to 0.5
0.6 to 1.0
1.1 to 1.5
1.6 to 2.0
2.1 to 2.5
2.6 to 3.0
3.1 to 3.5
3.6 to 4.0
4.1 to 4.5
4.6 to 5.0

Southern Sky

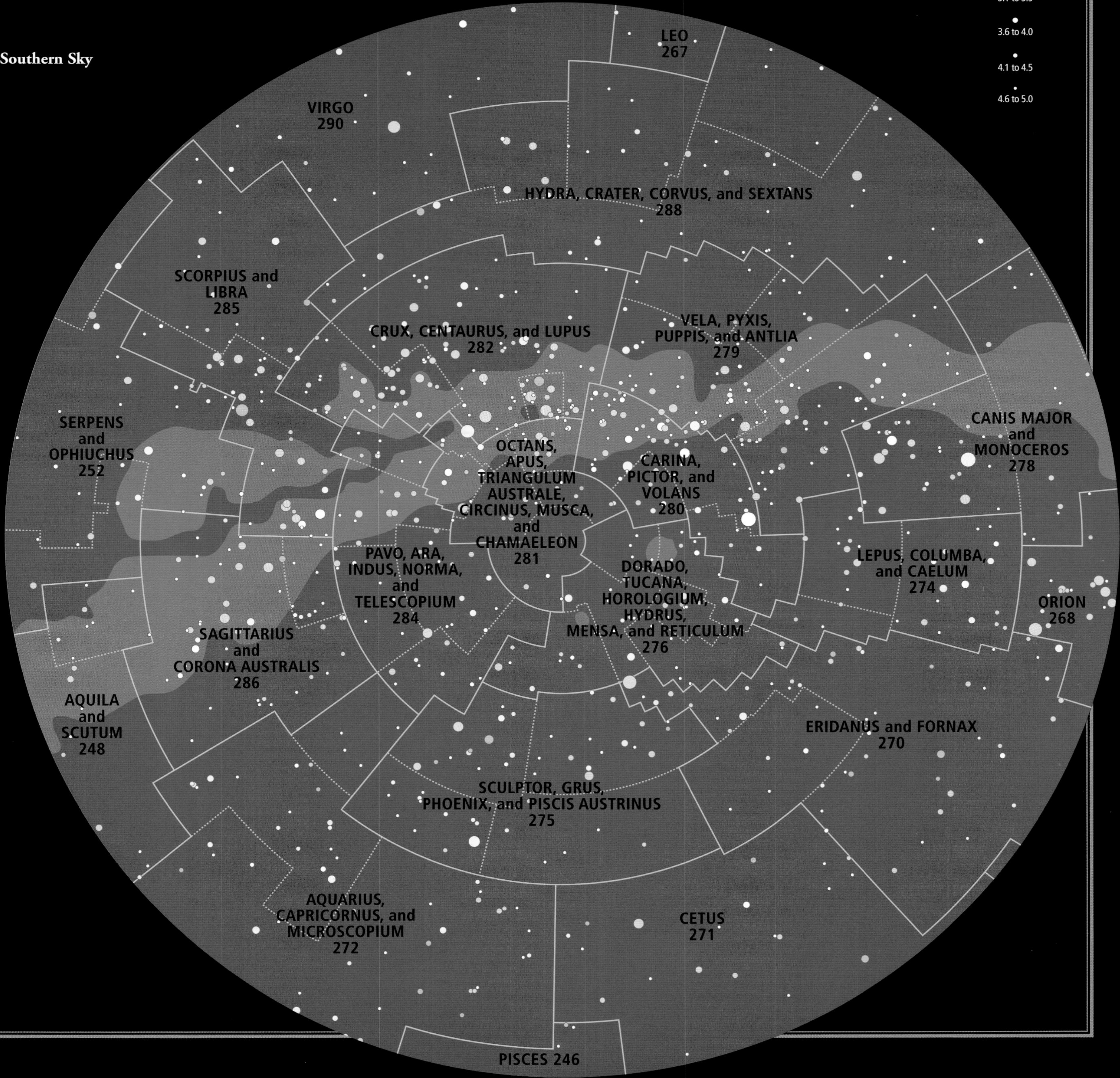

LEO 267

VIRGO 290

HYDRA, CRATER, CORVUS, and SEXTANS 288

SCORPIUS and LIBRA 285

CRUX, CENTAURUS, and LUPUS 282

VELA, PYXIS, PUPPIS, and ANTLIA 279

SERPENS and OPHIUCHUS 252

OCTANS, APUS, TRIANGULUM AUSTRALE, CIRCINUS, MUSCA, and CHAMAELEON 281

CARINA, PICTOR, and VOLANS 280

CANIS MAJOR and MONOCEROS 278

PAVO, ARA, INDUS, NORMA, and TELESCOPIUM 284

DORADO, TUCANA, HOROLOGIUM, HYDRUS, MENSA, and RETICULUM 276

LEPUS, COLUMBA, and CAELUM 274

ORION 268

SAGITTARIUS and CORONA AUSTRALIS 286

AQUILA and SCUTUM 248

ERIDANUS and FORNAX 270

SCULPTOR, GRUS, PHOENIX, and PISCIS AUSTRINUS 275

AQUARIUS, CAPRICORNUS, and MICROSCOPIUM 272

CETUS 271

PISCES 246

ANDROMEDA

Andromeda (the Princess, pictured right) is not a particularly conspicuous constellation, but it is easy to find, immediately south of the W of Cassiopeia and to the northeast of the Great Square of Pegasus. The Princess is essentially a very long, narrow V-shape, with the southernmost leg of the V containing the four brightest stars. Of course, this constellation is most famous for the galaxy of the same name. The Andromeda Galaxy (M31) is a spiral galaxy slightly larger than our own Milky Way and, lying 2.9 million light-years away, has the distinction of being the most distant object visible to the naked eye (although you will need a dark sky to spot it). Some argue that the more distant and fainter M33 in Triangulum is discernible also, but only to the very keenest eye. Both M31 and M33 are members of the Local Group cluster of galaxies. Other objects of interest in this constellation include the planetary nebula NGC 7662 and the open cluster NGC 752.

MAGNITUDE
SCALE

● −0.5 and brighter

● 0.0 to −0.4

● 0.1 to 0.5

● 0.6 to 1.0

● 1.1 to 1.5

● 1.6 to 2.0

● 2.1 to 2.5

● 2.6 to 3.0

● 3.1 to 3.5

● 3.6 to 4.0

● 4.1 to 4.5

● 4.6 to 5.0

● 5.1 to 5.5

● 5.6 to 6.0

● 6.1 to 6.5

BRIGHTEST STARS

NAME	MAGNITUDE	DISTANCE (LY)	SPECTRUM
Alpheratz (α AND)	2.06	97	B8
Mirach (β AND)	2.06	199	M0
Almaak (γ AND)	2.26	355	K3+A0
δ AND	3.27	101	K3
51 AND	3.59	174	K3

OTHER FEATURES

NAME	TYPE	DISTANCE (LY)	ALSO KNOWN AS
NGC 752	Open cluster	1,300	Melotte 12
NGC 7662	Planetary nebula	5,600	Blue Snowball Nebula
M32	Satellite, elliptical galaxy	2.9 million	NGC 221
M110	Satellite, elliptical galaxy	2.9 million	NGC 205
Andromeda Galaxy	Spiral galaxy	2.9 million	M31, NGC 224

Andromeda Galaxy (right)
This great spiral galaxy, object number 31 in Charles Messier's catalog of celestial treasures and located some 2.9 million light-years away, is the closest large stellar island to our own Milky Way Galaxy. Also known as NGC 224, it is a spiral of class Sb, having moderately open arms. However, because we see it from an oblique vantage point, the arms are not as well defined as in some other galaxies. You can easily see M31 in binoculars, but even the naked eye will discern a large fuzzy patch if the sky is sufficiently dark.

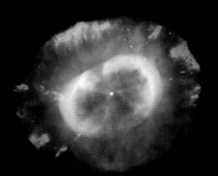

The Blue Snowball Nebula (left)
Observed through a small telescope, the Blue Snowball Nebula, NGC 7662, some 5,600 light-years distant, appears as a softly glowing blue disk. Closer up, as seen by the Hubble Space Telescope, NGC 7662 resembles an eye rather than a snowball. The "iris" is a bubble of recently expelled, fast-moving material pushing the older gas ahead of it to form a bright rim. The origins of the red outer streaks are unknown.

Black holes in the Andromeda Galaxy (M31) (below)
The heart of M31 is thought to be a black hole with the mass of 30 million Suns. Its location corresponds with the yellow dot—indicating an extremely hot X-ray source—just above the blue dot in this Chandra X-ray Observatory image. Why there should be a relatively cool X-ray source—the blue dot—just 10 light-years south of the black hole is a mystery. The other yellow dots are probably X-ray binary systems where a neutron star or black hole is in orbit around a normal star.

The Andromeda Galaxy companion (M32) (above)
This Hubble image of the heart of M32, taken in ultraviolet light, shows a swarm of about 8,000 blue stars surrounding the galactic core. These are extremely hot stars at a late stage in their lives. Unlike the Sun, which burns hydrogen into helium, these old stars exhausted their central hydrogen, and now burn helium into heavier elements. The strong concentration of stars toward the nucleus supports the notion that there is a supermassive black hole at the heart of M32.

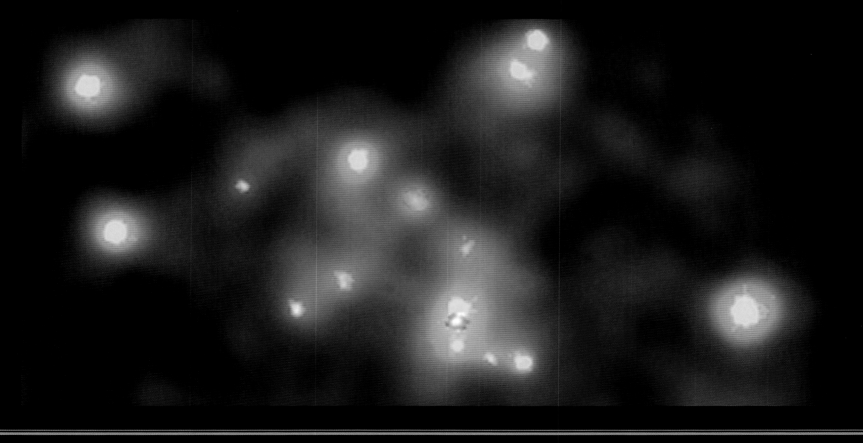

SPECTRA
KEY

O, B

A

F

G

K

M, N, R, S

STARS
Double star

Variable star

DEEP-SKY
OBJECTS

Open
star cluster

Globular
star cluster

Bright
nebula

Planetary
nebula

Galaxy

Large faint
galaxy

PISCES

Pisces (the Fish) is not a very eye-catching constellation, devoid of stars brighter than magnitude 3.5. Nevertheless it occupies a substantial portion of the sky and often plays host to the planets, as it is on the ecliptic and thus a zodiacal constellation. The ancients who named this V-shaped assemblage pictured it as two fish joined at the tails. The western fish, south of Pegasus, is the more conspicuous, its "head" composed of a ring of seven stars known as the Circlet. The eastern fish, however, adjacent to Andromeda, is little more than a haphazard string of faint stars. Zeta (ζ) Piscium, just a degree or so away from the ecliptic, is an attractive double star with a separation of about 23 arc seconds. There are a handful of galaxies here, with the prettiest being M74 (right). Also known as NGC 628, M74 is a face-on spiral galaxy, class Sc, about 30 million light-years away. However, you will need at least an 8-inch (200-mm) telescope to see it.

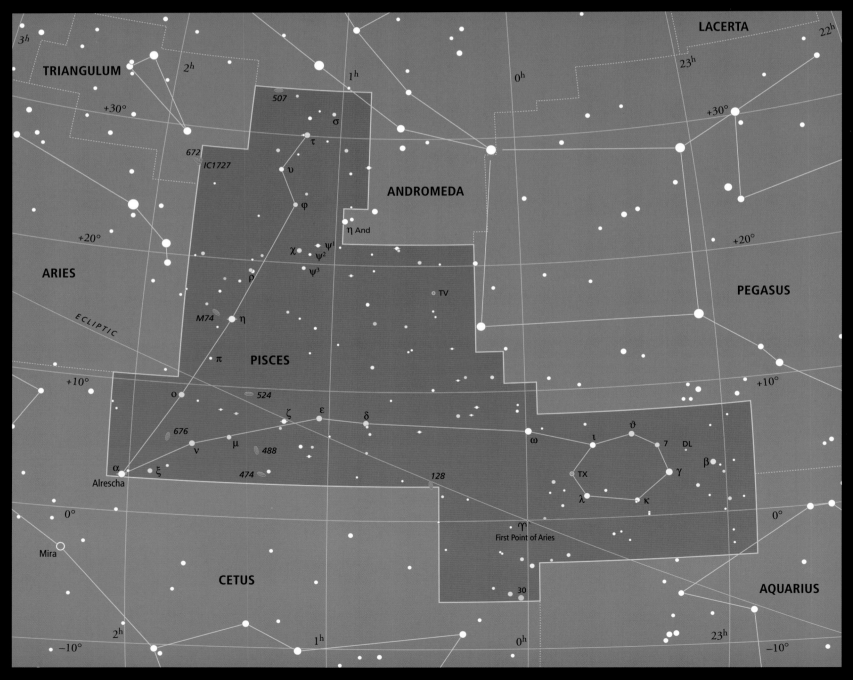

ARIES Triangulum

Aries (the Ram) is a small constellation of just a handful of stars—our ancestors who named it clearly had a great deal of imagination to picture it as a male sheep. The brightest stars, Hamal and Sheratan, denoting the ram's horns, are of magnitude 2.0 and 2.6 respectively. Aries is playground to a whole host of various galaxies; but they are very faint, typically between magnitudes 11 and 15. Close to Aries is another constellation whose three principal stars, forming a triangle, give the group its unsurprising name, Triangulum. Triangulum is small, but it has an ace up its sleeve in the form of the beautiful M33 (right), a spiral galaxy about 2.7 million light-years distant. Like the Andromeda Galaxy (about which M33 might be in orbit) and our own Milky Way, M33 belongs to the loose cluster of galaxies called the Local Group. M33 also has many regions of active star formation.

MAGNITUDE SCALE

- −0.5 and brighter
- 0.0 to −0.4
- 0.1 to 0.5
- 0.6 to 1.0
- 1.1 to 1.5
- 1.6 to 2.0
- 2.1 to 2.5
- 2.6 to 3.0
- 3.1 to 3.5
- 3.6 to 4.0
- 4.1 to 4.5
- 4.6 to 5.0
- 5.1 to 5.5
- 5.6 to 6.0
- 6.1 to 6.5

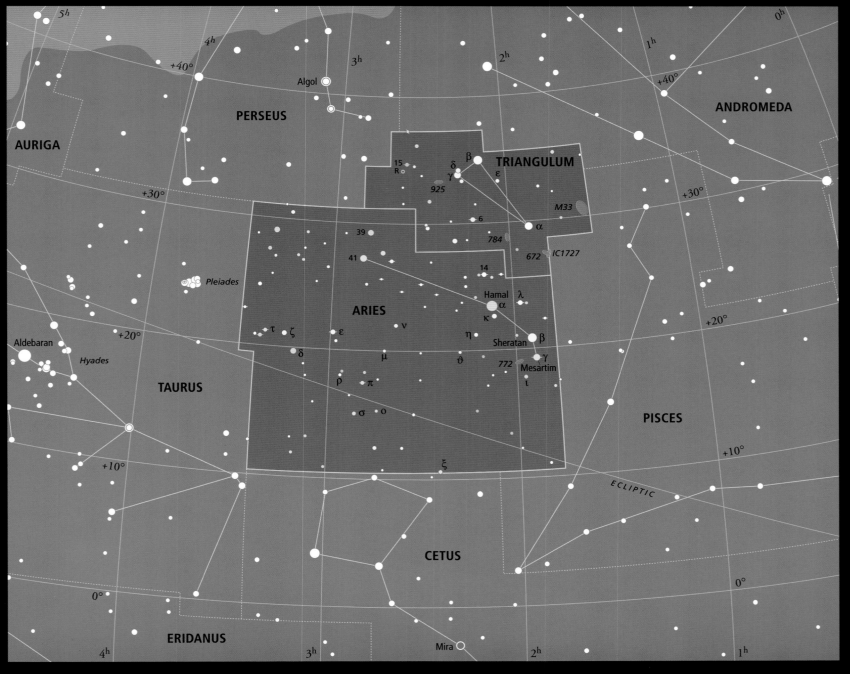

AQUILA

Delphinus, Equuleus, Sagitta, Scutum, Vulpecula

Aquila (the Eagle) is host to the sky's twelfth brightest star, Altair, although most of its main stars are fainter than third magnitude. Altair is actually a multiple star system, and one of our closest stellar neighbors at a distance of 17 light-years. This constellation is also home to several interesting objects including a supergiant star, Cepheid variable Eta (η) Aquilae, the open star cluster NGC 6709, and the striking (but small and faint) planetary nebula NGC 6751. Surrounding Aquila are a host of smaller constellations, notably Scutum (the Shield), home to M11, the spectacular open cluster; Delphinus (the Dolphin); Equuleus (the Little Horse); Sagitta (the Arrow); and Vulpecula (the Fox), which boasts the Dumbbell Nebula (right, as imaged by a 12.5-inch (317-mm) telescope), one of the finest planetary nebulas in the sky. Equuleus is the sky's second smallest constellation, after Crux.

SPECTRA KEY

- O, B
- A
- F
- G
- K
- M, N, R, S

STARS

- Double star
- Variable star

DEEP-SKY OBJECTS

- Open star cluster
- Globular star cluster
- Bright nebula
- Planetary nebula
- Galaxy
- Large faint galaxy

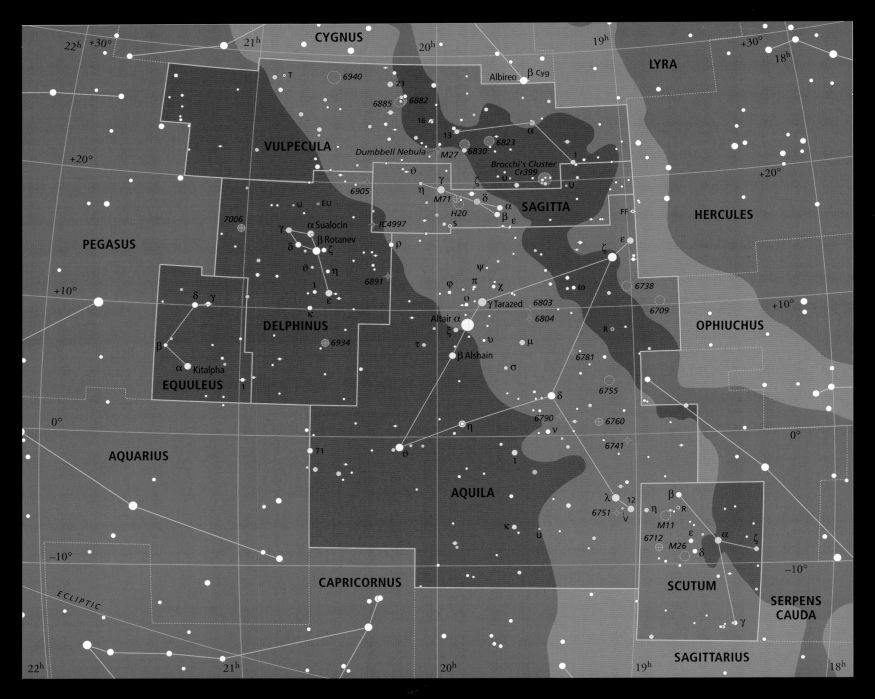

PEGASUS

Pegasus (the Winged Horse) is a large northern constellation adjacent to Pisces and Andromeda. Although its brightest stars are all fainter than magnitude 2.4, Pegasus is still recognizable for the famous Great Square of Pegasus—four stars describing a large quadrangle that spans about 15 degrees of sky. However, one of the four stars in the Great Square of Pegasus, Alpheratz, is not actually in that constellation, but belongs to neighboring Andromeda. Pegasus has many galaxies, including the face-on spiral NGC 7742 (as captured by the Hubble Space Telescope, right), but they are all faint. The brightest galaxy, but still at ninth magnitude, is NGC 7331. Happily, though, Pegasus is host to one of the nicest globular star clusters in northern skies. This is M15, the Pegasus Cluster. It is of magnitude 6.4 and spans about 12 arc minutes, or just over a third the diameter of the full Moon.

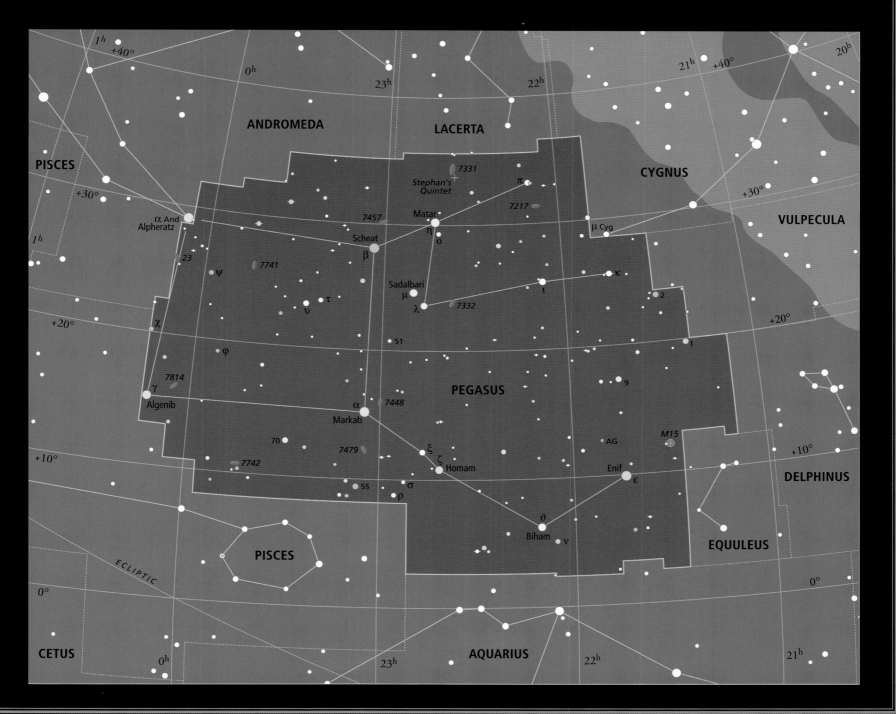

MAGNITUDE SCALE

−0.5 and brighter
0.0 to −0.4
0.1 to 0.5
0.6 to 1.0
1.1 to 1.5
1.6 to 2.0
2.1 to 2.5
2.6 to 3.0
3.1 to 3.5
3.6 to 4.0
4.1 to 4.5
4.6 to 5.0
5.1 to 5.5
5.6 to 6.0
6.1 to 6.5

CYGNUS *Lacerta*

Cygnus (the Swan) is an unmistakable northern constellation, a giant bird, wings outstretched, fleeing from neighboring Lacerta (the Lizard). The bright star Deneb marks the Swan's tail, Albireo or Beta (β) Cygni represents the head, while the wing tips are denoted by Kappa (κ) and Mu (μ) Cygni. Owing to its place against the backdrop of the Milky Way, Cygnus is a very rich constellation. Just scanning it with binoculars will resolve the Milky Way into clouds of countless stars. You will also note that the Milky Way here appears split into two parts. This is because of the presence of large clouds of dust that obscure the background stars—the so-called Great Rift. Some rewarding sites to explore in Cygnus are the North America Nebula (NGC 7000), the Pelican Nebula (IC 5067), and the Veil Nebula (NGC 6992, 6995, 6979, and 6960), which are just a few among numerous other nebulas and open clusters.

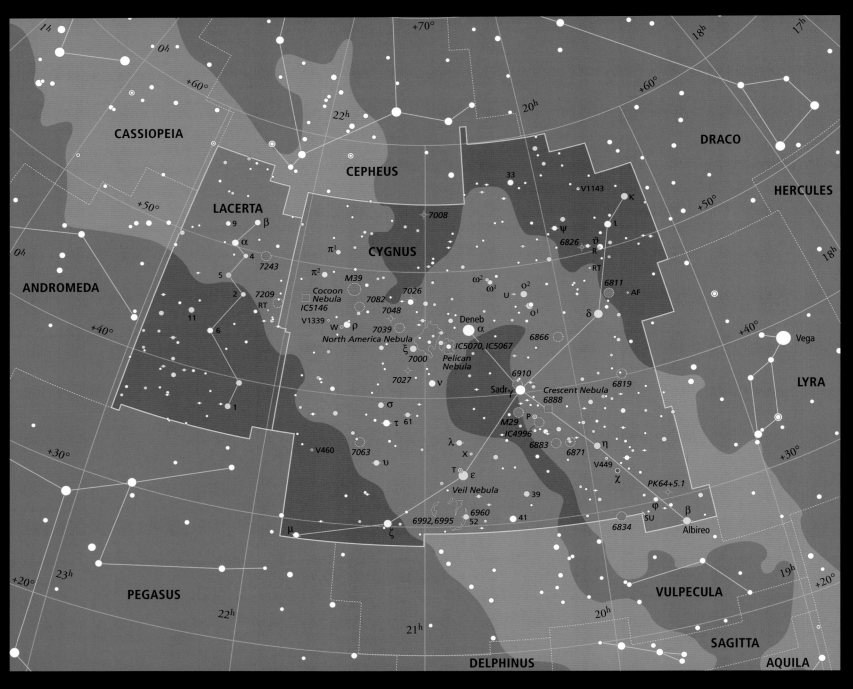

SPECTRA KEY
- O, B
- A
- F
- G
- K
- M, N, R, S

STARS
- Double star
- Variable star

DEEP-SKY OBJECTS
- Open star cluster
- Globular star cluster
- Bright nebula
- Planetary nebula
- Galaxy
- Large faint galaxy

Crescent Nebula (above)

The Crescent Nebula (NGC 6888) in Cygnus is a gaseous bubble blown off by a giant star some 250,000 years ago. The progenitor is WR 136, a member of a very powerful class of super-hot objects known as Wolf-Rayet stars. These stellar giants, more than ten times as massive as the Sun, literally rip themselves apart by their own energy production, blowing their outer layers into space as they evolve. This Hubble Space Telescope image shows how the central star has shredded the nebula into an intricate web of filaments.

Veil Nebula (left)

Some 15,000 years ago, a star 2,600 light-years away in the constellation of Cygnus suddenly blew itself apart. Today, the scattered remains of this stellar detonation have spread out to form a spherical shell of ionized gas, currently measuring about 130 light-years across and still expanding. This photo shows NGC 6960, just a portion of this well-known supernova remnant, the Veil Nebula. The bright star at the center is 52 Cygni.

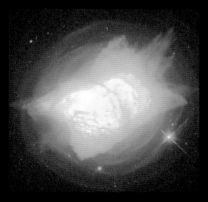

The galactic plane (below)

The plane of the Milky Way, like all spiral galaxies, is thick not only with stars, but also with vast quantities of dust. This photo shows the Milky Way in Cygnus, not as it appears in visible light, but as imaged in the infrared spectrum. The radiant filaments are wisps of gas and dust, while the denser knots are star-forming regions. This image covers about six by four degrees of sky.

Future of the Sun (above)

NGC 7027 is a planetary nebula, the cast-off outer shell of an aging low mass star. In five to eight billion years our Sun will likely end its life in this fashion, perhaps resembling the nebula in this false-color image. NGC 7027 is about 3,000 light-years away in Cygnus.

BRIGHTEST STARS

NAME	MAGNITUDE	DISTANCE (LY)	SPECTRUM
Deneb (α CYG)	1.25	3,230	A2
Sadr (γ CYG)	2.20	1,520	F8
ε CYG	2.46	165	K0
δ CYG	2.87	171	B9
Albireo (β CYG)	3.08	386	K3

OTHER FEATURES

NAME	TYPE	DISTANCE (LY)	ALSO KNOWN AS
North America Nebula	Bright nebula	1,600	NGC 7000
Pelican Nebula	Bright nebula	1,600	IC 5067, IC 5070
Veil Nebula	Bright nebula	2,600	NGC 6992, 6995, 6960, 6979
Crescent Nebula	Bright nebula	4,700	NGC 6888

SERPENS Ophiuchus

Serpens (the Serpent) is a faint, long, northern constellation. Curiously, it is split into two, the only constellation where this is the case. Serpens Cauda is the tail of the Serpent, while the head is Serpens Caput. Together they form a single constellation, even though they are separated by another constellation, Ophiuchus (the Serpent Carrier). Serpens Cauda is home to M16, a stunning combination of open star cluster and emission nebulosity also known as the Eagle Nebula. Ophiuchus has numerous globular clusters, a few faint planetary nebulas (such as NGC 6369, right), and is home to the second nearest star to the Sun. Called Barnard's Star, it is a red dwarf of magnitude 9.5, some 6 light-years away.

LYRA Hercules

Lyra represents a musical instrument called a lyre, a kind of ancient harp. This northern constellation is small, but contains the spectacularly bright star Vega, the prototype magnitude-zero star. Vega is only about 25 light-years away—on our doorstep as far as stellar distances go—and about 50 times as luminous as the Sun, shining with a steely blue hue. Lyra is famous also for the Ring Nebula (M57), a beautiful celestial "smoke ring" which is the jettisoned atmosphere of an old star. The Hubble Space Telescope recently captured a breathtaking image of this planetary nebula (right). Adjacent to Lyra is Hercules (the famous hero of Greek mythology), a fairly large constellation consisting of a main quadrangle of stars at its center representing the hero's torso from which his arms and legs radiate. This constellation is famed for its dramatic globular cluster, M13, visible to the naked eye as a fuzzy patch if the sky is dark.

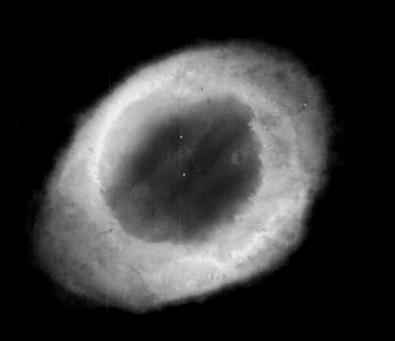

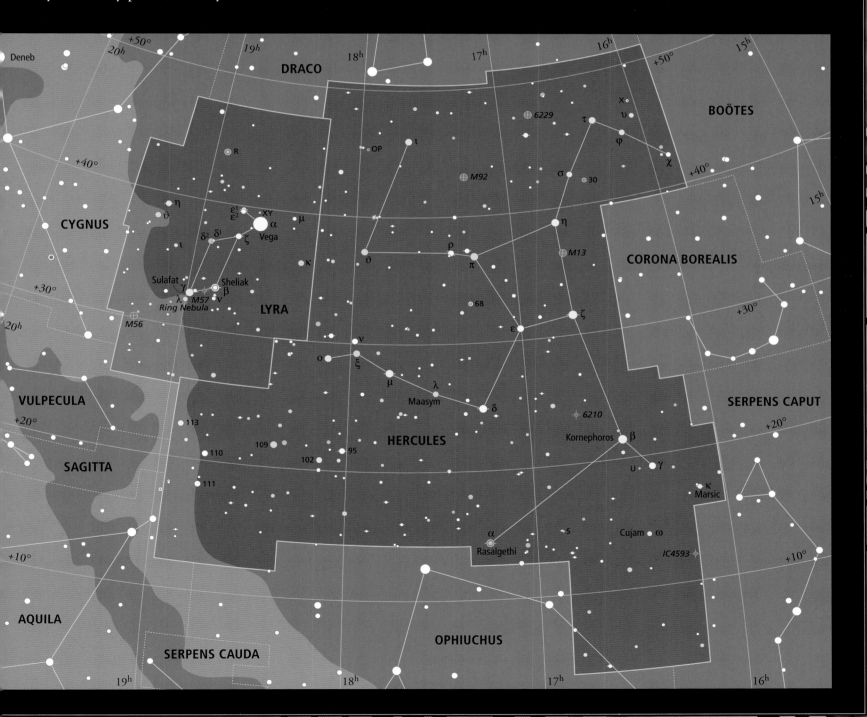

SPECTRA
KEY

O, B

A

F

G

K

M, N, R, S

STARS

Double star

Variable star

DEEP-SKY
OBJECTS

Open
star cluster

Globular
star cluster

Bright
nebula

Planetary
nebula

Galaxy

Large faint
galaxy

DRACO Ursa Minor

Draco (the Dragon) is a very long but faint constellation of the northern hemisphere, winding its way around the north celestial pole and neighboring constellation, Ursa Minor (the Little Bear). It hosts the annual meteor showers the Quadrantids and the Draconids, and contains the spectacular planetary nebula called the Cat's Eye Nebula (NGC 6543, captured on the right using the Hubble Space Telescope). Ursa Minor, itself also faint, is famous nonetheless, for it contains the pole star, Polaris, presently the brightest star close to the north celestial pole and an aid to terrestrial navigation. At a displacement of just 1.5 Moon diameters it is not right on the pole, but it is close enough for most purposes. Because Earth's axis precesses as Earth spins, the pole star changes with time. In ancient Egyptian times, Thuban, Alpha (α) Draconis, was almost on the pole, and in 11,500 years, the brilliant star Vega will be less than six degrees from the pole.

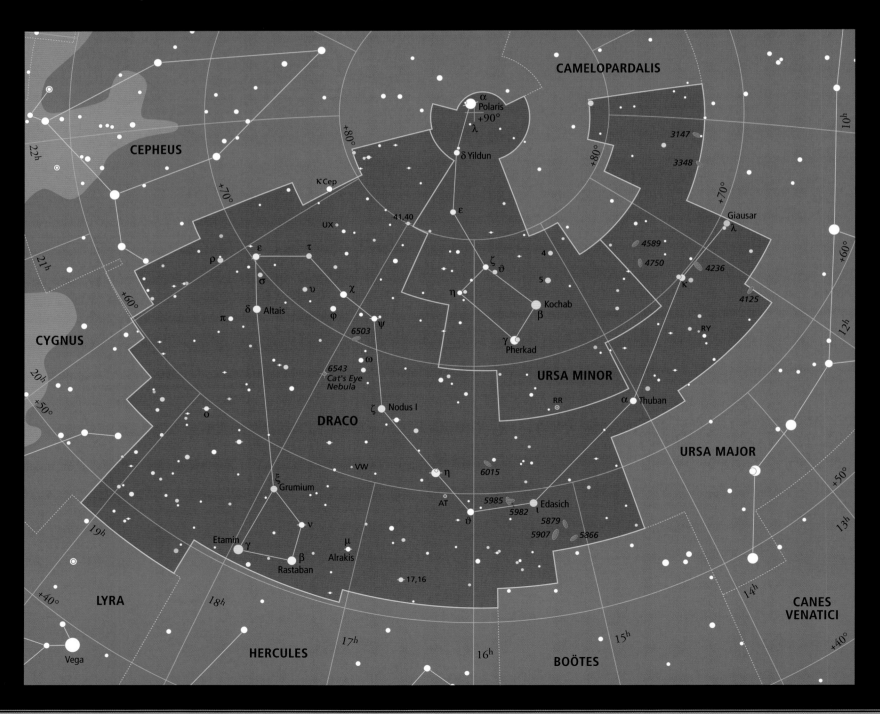

BOÖTES · Corona Borealis

Boötes (the Herdsman) is a largely unremarkable northern constellation, containing only two stars brighter than second magnitude. One of these, however, is the brilliant Arcturus which, with a magnitude of –0.05, is the brightest star north of the celestial equator and the fourth brightest in the entire sky. Arcturus, which is actually a multiple system, is an orange giant 34 times larger than the Sun and just 37 light-years away. Boötes contains few non-stellar objects of interest. There are some faint galaxies and a globular cluster (NGC 5466), and also a distant galaxy cluster called 3C 295, which is enveloped in a vast cloud of hot gas (right, photographed by the Chandra X-ray Observatory), but at magnitude 19 the latter is very faint. Between Boötes and Hercules is a small, faint, but easily identified constellation called Corona Borealis (the Northern Crown). It comprises a semicircle of seven principal stars.

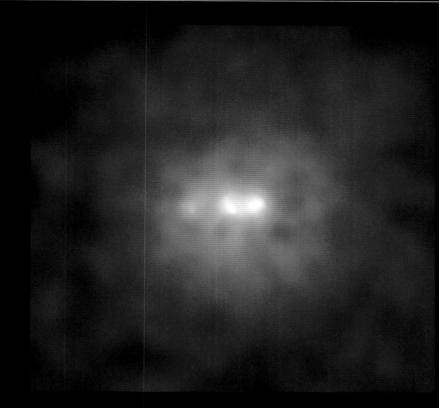

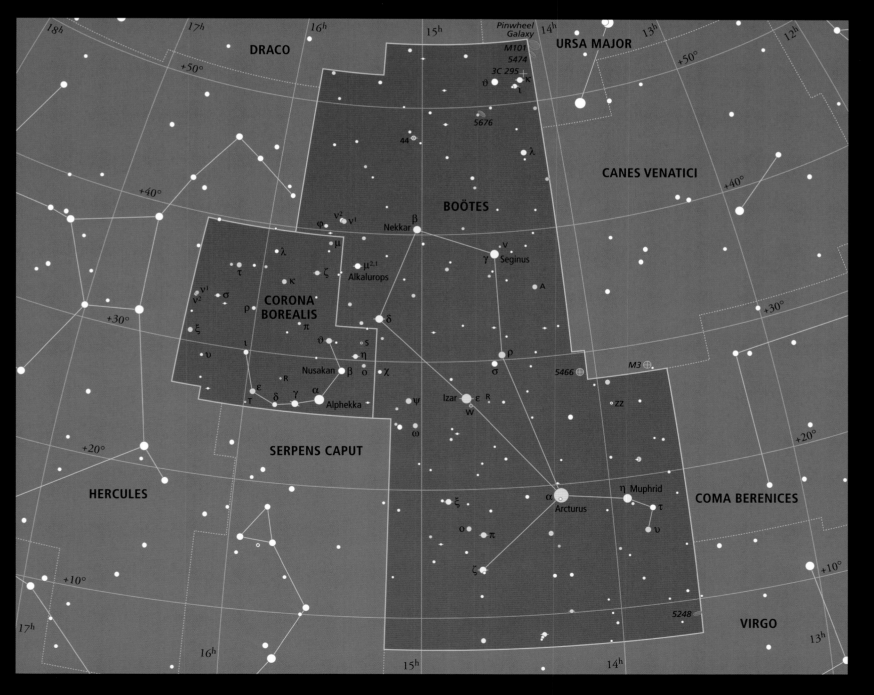

URSA MAJOR

The third largest constellation, Ursa Major (the Great Bear) needs little introduction to skywatchers in the northern hemisphere. It is most famous for the asterism (a recognizable pattern of stars, not a constellation in itself) formed by its seven brightest stars. In England this pattern is known as the Plough, while Americans refer to it as the Big Dipper. The second star in the handle of the Big Dipper, called Mizar, is actually a double. Paired with Alcor just 11 arc minutes away, the two are easily resolved with a keen naked eye. The Plough or Big Dipper has long been a useful guide to terrestrial navigation, because a line drawn from Merak (Beta (β) Ursae Majoris) past Dubhe (Alpha (α) Ursae Majoris) points almost directly to the pole star, Polaris. And if you follow the curve of the handle of the Big Dipper, it brings you to the brilliant orange Arcturus in Boötes. Ursa Major contains a wealth of NGC as well as Messier galaxies, such as the spiral galaxy M81.

SPECTRA KEY

- O, B
- A
- F
- G
- K
- M, N, R, S

STARS
- Double star
- Variable star

DEEP-SKY OBJECTS
- Open star cluster
- Globular star cluster
- Bright nebula
- Planetary nebula
- Galaxy
- Large faint galaxy

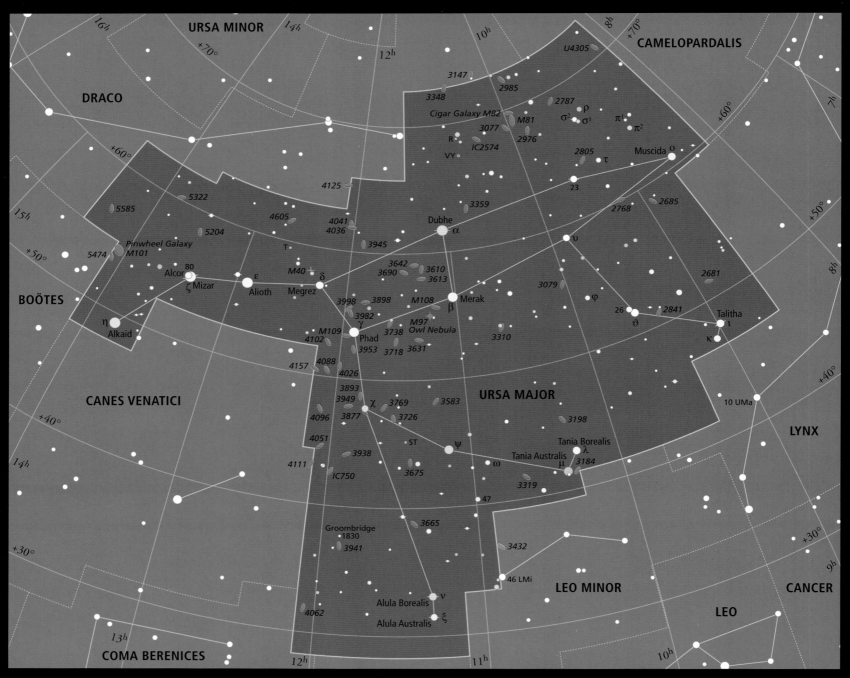

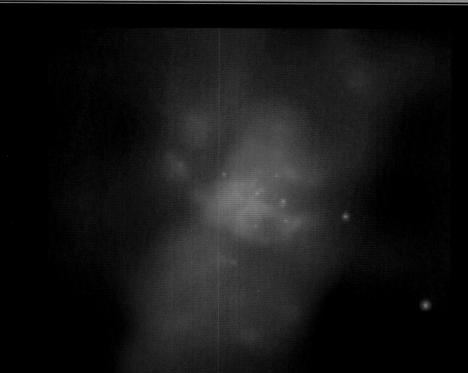

BRIGHTEST STARS			
NAME	MAGNITUDE	DISTANCE (LY)	SPECTRUM
Alioth (ε UMA)	1.77	81	A0
Dubhe (α UMA)	1.79	124	K0
Alkaid (η UMA)	1.86	101	B3
Mizar (ζ UMA)	2.27	78	A1
Merak (β UMA)	2.37	79	A1
OTHER FEATURES			
NAME	TYPE	DISTANCE (LY)	ALSO KNOWN AS
Owl Nebula	Planetary nebula	1,300	NGC 3587, M97
M81	Spiral galaxy	11 million	NGC 3031
Cigar Galaxy	Peculiar galaxy	12 million	NGC 3034, M82
Pinwheel Galaxy	Spiral galaxy	23 million	NGC 5457, M101
NGC 3079	Spiral galaxy	50 million	Bode's Galaxy

Cigar Galaxy (left)
M82 is a spiral galaxy seen edge-on, thus taking on a spindle-like appearance that has earned it the nickname of the Cigar Galaxy. This false-color image was taken by the orbiting Chandra X-ray Observatory. Some of the bright spots are X-ray binary stars—black holes or neutron stars orbiting (and simultaneously devouring) much larger companions. Other glowing patches are regions where it is thought that gas has been compressed by supernova shockwaves and made to produce X-rays.

NGC 3079 (right)
This is a close-up view of the spiral galaxy NGC 3079, 50 million light-years away. The galaxy itself is seen edge-on, running left to right at the bottom. The red formation above it is a bubble of hot gas released by a burst of star formation. Eventually it will rain back down on the disk and trigger more star birth.

Owl Nebula (below)
M97, as the Owl Nebula is also known, is a planetary nebula—the cast-off atmosphere of an aging Sun-like star. Such nebulas are often unusual and complex structures. The Owl Nebula is no exception and astronomers studying it have developed several competing theories to account for its present shape.

In our galactic neighborhood
M81 is a beautiful spiral galaxy located about 11 million light-years from Earth—on our doorstep as far as galaxies go. This false-color image taken by NASA's Spitzer Space Telescope shows M81 in infrared. The color of the galaxy's core (blue) indicates that it is replete with older stars. The spiral arms, meanwhile, are glowing strongly at a wavelength of eight microns (red). This indicates emissions, not from stars, but from lanes of gas and dust energized by the radiation of embedded hot stars.

Colliding galaxies
Here we see spirals M81 and M82 in a single frame and at optical wavelengths. Astronomers believe that these two galaxies are interacting gravitationally, periodically passing close to each other and then moving apart again. With each close pass, the galaxies exert forces on each other that cause interstellar gases to compress and form new stars. In several billion years, these galaxies will have completely merged into a single, larger entity.

CASSIOPEIA Cepheus

Cassiopeia (the Queen) is a distinctive constellation of the northern hemisphere, its five brightest stars forming an unmistakable—if slightly distorted—celestial W superimposed on the Milky Way. A scan of Cassiopeia with binoculars reveals rich star clouds and several open clusters, including NGC 663, M103, and M52, otherwise known as the Scorpion. There are also a few nebulas, including the curiously named Pacman Nebula (NGC 281) and NGC 7635, the Bubble Nebula (pictured right). Adjacent to Cassiopeia on the open side of the W is Cepheus (the King), looking a little like a box with a triangle on top. Cepheus also encroaches onto the Milky Way's star clouds, and is worth a scan with binoculars. Delta (δ) Cephei is the prototype for the so-called Cepheid variable stars which vary their brightness as they pulsate. Delta Cephei shows a 1-magnitude change in intensity over its 5.4-day cycle.

PERSEUS

Perseus (a hero of Greek mythology) is a constellation of the fall skies in the northern hemisphere, between Taurus and Cassiopeia. It is famous for two objects. First, it contains an eclipsing binary known as Algol or Beta (β) Persei. The two primary stars that comprise Algol orbit each other every 2.87 days, each eclipsing the other (as seen from Earth) as they do so. There are several binaries like these, all known as Algol systems after this prototype. The second object of interest is the striking Double Cluster. This is a pair of open clusters (NGC 869 and 884) superimposed on the star clouds of the Milky Way, and is a rewarding sight in binoculars or a low-power telescope. Perseus contains several other interesting objects, including the galaxy NGC 1275. The Hubble Space Telescope captured this galaxy, which in the image at right is the bright, face-on spiral just left of center. The dark lanes of dust belong to another galaxy in the foreground.

MAGNITUDE SCALE

- −0.5 and brighter
- 0.0 to −0.4
- 0.1 to 0.5
- 0.6 to 1.0
- 1.1 to 1.5
- 1.6 to 2.0
- 2.1 to 2.5
- 2.6 to 3.0
- 3.1 to 3.5
- 3.6 to 4.0
- 4.1 to 4.5
- 4.6 to 5.0
- 5.1 to 5.5
- 5.6 to 6.0
- 6.1 to 6.5

SPECTRA
KEY

O, B

A

F

G

K

M, N, R, S

STARS

Double star

Variable star

DEEP-SKY
OBJECTS

Open
star cluster

Globular
star cluster

Bright
nebula

Planetary
nebula

Galaxy

Large faint
galaxy

TAURUS

Taurus (the Bull) is an arresting, ancient zodiacal constellation of the northern hemisphere, sitting on the ecliptic between Gemini and Aries. It is a delight for the naked eye and even better seen through binoculars. Its brightest star is the brilliant Aldebaran, an orange giant about 150 times as luminous as the Sun. Aldebaran, Arabic for "the Follower," is situated against the backdrop of the V-shaped open cluster called the Hyades. This is the closest obvious open cluster to the Sun, but still twice as distant as Aldebaran. Another spectacular cluster is the Pleiades or Seven Sisters (M45), featuring a brilliant scattering of gems whose brightest members create a glowing patch about twice the Moon's apparent diameter. Taurus is also home to the Crab Nebula (M1), the shattered remains of a star that blew itself apart in a supernova explosion. This event was witnessed by Chinese astronomers in 1054 who recorded that it was bright enough to be seen by day.

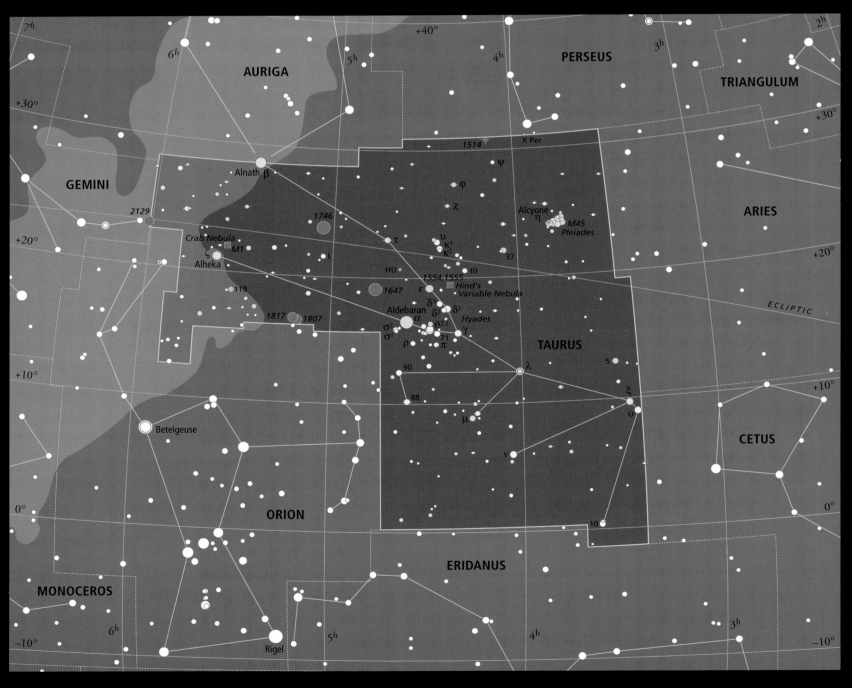

MAGNITUDE
SCALE

-0.5 and
brighter

0.0 to -0.4

0.1 to 0.5

0.6 to 1.0

1.1 to 1.5

1.6 to 2.0

2.1 to 2.5

2.6 to 3.0

3.1 to 3.5

3.6 to 4.0

4.1 to 4.5

4.6 to 5.0

5.1 to 5.5

5.6 to 6.0

6.1 to 6.5

Crab Pulsar (left)
During the explosive event of 1054 that produced the Crab Nebula, the progenitor star collapsed in on itself and metamorphosed into a super-dense, rapidly spinning, stellar object known as a pulsar. This Hubble optical (red) and Chandra X-ray (blue) composite image of the Crab Nebula reveals the rings and jets that are indicative of a pulsar.

Nebulosity in the Pleiades (below)
This unusual Hubble photo shows how one of the Pleiades stars, Merope (out of the frame, above right), is illuminating a nearby cloud of dust to paint spectacular glowing tendrils in space. This portion of the Pleiades is called Barnard's Merope Nebula (IC349).

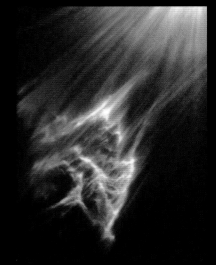

Crab Nebula (right)
This European Southern Observatory photo shows the famous Crab Nebula (M1). This was a star that in 1054 underwent a supernova explosion, scattering debris into space. Now, nearly a thousand years later, the supernova remnant has expanded and evolved to produce this bright nebula's intricate filamentary structure seen here.

The stunning Pleiades (below)
The Pleiades (M45) in Taurus is probably the most famous open cluster in the whole sky. Although it is sometimes called the Seven Sisters, this cluster is actually composed of several hundred young blue stars that formed together out of an interstellar cloud of dust and gas. Long-exposure photographs reveal the Pleiades bathed in a striking blue reflection nebula.

BRIGHTEST STARS			
NAME	MAGNITUDE	DISTANCE (LY)	SPECTRUM
Aldebaran (α TAU)	0.85	65	K5
Alnath (β TAU)	1.65	131	B7
Alcyone (η TAU)	2.87	368	B7
Alheka (ζ TAU)	3.00	417	B4
λ TAU	3.47	370	B3

OTHER FEATURES			
NAME	TYPE	DISTANCE (LY)	ALSO KNOWN AS
Hyades	Open cluster	150	Melotte 25
Pleiades	Open cluster	375	M45
Crab Nebula	Supernova remnant	6,300	M1
Crab Pulsar	Neutron star	6,300	NP0532

CAMELOPARDALIS

This polar constellation of the north, whose name means "the Giraffe," is largely unremarkable. Even its brightest star, Beta (β) Camelopardalis, is only magnitude 4. But while it contains no bright stars, Camelopardalis is nevertheless good for telescope owners, as it is replete with galaxies. The brightest of these is NGC 2403 at a magnitude of 8.4, while there are several others up to twelfth magnitude. One of these is a dwarf irregular galaxy, NGC 1569, shown on the right as portrayed by the Hubble Space Telescope. The bright stars left of center in the image have sculpted holes in the local interstellar medium by the power of their outflowing winds and blasts from supernova explosions. The holes show up as darker areas in the glowing red gas surrounding the stars. Camelopardalis also plays host to an open cluster NGC 1502, with a neighboring planetary nebula, NGC 1501.

AURIGA · Lynx

Auriga (the Charioteer) is a bright constellation of northern skies superimposed on the star fields of the Milky Way, adjacent to Taurus. Its brightest star, and sixth brightest in the whole sky, is the brilliant yellow Capella, which is actually a binary system comprising two stars that are each very similar to our own Sun. Owing to its Milky Way backdrop, Auriga is a treasure trove for binocular owners or those with small to moderately powered telescopes. There are several fine open clusters here, including M36, M37, M38, and a scattering of NGC and IC clusters too. The star AE Aurigae (right) is curious, often called the Flaming Star as it appears to be surrounded by "smoke" which is actually composed of hydrogen gas and carbon grains. Auriga is bordered by, among others, the constellation Lynx. Lynx has only one third-magnitude star. But while not particularly striking, it does contain a few galaxies brighter than thirteenth magnitude.

MAGNITUDE SCALE

- −0.5 and brighter
- 0.0 to −0.4
- 0.1 to 0.5
- 0.6 to 1.0
- 1.1 to 1.5
- 1.6 to 2.0
- 2.1 to 2.5
- 2.6 to 3.0
- 3.1 to 3.5
- 3.6 to 4.0
- 4.1 to 4.5
- 4.6 to 5.0
- 5.1 to 5.5
- 5.6 to 6.0
- 6.1 to 6.5

SPECTRA KEY

O, B

A

F

G

K

M, N, R, S

STARS

Double star

⊚ ○
Variable star

DEEP-SKY OBJECTS

Open
star cluster

Globular
star cluster

□ ♋
Bright
nebula

Planetary
nebula

Galaxy

Large faint
galaxy

GEMINI Cancer

Gemini is a zodiacal constellation, representing a pair of twins from Greek mythology. The twins are immortalized in the constellation's two brightest stars, Castor and Pollux. Castor is a sextuple star 52 light-years away, a multiple system of three stellar pairs, all bound together by gravity. Pollux is distinctly yellow and 18 light-years closer than Castor—so the "twins" are not actually related. Gemini has several interesting sights, including the open cluster M35, visible to the naked eye on a dark night. Gemini is bordered by two other zodiac signs, Cancer (the Crab) on one side and Taurus (the Bull) on the other. Cancer is not a striking grouping, its four brightest stars all being around fourth magnitude. But one interesting feature for binocular owners is Praesepe (M44 or NGC 2362), also known as the Beehive Cluster. M44 is about three times the apparent size of the Moon and contains some 40 visible stars.

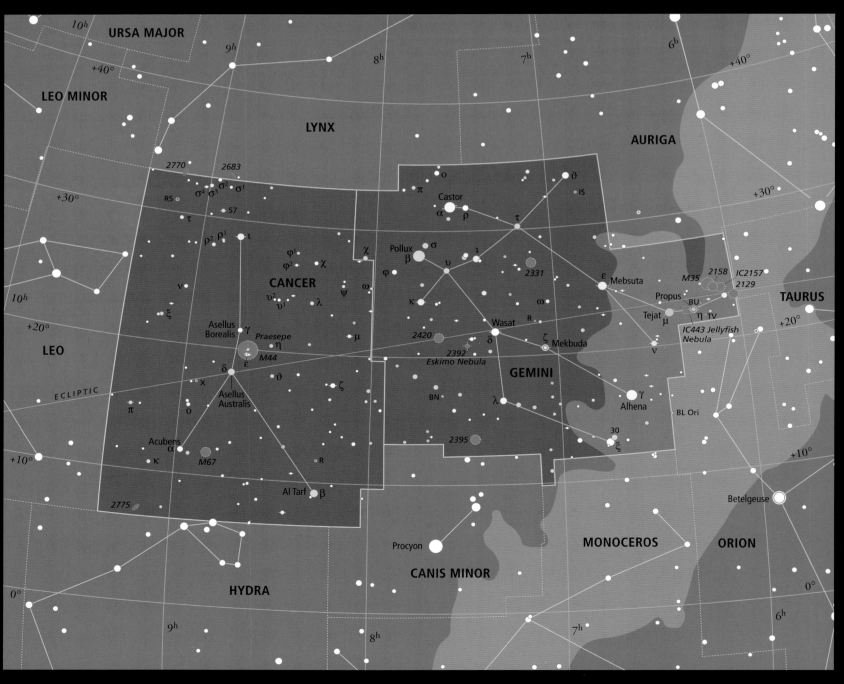

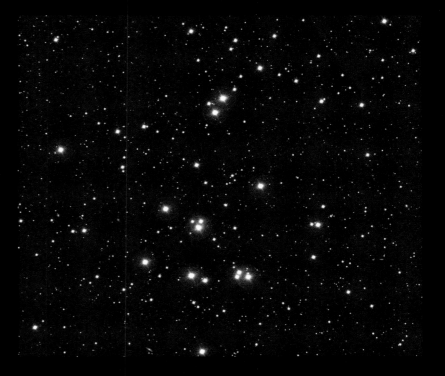

MAGNITUDE
SCALE

⬤
−0.5 and
brighter

⬤
0.0 to −0.4

⬤
0.1 to 0.5

⬤
0.6 to 1.0

⬤
1.1 to 1.5

⬤
1.6 to 2.0

⬤
2.1 to 2.5

●
2.6 to 3.0

●
3.1 to 3.5

●
3.6 to 4.0

•
4.1 to 4.5

•
4.6 to 5.0

·
5.1 to 5.5

·
5.6 to 6.0

·
6.1 to 6.5

Eskimo Nebula (left)

The Eskimo Nebula (NGC 2392) in Gemini is a complex planetary nebula, a gas bubble jettisoned by a dying star about 10,000 years ago. This nebula—named because it resembles the face of an Inuit, complete with a parka hood—was discovered by German-born British astronomer Sir William Herschel in 1787. The "parka" is studded with comet-like objects (but much larger than comets), their tails pointing toward the dying star at the center. Astronomers believe that these objects were formed when a more recently expelled, rapidly moving shell of gas collided with an earlier, relatively slower bubble.

Praesepe (below)

Praesepe (also M44 or the Beehive Cluster), 577 light-years distant in Cancer, is a large, bright cluster of approximately 200 stars. Easily visible to the naked eye, it is best seen through binoculars.

Open Cluster M35 (below left)

M35, 2,800 light-years distant in Gemini, is a rewarding sight for northern hemisphere viewers. Below it and to the left in this striking photograph from the Canada-France-Hawaii Telescope is NGC 2158—a much older, more compact cluster some six times more distant.

BRIGHTEST STARS			
NAME	MAGNITUDE	DISTANCE (LY)	SPECTRUM
Pollux (β GEM)	1.14	34	K0
Castor (α GEM)	1.58	52	A2+A1
Alhena (γ GEM)	1.93	105	A0
Tejat (μ GEM)	2.88	232	M3
Mebsuta (ε GEM)	2.98	904	G8
OTHER FEATURES			
NAME	TYPE	DISTANCE (LY)	ALSO KNOWN AS
Praesepe (Cnc)	Open cluster	577	M44, Beehive Cluster
M35 (Gem)	Open cluster	2,800	NGC 2168
Eskimo Nebula (Gem)	Planetary nebula	3,000	NGC 2392, Clownface Nebula
Jellyfish Nebula (Gem)	Supernova remnant	5,000	IC443

SPECTRA
KEY

O, B

A

F

G

K

M, N, R, S

STARS

Double star

Variable star

DEEP-SKY
OBJECTS

Open
star cluster

Globular
star cluster

Bright
nebula

Planetary
nebula

Galaxy

Large faint
galaxy

CANES VENATICI Coma Berenices

Canes Venatici (the Hunting Dogs) is a modern grouping dating from the 17th century. The dogs supposedly belong to the Herdsman, Boötes, a neighboring constellation. Canes Venatici is a small, faint assemblage whose brightest star, Cor Caroli or Alpha (α) Canum Venaticorum, is magnitude 2.9. Even so, there are many deep-sky objects, such as the striking face-on Whirlpool Galaxy (M51); the seventh-magnitude M3—a brilliant globular cluster containing an estimated half million stars; and many other NGC objects, mostly galaxies. The neighboring, and similarly faint constellation, Coma Berenices (Berenice's Hair) is even more abundant, with a generous sprinkling of galaxies between ninth and eleventh magnitudes. One of them is M64, seen on the right captured by the Hubble Space Telescope in 2001. Known also as the Blackeye Galaxy, the Sleeping Beauty Galaxy, or NGC 4826, M64 is surrounded by a curiously thick band of dust and gas.

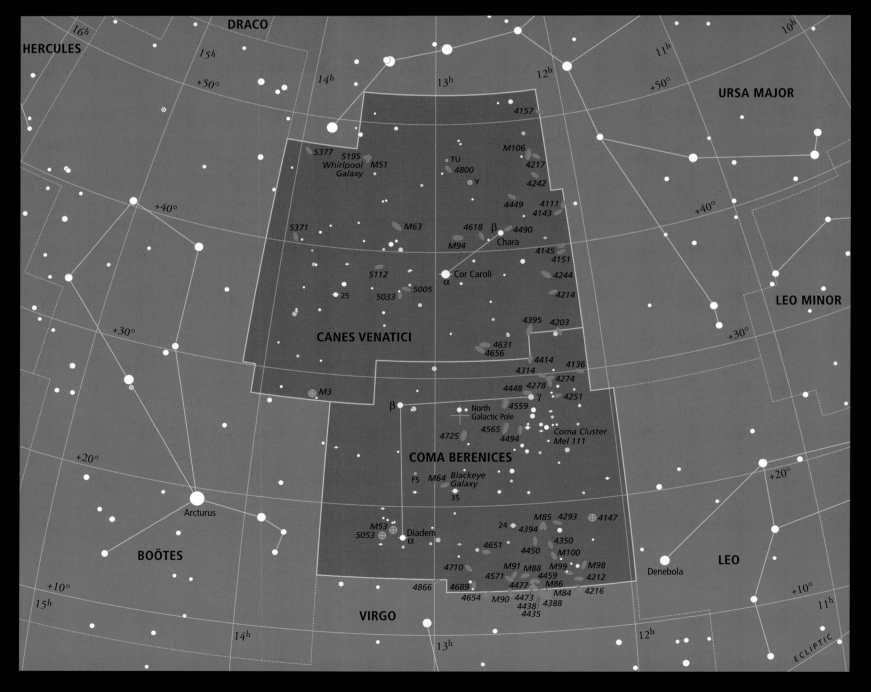

LEO Leo Minor

Leo, a constellation of the zodiac, is one of the few that bears some resemblance to what it was named after, a giant celestial lion. The brightest star, Regulus or Alpha (α) Leonis, forms one of Leo's front feet with Omicron (ο) Leonis making up the pair. Gamma (γ) Leonis marks his shoulder while Denebola or Beta (β) Leonis is at the tip of the tail. Leo contains several galaxies. M95, M96, and M105 are all between tenth and eleventh magnitude, similar to the three galaxies that comprise the so-called Leo Triplet: M65, M66 (right), and NGC 3628. The Triplet galaxies are sufficiently close to one another that it is possible to observe them in the same field of view using a low-power telescope. Leo's neighbor is Leo Minor (the Little Lion), a poor constellation with no bright stars. But like its bigger brother, Leo Minor contains a few satisfying galaxies for deep-space observers.

MAGNITUDE SCALE

−0.5 and brighter
0.0 to −0.4
0.1 to 0.5
0.6 to 1.0
1.1 to 1.5
1.6 to 2.0
2.1 to 2.5
2.6 to 3.0
3.1 to 3.5
3.6 to 4.0
4.1 to 4.5
4.6 to 5.0
5.1 to 5.5
5.6 to 6.0
6.1 to 6.5

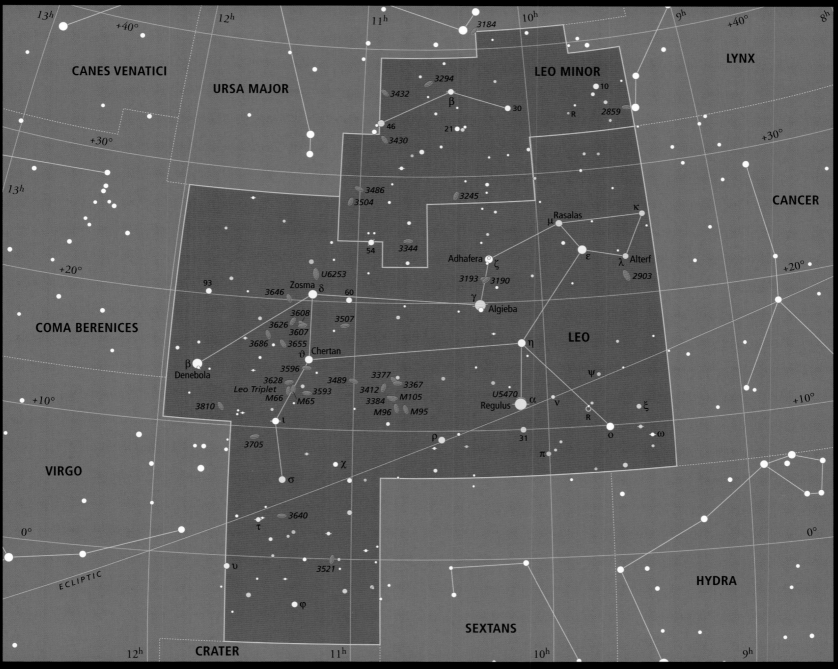

ORION

Along with Ursa Major, Orion (the Hunter) may be the most famous constellation of all, visible as it is from both hemispheres. Three bright stars in a near-straight line define the Hunter's belt, while two mark his shoulders and another two his feet. One of the shoulder stars is Betelgeuse. The tenth brightest star in the sky, Betelgeuse has a distinctly orange color to the naked eye. It is an extremely luminous variable red supergiant that can be 50,000 times brighter than the Sun and up to 650 times its diameter. Brighter still is Rigel, a steely blue star four or five times more intrinsically luminous even than Betelgeuse. Orion is also famous for the Orion Nebula, also known as the Great Nebula, and M42. It can be found below the belt and is said to represent the Hunter's sword. This active star factory is clearly visible as a bright smudge even from a light-polluted city—despite being some 1,500 light-years away.

Horsehead Nebula (above)

The Horsehead Nebula is one of the sky's most famous treasures. The Horsehead itself is a dark cloud of dust called Barnard 33. We see it only because it is superimposed on a bright red emission nebula, called IC434. Although the nebula is large—the region shown in this Canada-France-Hawaii Telescope photo spans an area about the same as that of the full Moon—it is faint and difficult to see with a telescope.

Orion's Belt (below)

This close up of Orion's Belt (defined by the bright stars Alnitak, Alnilam, and Mintaka) shows how the entire region is aglow with vibrant nebulosity. The Horsehead Nebula can be seen at lower left, just below the star Alnitak.

Betelgeuse (above)

Betelgeuse is among the sky's best known stars. It is a red supergiant so huge that if it replaced our Sun, it would swallow the orbits of all the planets out to, and including, Jupiter. Its size means that it is one of very few stars whose disk has been directly observed.

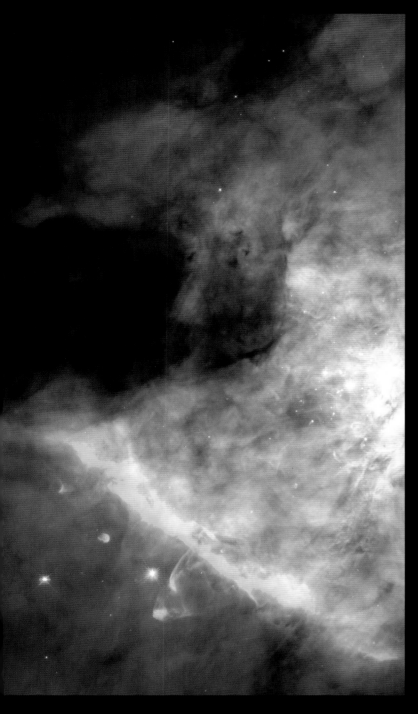

Orion Nebula (above)

The Orion Nebula (M42) is certainly the most famous nebula in the sky, mainly because it is easily visible to the naked eye from north or south of the equator as a bright, fuzzy patch—even from light-polluted skies. The photo above shows a close-up of part of the nebula studded with stars newly born and others still in formation.

BRIGHTEST STARS

NAME	MAGNITUDE	DISTANCE (LY)	SPECTRUM
Rigel (β ORI)	0.12	773	B8
Betelgeuse (α ORI)	0.50	427	M1
Bellatrix (γ ORI)	1.64	243	B2
Alnilam (ε ORI)	1.70	1,340	B0
Alnitak (ζ ORI)	2.05	817	O9

OTHER FEATURES

NAME	TYPE	DISTANCE (LY)	ALSO KNOWN AS
Orion Nebula	Bright nebula	1,500	Great Nebula, M42, NGC 1976
M43	Bright nebula	1,500	NGC 1982, de Mairan's Nebula
M78	Bright nebula	1,600	NGC 2068
Horsehead Nebula	Dark nebula	1,600	Barnard 33
Barnard's Loop	Reflection nebula	1,600	Sh2-276 (Sharpless 276)

ERIDANUS Fornax

Eridanus is a substantial constellation—the sixth largest in terms of area—that has been seen as a meandering river since ancient times. The spiral galaxy NGC 1232 (right, as seen from a large ground-based telescope) is a worthwhile sight for telescope owners as is the Fornax cluster of galaxies near the Eridanus–Fornax border. Fornax (the Furnace) is a modern constellation, tucked inside one of the bends of River Eridanus, featuring only faint stars but a number of spectacular galaxies.

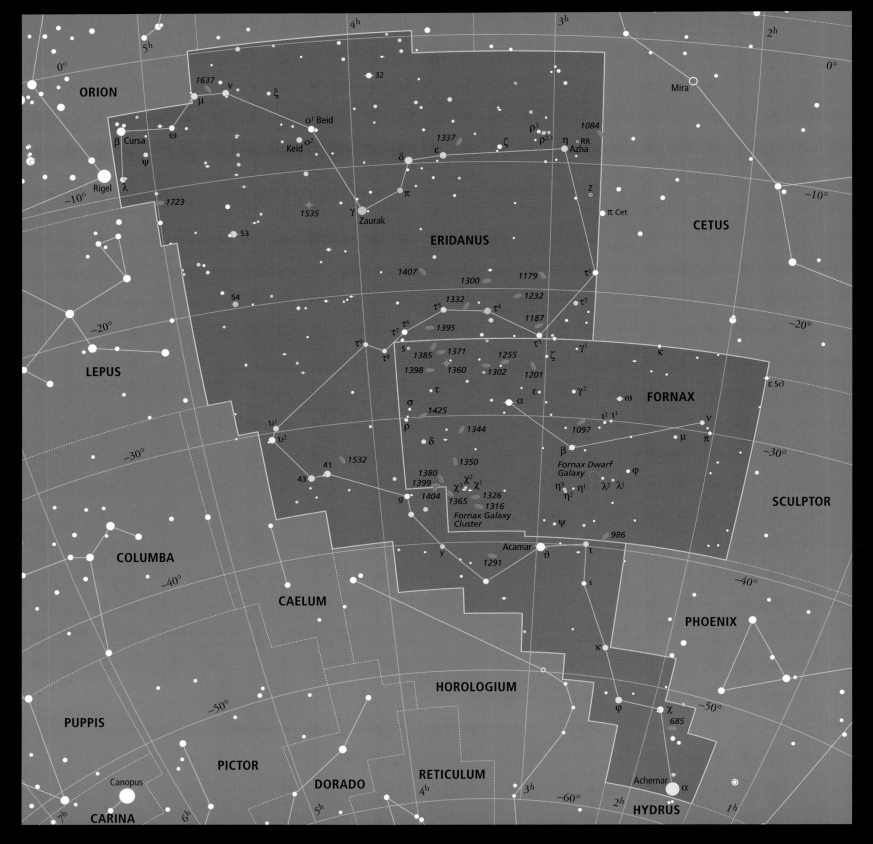

CETUS

Cetus (the Whale or the Sea Monster) is a large constellation —the fourth most extensive—that straddles the celestial equator. Cetus includes only three stars brighter than third magnitude. Nevertheless, this is the home of a famous stellar variable called Mira. Also known as Omicron (o) Ceti, Mira is a red giant that pulsates in and out of its average radius. As it pulsates, its brightness increases and decreases in sympathy. From Earth, Mira—which is the prototype of a whole class of stars with the same behavior—varies in visual magnitude from 3.4 to 9.3 over a period of 332 days, so for long periods of the year it is completely invisible to the naked eye. Cetus contains a faint planetary nebula, NGC 246, and a handful of galaxies. The brightest of these is M77, shown at right in a composite optical (red) and X-ray (green and blue) image revealing gas blowing away from a central supermassive black hole.

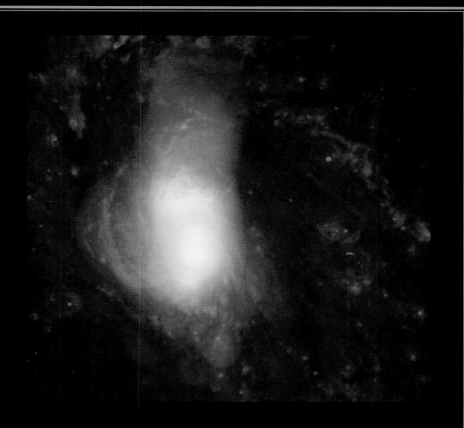

MAGNITUDE SCALE

-0.5 and brighter

0.0 to -0.4

0.1 to 0.5

0.6 to 1.0

1.1 to 1.5

1.6 to 2.0

2.1 to 2.5

2.6 to 3.0

3.1 to 3.5

3.6 to 4.0

4.1 to 4.5

4.6 to 5.0

5.1 to 5.5

5.6 to 6.0

6.1 to 6.5

SPECTRA
KEY
O, B
A
F
G
K
M, N, R, S

STARS
Double star
Variable star

DEEP-SKY
OBJECTS

Open
star cluster

Globular
star cluster

Bright
nebula

Planetary
nebula

Galaxy

Large faint
galaxy

AQUARIUS Capricornus, Microscopium

Aquarius (the Water Carrier) is on the ecliptic just south of the celestial equator, a zodiacal constellation in the middle of a whole group of similarly aquatic manifestations such as Delphinus (the Dolphin), Eridanus (the River), Pisces (the Fish), and Cetus (the Whale or Sea Monster). Aquarius has no bright stars, but it is home to planetary nebulas the likes of the Saturn Nebula (NGC 7009) and the Helix Nebula (NGC 7293), the latter of which has the largest apparent size of all such nebulas. Aquarius is adjacent to Capricornus (the Goat, or the Sea Goat), which in turn borders on the constellation Microscopium—no prizes for guessing what this 18th century group of faint stars was named after. Capricornus is faint but distinctive on a dark night, its principal stars forming a neat triangle. Microscopium, in turn, has no stars brighter than fourth magnitude, but contains a number of galaxies between twelfth and fourteenth magnitude.

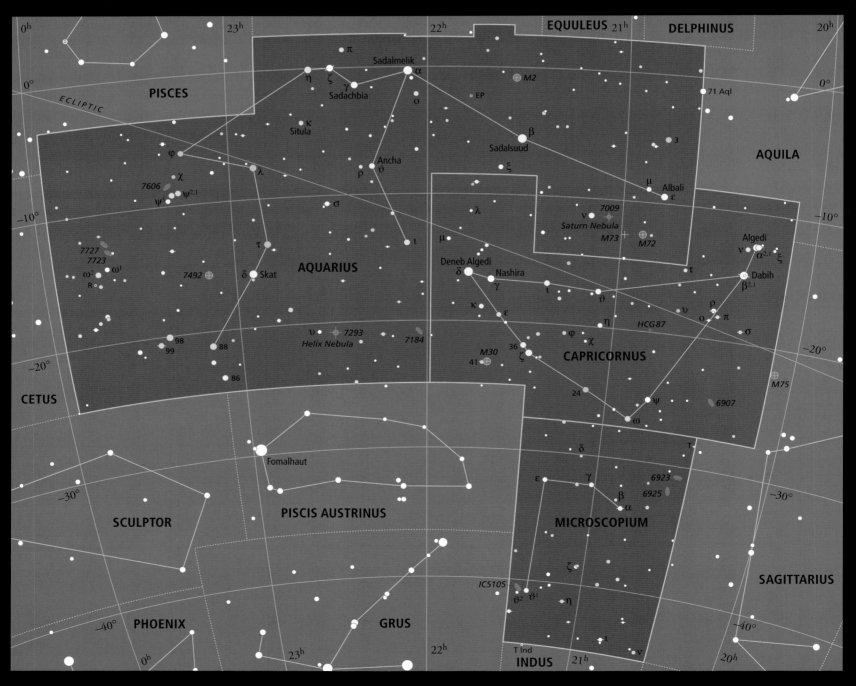

MAGNITUDE
SCALE

-0.5 and
brighter

0.0 to -0.4

0.1 to 0.5

0.6 to 1.0

1.1 to 1.5

1.6 to 2.0

2.1 to 2.5

2.6 to 3.0

3.1 to 3.5

3.6 to 4.0

4.1 to 4.5

4.6 to 5.0

5.1 to 5.5

5.6 to 6.0

6.1 to 6.5

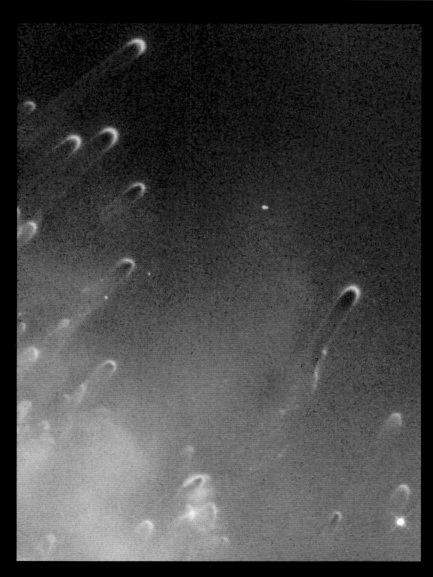

BRIGHTEST STARS

NAME	MAGNITUDE	DISTANCE (LY)	SPECTRUM
Deneb Algedi (δ CAP)	2.87	39	Amv
Sadalsuud (β AQR)	2.91	612	G0
Sadalmelik (α AQR)	2.96	759	G2
Dabih (β CAP)	3.08	344	F8 + A0
Skat (δ AQR)	3.27	160	A3

OTHER FEATURES

NAME	TYPE	DISTANCE (LY)	ALSO KNOWN AS
Helix Nebula (AQR)	Planetary nebula	450	NGC 7293
Saturn Nebula (AQR)	Planetary nebula	2,400	NGC 7009
M2 (AQR)	Globular cluster	37,500	NGC 7089
M72 (AQR)	Globular cluster	55,400	NGC 6981

Helix Nebula (below)
Because of its proximity, at just 450 light-years from Earth, the Helix Nebula (NGC 7293) in Aquarius has the largest apparent diameter of any planetary nebula in the sky. Measuring about three light-years across, it spans almost as much sky as a full Moon. This photo is a composite of images taken by the Hubble Space Telescope and a ground-based telescope at Kitt Peak National Observatory in the United States.

Cometary knots (above)
This is a close-up of the Helix Nebula (NGC 7293) as taken with the Hubble Space Telescope in 1994. The comet-like objects have been dubbed cometary knots but they are far larger than comets, the "head" of each measuring perhaps twice the diameter of the Solar System. The "knots" were formed when a more recent shell of gas was blown off by the nebula's central star, hitting, and shredding a slower moving shell laid down earlier.

Galaxy group in Capricornus (below)
HCG 87 is a loose group of galaxies bound together by gravity, situated some 400 million light-years away in Capricornus. This photo of the group, which includes an edge-on spiral (lower center), an elliptical galaxy (to its right), and another large spiral (top), was taken using the Gemini South Telescope at Cerro Pachón, in the Chilean Andes. Other galaxies in the photo, including the small central spiral, are background galaxies, not associated with the group.

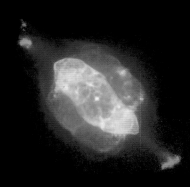

Saturn Nebula (above)
Another beautiful planetary nebula in Aquarius is the Saturn Nebula (NGC 7009), 2,400 light-years away. The center of the nebula is dominated by a brightly glowing, colorful shell of gas enclosing a cavity, with the progenitor star at the center. Farther out, a pair of "handles" comprised of low-density gas lie on either side of the nebula's long axis. These give the object the appearance of the ringed planet seen nearly edge-on, hence its name.

LEPUS Columba, Caelum

Lepus (the Hare) is only a moderately bright group of stars, and is fairly small; but it is easy to find because it lies immediately to the south of Orion. Its two brightest stars, Arneb and Nihal, are magnitude 2.56 and 2.78 respectively, while its other main stars are between third and fourth magnitude only. Lepus contains a globular cluster, M79, and is also home to the enigmatic Spirograph Nebula (IC418, seen on the right as captured by the Hubble Space Telescope). Just south of Lepus are the constellations Columba (the Dove) and Caelum (the Chisel). These constellations lie south of the celestial equator and are not easily observable by northern hemisphere skywatchers. Columba contains a globular cluster, NGC 1851, which is seventh magnitude, and a number of galaxies, all fainter than tenth magnitude. Caelum also boasts a couple of galaxies, but it has no stars brighter than magnitude 4.5.

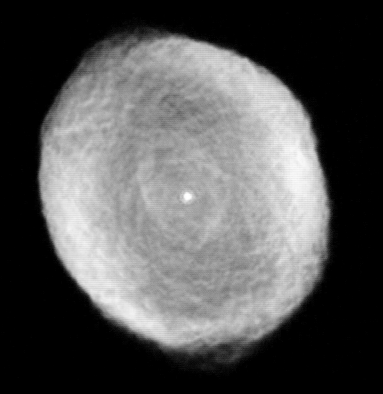

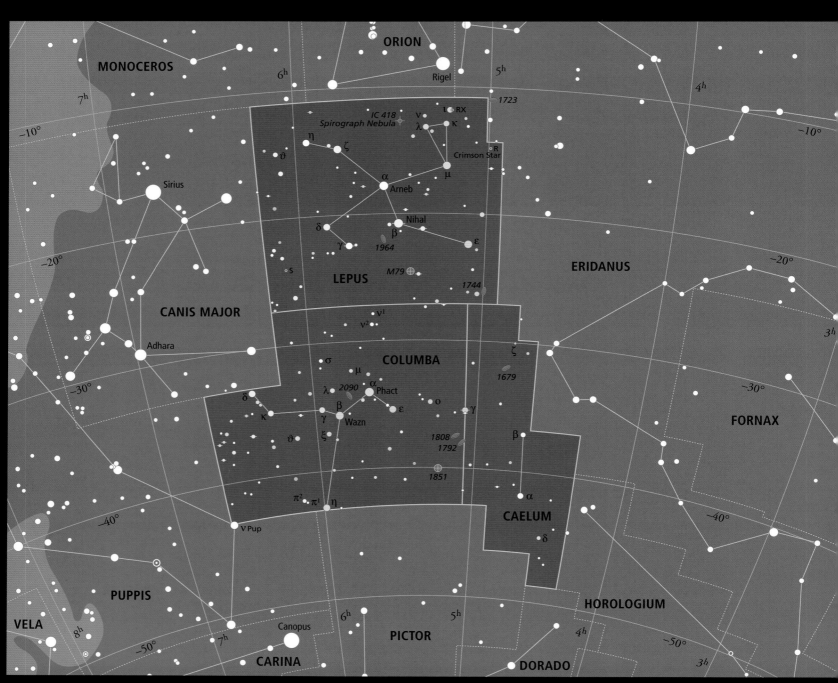

SCULPTOR

Grus, Phoenix, Piscis Austrinus

Sculptor (the Sculptor) is a modern constellation south of the celestial equator. Even in the southern latitudes this faint patch of stars is not distinctive for here we are looking directly out of the plane of our galaxy into intergalactic space. However, there are a number of interesting and quite bright galaxies here, NGC 613 (right), NGC 55, and NGC 253, among them. NGC 253 in particular is quite large, and easily discernible in binoculars as a thick bar. Sculptor's neighboring constellations include Phoenix (the Phoenix), Grus (the Crane), and Piscis Austrinus (the Southern Fish). Piscis Austrinus is home to the bright star Fomalhaut (sometimes called the Solitary One), at magnitude 1.15 the brightest star for some distance around this patch of sky. The two brightest stars in Grus, Alnair and Beta (β) Grus, are a fairly conspicuous pair at magnitudes 2.10 and 1.74 respectively.

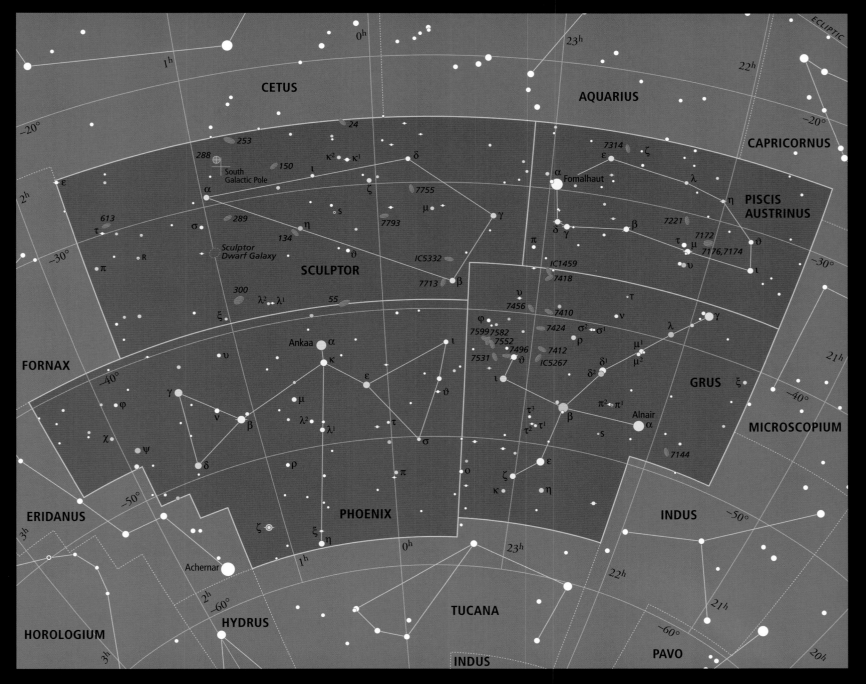

MAGNITUDE SCALE

- −0.5 and brighter
- 0.0 to −0.4
- 0.1 to 0.5
- 0.6 to 1.0
- 1.1 to 1.5
- 1.6 to 2.0
- 2.1 to 2.5
- 2.6 to 3.0
- 3.1 to 3.5
- 3.6 to 4.0
- 4.1 to 4.5
- 4.6 to 5.0
- 5.1 to 5.5
- 5.6 to 6.0
- 6.1 to 6.5

DORADO AND TUCANA

Horologium, Hydrus, Mensa, Reticulum

Deep in the southern hemisphere are two constellations that, while exhibiting no bright stars, are nonetheless home to two of the night sky's most awesome spectacles. The constellations are Dorado (variously the Goldfish, Swordfish, or Dolphinfish) and Tucana (the Toucan); and their treasures, the Large and Small Magellanic clouds, respectively. These bright smudges, resembling detached portions of the Milky Way, are actually satellite galaxies, irregular in shape, locked in orbit around our galaxy. Tucana is also famed for its globular cluster 47 Tucanae, the sky's second brightest, visible to the naked eye. Nearby constellations include Horologium (the Clock), Hydrus (the Water Serpent), Mensa (the only constellation named after a geological feature, namely Table Mountain), and Reticulum (the Reticule), but all are faint.

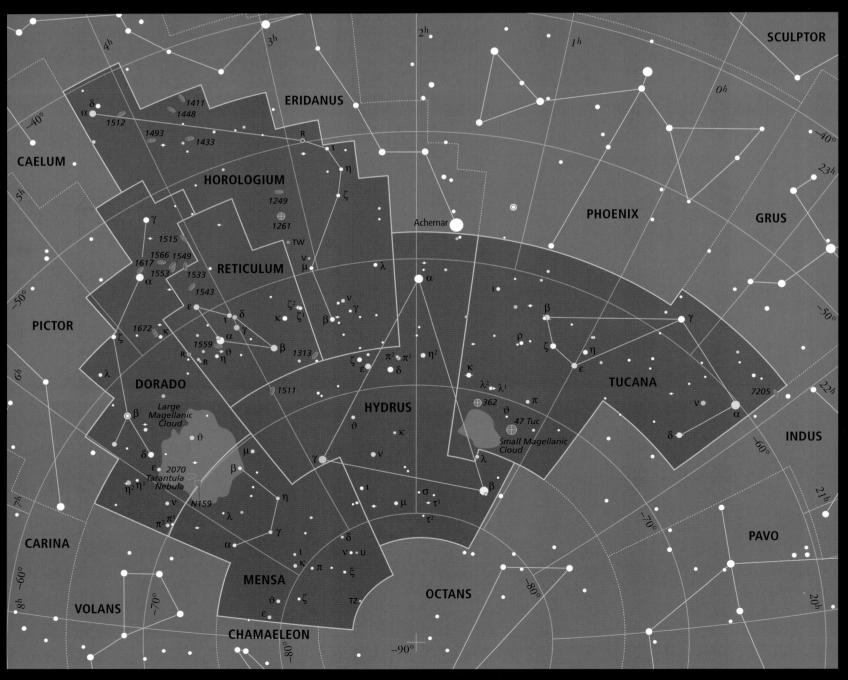

BRIGHTEST STARS			
NAME	MAGNITUDE	DISTANCE (LY)	SPECTRUM
β HYI	2.80	24	G2
α HYI	2.86	71	F0
α TUC	2.87	199	K3
γ HYI	3.24	214	M2
α DOR	3.27	176	A0
OTHER FEATURES			
NAME	TYPE	DISTANCE (LY)	ALSO KNOWN AS
47 Tucanae (TUC)	Globular cluster	13,400	NGC 104
Tarantula Nebula(DOR)	Emission nebula	179,000	30 Doradus, NGC 2070
Large Magellanic Cloud	Irregular satellite galaxy	180,000	LMC
Small Magellanic Cloud	Irregular satellite galaxy	210,000	SMC

159 (above)
his vast nebula is one of the numerous star factories embedded in the Large Magellanic Cloud.
alled N159—number 159 in a specific catalog of Large Magellanic Cloud objects—this cloud, over
50 light-years across, gets its red color from hydrogen gas, made to glow by young new stars within.

7 Tucanae (above)
his Hubble image shows a swarm of about 30,000 tightly packed stars near the heart of globular
uster 47 Tucanae. This cluster of several million mostly old stars is a gravitational captive of the
ilky Way but was formed long before our galaxy assumed its present shape. Clusters such as
7 Tucanae and Omega Centauri have some of the oldest known stars in the universe.

Tarantula Nebula (above)
The Large Magellanic Cloud is home to a vast patch of interstellar fog called the Tarantula Nebula (NGC 2070). It is easy to see why this sprawling web of stars and gas has been likened to a spider. The Tarantula is some 179,000 light-years away and so appears quite small, but if it were as close as the Orion Nebula it would span an impressive 30 degrees of sky—one-third of the distance from the horizon to the zenith. Within this vast gaseous labyrinth are some of the most massive stars known.

A thousand-year-old explosion (left)
E0102-72 is the memorable name given to the remnant of a supernova that exploded in the Small Magellanic Cloud about a thousand years ago. It is about 40 light-years across. This color composite is made from three images taken at different wavelengths: radio (red), optical (green), and X-ray (blue). The radio image shows the outward moving shockwave; oxygen and neon gas heated to millions of degrees Celsius by the rebounding wave is seen in the blue X-ray wavelengths; while clouds of cooler, though still super-heated, oxygen are seen in the visible wavelengths.

CANIS MAJOR Canis Minor, Monoceros

Canis Major (the Great Dog) is a gem of a constellation. It has the claim to fame that it is home to the brightest star of the entire sky and the eighth closest to Earth, Sirius, also called the Dog Star. Just north of Canis Major is Monoceros (the Unicorn), and slightly farther north again lies the Small Dog, Canis Minor. The latter contains another bright star called Procyon. This entire region—Canis Major, Monoceros, and Canis Minor— is particularly rich as it straddles the Milky Way. Open clusters and nebulas are everywhere, and this is a great place to go scanning with binoculars. Among some of the sights are the Rosette Nebula (NGC 2237), and the Christmas Tree Cluster (NGC 2264), both in Monoceros, and the outstanding open cluster M41 in Canis Major. On the right is another interesting feature of Canis Major: a pair of galaxies in collision, NGC 2207 and IC2163.

VELA

Pyxis, Puppis, Antlia

Vela (the Sail) sits amid an attractive piece of celestial real estate, right on top of the bright star clouds of the Milky Way in the southern hemisphere. This region is replete with open clusters. Most of them are rather faint, but an exception is the Omicron Velorum Cluster at magnitude 2.5. There is also a fine planetary nebula, NGC 3132 (right, as portrayed by the Hubble Space Telescope). NGC 3132 resembles the more famous Ring Nebula (M57) in the northern constellation Lyra, and has therefore often been called the Southern Ring Nebula. Adjacent to Vela are the constellations Pyxis (the Compass), Puppis (the Stern), and Antlia (the Air Pump). Puppis, like Vela, is rich in open clusters such, as M47, and is a delight to scan with binoculars or a low-power telescope. Originally, these four constellations, along with a fifth, Carina (the Keel) farther south, were envisioned as parts of a giant ship known as Argo.

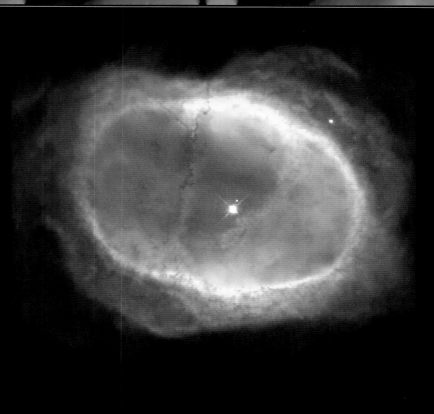

CARINA Pictor, Volans

Carina (the Keel) is a striking constellation of the southern skies which is also visible from the north, but only at low latitudes. Its most distinctive features are Canopus—a yellow-white supergiant and second brightest star in the sky after nearby Sirius—and the awesome Eta Carinae Nebula (NGC 3372) (right, as imaged by the Hubble Space Telescope). This nebula has been compared to the Great Nebula in Orion (M42), and some would argue that Eta Carinae is the more striking. It is a huge cloud of gas expelled by and surrounding the hypergiant star Eta (η) Carinae—a star that, in 1843, flared up to become almost as bright as Sirius despite being about 800 times more distant. Adjacent to Carina is the faint constellation Pictor (the Easel), which is noted for Beta (β) Pictoris, a star with a planetary system in formation. Meanwhile, south of Carina is another small and unremarkable constellation called Volans (the Flying Fish).

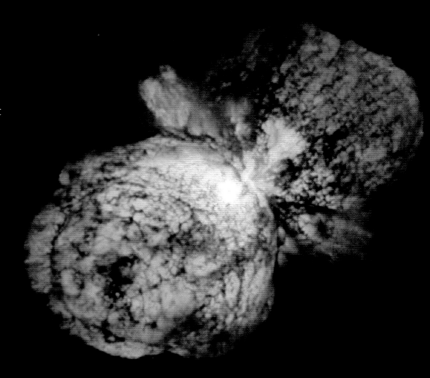

MAGNITUDE
SCALE

● −0.5 and
brighter

● 0.0 to −0.4

● 0.1 to 0.5

● 0.6 to 1.0

● 1.1 to 1.5

● 1.6 to 2.0

● 2.1 to 2.5

● 2.6 to 3.0

● 3.1 to 3.5

● 3.6 to 4.0

● 4.1 to 4.5

● 4.6 to 5.0

● 5.1 to 5.5

● 5.6 to 6.0

● 6.1 to 6.5

OCTANS
Apus, Triangulum Australe, Circinus, Musca, Chamaeleon

This region of the southern sky seems to contain nothing but small, dim constellations. Octans (the Octant) sits astride the south celestial pole and it is here that you will find the southern equivalent of Polaris—the south pole star, Sigma (σ) Octantis. But, being barely visible to the naked eye even in dark skies, it is not much of an aid to navigation. North of Octans is obscure Apus (the Bird of Paradise), with Triangulum Australe (the Southern Triangle) farther north again. Triangulum Australe, a medium-bright trio of stars, is a complement to its northern counterpart Triangulum. To the west of Triangulum Australe is Circinus (the Drawing Compass). Slightly farther west and south is the equally indistinct Musca (the Fly), home to the Hourglass Nebula (MyCn18) (right, as made famous by the Hubble Space Telescope). Between Musca and Octans is the faint constellation Chamaeleon, after the animal of the same name.

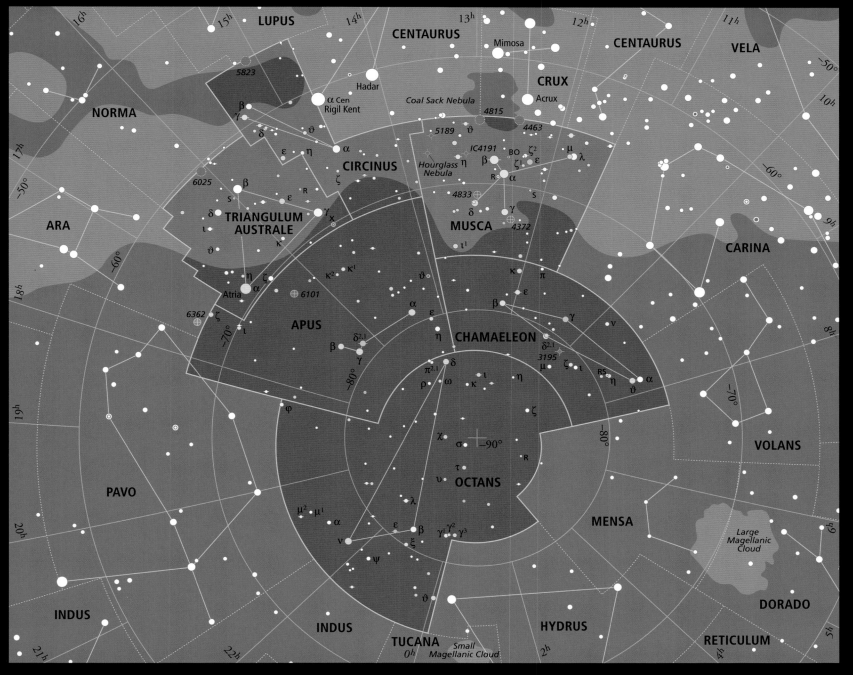

CRUX AND CENTAURUS

Lupus

The constellations Crux (the Southern Cross) and Centaurus (the Centaur) need little introduction to southern observers. Crux is the smallest constellation in terms of area—but what an assemblage! Superimposed on the dense background of the Milky Way, its principal four stars form a brilliant and compact celestial cross. This is the home of the strikingly beautiful Jewel Box Cluster and the dark Coal Sack Nebula. Centaurus features the splendid Omega Centauri cluster and several bright stars including Alpha (α) and Beta (β) Centauri—also known as Rigil Kent and Hadar respectively. Rigil Kent is a close binary system comprising two Sun-like stars that are in turn encircled by a faint red dwarf called Proxima Centauri, the closest known star to the Sun. Lupus (the Wolf) is a third constellation in this region, boasting a few second-magnitude stars and some deep-sky objects.

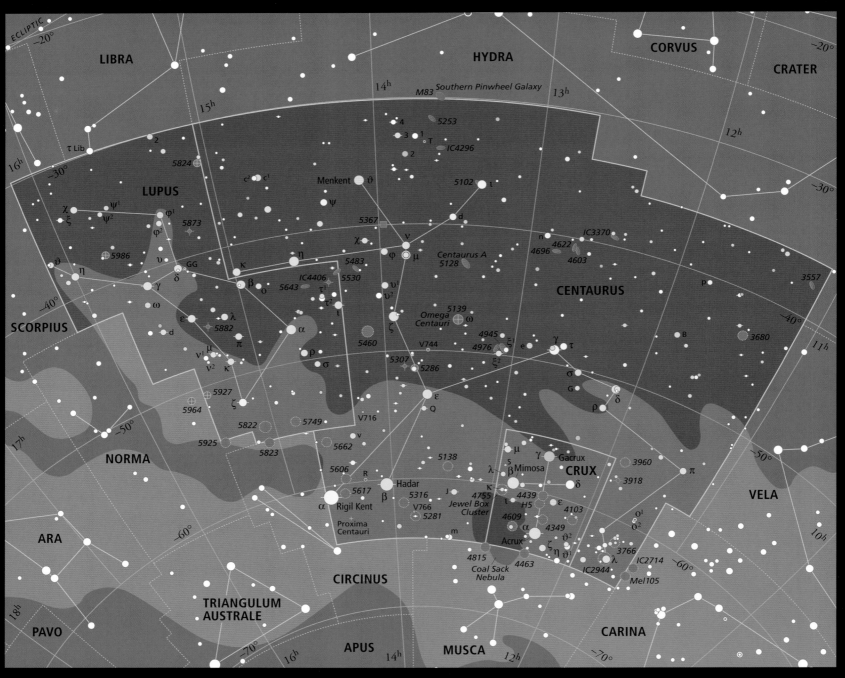

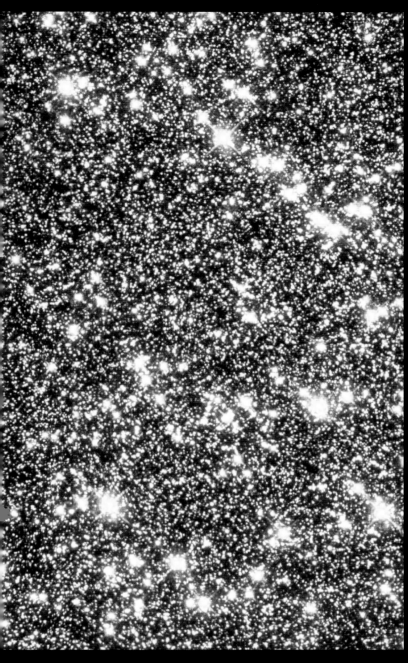

NGC 4603 (above)

NGC 4603, photographed by the Hubble Space Telescope, is a spiral galaxy in the constellation of Centaurus whose arms can been seen here bejeweled by clusters of bright young blue stars. It is just one of many galaxies bound together by gravity and forming the Centaurus galaxy cluster.

Omega Centauri (left)

This Hubble image shows some 20,000 stars packed into a small section (about five by nine light-years) at the heart of Omega Centauri, the most luminous and massive globular star cluster in the Milky Way. A similarly sized region centered on the Sun would contain fewer than a half-dozen stars. The cluster, as this image shows, is dominated by faint, yellow-white dwarf stars, similar to our Sun. The bright yellow-orange stars dotted throughout are red giants that have expanded to diameters about a hundred times that of the Sun, and the faint blue stars have been captured in a momentary stage of star evolution between dwarf and red giant.

Centaurus A (below)

This photograph shows the elliptical galaxy Centaurus A (NGC 5128) in the infrared—and the contents of its celestial "stomach." Inside are the remains of a spiral galaxy, seen here as the central red shape, that was cannibalized in a collision with Centaurus A. The Spitzer Space Telescope, whose infrared camera is able to see into and through interstellar dust at objects otherwise hidden, took this image.

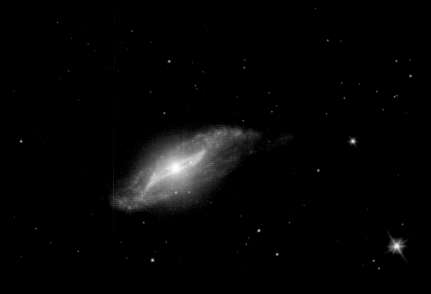

Thackeray's Globules (above)

The red background in this Hubble image is the star-forming nebula known as IC2944, located about 5,900 light-years away in Centaurus. Superimposed on it are several curious dark blotches known as Thackeray's Globules, after the scientist who first drew attention to them. Globules are small patches of interstellar dust, some of which are cocoons for newly forming stars. The large globule at the top is actually two overlapping clouds, each about one light-year across, typical sizes for globules.

BRIGHTEST STARS			
NAME	**MAGNITUDE**	**DISTANCE (LY)**	**SPECTRUM**
Rigil Kent (α CEN)	−0.27	4.39	G2+K1
Hadar (β CEN)	0.61	525	B1
Acrux (α CRU)	0.77	321	B0+B1
Mimosa (β CRU)	1.25	353	B0
Gacrux (γ CRU)	1.63	88	M3

OTHER FEATURES			
NAME	**TYPE**	**DISTANCE (LY)**	**ALSO KNOWN AS**
Proxima Centauri (CEN)	Red dwarf	4.22	Alpha Centauri C
Coal Sack Nebula (CRU)	Dark nebula	550	—
Jewel Box Cluster (CRU)	Open cluster	7,600	NGC 4755
Omega Centauri (CRU)	Globular cluster	16,000	NGC 5139
Centaurus A (CEN)	Elliptical galaxy	15 million	NGC 5128

PAVO

Ara, Indus, Norma, Telescopium

The five constellations Pavo (the Peacock), Ara (the Altar), Indus (the Indian), Norma (the Surveyor's Level), and Telescopium (the Telescope) cover a large patch of the southern sky between Centaurus and Grus. This is a dim group: only Pavo has a star brighter than second magnitude—Alpha (α) Pavonis, the Peacock Star. Nevertheless, there are still some worthwhile sites here for telescope owners. Ara and Norma, lying in front of the Milky Way, are rich in open clusters. The brightest of these—NGC 6087, 6067, and 6025—are all around fifth magnitude. Meanwhile, for a look at a nearby globular cluster—possibly the closest, at just 8,200 light-years distant—aim your telescope at NGC 6397, whose core is shown at right, located between Beta (β) and Theta (ϑ) Arae. The stars here are packed together with a density around a million times greater than that of the solar neighborhood.

SCORPIUS Libra

Scorpius (the Scorpion), its barb embedded in the Milky Way, is a distinctive zodiacal constellation with some bright to medium-bright stars. Most notable among them is the brilliant Antares—a highly luminous red supergiant 400 times as large as the Sun and 10,000 times as bright. Antares means "rival of Mars," and indeed it has a definite orange hue to it just like the planet. Nearby is the striking globular cluster M4, one of the best such clusters to view with a small telescope. The photo on the right shows Antares at lower left with M4 immediately to the right of it and Sigma (σ) Scorpii, enveloped in gas, at top right. Other delights of Scorpius include M6 and M7, a pair of large, bright open clusters. West of Scorpius lies one of its two neighboring zodiac signs, Libra (the Scales), while Sagittarius lies on the eastern border. Libra is not a very bright constellation, but it is large, and contains several galaxies around magnitude 12.

Straddling both the ecliptic and the Milky Way, Sagittarius is a constellation of the zodiac representing an archer. This is a large assemblage with a huge array of striking star clusters and nebulas, and a number of medium-bright stars. Sagittarius is well known, for it pinpoints the location of the center of our galaxy. You cannot see the center itself because it is behind the Sagittarius star and dust clouds. But if you traveled in a straight line toward Sagittarius and beyond, you would eventually reach the very heart of our galaxy. Owing to the density of the Milky Way in Sagittarius, this is one of the best places to point your binoculars and scan around for celestial treasures. Immediately south is a fairly small constellation called Corona Australis (the Southern Crown). It is as faint as it is petite, but it does bear an interesting similarity to its northern counterpart, Corona Borealis.

SPECTRA KEY

- O, B
- A
- F
- G
- K
- M, N, R, S

STARS

- Star
- Double star
- Variable star

DEEP-SKY OBJECTS

- Open star cluster
- Globular star cluster
- Bright nebula
- Planetary nebula
- Galaxy
- Large faint galaxy

MAGNITUDE
SCALE

● −0.5 and brighter

● 0.0 to −0.4

● 0.1 to 0.5

● 0.6 to 1.0

● 1.1 to 1.5

● 1.6 to 2.0

● 2.1 to 2.5

● 2.6 to 3.0

● 3.1 to 3.5

● 3.6 to 4.0

● 4.1 to 4.5

● 4.6 to 5.0

● 5.1 to 5.5

· 5.6 to 6.0

· 6.1 to 6.5

In the center of NGC 6559 (above)

NGC 6559 is a celestial cloud in Sagittarius. This photo, in one frame, shows the three classic types of nebulas: a reflection nebula, an emission nebula, and several dark nebulas. The emission nebula produces the overall red glow—it is hydrogen gas made to glow by bright stars embedded within it. The blue glow is light reflected from stars off dust, producing a reflection nebula. And the dark regions are dense patches in the nebula that do not shine but rather block the background light to show up only in silhouette.

Center of the Omega Nebula (left)

The Omega Nebula, object number 17 in Charles Messier's celestial catalog and an active star-forming region, is found just inside the border of Sagittarius. This European Southern Observatory photo reveals the glow of ionized hydrogen gas and dark dust clouds characteristic of such regions.

BRIGHTEST STARS

NAME	MAGNITUDE	DISTANCE (LY)	SPECTRUM
Kaus Australis (ε SGR)	1.85	145	B9
Nunki (σ SGR)	2.02	224	B2
Ascella (ζ SGR)	2.60	89	A2+A4
Kaus Media (δ SGR)	2.70	306	K3
Kaus Borealis (λ SGR)	2.81	77	K1

OTHER FEATURES

NAME	TYPE	DISTANCE (LY)	ALSO KNOWN AS
Omega Nebula (SGR)	Emission nebula	5,000	M17, NGC 6618, Swan Nebula
Lagoon Nebula (SGR)	Emission nebula	5,200	M8, NGC 6523
Trifid Nebula (SGR)	Complex nebula	5,200	M20, NGC 6514
Sagittarius Star Cloud (SGR)	Star cloud	10,000–16,000	M24

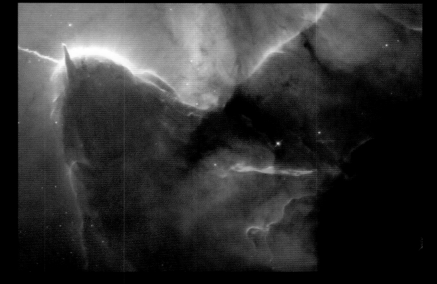

Trifid Nebula—pillars and jets (above)

The Trifid Nebula (M20 or NGC 6514) is a well-known emission nebula in Sagittarius. This close-up photo taken by the Hubble Space Telescope shows what appears to be a giant celestial slug, complete with antennae. The slug is, in fact, a vast pillar of gas and dust, illuminated by the stars that surround it. Some of these stars are so powerful that their radiation is slowly eroding the pillar. The two "antennae" contain in their tips newly forming stars. It is likely that in a few thousand years the antennae will erode completely, revealing the new-born stars within.

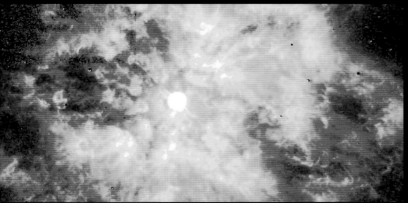

Wolf-Rayet stars (above)

WR124 belongs to an extremely energetic class of objects known as Wolf-Rayet stars. These stars, which are nearing the end of their lives and are at least ten times more massive than the Sun, emit so much energy that they blow out their outermost layers. In the case of WR124, located in Sagittarius, this has created a bright celestial firework with gas rushing outward from the central star at speeds of up to 100,000 miles per hour (160,000 km/h).

Window on the Milky Way (left)

The Sagittarius Star Cloud (M24) is not an open cluster or true deep-sky object at all; rather, it is a window where our view toward the center of the Milky Way is less obscured by dust than elsewhere. This Hubble Space Telescope view reveals a dazzling array of stars. Along with numerous yellow stars much like our Sun, are hot, relatively short-lived blue stars, and red stars which can be either nearby small stars slowly burning their fuel or more distant red giants at the end of their life cycle.

SPECTRA
KEY

O, B

A

F

G

K

M, N, R, S

STARS

Double star

Variable star

DEEP-SKY
OBJECTS

Open
star cluster

Globular
star cluster

Bright
nebula

Planetary
nebula

Galaxy

Large faint
galaxy

HYDRA · Crater, Corvus, Sextans

Hydra is a truly enormous constellation representing a mythical sea serpent. It snakes its way across 100 degrees of sky, from Cancer in the west—where its head rests—to Libra in the east. But despite its size, Hydra is difficult to trace because of the relative faintness of its stars. The brightest star, in the western portion of the constellation, is Alphard (the green star in the photo of Hydra, right). Hydra is home to the binocular object M83, a face-on barred spiral galaxy known as the Southern Pinwheel, and the open cluster M48 (NGC 2548). On the northern border of Hydra, from east to west, can be found three much smaller constellations: Corvus (the Crow), Crater (the Cup, which does indeed resemble a goblet), and Sextans (the Sextant). Sextans is home to the Spindle Galaxy (NGC 3115), an edge-on spiral, and Corvus contains the famous Antennae Galaxies (NGC 4038 and NGC 4039)—a pair of spirals engaged in a stately collision.

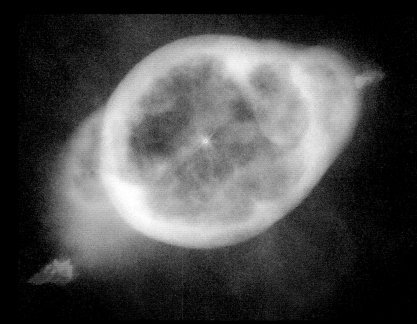

Brightest Stars

Name	Magnitude	Distance (ly)	Spectrum
Alphard (α Hya)	1.98	177	K3
Gienah (γ Crv)	2.59	165	B8
Kraz (β Crv)	2.65	140	G5
Algorab (δ Crv)	2.95	88	B9
γ Hya	3.00	132	G8

Other Features

Name	Type	Distance (ly)	Also known as
M48 (Hya)	Open cluster	2,000	NGC 2548
Southern Pinwheel (Hya)	Spiral galaxy	15 million	M83, NGC 5236
Spindle Galaxy (Sex)	Spiral galaxy	30 million	M102, NGC 3115
Antennae Galaxies (Crv)	Merging galaxies	60 million	NGC 4038 and NGC 4039

Ghost of Jupiter (above)

NGC 3242, sometimes called the Ghost of Jupiter for its resemblance to that planet as seen in a telescope, is a planetary nebula in Hydra. It is the remains of a star (center) that has thrown off its outer shell, an event that will one day befall the Sun. Astronomers are unsure of the origin of the gas producing the red emission on the sides.

The Southern Pinwheel (above)

This image shows the central portion of the spectacular face-on galaxy the Southern Pinwheel (M83) in Hydra which lies 15 million light-years distant and is 30,000 light-years across. The Southern Pinwheel is known for its unusually high incidence of supernovae: five or six have been observed in the last century when only one might have been expected.

Collision of galaxies (below)

Around 60 million light-years away in Corvus is a pair of galaxies that, for 800 million years, have been slowly merging into a single, larger unit. The two galaxies are NGC 4038 and NGC 4039, known together as the Antennae Galaxies.

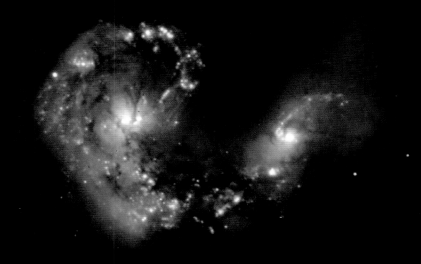

VIRGO

Virgo (the Virgin or the Maiden), on the zodiac and bridging the celestial equator, is the second largest constellation, after Hydra. Virgo has few bright stars but boasts a great many galaxies, including a group known as the Virgo Cluster. This is a truly huge assemblage: many thousands of galaxies, all held together by gravity. Also known as the Coma–Virgo Cluster because it encroaches into the adjacent constellation of Coma Berenices, this gravitational huddling is a delight for telescope owners. The famous Sombrero Galaxy (M104) and M87 (or Virgo A) are just two of the objects found here. M87 is one of the most massive galaxies in the known universe. South of the Virgo Cluster at magnitude 12.8 is the closest and brightest quasar in the sky, 3C 273. Shining 100 times brighter than the Milky Way and about 2.5 billion light-years away, this is one of the most distant objects observable to most amateur astronomers.

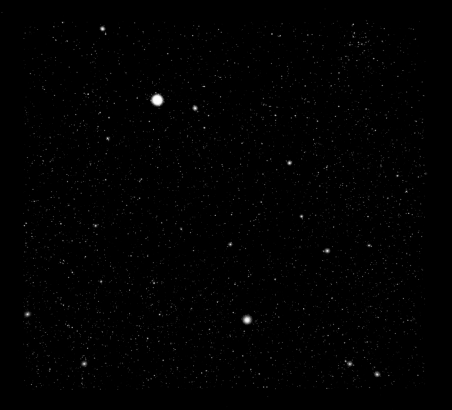

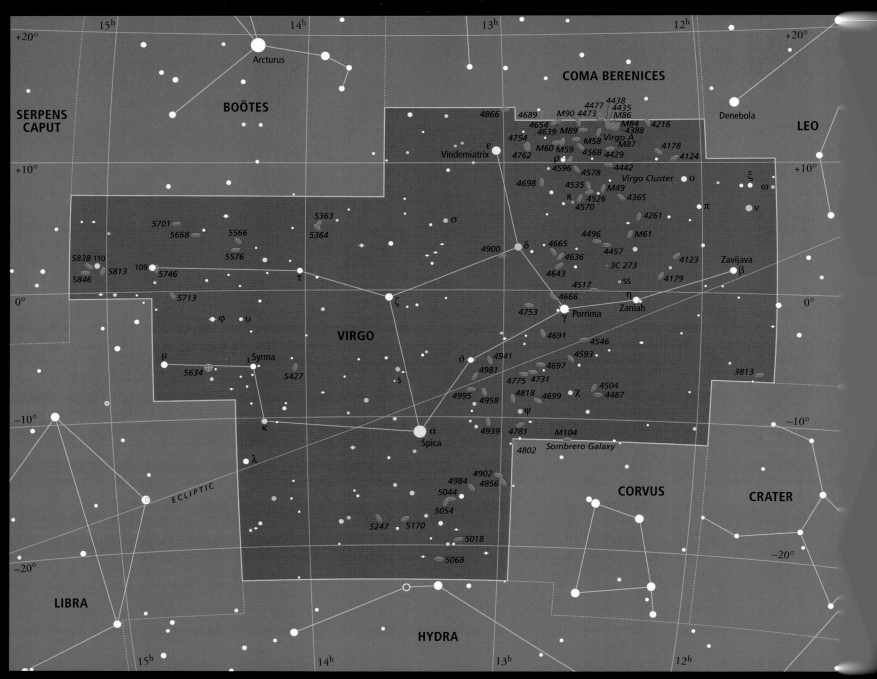

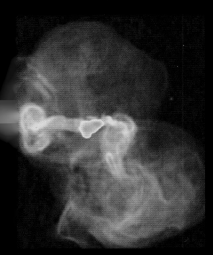

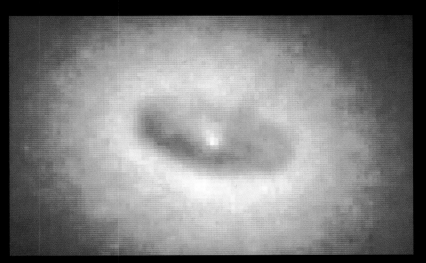

Virgo A in radio waves (above)
This image, taken using the group of radio
telescopes in New Mexico known as the Very
Large Array, reveals the complex structure
of a jet of subatomic particles, emanating
from the core of the giant elliptical galaxy
Virgo A. The false-colors correspond to the
intensity of the detected radio emissions. Also
known as M87, this galaxy almost certainly
contains in its heart a supermassive black
hole, which would be responsible for the jet.

Sombrero Galaxy (above)
Situated just inside the border of Virgo, the
Sombrero Galaxy (M104) is a famous galaxy
that is thought to resemble the distinctive
Mexican hat after which it is named. M104
is a spiral galaxy seen almost edge-on, the
"rim" of the hat corresponding to a thick
layer of gas and dust in the galaxy's disk.

BRIGHTEST STARS			
NAME	MAGNITUDE	DISTANCE (LY)	SPECTRUM
Spica (α VIR)	0.98	262	B1
Porrima (γ VIR)	2.60	39	F0+F0
Vindemiatrix (ε VIR)	2.83	102	G8
Heze (ζ VIR)	3.37	45	A3
Minelauva (δ VIR)	3.38	202	M3

OTHER FEATURES			
NAME	TYPE	DISTANCE (LY)	ALSO KNOWN AS
Virgo Cluster	Galaxy cluster	49–72 million	Coma–Virgo Cluster
Sombrero Galaxy	Edge-on spiral	50 million	M104, NGC 4594
Virgo A	Elliptical galaxy	60 million	M87, NGC 4486
3C 273	Quasar	2.5 billion	—

M61 (below)
M61 is a spiral galaxy approximately 60 million
light-years away, just one of perhaps 2,000
members of the massive Virgo Cluster. The
pink specks in the spiral arms are regions of
active star formation powered by hot young
stars. The photo was taken using a 20-inch
(500-mm) telescope.

NGC 4261 (above)
Current theories suggest that many, perhaps
all, galaxies have supergiant black holes
lurking in their cores, shredding stars apart
to form vast pancakes of gas and dust known
as accretion disks. This Hubble photo from
1992 clearly shows such a disk, encircling
a probable black hole in the center of the
galaxy NGC 4261. This monster black hole has
more than a billion times the mass of the Sun.

Quasar 3C 273 (below)
3C 273 is a fascinating deep-sky object known
as a quasar—a type of bright active galactic
nucleus, probably powered by a black hole.
This photo shows the quasar as seen by the
Hubble Space Telescope. A black disk has been
used to block the bright emissions from the
central core, so that otherwise invisble details
in the rest of the galaxy are revealed—such
as the ring of red dust seen here.

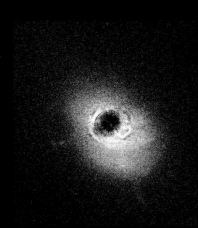

Universal Records

HOTTEST PLANET SURFACE IN THE SOLAR SYSTEM

The surface of Venus, 867°F (464°C). At its hottest, Mercury comes close: 800°F (430°C). Venus's thick atmosphere traps the Sun's heat, so midnight temperatures are as hot as those at noontime. (And the rocks are hot enough to glow dull red!)

COLDEST RECORDED SURFACE IN THE SOLAR SYSTEM

The surface of Triton, the largest satellite of Neptune. When the Voyager 2 probe passed this world in 1989, it found a frigid surface with a temperature measured at –391°F (–235°C).

BIGGEST CRATER IN THE SOLAR SYSTEM

The Aitken Basin near the Moon's southern pole, 1,600 miles (2,500 km) in diameter. This ancient impact scar is so heavily marked with smaller craters that its existence was not confirmed until the Lunar Orbiter program in the 1960s. Detailed mapping from the 1994 Clementine lunar orbiter mission revealed that this broad depression in the lunar far side is an average of 6.2 miles (10 km) lower than the surrounding highlands.

HIGHEST MOUNTAIN IN THE SOLAR SYSTEM

Olympus Mons on the western hemisphere of Mars, rising 17 miles (27 km) above the local surface, its base about 340 miles (550 km) across. The second highest is Maxwell Montes on the eastern hemisphere of Venus, which rises 7 miles (11 km) above the planet's average surface. Earth's highest peak is officially Mount Everest, 5.5 miles (8.8 km) above sea level. However, Hawaii's Mauna Kea can also claim to be the highest, since it rises about 5.6 miles (9 km) above the ocean floor.

LARGEST CANYON IN THE SOLAR SYSTEM

Valles Marineris on Mars, roughly 2,400 miles (3,800 km) long, with a maximum width of about 370 miles (600 km) and a maximum depth of 4.5 miles (7 km). If it were in the United States, this canyon would extend from San Francisco on the west coast to the Appalachian Mountains in Virginia near the east coast. In Europe, it would stretch from Paris to Russia's Ural Mountains.

LARGEST PLANET IN THE SOLAR SYSTEM

Jupiter, with 317.8 times the mass of Earth, and just under 11 times its diameter. Jupiter contains more mass than all the rest of the planets, satellites, comets, and asteroids combined.

LARGEST KNOWN PLANET

An unnamed planet orbiting the star HD 114762. This planet appears to have 11 times the mass of Jupiter, but some astronomers think it may actually be a brown dwarf, an object that is like a small, dim, cool star. If it is a brown dwarf, then the most massive planet would be one with 6.6 times Jupiter's mass that orbits the star 70 Virginis.

LARGEST SATELLITE IN THE SOLAR SYSTEM

Jupiter's Ganymede, 3,270 miles (5,262 km) in diameter. If Ganymede orbited the Sun instead of Jupiter, it would easily qualify as a planet. It is larger than either Mercury or Pluto.

LARGEST METEORITE

Hoba meteorite in Namibia, weighing 65 metric tons—about as heavy as ten elephants. Discovered in 1920, this iron meteorite almost 10 feet (3 m) long still lies in the ground where it landed. It was originally even larger—part of the meteorite has weathered away.

GREATEST METEOR SHOWER

The Leonids on November 13, 1833, with up to 200,000 meteors per hour. Onlookers said that the meteors "fell like snowflakes," while many thought the world was about to come to an end. The remarkable display helped astronomers realize that meteors were entering Earth's atmosphere from outer space, and were not just an Earth-based event like rain.

LARGEST ASTEROID

1 Ceres, 580 miles (933 km) in diameter. This largest of all asteroids was also the first to be found—and its discovery came on the first day of the 19th century: January 1, 1801. It was discovered by Giuseppe Piazzi (1746–1826) at the Palermo Observatory.

LARGEST KUIPER BELT OBJECT (KBO)

The diameter of an unnamed object cataloged 2003 UB313 is as yet undetermined, but estimates range from about 1,500 to over 3,000 miles (2,400–5,000 km). Even the lower figure would make this object larger than Pluto, which some astronomers consider a KBO. UB313 orbits the Sun between 38 and 97 AU with a period of 560 years. The largest known KBO that keeps within the outer edge of the Kuiper Belt throughout its orbit is Quaoar, with a diameter of 800 miles (1,300 km).

CLOSEST COMET TO EARTH

Comet Lexell in 1770, at a distance of 1.4 million miles (2.2 million km) from Earth—less than six times the distance to the Moon. Despite coming so close, this comet never developed much of a tail and its head looked no bigger than five times the size of the Moon in our night sky.

LONGEST COMET TAIL

Great Comet of March 1843, 190 million miles (300 million km) long. This tail was long enough to reach from the Sun to well past the orbit of Mars.

MOST MASSIVE STAR IN OUR NIGHT SKY

Eta Carinae, approximately 150 times as massive as the Sun. Astronomers are not certain if Eta Carinae is one star or a binary system.

LEAST MASSIVE KNOWN STAR

Gliese 105C, about 10 percent as massive as the Sun. This is about as small as a star can be and still be a true star (an object that fuses hydrogen into helium).

NEAREST STAR

Proxima Centauri, possible third member of the Alpha Centauri system. This cool red dwarf star lies about 4.22 light-years away in the constellation Centaurus.

BROADEST STAR IN OUR NIGHT SKY

Betelgeuse in Orion, about 800 times the Sun's diameter. If it replaced the Sun in the Solar System, this bloated red supergiant star would reach past the orbit of Jupiter.

BRIGHTEST STAR IN OUR NIGHT SKY

Sirius with an apparent magnitude of –1.46. Sirius is a binary star 8.6 light-years away in Canis Major. The brightest star north of the celestial equator (and fourth brightest overall) is Arcturus in Boötes with an apparent magnitude of –0.04.

GLOBULAR STAR CLUSTER WITH THE MOST STARS

Omega Centauri, with some estimates of over 10 million stars. This globular cluster measures over 600 light-years from one extreme to the other, and is about 16,000 light-years away. Some astronomers believe that Omega Centauri is the remnant core of a dwarf galaxy consumed by the Milky Way in the distant past.

LARGEST CONSTELLATION

Hydra (the Sea Serpent) at 1,302.844 sq degrees, or 3.16 percent of the sky. Hydra snakes its way across 100 degrees of sky but its stars are faint: fewer than 100 are visible to the naked eye.

SMALLEST CONSTELLATION

Crux (the Southern Cross) at 68.477 square degrees, or 0.16 percent of the sky. Despite its small size, Crux, superimposed on the Milky Way, is a rich site for astronomers, and its distinctive pattern of four bright stars appears on the flags of four nations.

MOST MASSIVE GALAXY

Giant elliptical M87 in the constellation of Virgo, with at least 800 billion Suns' worth of mass. M87 is a member of the Virgo cluster of galaxies.

LEAST MASSIVE GALAXY

The Pegasus II dwarf elliptical, about 10 million solar masses. Smaller galaxies may exist, but as they are not very luminous, astronomers cannot detect them unless they lie close to us.

NEAREST GALAXY

The Canis Major dwarf galaxy. This galaxy in Canis Major is 25,000 light-years away from the Solar System and 42,000 light-years from the center of the Milky Way. It is the current record holder, but surveys find new dwarf elliptical galaxies every year or so, and an even closer galaxy may yet be found.

MOST DISTANT OBJECT VISIBLE TO THE NAKED EYE

Andromeda galaxy (M31), 2.9 million light-years away. When you look at this galaxy, you are seeing light that left the galaxy when the most recent great Ice Ages were beginning on Earth. The spiral galaxy M33 in Triangulum is farther and fainter, and may be visible to the very keenest eye.

MOST DISTANT OBJECT DETECTED

An unnamed galaxy in the constellation Fornax, 13 billion light-years away, and only 2,000 light-years across. This galaxy showed up in a Hubble Space Telescope image, gravitationally lensed by a much closer galaxy cluster. It is so distant that its light must have set out when the universe was just 750 million years old.

Satellites Of Earth

Name	Mean Distance From Earth Miles (km)	Mean Diameter Miles (km)	Orbital Period Days	Disc.
The Moon	238,855 (384,400)	2,160 (3,476)	27.322	—

Satellites Of Mars

Name	Mean Distance From Mars Miles (km)	Mean Diameter Miles (km)	Orbital Period Days	Disc.
Phobos	5,827 (9,378)	15 (24)	0.319	1877
Deimos	14,577 (23,459)	8 (13)	1.262	1877

Known Satellites Of Jupiter (satellites with mean diameters under 6 miles [10 km] not listed)

Name	Mean Distance From Jupiter Miles (km)	Mean Diameter Miles (km)	Orbital Period Days	Disc.
Metis	79,500 (127,960)	25 (40)	0.295	1979
Adrastea	80,000 (128,980)	12 (20)	0.298	1979
Amalthea	112,700 (181,300)	117 (189)	0.498	1892
Thebe	138,000 (221,900)	60 (100)	0.675	1979
Io	261,970 (421,600)	2,264 (3,643)	1.769	1610
Europa	416,878 (670,900)	1,940 (3,122)	3.551	1610
Ganymede	665,100 (1,070,400)	3,270 (5,262)	7.155	1610
Callisto	1,169,855 (1,882,700)	2,996 (4,821)	16.689	1610
Leda	6,937,500 (11,165,000)	11 (18)	240.92	1974
Himalia	7,121,500 (11,461,000)	114 (184)	250.56	1904
Lysithea	7,280,500 (11,717,000)	25 (38)	259.22	1938
Elara	7,295,000 (11,741,000)	48 (78)	259.65	1905
Ananke	13,220,000 (21,280,000)	12 (20)	629.8[R]	1951
Carme	14,540,000 (23,400,000)	19 (30)	734.2[R]	1938
Pasiphae	14,680,000 (23,620,000)	22 (36)	743.6[R]	1908
Sinope	14,875,000 (23,940,000)	17 (28)	758.9[R]	1914

Known Satellites Of Saturn (satellites with mean diameters under 6 miles [10 km] not listed)

Name	Mean Distance From Saturn Miles (km)	Mean Diameter Miles (km)	Orbital Period Days	Disc.
Pan	83,005 (133,583)	12 (20)	0.575	1990
Atlas	85,545 (137,670)	21 (33)	0.602	1980
Prometheus	86,550 (139,350)	56 (91)	0.613	1980
Pandora	88,000 (141,700)	52 (84)	0.629	1980
Epimetheus	94,050 (151,422)	71 (115)	0.694	1980
Janus	94,081 (151,472)	110 (178)	0.695	1966
Mimas	115,280 (185,520)	247 (397)	0.942	1789
Enceladus	147,900 (238,020)	310 (499)	1.370	1789
Telesto	183,090 (294,660)	14 (23)	1.888	1980
Tethys	183,090 (294,660)	659 (1,060)	1.888	1684
Calypso	183,090 (294,660)	13 (21)	1.888	1980
Helene	234,500 (377,400)	20 (33)	2.737	1980
Dione	234,500 (377,400)	696 (1,120)	2.737	1684
Rhea	327,490 (527,040)	949 (1,528)	4.518	1672
Titan	759,210 (1,221,830)	3,200 (5,150)	15.95	1672
Hyperion	920,000 (1,481,100)	177 (286)	21.28	1848
Iapetus	2,212,890 (3,561,300)	892 (1,436)	79.33	1671
Kiviuq	7,065,000 (11,370,000)	9 (14)	450.44	2000
Ijiraq	7,108,000 (11,440,000)	6 (10)	452.76	2000
Phoebe	8,045,000 (12,952,000)	136 (220)	549.83[R]	1899
Paaliaq	9,440,000 (15,200,000)	14 (22)	680.67	2000
Albiorix	10,180,000 (16,390,000)	20 (32)	784.23	2000
Siarnaq	11,280,000 (18,160,000)	20 (32)	894.54	2000
Tarvos	11,329,000 (18,240,000)	9 (14)	913.66	2000
Ymir	14,348,000 (23,100,000)	10 (16)	1317.14[R]	2000

Known Satellites Of Uranus

Name	Mean Distance From Uranus Miles (km)	Mean Diameter Miles (km)	Orbital Period Days	Disc.
Cordelia	30,930 (49,770)	12 (20)	0.335	1986
Ophelia	33,420 (53,790)	13 (21)	0.376	1986
Bianca	36,770 (59,170)	17 (27)	0.435	1986
Cressida	38,390 (61,780)	25 (40)	0.464	1986
Desdemona	38,950 (62,680)	20 (32)	0.474	1986
Juliet	39,990 (64,350)	29 (47)	0.493	1986
Portia	41,070 (66,090)	42 (68)	0.513	1986
Rosalind	43,460 (69,940)	22 (36)	0.559	1986
S/2003U2	46,480 (74,800)	7 (12)	0.618	2003
Belinda	46,770 (75,260)	25 (40)	0.624	1986
S/1986U10	47,500 (76,400)	50 (80)	0.638	1999
Puck	53,450 (86,010)	50 (81)	0.762	1986
S/2003/U1	60,710 (97,700)	10 (16)	0.923	2003
Miranda	80,400 (129,300)	293 (472)	1.413	1948
Ariel	118,690 (191,020)	720 (1,158)	2.520	1851
Umbriel	165,470 (266,300)	726 (1,169)	4.144	1851
Titania	270,860 (435,910)	981 (1,578)	8.706	1787
Oberon	362,580 (583,520)	946 (1,523)	13.463	1787
S/2001U3	266,000 (4,280,000)	7 (12)	266.6[R]	2001
Caliban	4,493,000 (7,230,000)	60 (96)	579.5[R]	1986
Stephano	4,972,000 (8,002,000)	12 (20)	676.5[R]	1999
Trinculo	5,326,000 (8,571,000)	6 (10)	758.1[R]	2001
Sycorax	7,568,000 (12,179,000)	118 (190)	1283.4[R]	1997
S/2003U3	8,914,000 (14,345,000)	7 (12)	1694.8	2003
Prospero	10,202,000 (16,418,000)	19 (30)	1992.8[R]	1999
Setebos	10,849,000 (17,459,000)	19 (30)	2202.3[R]	1999
S/2001U2	13,050,000 (21,000,000)	7 (12)	2823.4[R]	2001

Known Satellites Of Neptune

Name	Mean Distance From Neptune Miles (km)	Mean Diameter Miles (km)	Orbital Period Days	Disc.
Naiad	30,000 (48,200)	43 (69)	0.294	1989
Thalassa	31,100 (50,100)	54 (87)	0.311	1989
Despina	32,600 (52,500)	94 (152)	0.335	1989
Galatea	38,500 (62,000)	110 (177)	0.429	1989
Larissa	45,701 (73,548)	122 (196)	0.555	1981
Proteus	73,102 (117,647)	261 (420)	1.122	1989
Triton	220,438 (354,760)	1,682 (2,707)	5.877[R]	1846
Nereid	3,425,870 (5,513,400)	211 (340)	360.136	1949
S/2002 N1	9,747,000 (15,686,000)	30 (48)	1874.8	2002
S/2002 N2	13,952,000 (22,452,000)	30 (48)	2918.9	2002
S/2002 N3	13,952,000 (22,452,000)	30 (48)	2918.9	2002
S/2002 N4	28,937,000 (46,570,000)	37 (60)	9136.1[R]	2003
S/2003 N1	29,042,000 (46,738,000)	17 (28)	9136.1[R]	2003

Largest Known Asteroids

Name	Mean Diameter Miles (km)	Mean Distance From Sun (au)	Orbital Period Years	Disc.
1 Ceres	580 (933)	2.766	4.60	1801
2 Pallas	331 (532)	2.773	4.62	1802
4 Vesta	329 (530)	2.361	3.63	1807
10 Hygiea	275 (443)	3.140	5.56	1849
511 Davida	203 (326)	3.169	5.64	1903
704 Interamnia	197 (317)	3.062	5.36	1910

[R] indicates retrograde motion

GLOSSARY

Absolute magnitude

How bright a star would appear, in magnitudes, at a standard distance of 10 parsecs (32.6 light-years) from Earth.

Accretion disk

A swirling disk of matter that can surround either a star, a small black hole in a binary star system, or a supergiant black hole at the center of an active galaxy.

Active Galactic Nucleus (AGN)

The supermassive black hole at the heart of an active galaxy.

Active galaxy

A galaxy with a central black hole that is emitting a large amount of radiation that is non-stellar in origin.

Adaptive optics

A technology used with ground-based telescopes that provides real-time correction of atmospheric distortion.

Albedo

A measure of the light (or other radiation) reflected by a non-luminous body.

Antimatter

Matter composed of the antiparticles to those that constitute normal matter: antielectrons, antiprotons, and antineutrons.

Aperture

The diameter of a telescope's main light-collecting optics. Also, the diameter of a binocular lens.

Aphelion

The farthest distance from the Sun in the elliptical orbit of a comet, asteroid, or planet.

Apogee

The point in the orbit of the Moon or an artificial satellite at which it is farthest from Earth.

Apparent magnitude

The visible brightness of a star or other celestial object as seen from Earth.

Arcminute

A unit of angular measure equal to 1/60 of a degree; the Moon and Sun are about 30 arcminutes across.

Arcsecond

A unit of angular measure equal to 1/60 of an arcminute. Jupiter averages some 44 arcseconds across.

Asterism

A distinctive pattern of stars that forms part of one or more constellations but is not itself a constellation.

Asteroid

Also called a minor planet, a small stony and/or metallic object with a diameter of less than 600 miles (1,000 km) orbiting the Sun, usually in the Asteroid Belt.

Asteroid Belt

A reservoir of asteroids orbiting the Sun in the ecliptic between the orbits of Mars and Jupiter.

Astronomical unit (AU)

The mean distance between Earth and the Sun, about 93 million miles (150 million km).

Astrophysics

The study of the dynamics, chemical properties, and evolution of celestial bodies.

Atmosphere

A layer of gases attached to a planet or moon by the body's gravity.

Aurora (pl Aurorae)

Curtains and arcs of light in the sky over middle and high latitudes. They are caused by particles from the Sun hitting Earth's or another body's atmosphere and causing some of its gases to glow.

Axis

The imaginary line through the center of a planet, star, or galaxy around which it rotates.

Big Bang

The event about 13.7 billion years ago that marked the birth of the universe, according to our best cosmological theory.

Billion

One thousand million.

Binary asteroid

A system in which two asteroids of approximately equal size orbit each other around a common center of gravity.

Binary star

Two stars linked by mutual gravity and revolving around a common center of mass (see double star).

Bipolar outflow

A stream of matter in two opposite directions flowing from a T Tauri star or from a red giant just prior to the creation of a planetary nebula.

Black hole

An object so dense that no light or other radiation can escape it.

Blazar

A type of quasar (quasi-stellar radio source) characterized by extreme and rapidly changing output across a range of wavelengths.

Blue giant

A giant, hot, luminous blue star of spectral type O or B.

Blue straggler

A star within a globular cluster that is hotter and bluer than other cluster stars. They probably result from star mergers or interacting binaries.

Bow shock

The interface between a fast-moving body of gas or fluid and an obstacle. Examples in astronomy include the zone where the heliosphere runs into the interstellar medium or where expulsions of gas from an energetic star collide with another, neighboring star.

Brown dwarf

A starlike object not large enough to start hydrogen fusion reactions. They are one possible candidate for a form of dark matter.

Cataclysmic variable

A binary star system in which a white dwarf pulls matter from its companion, usually a red dwarf. As material enters the accretion disk of the white dwarf, nuclear fusion reactions result.

Celestial equator

The imaginary line encircling the sky midway between the celestial poles.

Celestial poles

The imaginary points on the sky where Earth's rotation axis, extended infinitely, would touch the imaginary celestial sphere.

Celestial sphere

The imaginary sphere enveloping Earth upon which the stars, galaxies, and other objects all appear to lie.

Cepheid variable

A variable star whose brightness varies over a period of a few days. The brightness is directly related to the period of pulsation, making Cepheids good indicators of distance in astronomy.

Chromosphere

In the Sun, the thin layer of atmosphere lying just above the photosphere (visible surface) and below the corona.

Cluster

A group of stars or galaxies held together by gravity.

Comet

A small body composed of ice and dust that orbits the Sun on an elongated path.

Conjunction

The moment when a given two celestial objects lie closest together in the sky.

Constellation

One of the 88 officially recognized patterns of stars that divide the sky into sections.

Convection

A heat-driven process that causes hotter material to move upward while lighter material sinks.

Corona

The high-temperature, outermost atmosphere of the Sun, visible from Earth only during a total solar eclipse.

Coronal Mass Ejection (CME)

A massive eruption of material from the Sun's corona over a period of several hours.

Cosmology

A branch of astronomy that deals with the origins, structure, and space-time dynamics of the universe.

Dark energy

A hypothetical type of energy with anti-gravitational properties that pervades the universe and may account for its accelerating expansion.

Dark matter

A form of matter which does not emit light or any other radiation. Dark matter far outweighs normal, visible matter in the universe.

Dark nebula

A cloud of interstellar dust that blocks the light of stars and nebulas behind it, appearing in silhouette.

Declination

The angular distance of a celestial object north or south of the celestial equator.

Deepsky object

A celestial object located beyond the Solar System.

Degree

A unit of angular measure equal to 1/360 of a circle.

Disk galaxy

Galaxies that have a flattened circular disk of stars. This description applies to spiral galaxies and lenticular galaxies.

Double star

Two stars that appear close together in the sky. Optical doubles are chance alignments of the stars; binary or multiple systems are linked by gravity.

Dust lane

The dark swathe of gas and dust seen within the disk of a spiral galaxy when viewed edge-on.

Dwarf galaxy

A small faint galaxy.

Dwarf planet

A small world, orbiting the Sun, which is almost spherical but whose orbit crosses those of other bodies. Pluto, Eris and Ceres are examples.

Dwarf star

Any star of average to low size, mass, and luminosity. These include red dwarfs, brown dwarfs, white dwarfs, and most main sequence stars such as the Sun.

Eccentricity

A measure of how far an orbit deviates from circularity; defined as the ratio of the distance between the foci and the major axis of the ellipse.

Eclipse

When one celestial body passes in front of another, dimming or obscuring its light.

Eclipsing binary

A binary star system whose components regularly pass in front of each other as seen from Earth therefore changing in luminosity.

Ecliptic

The apparent path of the Sun around the celestial sphere. Because we view this from Earth, it is the equivalent of the Earth's orbital plane.

Ejecta

Material thrown out of a crater during an impact event or, alternatively, ejected by a volcano.

Electromagnetic spectrum

The name given to the entire range of radiation that includes radio waves, infrared, optical light, ultraviolet light, X-rays, and gamma rays.

Ellipse

The oval, closed path followed by a celestial object moving under the influence of gravity.

Elliptical galaxy

Galaxies with a spheroidal shape and smooth appearance, consisting mostly of aging stars.

Emission nebula

A cloud of gas glowing as it re-emits energy absorbed from a nearby hot star.

Equator

The imaginary line on a celestial body that lies halfway between its two poles.

Equinox

The moment when the Sun appears to stand directly above a planet's equator.

Escape velocity

The minimum speed an object (such as a rocket) must attain in order to travel from the surface of a planet, moon, or other body, and into space. If the speed is too low, gravity will pull the object back down.

Event horizon

The region surrounding a black hole, beyond which no signal emitted either by the hole or an object falling into it can ever reach an outside observer. Beyond the event horizon, the escape velocity exceeds the speed of light.

Extrinsic variable

Stars that change luminosity as seen from Earth due to external factors such as rotation or the presence of an eclipsing binary companion star.

Galactic halo

A spherical region of space surrounding a disk galaxy believed to consist of gas, stars, and dark matter.

Galaxy

A huge gathering of stars, gas, and dust, bound by gravity and having a mass ranging from 100,000 to 10 trillion times that of the Sun.

Galilean moons

The four largest moons of Jupiter discovered by Galileo Galilei in 1610. They are, in order of distance from Jupiter: Io, Europa, Ganymede, and Callisto.

Gamma rays

Radiation with a wavelength shorter than X-rays.

Gas giant

A planet whose composition is dominated by hydrogen and helium (such as Jupiter and Saturn).

Gibbous

The phase of a moon or a planet when it appears greater than a half disk, but less than a full disk.

Globular star cluster

A spherical cluster that may contain over a million stars, most of them old and red.

Globule

A small, dark, roughly spherical cloud of gas and dust. Many globules are thought to be sites of star formation. Also known as Bok globules.

Heliosphere

A bubble blown in the interstellar medium by the pressure of the Sun's solar wind.

Herbig-Haro object (HH)

A bright emission nebula associated with bipolar jets of charged particles emitted by young stellar objects.

Hipparcos Catalog

A highly accurate catalog of 118,218 stars surveyed by the Hipparcos satellite and first published in 1997.

Hubble constant

The ratio of the speed of recession of a galaxy to its distance from the Solar System. A measure of the Hubble constant is essential in determining the age of the universe.

Ice giant

A planet whose composition is similar to that of a gas giant but includes a large proportion of rock and slushy ice.

Infrared (IR)

Radiation with wavelengths just longer than those of visible light.

Infrared galaxy

A galaxy that is visible primarily or only at infrared wavelengths.

Interferometry

A technique for linking two or more telescopes together to obtain a higher resolution image than would be possible with a single instrument.

Intergalactic medium (IGM)

The matter found in the space between galaxies. Most detected IGM is in the form of diffuse hot gas.

Interstellar medium (ISM)

The matter found in the space between stars. ISM in the disk of the Milky Way is about 90 percent gas, 10 percent dust.

Ionization

The loss or gain by an atom of one or more electrons resulting in the atom having a positive or negative electrical charge.

Kuiper Belt

The region of the Solar System, outside the orbits of the planets, that contains icy planetesimals.

Light-year

The distance that light travels in one year, about 6 trillion miles (9.5 trillion km).

Local Group

A galaxy cluster of about 40 nearby galaxies, including the Milky Way.

Luminosity

The amount of energy radiated by an object, such as a star, per unit of time. Luminosity depends on both the temperature and surface area of the object.

M objects

Star clusters, nebulas, and galaxies listed in the Messier catalog.

Magnetic field

A region surrounding a magnetic object, within which an iron-rich body will experience a magnetic force.

Magnetosphere

A region of space surrounding a planet or star that is dominated by the magnetic field of that planet or star.

Magnitude

A logarithmic unit used to measure the brightness of celestial objects. Apparent magnitude describes how bright a star looks from Earth, while absolute magnitude is its brightness if placed at a distance of 10 parsecs (32.6 light-years). The lower the magnitude, the brighter the star.

Main sequence

The longest-lived period in the lifecycle of a star, during which it converts hydrogen into helium. This generates the outward pressure that counterbalances the inward pull of the star's gravity.

Mantle

The main part of a planet or satellite lying between the crust (or outer atmosphere of a gas or ice planet) and the core.

Mare (plural maria)

A plain of solidified lava on the surface of the Moon, darker than the surrounding areas.

Meridian

An imaginary line on the sky that runs due north and south, passing through the zenith.

Meteor

The bright, transient streak of light produced by a meteoroid, a piece of space debris, burning up as it enters Earth's atmosphere at high speed.

Meteorite

The name given to any piece of interplanetary debris that reaches Earth's surface intact.

Meteoroid

Any small debris traveling through space, usually from a comet or asteroid.

Multiple star

Three or more stars linked by gravity.

Near Earth Asteroid (NEA)

An asteroid that orbits within 1.3 AU of the Sun. The orbits of many NEAs come close to or intersect the orbit of Earth.

Nebula

A cloud of gas or dust in space. They may appear dark or luminous.

Nebulosity

The presence of gas and/or dust.

Neutron star

A massive star's collapsed remnant, consisting almost wholly of very densely packed neutrons. May be visible as a pulsar.

NGC objects

Galaxies, star clusters, and nebulas listed in the New General Catalog.

Node (orbital)

The points in the orbit of a planet or other body where the orbit crosses the ecliptic.

Nova

A white dwarf star in a binary system which brightens suddenly by several magnitudes as gas pulled away from its companion star explodes in a thermonuclear reaction.

Nucleus

The central core of a galaxy or comet.

Oort Cloud

A sphere of trillions of potential comet nuclei extending about 1.5 light-years from the outer edge of the Kuiper Belt.

Open star cluster

A group of young stars, from dozens to a few hundred in number, bound together by gravity.

Opposition

The point in a planet's orbit when it appears opposite the Sun in the sky.

Optical telescope

Any telescope that collects visible light.

Orbit

The path of an object as it moves through space under the control of another object's gravity.

Parallax

The apparent change in position of a nearby object relative to a more distant background when viewed from different points. Parallax is used to determine distances to nearby stars.

Parsec

A unit of distance equal to the distance to an object that has a parallax of one second. Equivalent to 3.26 light-years.

Penumbra

The outer part of an eclipse shadow. Also, the lighter area surrounding a sunspot.

Perigee

The point in the orbit of the Moon or an artificial satellite at which it is closest to Earth.

Perihelion

The closest distance to the Sun in the elliptical orbit of a comet, asteroid, or planet.

Photosphere

The visible surface of the Sun or any other star.

Planetary nebula

A shell of gas blown off by a low-mass star when it runs out of fuel in its core.

Planetesimal

A small rocky or icy body; one of the small bodies that coalesced to form the planets.

Plasma

A gaseous state of matter in which atoms have been ionized and therefore display electromagnetic properties.

Plutoid

Any dwarf planet found beyond Neptune. Pluto is the prototype.

Precession

A slow, periodic wobble in Earth's axis caused by the pull of the Sun, the Moon, and other planets.

Prograde motion

The counterclockwise orbital or rotational motion of a satellite as seen from a position north of the ecliptic; the motion of most satellites in the Solar System.

Prominence

Short-lived structures of cooler gas embedded within the Sun's corona.

Protoplanetary disk

A disk of gas and dust surrounding a newborn star. Protoplanetary disks are thought to be the progenitors of planetary systems.

Pulsar

A rapidly-spinning neutron star that flashes bursts of radio (and occasionally optical) energy.

Pulsating variable

A star that changes its brightness as it expands and shrinks regularly.

Quasar

Short for quasi-stellar radio source, quasars are thought to be the active nuclei of very distant galaxies.

Radiation

Energy radiated from a source in the form of wavelengths or particles.

Radio galaxy

A type of active galaxy that is a strong source of radio energy.

Red dwarf

A small and relatively cool main sequence star of spectral class M or late K. Red dwarfs are the most common type of star in the universe.

Red giant

A large, cool, red star in a late stage of its life.

Reflection nebula

A cloud of dust or gas visible because it reflects light from nearby stars.

Reflector

A telescope that uses mirrors to magnify and focus an image into an eyepiece.

Refractor

A telescope that forms an image using lenses.

Retrograde motion

The clockwise orbital or rotational motion of a satellite as seen from a position north of the ecliptic; the opposite to most satellites in the Solar System.

Right ascension (RA)

The celestial coordinate analogous to longitude on Earth measured in hours and minutes.

Rotation

The spin of a planet, satellite, or star, on its axis.

RR Lyrae star

A large yellow or white pulsating variable star whose period relates to its absolute magnitude. RR Lyrae stars can be used as standard candles.

Satellite

Any small object orbiting a larger one, although the term is most often used for rocky or artificial objects orbiting a planet.

Seyfert galaxy

A type of active galaxy with extremely bright, often violent, core activity.

Sidereal time

The rotation or orbital motion of a planet or satellite measured with respect to stars. On Earth a sidereal day, month, and year differs slightly from the more familiar solar day, synodic month, and Julian year, respectively.

Singularity

A point in space-time where our laws of mathematics and physics cannot operate. Singularities exist at the centers of black holes.

Solar flare

A sudden release of energy in or near the Sun's corona emitting radiation into space.

Solar wind

A ceaseless, but variable, high-speed stream of charged particles flowing out into space from the Sun.

Solstice

The moment when a planet's pole tilts most directly toward (or away from) the Sun.

Spectroscopy

The analysis of light to determine, by studying the spectral lines, the chemical composition and conditions of the object producing it, as well as that object's motion and velocity toward or away from Earth.

Spicule

A narrow, short-lived jet of gas in the Sun's chromosphere.

Standard candle

An astronomical object (usually a star or a galaxy) of known absolute magnitude. By measuring the apparent magnitude of a standard candle, its distance from Earth can be calculated.

Sunspot

A dark, highly magnetic region on the Sun's surface that is cooler than the surrounding area.

Supercluster

A cluster of clusters: a vast assemblage of entire clusters of galaxies.

Supernova

The explosion of a massive star, which can briefly outshine entire galaxies, that occurs when the star reaches the end of its fuel supply.

Supernova remnant

An expanding cloud of gas thrown into space by a supernova explosion.

T Tauri star

A very young star distinguished by rapid spin, erratic changes in brightness, and intense, variable X-ray and radio emissions.

Tectonic

Relating to the structural deformation of the crust of a planet or large moon.

Terrestrial planet

A planet with a mainly rocky composition (Mercury, Venus, Earth, and Mars).

Transit

The passage of an astronomical body in front of another. Often, Venus and Mercury can be seen silhouetted against the Sun during transits.

Trillion

One thousand billion.

Umbra

The dark, inner part of an eclipse shadow. Also, the dark central part of a sunspot.

Variable star

Any star whose brightness appears to change.

Wavelength

The distance between two successive crests or troughs in a wave.

White dwarf

A small, dense, very hot but faint star. The final state of all but the most massive stars.

Wormholes

Theoretical tunnels through space and time. They could provide a short cut to a distant place in our universe or to another universe entirely.

X-ray binary

A binary system in which a neutron star or a small black hole is in orbit around (and simultaneously accretes matter from) a much larger companion.

X-rays

Radiation with wavelengths between ultraviolet and gamma rays.

Zenith

The point directly over an observer's head, 90 degrees perpendicular to the horizon.

Zodiac

Name given to the twelve constellations that lie along the path of the Sun on the sky or the ecliptic.

SCIENTIFIC NOTATION

When expressing the very large (and very small) numbers frequently encountered in astronomy, a system called scientific notation is often used. Scientific notation avoids the confusion that might arise from very long series of digits or the use of words like "billion" and "trillion" that can have different meanings in different parts of the world or have stood for different values in the past. Scientific notation is based on powers of the base number ten. A billion (1,000,000,000) is written 10^9, signifying a 1 followed by 9 zeros. One-billionth is written 10^{-9} signifying a 1 preceded by a decimal point and 9 zeros. Numbers that are not powers of ten (in this case the volume of the Sun in cubic miles) are written in this style: 3.38×10^{17}, indicating the number 3.38 with the decimal point moved seventeen places to the right.

ACKNOWLEDGMENTS

Weldon Owen would like to thank the following people for their assistance in the production of this book: Angela Handley, Jennifer Losco, Irene Mickaiel, Sarah Plant (Puddingburn Publishing Services), Juliana Titin, Melanie Young.

Key t=top; l=left; r=right; tl=top left; tcl=top center left; tc=top center; tcr=top center right; tr=top right; cl=center left; c=center; cr=center right; b=bottom; bl=bottom left; bcl=bottom center left; bc=bottom center; bcr=bottom center right; br=bottom right

PHOTO CREDITS

2MASS = Two Micron All Sky Survey; APL = Australian Picture Library; APL/CBT = Australian Picture Library/Corbis; AURA = Association of Universities for Research in Astronomy; CfA = Harvard-Smithsonian Center for Astrophysics; CFHT = Canada France Hawaii Telescope; ESA = European Space Agency; ESO = European Southern Observatory; GSFC = NASA Goddard Space Flight Center; ING = Isaac Newton Group of Telescopes; ISP = Institute for Solar Physics; JHU = John Hopkins University; LPI = Lunar and Planetary Institute; MSSS = Malin Space Science Systems; N_A = NASA/Astronomy Picture of the Day; N_CH = NASA/Chandra X-ray Observatory; N_EO = NASA Earth Observatory; N_G = NASA/Great Images in NASA; N_H = NASA/Hubble Space Telescope; N_HI = NASA History Division; N_J = NASA/Jet Propulsion Laboratory; N_N = NIX/NASA Image Exchange; N_NC = NASA/National Space Science Data Center; N_O = NASA Observatorium; N_SE = NASA Solar System Exploration; N_SP = NASA/Spitzer Space Telescope; NAOJ = National Astronomical Observatory of Japan; NASA = National Aeronautics and Space Administration; NOAO = National Optical Astronomy Observatory; NRAO = National Radio Astronomy Observatory; PL/SPL = photolibrary.com/Science Photo Library; RSA = Royal Swedish Academy of Sciences; SOHO = NASA Solar and Heliospheric Observatory; SSI = Space Science Institute; STScI = Space Telescope Science Institute

2–3c N_H/ESA/AURA/Caltech **4**c APL **6**tl, tcl PL/SPL tcr GSFC/WMAP Science Team tr APL **7**tl PL/SPL tcl APL/CBT tcr 2MASS/G.Kopan/R.Hurt tr ISP/RSA **8**bl Robert Gendler br N_J/University of Colorado c N_J tcl PL/SPL tr ESA **14**c PL/SPL **16**cl PL/SPL **17**tl NASA/GSFC/METI/ERSDAC/JAROS/US-Japan ASTER Science Team tr N_A **18**cl GSFC **19**bl NASA tr PL/SPL **20**c LPI cl PL/SPL tr N_EO **22**cl cr PL/SPL tr N_EO **26**cl N_N/HQ/GRIN tr N_G **27**cr, tl N_J **28**bl N_N/Johnson Space Center tr PL/SPL **29**br N_NC tl LPI **30**bl N_G br N_HI cr NRAO/AUI/Bruce Campbell/Smithsonian Institution tr N_SE/Celementine Science Group/LPI tr N_J **32**bl N_G br N_SE/HQ/N_G cl N_A cr, tr N_NC **33**br N_J tr N_G **34**c PL/SPL **36**c NASA Visible Earth c N_J cl PL/SPL **37**tl Photo Researcher's Inc. **39**bl N_J/Northwestern University tr N_A/SOHO/LASCO Consortium/ESA **40**cl N_J **42**bl, br, cr N_J/Northwestern University **43**bl N_O br N_NC tr N_HI **44**bl N_J/Northwestern University/The Planetarium cr N_J **47**bl N_N tr N_NC **48**cl N_NC tr N_J **50**cl N_NC **52**bc N_J bl N_J/Caltech tr N_N **53**b N_N tl, tr N_J **54**br, tr PL/SPL **55**cl N_J **57**bl N_J/MSSS **58**cl N_J **60**cl N_A/MGS/MOC/MSSS **62**br N_J br, cl N_J/MSSS **63**bl N_J/GSFC br N_J/MSSS tr N_SE/ESA **64**b, cl N_J cr N_J/MSSS **65**bcr PL/SPL c N_J/Cornell tc N_J/MSSS tr N_A/J_H/Viking Project **66**b Mark Robinson/JHU Applied Physics Laboratory cl N_A/Near Project/NLR/JHU Applied Physics Laboratory/Goddard SVS **67**br N_A/Dr. William J.Merline–Southwest Research Institute, Boulder CO/Dr Laird M.Close–University of Arizona, Tucson AZ/Images acquired at the W.M.Keck Observatory/Mauna Kea, Hawaii cl N_A/NEAR cl N_A/US Geological Survey cr N_J/Northwestern University **68**bc N_J bl N_SE/JPL cr PL/SPL tc N_H/Ben Zellner/Peter Thomas tl N_H /R.Kempton/New England Meteoritical Services **69**br N_H/ESA/Y.Momany c N_A/NEAR Project/JHU Applied Physics Laboratory **70**c N_J **73**tr N_J tr N_J/Heidi Hammel–Massachusetts Institute of Technology **75**tr N_H **76**cr N_J t N_H/John Clarke–University of Michigan/ESA **78**b N_H/H.A.Weaver/T.E.Smith–STScI/J.T.Trauger/R.W.Evans/N_J c N_H cl, cr, tr N_J **79**bl N_J br N_J/SSI **80**bl, br, cl N_J cr N_J/Arizona State University–Academic Research Lab **81**br, cl, cr, t, tr N_J **82**bl, br, cl, tr N_J **85**bl N_J tr N_H **86**c N_J t N_J/SSI **88**bl University of Utrecht cl N_SE cr N_J tr NASA **89**c N_J/SSI t N_J/University of Colorado **90**b N_A/Voyager 1 b N_A/Voyager 2/Calvin J.Hamilton b, c, cl N_J/SSI bl N_A/SSI br, c, cr N_J **91**bl N_J/SSI br N_J/ESA/University of Arizona tl N_A/Voyager 2/Calvin J.Hamilton **93**bl N_J tr N_J/Kenneth Seidelmann–US Naval Observatory **94**br, cr N_J tr Madison Space Science and Engineering Center/Lawrence Sromovsky **95**bl, br N_J **96**b, bl, cl N_J br N_A/Astrogeology Team–USGS/The Voyager Project **97**bc, bl, br N_J **99**bl N_J tr N_J/Voyager Project **100**c, t N_A/Voyager 2 c N_A/Lawrence Sromovsky/P.Fry–University of Wisconsin **102**bl N_A/Voyager 2 br N_NC br N_J **103**bl N_J br N_A/Voyager 2 **105**bl N_A/Eliot Young–SwRI cr N_NC **106**c, cl N_J/Caltech **107**tr N_J/Caltech/UMD **109**bl N_J br N_H/M.Combi–University of Michigan c PL/SPL tr N_A/The Voyager Project **112**c, ISP/RSA **117**bl N_N/Johnson Space Center/Earth Sciences and Image Analysis **118**tr NASA/Yohkoh Mission–ISAS/Lockheed-Martin Solar and Astrophysics Laboratory/NAOJ/University of Tokyo **119**b, cr ISP **120**bl, br PL/SPL tr N_A/TRACE Project **121**c SOHO/ESA tl N_A/SOHO/EIT Consortium/ESA **122**b PL/SPL tr New Mexico State University/A.Klypin–New Mexico State University **123**bl NASA/Yohkoh Mission–ISAS/Lockheed-Martin Solar and Astrophysics Laboratory/NAOJ/University of Tokyo cl, t PL/SPL **124**cl, tr Museum History Science, Oxford, UK **128**bl PL/SPL cl N_CH/McDonald Observatory **130**cl ESO **132**b Northwind Picture Archives tr Bridgeman Art Library **133**bc University of St Andrews/A.Cameron/M.Jardine/K.Wood bl NOAO cr N_H/Rodger Thompson/Marcia Rieke/Glenn Schneider/Susan Stolovy–University of Arizona/Edwin Erickson–SETI Institute, Ames Research Center/David Axon–STScI t National Maritime Museum, Greenwich, UK **134**b NRAO/AUI/Kelly Gatlin/Patricia Smiley c CFHT/Jean-Charles Cuillandre **135**cl PL/SPL r N_H/ESA/H.E.Bond–STScI/AURA **136**c PL/SPL **138**bl N_A/Subaru Telescope/NAOJ/All Rights Reserved cl PL/SPL **140**br PL/SPL tr N_SP/MSX/IPAC **141**br N_A/CFHT/Hawaiian Starlight **142**bl N_A/Russell Croman br N_A/Joint Astronomy Center/Image Processing by C.Davis/W.Varricatt tr Atlas Image obtained as part of the 2MASS Survey–a joint project of the University of Massachusetts and the Infrared Processing and Analysis Center/California Institute of Technology/funded by NASA and the National Science Foundation **143**bl PL/SPL cr N_A/Loke Kun Tan/StarryScapes **144**br, cr N_H/AURA/STScI cl ESO tcr N_SP/JPL/Caltech/V.Gorjian/NOAO **146**cl N_SP/visible: Howard McCallon/infrared: NASA/IRAS r PL/SPL **147**bl PL/SPL cl N_A/J.Bally/D.Devine/R.Sutherland/D.Johnson/Canadian Institute for Theoretical Astrophysics/HST r Robert Gendler tl ESO/ISAAC/Very Large Telescope **148**bcl N_SP/JPL/Caltech/G.Melnick/CfA br PL/SPL cl N_A/Bessell, Sutherland, and Buxton–Australian National University Research School of Astronomy and Astrophysics tr Robert Gendler **149**bl, br, cr, tr PL/SPL **150**b, c, tcl, tr PL/SPL **151**bl N_A/Jeffrey Newman–University of California Berkeley br N_A/Christine Pulliam–CfA/Volker Springel/Max Planck Institute for Astrophysics/Lars Hernquist–CfA cr N_H/Margarita Karovska/CfA tr N_CH/CXC/SAO/M.Karovska et al. **152**bl N_A/Adam Block–NOAO/KPNO Visitor Program/AURA/NSF cl N_H/J.Hester/Arizona state University **154**bl N_A/Hubble European Space Agency Information Center/Valentin Bujarrabal br PL/SPL cl N_A/R.Corradi–ING/D.Goncalves–Institute Astrofisica de Canarias tr N_H/ESA/A.Zijlstra–UMIST, Manchester, UK **155**br N_A/H.Van Winckel–KU Leuven/M.Cohen–UC Berkeley/H.Bond–STScI/T.Gull–GSFC/ESA